OLD AND NEW BIRMINGHAM.

"Ask Britain who gives her the spear and the shield,
The helmet, the sword—her defence in the field?
Ask Science (from Science the tribute is due)
Who gives her the lever, the wedge, and the screw?
Ask Ceres (for Ceres the claim will allow)
Who gives her the sickle, the scythe, and the plough?
  'Tis Birmingham!"

—WILLIAM HAMPER

OLD AND NEW BIRMINGHAM:

A HISTORY OF
THE TOWN AND ITS PEOPLE.

BY
ROBERT K. DENT.

VOLUME II

"So describe,
That you shall fairly streets and buildings trace,
And all that gives distinction to the place."
—CRABBE.

Republished by
EP Publishing Limited
1973

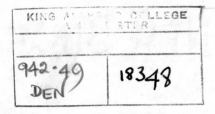
Publisher's Notes

Volume I is a reprint of the first 33 chapters of 'Old
and New Birmingham' covering the period up to 1760
and includes a new introduction by Dorothy H.
McCulla.

This Volume includes chapters 34 to 60 and covers
the period 1760–1832.

Volume III includes chapters 61 to 68 and the 10
chapters comprising part 2, and covers the period
1832–1880.

The work was originally published in weekly numbers
between 1878 and 1880 by Houghton and Hammond,
Scotland Passage, Birmingham.

Facsimiles of some of the original covers for this
work are reproduced at the end of each volume.

This volume has been reproduced from Birmingham Public Library copy number 242137. The small
corrections mentioned in the original errata have
been corrected in this reprint.

Reprint © 1973 EP Publishing Limited

East Ardsley, Wakefield

Yorkshire, England

ISBN 0 85409 884 4

Please address all enquiries to EP Publishing Ltd.

(address as above)

Reprinted in Great Britain by
The Scolar Press Limited, Menston, Yorkshire

CONTENTS.

LIST OF ILLUSTRATIONS.

CHAPTER XXXIV.

WHAT LED TO THE RIOTS OF 1791.

History of the Churches and Sects, 1781-1791—Dr. Priestley and Catherine Hutton—Growth of Dissent—The Test Acts—Dr. Priestley and his opponents—Wilful misconstruction—Sympathy with the French Revolution—Gillray's Cartoon: "A Birmingham Toast"—An inflammatory hand-bill and its results—Announcement of the Meeting of July 14.

In entering upon the religious and political history of the few years which preceded that event which darkens our local history, with an indelible stain, and which seriously retarded the progress, civil, intellectual, and religious, of our town, we would endeavour to the utmost of our ability to free ourselves from all bias against, or in favour of any party whatever, to narrate the facts with truth and simplicity, to extenuate nothing, nor set down aught in malice.

The decade which preceded the riots was one of great prosperity for the dissenters in Birmingham. In 1781 the Methodists, who had hitherto used the cast-off theatre in Moor Street, began for the first time to build for themselves, and completed the old meeting house in Cherry Street, (which was taken down in 1823,) ready for opening on the 7th of July 1782, the cost of its erection being about £1,200. The venerable founder of the society visited Birmingham on several occasions during the last few years of his life. He preached at the opening of the above-named meeting house; again in March 1783, although "dangerously ill," he preached, under considerable temporary excitement, being "electrified, [not literally, we presume,] during the service," and ventured to preach three quarters of an hour. In 1786 he spent more than a week in Birmingham; he again administered the sacrament to nearly seven hundred persons in 1787. In the same year he met with more than one unpleasant adventure during a stage-coach journey from Manchester to this town. He had secured, says his latest biographer, Mr. Tyerman, the whole of the coach that ran between Manchester and Birmingham for himself and friends. "Six packed themselves within, and eight arranged themselves without, and off they all set at midnight; but even the presence of fourteen Methodist preachers was not an insurance against accident. No doubt, many a hymn was sung as they whisked away through beautiful Cheshire scenery, the stars shining approvingly, and the fields all around wrapped in solemn silence; but, a little before three in the morning, when approaching Congleton, the coach broke beneath its unwonted burden, and had to be abandoned for another. In about an hour, number two was crippled like number one; while one of the horses was so knocked up as to be scarcely able to move at all. This Methodist monopoly of the Birmingham stage coach issued, not an a moonlight pleasure trip, but in a series of disasters which men so pious and so good had not expected. The distance was not great; but nineteen hours were spent in getting over it. The party arrived in Birmingham at 7 p.m.; Wesley, found a congregation waiting; he stepped out of the coach into the chapel, and began preaching without delay. 'And such,' says he, 'was the goodness of God, that I found no more weariness when I had done than if I had rested all the day.'"

In 1789 Wesley was present at the opening of the second chapel of Methodism in Birmingham, in Bradford Street.

The Baptists and Independents also extended their sphere of labour in Birmingham, the former by the erection of a second meeting-house in Bond Street, which was opened November 15th, 1786; and the latter by the erection of a small meeting-house in Paradise Street, opened on Whit-Sunday, 1787.

The members of the Countess of Huntingdon's connection, few though they were in number, had during this decade erected a small chapel in Peck Lane, and probably another in Bartholomew Street, but this latter may have been erected subsequent to the riots; it is included in Hutton's list in 1795.

In 1789 the Roman Catholics found a home once more within the borders of the town from whence they had been banished just a century. A place of worship was erected (chiefly owing to the exertions of the Rev. John Nutt, the first pastor) on the borders of the Easy Hill estate, and dedicated to St. Peter.

The Jews, doubtless having grown a-weary of the miserable surroundings of their little synagogue in the Froggary, with its "drooping ensigns of poverty," erected a new and and larger synagogue in Severn Street, which was then pleasantly situated on the outskirts of the town, with an almost uninterrupted view of the country away as far as Edgbaston. The new building was dedicated September 23rd, 1791; the ceremony being performed by Mr. Phillips, Mr. Yates, and Mr. Levy, who, says the *Gazette* of that date, "sung the appointed psalms and songs in the sacred language with great judgment and melody."

The latest of the new sects to erect a place of worship in the town was that of the Swedenborgians. According to an interesting account of the early Swedenborgians in Birmingham, contributed by Mr. John Rabone to the *Century of Birmingham Life;** the first building ever erected for this sect in England, or indeed in any part of the world, was in Birmingham, viz., the chapel in Newhall Street now known as Zion Chapel; which was consecrated and opened June

* Vol. i, pp. 369-70.

19th, 1794—only a few weeks before the outbreak of the riots. The officiating ministers were the Revds. Robert Hindmarsh and Joseph Proud; and among those present at the opening services, were several prominent members of the New Meeting congregation, with their pastor, Dr. Priestley.

In our last notice of the churches and sects we referred to Catherine Hutton's proposed migration to the 'Old Meeting' in the event of Dr. Priestley's becoming pastor of that congregation. That migration took place very soon after the doctor's acceptance of the charge, and in a letter to a friend at Leicester, during 1781, Miss Hutton speaks in glowing terms of the new pastor. "I have much to say to you," she writes, "on the subject of Dr. Priestley. I look upon his character as a preacher to be as amiable, as his character as a philosopher is great. In the pulpit he is mild, persuasive, and unaffected, as his sermons are full of sound reasoning and good sense. He is not what is called an orator; he uses no action, no declamation; but his voice and manner are those of one friend speaking to another. If you will come to Birmingham, I will promise that you shall hear him preach; for my brother and I have formally become a part of his congregation. I cannot promise to introduce you to him, as at present I have not the honor of his acquaintance; but I shall lose no opportunity of procuring it."*

This honour Miss Hutton was not long in procuring, as will be seen from the following extract from another letter to the same lady, dated July 16th, 1783: "Your letter contains the second proof I have that I am spoken handsomely of by Dr. Priestley; the first was so much in my favour that I dare not repeat it. You may be assured it gives me pleasure to be praised by him whom all men praise; but I cannot help confessing that not more praise is due

* MS. copies of Miss Hutton's letters in the possession of Mrs. W. Franks Beale; the whole of which have been kindly placed at our disposal, and from which interesting extracts will be made from time to time.

to my talents than to the Doctor's penetration in finding them out; for I have not been in his company more than three times, and during them all I was awed by the consciousness of my own great inferiority."

While all the dissenting sects were thus making considerable progress, not a single new place of worship was erected in connection with the Established Church—although a small chapel, "converted" from a private residence, was opened a few months subsequent to the riots—and this rapid growth of dissent may possibly have alarmed the Church party; as in those days, when toleration was almost unknown, all dissenters were looked upon as dangerous to the welfare of the State—especially as there had been during the same period repeated endeavours on the part of the latter to obtain a repeal of the Corporation and Tests Acts. In these endeavours the name of Dr. Priestley was at all times prominent. Nor was he silent on local matters, as we have already seen in the question of the introduction of controversial theology into the Birmingham Library. He fearlessly proclaimed to the world, in his innumerable books and tracts, his religious and political convictions; and perhaps in this he was unwisely over-zealous, as even so ardent an admirer as Catherine Hutton, admits. "A circumstance," she says, "which particularly rendered Birmingham a likely theatre for mischief was the zeal of Dr. Priestley—fervent, though not intemperate. Having fully assured himself of the truth in religion, he conceived it his duty to go abroad into the world and endeavour to persuade all mortals to embrace it, an idea which has done more mischief than any which ever entered the erring mind of man. He sometimes, too, in his sermons, glanced at politics—a subject that should never be mingled with religion—and this treasured up wrath for him against the day of wrath. I look upon Dr. Priestley as a good man, attached to his King and country, and meaning well to every creature; but, though unintentionally, and

himself the first sufferer, he was, I think, one of the primary causes of the riots in Birmingham, by rousing the spirit of bigotry and all uncharitableness in others. He was himself so unconscious of having done wrong, nay, he was so certain of having done only right, that his friends took him almost by force from his house, and saved him from the vengeance of a mob who would have torn him to pieces."

He held a controversy with the Revds. S. Madan and E. Burn—two of the Episcopalian clergy of the town—and the paper warfare on both sides waged hotly. "To dispute with the Doctor," says Hutton drily, "was deemed the road to preferment. He had already made two bishops, and there were still several heads which wanted mitres, and others who cast a more humble eye upon tithes and glebe lands." Several of the clergy did not hesitate to stoop to a wilful, and, it is to be feared, malignant misconstruction of his words. In one of his pamphlets the Doctor had instituted a comparison between the progress of free inquiry and the action of gunpowder; he writes:

"The present silent propogation of truth may even be compared to those causes in nature which lie dormant for a time, but which in proper circumstances act with the greatest violence. We are, as it were, laying gunpowder, grain by grain, under the old building of error and superstition, which a single spark may hereafter inflame, so as to produce an instantaneous explosion; in consequence of which, that edifice, the erection of which has been the work of ages, may be overturned in a moment, and so effectually, as that the same foundation can never be built upon again."

This obviously figurative expression was actually laid hold of by the clergy as a covert threat of *a new Gunpowder Plot, for blowing up all the churches of the Establishment!* * It was in vain that the Doctor expostulated against such misinterpretation of his words, and explained that he referred merely to the powerful force of

---

* This passage is referred to in an old poem entitled "Topsy-Turvy," published in 1793:—

" E'en now is your church undermined,
   With Priestley's Polemical Nitre,
 Which exploded you'll presently find,
   The red night-cap take place of the Mitre."

THE ATTACK ON THE OLD MEETING HOUSE, JULY 14TH, 1791.

29

argument; it was in vain that he pointed out the blamelessness of his life among them; the ignorant masses—and, alas! *how* ignorant those masses were, *how* blindly they were led by their spiritual pastors and masters, we of the present age can never fully realize—believed the libellous charges, and hated Priestley and all "Socinians" (or "*Priestleyans,*" as they were beginning to be styled), as became good Churchmen and loyal subjects of King George. Right or wrong, the parsons were against this "formidable Heresiarch," as he had been dubbed, and as they had the consciences of the masses in their keeping, it behoved the latter to follow their leaders without question; and "D—n Priestley" was the loyal and patriotic sentiment chalked up on every blank wall in Birmingham.

But by far the greatest crime of all which Dr. Priestley and the "Socinians" had committed, was that of sympathising with the lovers of freedom who had just succeeded in overturning the throne of Louis XVI. in France. This sympathy Gillray, the caricaturist, turned to account in a bitterly hostile and infamously libellous print—on the occasion of the memorable dinner to which we shall refer presently—representing the leading "Jacobins" of the day drinking "A Birmingham Toast," proposed by Dr. Priestley, "The —— Head *here!*" i.e., in a Communion salver which he holds aloft, himself drinking the toast from a chalice. The Jacobins are represented as eagerly welcoming this toast; Sheridan, pouring out a fresh glass of sherry, of which he has already emptied several bottles, is made to say (in one of those inartistic "balloon" inscriptions which disfigure all the older caricatures), "I'll pledge you that toast," his remark being further garnished with choice flowers of speech which we need not quote here; Sir Cecil Wray, frugally drinking small-beer, exclaims, "O heav'ns! why I would empty a Chelsea Pensioner's small-beer barrel in such a cause;" Fox, as chairman, with punch-bowl before him, cries, "My soul and body, both upon the toast!"

Horne Tooke, who sits next him, drinking "Hollands" says, "I have not drank so glorious a toast since I was Parson of Brentford;" while in the corner, opposite Dr. Priestley, his co-religionist, Dr. Theophilus Lindsey cries "Amen! Amen!" as he drinks the toast in brandy. In the background are several cadaverous-looking pietists, supposed to represent Dr. Priestley's congregation. The print is exceedingly vigorous in design and execution, but as full of venom as an etching from Gillray's needle could possibly be. A carefully engraved copy of this plate, divested of the balloon-like scrolls containing the inscriptions, appears on page 215.

But Gillray was not alone in thus taking advantage of Priestley's sympathy with the Revolutionists of France. An inflammatory hand-bill, purporting to come from the Doctor, was fabricated in London, brought to Birmingham, and a few copies privately scattered under the table at an inn. It ran as follows:

"My Countrymen—The second year of Gallic Liberty is nearly expired. At the commencement of the third, on the 14th of this month, it is devoutly to be wished that every enemy to civil and religious despotism would give his sanction to the *majestic common cause* by a public celebration of the anniversary. Remember that on the 14th of July, the Bastille, that 'high altar and castle of despotism,' fell. Remember the enthusiasm peculiar to the cause of liberty, with which it was attacked. Remember that generous humanity that taught the oppressed, groaning under the weight of insulted rights, to save the lives of oppressors! Extinguish the mean prejudices of nations! and let your numbers be collected and sent as a free-will offering to the National Assembly.

"But is it possible to forget that our own Parliament is venal? your Minister hypocritical? your clergy legal oppressors? the Reigning Family extravagant? the crown of a certain great personage becoming every day too weighty for the head that wears it? Too weighty for the people who *gave* it? Your taxes partial and excessive? Your Representation a cruel *insult* upon the Sacred Rights of Property, Religion, and Freedom?

"But on the 14th of this month, prove to the political sycophants of the day that you reverence the Olive Branch; that you *will* sacrifice to public tranquility, till the majority *shall* exclaim, *The Peace of Slavery is worse than the War of Freedom.* Of that moment let tyrants beware!"

This seditious hand-bill, as may be imagined, added fuel to the fire of hatred which burned in the hearts of the masses against the dissenters. The latter immediately offered a reward of one hundred guineas for the discovery of the writer, printer, publisher, or distributor of the inflammatory address, and disclaimed all complicity in the matter, or concurrence in the sentiments of the writer thereof.* But this was all in vain; the incensed multitude refused to believe in the innocence or loyalty of the dissenters, and watched their opportunity to punish the supposed traitors. This was soon afforded, by the announcement of a meeting to take place at the Hotel in Temple Row, on the 14th of July, 1791, to celebrate the anniversary of the destruction of the Bastille. Dr. Priestley and his followers were at once identified with this celebration, by the masses of the people, (who were opposed to the French Revolution,) inasmuch as the worthy doctor had been nominated as a citizen of the new Republic, in recognition of his able reply to Burke's *Reflections on the French Revolution.* The meeting was announced in the *Gazette,* (in an advertisement dated "Hotel, Birmingham, July 7," a week previous to the date fixed for the celebration,) and immediately under it appeared another advertisement to the effect that a list of the gentlemen who were present at the meeting should be published on the following day. This latter announcement was evidently intended to intimidate the projectors of the meeting, and to alarm the inhabitants.

In a most interesting narrative of the sufferings

* Another reward of a hundred guineas was also offered by the local authorities, and a third hundred by the Government.

of the Hutton family during the Riots, written by the historian's daughter, Catherine, she says:

"Dr. Priestley admired my father, and frequently took tea with us, without ceremony. On Wednesday, the 6th, he drank tea with us, and asked my father to join the party at the dinner. 'I wish well to liberty everywhere,' replied my father, 'but public dinners are out of my way.' The doctor then asked Mr. Berington, the author of *Lives of Henry the Second,* and of *Abelard and Heloise,* who was also with us, if he would dine. 'No,' said Mr. Berington, 'we Catholics stand better with government than you Dissenters, and we will not make common cause with you.' On Monday, the 11th, the advertisement respecting the dinner appeared again in the Birmingham newspaper, and immediately under it was another informing the public that the names of the gentlemen who should dine at the hotel on Thursday would be published, price one halfpenny. This seemed a signal for mischief; but mischief was unknown in Birmingham, and no one regarded it.

"On Tuesday, the 12th, I went to Bennett's Hill [Washwood Heath], to pass a few days with my mother. In the evening my brother [Thomas Hutton] came, and told us that a riot was expected on Thursday; but so little was I interested by the intelligence, that it left no impression on my mind. The word *riot,* since so dreadful, conveyed no other idea than that of verbal abuse."

The Huttons were not alone in disregarding the rumours of a disturbance, as we shall see in our next chapter.

CHAPTER XXXV.

THE FOURTEENTH OF JULY, AND ITS EVENTS.

A Conciliatory Announcement—Proposed postponement of the dinner—The idea of postponement abandoned—The Dinner and the Toasts—An Opposition Meeting—Commencement of Hostilities—Attack on the Hotel—The New Meeting House—The Old Meeting House—Narrow Escapes—"To Dr. Priestley's!"—Mr. Russell's attempt to save the house—The house destroyed—Conduct of Dr. Priestley.

THE momentous fourteenth of July at length arrived, and fears of a disturbance were rife on every hand. The peace-loving dissenters, anxious to allay the fears of the populace as to their intentions, published, in the *Birmingham Chronicle*, on the morning of the 14th, the following address :

BIRMINGHAM COMMEMORATION OF THE FRENCH REVOLUTION.

Several hand-bills having been circulated in the town, which can only be intended to create distrust concerning the intention of the meeting, to disturb its harmony, and inflame the minds of the people, the gentlemen, who proposed it, think it necessary to declare their entire disapprobation of all such hand-bills, and their ignorance of the authors. Sensible themselves of the advantages of a free government, they rejoice in the extension of liberty to their neighbours; at the same time avowing, in the most explicit manner, their firm attachment to the constitution of their own country, as vested in the three estates of King, Lords, and Commons. Surely no free-born Englishman can refrain from exulting in this addition to the general mass of human happiness. It is the cause of humanity ! It is the cause of the people !
Birmingham, July 13, 1791.

This, however, failed to reassure the people,— or, more probably, the movers of the projected attack on the dissenters,—and the disturbing rumours increased as the day advanced; the friends of the proposed celebration, therefore, agreed to postpone the matter until a more peaceable feeling should prevail, and to this end, prepared a hand-bill as follows :

INTENDED COMMEMORATION OF THE FRENCH REVOLUTION.

The friends of the intended festivity finding that their views and intentions, in consequence of being misconceived by some, and misrepresented by others, have created an alarm in the minds of the majority of the town, and, it is thought, endangered its tranquillity, inform their neigh-bours that they value the peace of the town far beyond the gratification of a festival, and therefore have determined to give up their intentions of dining at the hotel upon this occasion ; and they very gladly improve this renewed opportunity of declaring that they are to this hour ignorant of the author, printer, or publisher of the inflammatory hand-bill circulated on Monday.

This notice of postponement was actually put into the hands of the printer, but before it was set up, Mr. Dadley, the proprietor of the hotel, attended, in consequence of his having received an order countermanding the dinner, and represented that there was no ground for fear, and no danger of any serious disturbance ; he therefore recommended that the idea of postponement should be abandoned, but that, in order to prevent the possibility of danger, "the gentlemen should take care to break up early." This advice was listened to, and orders were given for the suppression of the bill announcing the postponement. The meeting was most orderly,—far more so than many a vestry meeting where "Church and King" are duly honoured,—and the toasts were of a loyal and patriotic character ; and, as much was said as to the revolutionary tendency of the sentiments expressed therein, we append a list of them, as furnished by Mr. William Russell, (one of the sufferers), in answer to the calumnious misstatements of certain newspapers of the opposite party. The toasts were as follows :

1. The King and Constitution.
2. The National Assembly and Patriots of France, whose virtue and wisdom have raised twenty-six millions from the mean condition of subjects of despotism, to the dignity and happiness of free men.
3. The Majesty of the People.
4. May the New Constitution of France be rendered perfect and perpetual.

5. May Great Britain, Ireland, and France, unite in perpetual friendship; and may their only rivalship be the extension of peace and liberty, wisdom and virtue.

6. The Rights of Man. May all nations have the wisdom to understand, and the courage to assert and defend them.

7. The true Friends of the Constitution of this Country, who wish to preserve its spirit, by correcting its abuses.

8. May the people of England never cease to remonstrate, till their Parliament becomes a true National Representation.

9. The Prince of Wales.

10. The United States of America. May they for ever enjoy the liberty which they have so honourably acquired.

11. May the late Revolution in Poland prove the harbinger of a more perfect system of liberty extending to that great kingdom.

12. May the Nations of Europe become so enlightened as never more to be deluded into savage wars, by the mad ambition of their rulers.

13. May the sword be never unsheathed, but for the defence and liberty of our country; and then may every man cast away the scabbard until the people are safe and free.

14. To the glorious memory of Hampden and Sydney, and other heroes of all ages and nations, who have fought and bled for liberty.

15. To the memory of Dr. Price, and of all those illustrious sages who have enlightened mankind on the true principles of civil society.

16. Peace and good-will to all mankind.

17. Prosperity to the town of Birmingham.

18. A happy Meeting to all the Friends of Liberty on the 14th of July, 1792.

About eighty gentlemen sat down to dinner, at three o'clock. The room was appropriately decorated, " with three elegant emblematical pieces of sculpture, mixed with painting, in a new style of composition." The centre-piece was a " finely-executed portrait of His Majesty, encircled with a glory," and on either side was an alabaster obelisk,—the one representing Gallic liberty breaking the bands of despotism, and the other British liberty in its present enjoyment.

Meanwhile, their opponents—the Anti-Jacobins,—were holding a by no means orderly meeting at an inn not far from Dadley's Hotel,* and drinking confusion (and something worse) to Priestley and his followers ; keeping up a con-

tinual cry of " Church and King for ever."* This was to be the war cry of the rabble, " people," says Hutton, " who would have sold their King for a jug of ale, and demolished the Church for a bottle of gin."

A spy had obtained admission to the hotel, and brought word (referring no doubt to the central ornament already mentioned,) " *that they had cut off the King's head and set it on the table!* Whether this was a mere pleasantry, or intended to work upon the feelings of the ignorant mob, we cannot say ; but if the latter, it was speedily successful. The crowd had hissed and hustled the gentlemen as they went into the hotel, and, when the meeting broke up, at about five o'clock, those who had attended it found greater difficulty in returning to their homes. The mob re-assembled in larger numbers at about eight o'clock, and at once commenced an attack upon the hotel, breaking all the windows and damaging most of the furniture in the room in which the meeting had been held. They had watched the house during the whole of the evening, to see if Dr. Priestley came out, and probably their chief object in attacking the Hotel was to find him. But he had not been present at the dinner at all ; " public assemblages of a political or convivial nature," says Mr. Hawkes Smith, " were not the chosen recreation of the philosopher and theologian." And so they wreaked their vengeance upon the building in which the Dissenters had met ; it was in vain that the better-disposed among them cried out " Don't break Dadley's windows ! he's a Churchman !" They had determined upon creating a disturbance, and proving their loyal attachment to the Church and King.

Disappointed and foiled in their endeavours to find Dr. Priestley, they proceeded to the

---

* Afterwards, and more commonly known as " Dee's Royal Hotel," Temple Row.

* At a Municipal dinner shortly after the Riots, at which Dr. Samuel Parr was present, the toast " Church and King " having been proposed, the doctor immediately rose to his feet and loudly proclaimed his dissent. " No, sir !" said he, " I will not drink that toast. It was the cry of Jacobites ; it is the cry of incendiaries. It means a Church without the Gospel, and a King above the Law ! "

building in which he ministered,—the New Meeting House, in Moor Street. The gates and doors were soon burst open, the pews demolished, the cushions and other fittings taken and burnt in the open space in front, and they then commenced to demonstrate their "burning love" upon the building itself, and in a very short period left nothing but the four blackened outside walls, which were of such thickness and solidity as to resist the action of the flames. A valuable library of theological books, (in the vestry,) belonging to the society, was also destroyed.

While this scene was taking place in Moor Street, a second party of rioters were attacking the Old Meeting House; they tore down, with crowbars and other implements, the pulpit, pews, galleries, etc., and set fire to them in the burial ground. Then, after demolishing portions of the building, they set fire to its walls, and razed it to the ground, so that not a vestige remained. Their systematic mode of conducting these disgraceful proceedings is shown in the fact that they exerted themselves to the utmost to prevent injury to the surrounding houses, being determined that only the dissenters should suffer; also, that they had prepared a list of the various houses which they had determined to attack, and included those of every known dissenter in the neighbourhood.

Another party had meanwhile proceeded to Newhall Street, and surrounded the newly erected Church of the Swedenborgians, with the intention of destroying it, but were diverted from their purpose by the presence of mind of the minister, the Rev. Joseph Proud, who lived at the house adjoining. A collection had been made in the church on the preceding day, and the minister, standing on the elevated steps in front of his house, scattered the money among the throng of would-be incendiaries, telling them that his congregation were not Unitarians, but that they were loyal to the Throne and the Government. A shout of "the New Jerusalem for ever" was immediately raised, and the crowd passed on with-

out injuring either the church or its courageous minister.

A similar incident occurred at the meeting-house of Lady Huntingdon's Connexion, in King Street. The mob had gathered round the building in order to destroy it, when someone among them cried out, "Don't burn it, they're good 'Church and King' men."

Meanwhile, among those who had destroyed the two Meeting-Houses of the Unitarians, the cry was "*To Dr. Priestley's!*"

In a vivid and picturesque narrative of the riots, written by Miss Russell, (daughter of William Russell, Esq., of Showell Green,) we read that her father "went first," on hearing of the riots, "to Dr. Priestley's house, where he found William Priestley, whom he instructed to begin and move all the Doctor's manuscripts he thought most likely to be valuable, by means of persons in the neighbourhood whom my father had brought for that purpose, and on whom he could rely, to a place in the vicinity he had fixed upon as secret and secure. This he urged him to do as expeditiously and quietly as possible, and to continue this employ, including also any other valuables he recollected, till my father should send him word to stop, not attending to any reports that might be brought him.

"My father," continues Miss Russell, "then rode on to town as far as Digbeth, and there, meeting the mob, he tried in vain to proceed. He met many of his friends, all of whom requested him to return, telling him he did not hear the threats that were uttered against him. At length, one of them, I believe Mr. J. F——, suddenly turned his horse, and, giving him a cut with his whip, the press was so great, and the spirit of the horse so roused, my father found himself obliged in a manner to return. Arriving at Dr. Priestley's gate before the mob, he stationed himself within-side till the mob came up and then addressed them, endeavouring to induce them, by fair words and money, to desist and return home. At first they seemed a little pacified and inclined to listen, till one more loud than the rest, and who had the appearance of a ringleader, cried out, 'Don't take a sixpence of his money; in the riots of '80 in London, a man was hanged for only taking sixpence.' They all then vociferated, 'Stone him, stone him!' and began to fling stones. My father then, finding it rashness to brave two or three thousand men, turned his horse and rode up to the house, telling W. P. that he must desist, and take as much care of the house as he could, and advising him to make all the doors and windows as secure as possible. He then rode off home."

The mob then commenced their attack upon the house, "with the most incredible fury," says the *Gazette*. They began by breaking down the doors and windows, and throwing out the furniture from every part of the house; tearing and burning all the books and manuscripts in the doctor's library, including, among the latter, the results of many years of patient research in natural philosophy, such as could never be restored or recovered. As they went from room to room throughout the house, in the hope of finding Dr. Priestley, (who with Mrs. Priestley and Mr. S. Ryland had escaped to the residence of Mr. Russell, at Showell Green, an hour or more previously,) they vented their disappointment in curses and imprecations on him, and redoubled their fiendish energies in the total demolition of his house and property. His valuable library was scattered to the winds, so that, according to an eye-witness, "the highroads for full half a mile of the house were strewed with books, and that on entering the library there was not a dozen volumes on the shelves, while the floor was covered several inches deep with the torn manuscripts."

The shrubs, trees, etc., in the garden were all trampled down or torn up, and the desolate appearance of the place was thus rendered complete; but there was still a gleam of hope that the laboratory, with all the doctor's valuable apparatus, would escape uninjured, as the mob, having entered the cellars, had become so intoxicated as to be, in most cases, almost senseless, whilst the remainder had been rendered so quarrelsome, by the plentiful draughts of wine and ale, that, according to the *Gazette* report, no less than nine or ten different battles among themselves were at one time being fought in the adjoining field. But, after they had spent their vinous strength on the inglorious battle-field, they returned once more to the scene of destruction, broke into the laboratory, and destroyed the whole of the philosophical instruments, which, according to the doctor's declaration, were the most valuable that any individual in this or any other country was ever possessed of. They then set fire to the whole building; and in a few hours nothing remained of the house, offices, etc., but the bare walls. One man was killed on the spot by the falling of a cornice pole. This brought Thursday's proceedings to a close; and most of the rioters remained, sleeping, or in a state of helpless intoxication, in the fields around the house until morning.

We return for a few moments to Miss Russell's narrative. After Mr. Russell had returned home from his interview with the rioters, at Fair Hill, he, with his own family and the refugees, walked on to Mr. Hawkes's. "Here," says Miss Russell, "we found the family up, and under great apprehension; and here we soon heard the shouts of the mob at Dr. Priestley's house (and I shall never forget what dreadful and hideous shouts they were), intermingled with a loud noise of battering against the walls, and such a confusion of cries, huzzas, &c., as cannot be imagined. Soon the flames burst forth, and then all seemed quiet. What were the emotions of our mind at this moment no one can imagine, unless they had beheld our countenances and heard the broken, short sentences that formed all the conversation which passed amongst us : yet the extreme agitation of our minds did not prevent us from admiring the divine appearance of the excellent Dr. Priestley. No human being could, in my opinion, appear in any trial more like divine, or show a nearer resemblance to our Saviour, than he did then. Undaunted he heard the blows which were destroying the house and laboratory that contained all his valuable and rare apparatus and their effects, which it had been the business of his life to collect and use. All this apparatus, together with the uses he had made of them, the laborious exertions of his whole life, were being destroyed by a set of merciless, ignorant, lawless banditti, whilst he, tranquil and serene, walked up and down the road with a firm yet gentle pace that evinced his entire self-possession, and a complete self-satisfaction and consciousness which rendered him thus firm and resigned under the unjust and cruel persecution of his enemies; and with a countenance expressing the highest devotion, turned as it were from this scene, and fixed with pure and calm resignation on Him who suffered the administration of this bitter cup. Not one hasty or impatient expression, not one look expressive of murmur or complaint, not one tear or sigh escaped him; resignation and a conscious innocence and virtue seemed to subdue all these feelings of humanity.

"About four o'clock my father returned and informed us that the fire had consumed the Doctor's house, the mob were nearly dispersed, half drunk, having been up to their ankles in wine in his cellar, where they had broke the necks off all the bottles, and inundated the cellar with that portion of their contents they could not drink—that the fields round were now covered with these fiends sleeping from drunkenness and fatigue, and that, as day was now come, he thought it most likely they would disperse entirely, and that consequently we might return home again. Accordingly we set off, and never shall I forget the joy with which I entered our own gates once more. That our house was spared I was grateful beyond measure; it seemed as an old dear friend restored to life from a dangerous disorder. I rejoiced also because it enabled us to afford an asylum to our exemplary fellow-sufferer."

A hurried letter was despatched from the town, apparently in the morning of each day, to London; and, although, from their having been written in the heat of the strife, they are necessarily imperfect and inaccurate, they are brief but exceedingly graphic journals of the events of each day; we cannot therefore do better than summarise each day's proceedings by quoting these letters; taking care, as far as possible, to correct their errors. On Friday morning this correspondent wrote of the doings on Thursday, as follows:—

"*Ten o'Clock in the Morning.*—The meeting at the hotel yesterday, to celebrate the French Revolution, was not so numerously attended as the friends to it expected. Eighty gentlemen only dined at the hotel, all of whom departed soon after five o'clock. The mob, that had began to assemble before, now commenced hostilities, by breaking all the windows of the hotel; and from thence they paraded to Dr. Priestley's Meeting House, which they set fire to. Another party, at the same time, set fire to the Old Meeting House; and both these places were soon burnt to the ground. [The outside walls only of the New Meeting were left standing.] Some adjoining houses took fire by accident, and were also consumed. [All other accounts state that the rioters permitted the occupiers of all the adjoining houses to extinguish the flames, and so saved them from serious injury.]

"The mob then went to Dr. Priestley's dwelling house, at Fair Hill, about a mile and a half on this side Birmingham, which they completely gutted, burnt the inside, all his furniture, books, manuscripts, and philosophical apparatus, and drank out all his wines, &c. They are at this minute pulling the next house down.

"The mob now get valiant, and swear that every Priestley's man here must *come down*. In short, the whole place is in the utmost confusion."

HOUSES DESTROYED BY THE RIOTERS, JULY, 1791.

CHAPTER XXXVI.

THE SECOND DAY OF THE RIOTS.

The reign of terror—William Hutton's Advice—Attack on Baskerville House—Special Constables sworn—Conflict with the rioters—Attack on Bordesley Hall—William Hutton's place of business sacked—End of Friday's proceedings.

ON Friday morning, as they recovered from the fatigue and intoxication of the previous night, different parties of the rioters returned into the town, to the great consternation of all the inhabitants. Business was totally suspended, and all the shops closed ; while on almost every door was chalked the Shibboleth of the attacking party, " Church and King,"—a talisman which failed not to secure for the inhabitants an immunity from destruction or injury.

The doors of the Bridewell and other places of confinement were thrown open, and the mob, joined by this reinforcement from the dangerous classes, paraded the streets armed with bludgeons, shouting " Church and King ! "

The affrighted inhabitants ran hither and thither for advice, but as yet no active steps had been taken to quell the riot. In their terror, many sought advice of William Hutton, who was esteemed for his sound wisdom by every right-thinking man. " As the danger admitted of no delay," says Hutton, " I gave this short answer, —' Apply to the magistrates, and request four things : to swear in as many special constables as are willing, and arm them ; to apply to the commanding officer of the recruiting parties for his assistance ; to apply to Lord Beauchamp to call out the militia in the neighbourhood ; and to write to the Secretary-at-War for a military force.' What became of my four hints is uncertain, but the result proved that they were lost."

In the course of the morning the Earl of Aylesford arrived at Fair Hill, (the residence of Dr. Priestley,) and harrangued what remained of the mob there. He then brought them into the town, and endeavoured to persuade them to disperse, and return to their homes and occupations ; but it was all in vain. Like the wild beast who has tasted blood, they were now insatiable. It was in vain that they were told, that having destroyed the meeting house and the home of Dr. Priestley, "they had *now* done enough ! " It was in vain that the magistrates and other principal inhabitants harrangued them in St. Philip's Churchyard, beseeching them to desist from violence ; they were now mad for rapine and plunder, free from the law, (for as the author of *John Halifax* says, in the narrative of the bread riot at Norton Bury Mill, the law would not, at that time, readily interfere on behalf of dissenters,) and they had still a long list of houses which needed to be burnt in honour of " Church and King."

At two o'clock they attacked Baskerville House, the residence of J. Ryland, Esq. This was still a pleasantly situated mansion ; it stood " in the midst of a luxuriant meadow," and was approached by a fine avenue of trees. Other trees surrounded it on every side ; and, although so near as to be almost *within* the town, it must have been at that time as fair a residence as any on which the mad fury of the rioters fell.

The house which John Baskerville had erected for himself, and which was even in its original state a most commodious dwelling, it was now much more spacious and elegant, having been enlarged and improved by Mr. Ryland, and was actually " receiving its last improvements, from the hand of its unoffending possessor," when it was attacked by the rioters. They were several times repulsed, and, in one instance, the house was entirely cleared of them, by the unassisted arm of a single individual. And it must be remembered that even the defence of their own property by the dissenters was hedged about with legal difficulties. One gentleman asked "if he might arm his dependents?" The answer was, "The hazard will be yours." Again, "Whether he might carry a brace of pistols in his own defence?" "If you kill a man,"—was the reply —"you must be responsible." And so the attack continued. The rioters were strengthened by a reinforcement, bringing their number up to nearly a thousand; every room was entered, and in the cellar, (where were stored wines to the value of three hundred pounds,) they remained, drinking, long after the building was fired,—some even until the roof fell in. Such a sight, perhaps, has seldom been witnessed; the furious rabble, maddened and inflamed with drink, cursing, yelling, dying, amid the blazing ruins; the scene, a few hours previous so fair to look upon, now blackened and disfigured in every direction,—a scene of desolation without, a pandemonium within the house. Seven persons were burnt to death in the cellar, and when dug out of the ruins were so mutilated as scarcely to be recognised. One poor wretch was buried in one of the vaults, and was unable to get out until the following Monday, when he expired, soon after his release, on the grass in front of the house. Many were terribly scorched and bruised, and were carried away to the hospital.

Meanwhile the magistrates had summoned (by the town crier,) the more peaceable inhabitants to meet in St. Philip's Churchyard, and commenced to swear in as many of them as were willing, as special constables. A large body of these were immediately despatched to Baskerville House, where a fierce struggle ensued, the rioters attacking them with bludgeons and stones, and soon caused them to beat a retreat. One of the gentlemen who acted as a special constable (Mr. Thomas Ashwin) was so severely wounded in this fight, that he died shortly afterwards.

At the same time, information having been received that another party of rioters had commenced an attack on the house of Mr. John Taylor,* (Bordesley Hall,) a second detachment of constables, headed by Captain Carver, repaired to the place, and succeeded in driving out the rioters, whom they found in the cellar, from the premises. Having got possession of the house, they kept the lawless mob at bay while the title deeds, writings, etc., belonging to Mr. Taylor, were removed, together with a portion of the furniture. But as evening drew near, the attacking party were joined by those who had just left the ruins of Baskerville House, with others, and so were enabled to overpower the constables by force of numbers. As a last resource, Captain Carver offered the mob the immediate payment of one hundred guineas, but was at once met with the cry of "No bribery!" He immediately threw himself into the midst of them, and narrowly escaped their fury. As the night advanced, the flames appeared through the roof, and this fine mansion was in a short time entirely gutted.

Friday's work of destruction was brought to a close by an attack on the house of business of William Hutton, in High Street. It had been attempted several times during the afternoon.

"About noon," says Hutton, "some of my friends advised me 'to take care of my goods, for my house must come down.' I treated the advice as ridiculous, and replied, ' That was their duty, and the duty of every inhabitant, for my case was theirs; I had only the power of an individual. Besides, fifty wagons could not have carried off my stock in trade, exclusive of the furniture of my house; and if they could, where must I deposit it?' I sent, however, a small quantity of paper to a neighbour, who returned it, and the whole afterwards fell a prey to rapine."

---

* Son of the John Taylor mentioned in our chapter of Birmingham Worthies.

It may be asked, why the property of William Hutton, a man honoured and esteemed by his fellow-townsmen, moderate in his opinions on all subjects, and *not a Unitarian*, (for as we have previously said, he attended the Independent Meeting House in Carr's Lane,) should have been singled out for attack? Not for his religious or political opinions, certainly, but for the part he took as a Commissioner of the Court of Requests, or, as it was popularly called, the Court of Conscience. He says, in his narrative, " Some gentlemen advised the insurgents assembled in New Street to disperse; when one, whom I well knew, said, ' Do not disperse, they want to sell us. If you will pull down Hutton's house, I will give you two guineas to drink, for it was owing to him I lost a cause in the Court.' The bargain was struck, and my building fell."

The mob attacked the house three or four times, and were brought off repeatedly, by William Hutton himself first, and afterwards by his son Thomas. On the fourth attack, however, they refused all attempts at conciliation. They entered the building, and stripped it of its contents; the different pieces of furniture were hoisted to the upper windows, and then allowed to fall into the street, in order to complete their destruction; and those which survived the fall were smashed to pieces with bludgeons, by three strong men who were stationed below for that purpose. As they went about their work of destruction, they shouted, " Down with the Court of Conscience!" "No more ale-scores to be paid!" Church and King were forgotten now by the dishonest rogues who saw in the riots a grand opportunity of taking vengeance upon the man who had compelled them to pay their just debts.

The rioters completed their work of destruction at this house just before daylight, having destroyed or carried away all the furniture, the large stock of paper, and a library of valuable books belonging to Hutton's son Thomas. They left the house stripped of its roof, doors, chimney-pieces, windows, and window frames, and were only deterred from setting fire to the building itself by the fear of injuring those adjoining it.

The work of Friday, which was brought to a close with this act of vandalism, is thus summarised by the correspondent quoted at the end of the last chapter :—

" *Friday, July 15.—Three o'clock in the Afternoon.*— Since my last, the following houses have been pulled down, and the furniture removed and burnt; viz. : Messrs. Ryland's, (late Baskerville's,) Humphreys', and Taylor's. All these gentlemen are dissenters, and men of great property. The house of Mr. Humphreys, which is near Dr. Priestley's, was admired as an elegant structure, but now is a heap of ruins. [*This is an error ; Mr. Humphreys' house was not destroyed until Saturday.*]

" *Lord Aylesford* come into town this morning, and harangued the mob. What his Lordship said appeared at first to have a good effect, and they promised him and the magistrates they would disperse peaceably. They did not, however, keep their words, but increased in numbers, and became more riotous. We dread the night, as we have no military with us.

" This instant a large party of gentlemen, on horseback, are going to endeavour to save Mr. Ryland's house, or his furniture ; but it is now known they are too late.

" *Six o'clock in the Evening.*—The rioters being divided into two parties, and meditating the destruction of several other houses, about three o'clock in the afternoon, consternation and alarm seemed to have suspersded all other sensations in the minds of the inhabitants ; business was given over, and the shops were all shut up. The inhabitants were traversing the streets in crowds, not knowing what to do, and horror was visible in every countenance.

" About half-past three the inhabitants were summoned by the bell-man to assemble in the New Church Yard. [*St. Philip's*]. Two magistrates attended in an adjacent room, [*the Swan Inn, in Bull Street*] and swore in several hundred constables, composed of every description of inhabitants, who marched away to disperse the rioters, who were beginning to attack the house of Mr. Hutton, paper merchant, in the High Street. This was easily effected, there being not more than half-a-dozen drunken wretches then assembled on the spot.

" From thence they proceeded to disperse the grand body, who were employed in the destruction of Mr. Ryland's house. On entering the walls which surround the house, then all in a blaze, a most dreadful conflict took place, in which it is impossible to ascertain the number of the wounded. The constables were attacked with such a shower of stones and brickbats as it was impossible to resist. The rioters then possessing themselves of bludgeons, the constables were entirely defeated, many of them being much wounded. One person was killed, but of which party it is not yet known.

" *Eleven o'clock at Night.*—The mob being now victorious, and heated with liquor, everything was dreaded.

Several attempts were made to amuse them, but in vain. They exacted money from the inhabitants; and at ten o'clock at night, they began and soon effected the destruction of Mr. Hutton's house, in the High Street, plundering it of all its property.

"From thence they proceeded to the seat of John Taylor, Esq., banker. [*These two events are transposed;*

the house of Mr. Taylor was attacked and destroyed before *that of Mr. Hutton.*] There five hundred pounds [*all other accounts say one hundred*] were offered them to desist, but to no purpose, for they immediately set fire to that beautiful mansion, which, together with its superb furniture, stables, offices, greenhouse, hot-house, &c., are reduced to a heap of ruins."

CHAPTER XXXVII.

THE THIRD DAY OF THE RIOTS.

Attack on Hutton's House at Washwood Heath—Catherine Hutton's narrative—The Magistrates at length aroused—An extraordinary appeal—Mr. Humphrey's House attacked—Miss Russell's narrative—Other events of Saturday.

AFTER the mob had sufficiently wreaked their vengeance on Mr. Hutton's place of business, they set off at early dawn on Saturday morning, to his country residence, at Bennett's Hill, Washwood Heath. The story of the attack on this house has been so well told by the historian's daughter, Catherine, that we cannot do better than give her narrative entire, — the more especially as it has hitherto been known only to the members of the family and the select circle to whom Mrs. Franks-Beale's private reprint of the narrative* has found its way.

The first news of the proposed attack on Mr. Hutton's house reached his family on the previous morning: Miss Hutton says:—

"On Friday morning, at seven o'clock, when I no more expected mischief than if I had been in heaven, my mother came into my room and told me that the Old and New Meeting Houses and Dr. Priestley's house were burnt to the ground. I heard it with grief and astonishment, but without any alarm for ourselves, who, I believed, had injured no one. My mother added, 'Now they are going to attack the houses of the Dissenters.' I saw in a moment which way her fears pointed,

and I said, 'They cannot injure us. My father was not at the dinner; and though a Dissenter, he is a very moderate man.' 'Ah!' said my mother, 'you forget the Court of Conscience!'

"My mother was much alarmed, and I not perfectly at ease, though I endeavoured to comfort her, till eleven o'clock, when two men, strangers to us, came to tell us that Mr. Ryland's house was then on fire, that our house was to be the next, and that if we pleased, they would assist in removing the furniture to a place of safety. It was now time to act. I employed them to take down valences, and take to pieces bedsteads, under the superintendence of my mother; I sent my keys to Birmingham by our coachman, with orders to the maids there to secure the plate, linen, and clothes, and I went myself to the houses of three different farmers in the neighbourhood to request them to receive our goods. The first replied, 'No, I've no room here.' The second said, 'Aye, yo may send 'em.' But a third joining us, and saying, 'But don't you think you bayn't in no danger yourself if you take 'em in?' the friendly neighbour said, 'Why, aye, I dayn't think o' that; yo moan't send 'em.' It then first occurred to me that I was a humble suppliant. Till now, I had imagined that anyone

* A Narrative of the Riots in Birmingham, July, 1791. Birmingham: [" Printed for private circulation among the descendants of those who suffered in those troublous times."] S.A.

who was not of the mob himself, would cheer-
fully assist us to escape the depredations of the
mob.   The next man to whom I applied allowed
me to fill his house and barn.

"We now repaired each to his post.   My
mother sent different articles of furniture; Ann
C——, our maid servant, and our two assistants
carried them, and I received them, till our neighbour would take no more, and I returned home.
I now packed up china as fast as two persons
could give me the different pieces, and pieces of
paper to put between them.   My mother's sister,
my uncle's wife, and a female neighbour, having
heard of the misfortune which hung over our
heads, came to tender their services, and the
latter took some of our property, so that when
our coachman returned, and I ordered him to
drive the carriage to the inn at Castle Bromwich,
there was nothing left to put in it except a carpet
and some tins and coppers.

"A farmer's wife, who lived at the distance of
a mile and a half, dressed herself in her holiday
clothes, and came in her dung cart, with a party
of her friends, to enjoy the spectacle of a house
in a blaze, and appeared in some confusion when
she found we were yet in possession of it, and she
was obliged to explain the motive of her visit.

"A sudden panic now seized our neighbour,
and he insisted upon our furniture being taken
out of his house.   My father, finding himself
unable to secure our house at Birmingham, came
to us accompanied by ten men, determined to
defend this, and the first service they were
employed in was to bring back the goods.   Exhausted by fatigue, disappointment, and fasting,
we sat down in despair, and consigned our furniture to the fate of our house.

"A hackney coach, which had been sent for,
now stood at our gate; my mother and my aunt
got into it; I spread a sheet on the floor, and
having thrown into it such of my mother's clothes
as were next me, I carried it in my hand and
followed.   Our maid and a woman who had two
days' employment at our house every week, both

exceedingly drunk, attended at the coach door,
with a hypocritical whine.   The maid returned
like the dog, to her vomit; the woman to plunder.
A search warrant has since found our new carpet
hidden under her bed, and some earthenware and
kettles in her cottage.   I might here add that our
coachman, by whom I had sent the keys to Birmingham, never delivered them, and stood by
while the maids there broke open the drawers,
though he had the keys in his pocket.

"Our day had not been distinguished by the
common divisions of dinner-time and tea-time.
We had known no hour; we had tasted no food;
I was surprised when I saw the sun near its
setting, and it was nine o'clock when we arrived
at the house of my aunt's son, with whom she
lives.   There we tried to eat, and could not.

"From hence we despatched a messenger into
High Street, to bring us tidings of the state of
our house.   These were that the doors were fast,
the windows were broken, and a mob was assembled before it, who said that they would not burn
the house on account of the adjoining houses.
Our next intelligence was, that a panel of the
door was broken; and the next that the mob had
entered; paper was being thrown out of the
drawing-room windows; and women were carrying out aprons' full of our property.   This was a
dreadful moment indeed.   I thought I should
sink upon the floor; but I recollected that I had
a mother, and, instead of giving way to despair,
I ran to comfort her.

"At one o'clock in the morning we were joined
by my father and my brother.   My father's men
had become intoxicated and refractory, and he
had been obliged to abandon the house at
Bennett's Hill.   Between three and four o'clock
we all retired to bed, but not to sleep.   Between
five and six my aunt came into the room in which
my mother and I were lying, and told us that she
had been in High Street, where the mob were
still employed; that drawers, wardrobes, and
clothes were being thrown out of the windows,
and prints being trampled in the street.   She

added that my father's life was threatened. I rose instantly and went into his room, when I found him dressed and sitting on a chair. I told him what I had heard, and begged he would let me order a post chaise to take us to Sutton, a small town about seven miles distant, for I had now only one object in view, which was to save my father. With great difficulty he consented, and at seven o'clock, he, my mother, and myself, were seated in the chaise. We placed ourselves as much as possible before my father, and endeavoured to hide him as if he were flying from justice, while he was most indignant. 'What,' said he, 'have I been giving my time and my best services to the town, without fee or reward, to skulk from it like a malefactor! Let me go and face the mob, and set them at defiance!'

"Our prayers and entreaties, in some measure, calmed my father, and we breakfasted at the Three Tuns, at Sutton, not having eaten anything since breakfast the day before. After breakfast I set out lodging hunting, and I engaged, at a butchers, a parlour, just decent, and a bedroom far from it—being open to the stairs and roof, and containing two tattered, moth-eaten stuff beds. I then went to purchase muslin for a night-cap, otherwise my pocket handkerchief must have been the substitute, as it had been the night before. I now seated myself with my father and mother, and we reflected more at leisure on our misfortunes.

"In the early part of the evening my brother had seen a mob advancing to attack our house in Birmingham, and he had gone out to meet them, when a bludgeon was raised to knock him down, and he would probably have been killed had not a butcher arrested the uplifted arm, and cried, 'D——n you, don't you know he's Church and King? I went to school with him!' My brother then represented to the people that they might be much more worthily employed in rescuing the property of Mr. Taylor, of Bordesley, whose house was then beset by another party of rioters, than in destroying the house belonging to him

never offended them. Mob as they were, for a moment they listened to reason, and from their intended victim, my brother became their hero. They placed him at their head, and with a fiddle playing before him, they marched to Bordesley; but the moment they saw their fellow-mob engaged in the fascinating work of destruction, they deserted their leader, and joined the destroyers.

"My brother employed and assisted some spectators of a better sort to deposit Mr. Taylor's property in the neighbouring houses, till they would take no more; he then returned, alone, towards our house in Birmingham. In a short time he saw flying feathers, but whether from our beds he knew not; in Digbeth he saw one of our drawing-room chairs, which put the matter out of doubt. At the door of Mr. Carless, a respectable druggist, who lives near our house, he saw a bundle of writing paper, worth about five pounds, standing in the street. He took it up, and requested Mr. Carless to allow him to deposit it in his house. This Mr. Carless refused; and the paper was left in the street and destroyed. Exhausted with fatigue and thirst, my brother begged for a draught of water, and this Mr. Carless also refused. My brother's last request—and I wonder how he had the courage to make it—was for leave to pass through Mr. Carless's house, in order to avoid the rioters assembled before ours; this was, of course, refused, and my brother happily made his way through the mob undiscovered, while they were throwing furniture from the windows into the street. He now joined us, at twelve o'clock, at Sutton. He told us that the destruction of our house at Birmingham was completed, but that the neighbours had prevented its being set on fire, for fear of injury to themselves; that a party of rioters had attacked the house at Bennett's Hill at four o'clock in the morning, and my uncle had prevailed upon them to desist, by giving them ale at the village; that another party had appeared at seven o'clock, and had reduced the whole of the buildings to ashes. He added that it was no longer safe for him to remain in Birmingham.

"The mischief was now completed, and we encouraged each other to bear it. I had lost all I had collected, all that I had possessed; but I looked round me and saw my father, mother, and brother, and I was rich. I had been driven from two good homes; but I saw, in imagination, my mother and myself settled in our humble lodgings, my father visiting us every week, my brother occasionally, and I was content."

Another party, later in the morning, attacked the house of Mr. George Humphreys, at Sparkbrook, where the rioters were kept off for some time, but they at length entered and ransacked it, but did not burn it.

Meanwhile the magistrates, brought at length to see the danger to the town in general of the riots continuing any longer, issued, on Saturday morning, the following address:—

Birmingham, July 16th, 1791.—*Friends and Fellow-Countrymen,*—It is earnestly requested that every True Friend to the Church of England, and to the Laws of his Country, will reflect how much a continuance of the Present Proceedings must injure that Church and that King they are intended to support; and how highly Unlawful it is to destroy the Rights and Property of any of our Neighbours. And all True Friends to the Town and Trade of Birmingham, in particuar, are Intreated to Forbear immediately from all Riotous and Violent Proceedings; dispersing and returning peaceably to their Trades and Callings, as the only Way to do Credit to themselves and their Cause, and to promote the Peace, Happiness, and Prosperity of this Great and Flourishing Town.

The "True Friends to the Church of England and to the Laws of their Country" did not, however, regard this extraordinary entreaty to "do credit to themselves" by "returning peaceably to their trades and callings," but proceeded at once from Mr. Humphreys' to Showell Green, the residence of Mr. William Russell.

The news of the intended attack upon their house had reached the Russell family on the first night of the riots. "On that evening,"—says Miss Russell, in the narrative previously referred to,—"we walked up and down the foot-road

leading to town in a dreadful state of suspense and apprehension, clearly discerning the fire from the two Meeting-houses, and distinctly hearing the shouts of the mob. At length, my sister and I (our fears every minute strengthening) slipped away, and, hastily putting all our plate into a trunk without even locking the trunk, because in our haste we could not find the key, sent it by two of our servants to a neighbours."

We have already told, (from Miss Russell's narrative) how they watched the burning of Dr. Priestley's house, and how, when that was over, and the rioters were believed to have dispersed, they returned to their home, rejoicing that it was spared, and that they were thus enabled to offer a shelter to Dr. and Mrs. Priestley.

"On entering that house," continues Miss Russell, "thus so inexpressibly and strongly endeared to us, we began to think of rest. A room was prepared for the Doctor and Mrs. P. We all looked and felt all gratitude; but the Doctor appeared the happiest amongst us. Just as he was going to rest, expressing his thankfulness in being permitted to lie down again in peace and comfort, my father returned from Fair Hill, and brought the sad intelligence that they were collecting again, and their threats were more violent than ever—that they swore to find Dr. P. and take his life. The chaise was now ordered with all speed, and instead of the much-desired rest, the Doctor and Mrs. P. were obliged to dress again and get into it, scarcely knowing whither to go. Mr. R—— [Ryland] accompanied them, and it was thought most advisable to take a by-road to Heath, where Mrs. Finch, the Doctor's daughter, lived, near Dudley. Thus suddenly were our prospects changed! We now set to packing our beds, furniture of all sorts, and clothes, &c. The neighbourhood had by this time become all alarmed for us, and our poor neighbours for miles round were coming all through the day, requesting to assist us in packing, and to carry some of our things to their cottages, in order to

FORWARD

SAM: TIMMINS, ESQ., J.P.

PHOTOGRAPHED BY WHITLOCK.

BIRMINGHAM: HOUGHTON & CO., SCOTLAND PASSAGE.

The House of Gios Humphries Esq.— Spark Brook

William Hutton's House, Saltley.

The House of William Russell Esq. Showell Green

Moseley Hall

HOUSES INJURED OR DESTROYED DURING THE RIOTS, JULY, 1791.

31

secure them for us. Our house was filled with people from top to bottom, some packing one thing, some another; some hiding things about our own premises, others taking them to a barn fixed upon as a place of safety and secresy, and others again to their own homes, and thus endangering themselves by a risk of their being discovered, and suffering, in consequence, from the blind fury of the mob. These honest creatures bewailed our hard and undeserved lot much more than we did ourselves, though they did not feel it so much; and all of them voluntarily laboured and exerted themselves as much as if their own lives depended upon the saving our goods. By ten o'clock our house was nearly stripped, and its furniture scattered about the country. We now ran over to Mrs. B——'s, there took breath a little, and at her request some refreshment, and her affectionate solicitude caused us the relief and luxury of shedding tears, which agitation, hurry, and fatigue had hitherto prevented. Soon, however, did we return home, desirous to remain there as long as possible. Parties of the mob were constantly coming to the gates, but persons were stationed there to appease and send them away. We now heard that they were gone through the town to Mr. J—— R——'s [Ryland, Easy Hill], and this again gave us hope that our house might be spared; but my father much urged my brother, sister, and me to leave, and recommended our going to a neighbour's, who lived in a retired spot about half a mile off. He wished himself to remain at the house as long as possible. Accordingly, we loaded ourselves with cold meat, pies, &c., and set off, intending to take up our quarters there till all was over, thinking we should be near to hear how things went, and could profit by circumstances as they arose. As we passed across the fields we were alarmed by parties of men in their shirt sleeves, without hats, all half drunk; they were breaking the boughs from the trees and hedges, shouting, laughing, swearing, and singing in a manner

that seemed hideous beyond expression. After much alarm and frequently hiding ourselves behind the hedges and trees, we at length arrived at the place of our destination. We found our good neighbour Mrs. G. —— very ready to receive us, though we had never been upon anything of a sociable footing with her. Her house was a superior sort of cottage, and here we hoped to find an asylum till the storm was overblown. My father came and dined with us; he seemed full of hope that our house would escape, but was much distressed at not being able to get any communication with his friends at Birmingham. He had sent several notes to my uncle and other friends, as well as to the magistrates, but could get no answer. After dinner he went to town himself, having left the necessary directions for protecting the house; in the evening he returned to us, much hurt at the behaviour of the magistrates, and told us he could no longer think us safe there, but wished us to go to the house of B—— C—— [B. Cox, at Warstock], an old servant, who lived about five miles off, situate in a very obscure place; and as no time was to be lost, he requested we would set out on foot, whilst he went home and sent the coach after us; for there all our servants remained to take what care they could of what was left. Now the females all left it, the cook excepted, who remained to the last, and showed a degree of courage and spirit that astonished all who saw it. Walking up the common, we passed Mr. A——'s, [Anderton, Moseley Wake Green], a neighbour with whom we had been upon friendly terms, but who was of the Church-and-King party, and had refused to shelter a wagon-load of our goods in his barn, saying, he did not choose to risk his barn to save them; thus letting his poor illiterate neighbours outdo him in real friendship and charity. As we passed, he, with Mrs. A., &c., were on the lawn, and they had the assurance to accost us and express sorrow for our trouble. We received their compliment with coolness, and pursued our way. The carriage overtook us when we had proceeded about two miles, and my father with it. The evening was far advanced when we arrived at B. C.——'s, and on alighting we found even this obscure farm-house had been threatened, because there had been through the summer something of a Sunday evening's lecture held there, and also because it was reported some of our goods were collected here. It was true, that two wagon-loads had been sent, but they had been removed further up the country. The carriage was left here; the coachman returned on one of the horses, and B. C. on the other—the former to strengthen the guard at our house, the latter to return in a short time and bring us information of the state of things. Mrs. C., formerly a servant in our family, as well as her husband, was sincerely rejoiced to see us, and to have her house afford us an asylum. We took possession of an inner parlour, and meant to remain there concealed from any neighbours who might enter. A faithful little dog, who had accompanied us almost with-out our knowledge, seemed to be sensible of our plan, for he stationed himself at this parlour door almost as soon as we entered it, and when any person came near barked most violently; he soon got familiar with the different members of the family, and would suffer them to pass and repass quietly, but was really furious if any stranger entered the house and approached at all near the door; and this he continued all the time we remained here. At one o'clock in the morning B. C. returned, but the account he brought only increased our fears; the matter seemed to be without end. Mr. Ryland's house was gutted and set fire to; also Mr. Hutton's [historian of Bir-mingham], and the mob were then at Mr. Taylor's [Bordesley Hall], where they were committing the most inhuman depredations. My father now thought it right to go again himself and try if the magistrates could not by some means be persuaded to act. We did what we could to dissuade him from it, not now fearing for anything so much as his safety, and as there is no answering for the fury of a mob, and some envious, malicious spirits

had, we knew, spared no pains to inflame them against my father, our apprehensions for him when absent from us were cruel, for we were well aware that his active and bold daring spirit might lead him into danger before he was sensible of it. This we represented to him, and urged him as much as we could to remain in safety with us, but all in vain; go he would, promising to return soon. We did not think of going to bed, or even taking off our clothes, through the night, though this was the second we had passed in this state. To think of sleep or quiet was impossible in our state of mind, and all about us in the same state of agitation with ourselves. Things had gone so far, and were come to such a height, that the general security seemed in danger, pillage appeared the order of the day, and all parties now most likely would be involved. There was continual coming and going to this house, and we were tormented by a thousand reports, all sad, all distressing; which of them to believe we could not divine, and therefore suffered more or less from them all.

"The next morning, Saturday, about ten o'clock, our friend and neighbour Sarah S—— [Mrs. John Ryland] came on foot and alone; she had left her brother and sister with their children at a house on the common, and strolled hither herself for want of accommodation there. Mr. H. had left his house, having heard it was on the list of those to be pulled down. From S. S. [S. Smith] we heard many sad reports; the town and country was all under the greatest alarm, and all order and subordination seemed at an end. We received every now and then accounts that parties of the mob were on the road; sometimes they were said to be very near, coming to demolish the house we were in; at others they were going to Kingswood Meeting-house, about two miles from us. About twelve o'clock in the day poor Mrs. H. [Hobson] came, such a picture of fatigue and distress as I never saw before—a delicate little woman, without hat or cloak, in her nightcap, with a child on one arm and a large bundle under the other; she came in almost breathless, threw herself on a chair and nearly fainted. It was a long time before she could speak; at length we learned from her that Mr. H. [Rev. Mr. Hobson, minister of Kingswood Meeting-house] had gone off in disguise, and that she hurried from her house, having had information that the mob were very near. It was now near twelve hours since my father had left us. This was, sure, the longest morning I ever knew; we were strolling about the fields, listening to every sound that rose upon our ears, and with all the anxiety imaginable eyeing every person who appeared; and every noise we heard, every creature we saw, gave rise to a thousand thoughts and surmises. About one o'clock Mr. T— L—'s [T. Lee, attorney] family arrived; they fled here for safety, and brought, like all others, the most alarming accounts.

"About two o'clock, to our inexpressible joy, my father returned, but so changed by fatigue and alarm that his countenance was not at all like the same. He had been at Birmingham, trying to rouse the magistrates to exertion, and had met with such indifference from them as in the present state of things seemed almost incredible and quite unnatural. His friends were all dispersed, he could find none of them, a general panic had scattered them, and nothing was to be done but to submit. Having been thus disappointed at Birmingham, and finding it was impossible for him alone to do anything, he had returned home again, and remained there defending the house against parties of the mob who were continually coming to assault it, till, after having long disregarded the urgent entreaties of the servants and the friends there to leave, from their lively apprehensions for his safety, he was obliged to yield to them on receiving a message from a very respectable gentleman of the other party, who sent a friend privately to request of my father, if he valued his life, to quit his house and secrete himself, for the fury of the mob had become quite ungovernable. He now, therefore, thought it his duty to resign his premises to their fate, and save himself. About seven o'clock in the evening, we perceived a cloud of smoke arise from that quarter which almost amounted to a certainty with us to be our house in flames. Hence, we suppose, sprung the reason of the coachman's delay. Now a sort of melancholy filled our bosoms, hitherto torn by lively and different apprehensions. To contemplate the awful columns of smoke ascending from that beloved mansion where I had passed all my days in a calm, virtuous, and happy tranquillity, where all my pleasure seemed to centre, and where alone I felt as if happiness could be tasted, pierced me to the soul: it seemed as if a dear friend was expiring before me in whom my happiness centred. My whole soul was moved and distressed, but the luxury of tears was denied: spent and exhausted, my feelings, though not violent, were acute and quiet.

In this state we continued, looking towards the smoke, and wandering up and down the garden, till ten o'clock, till all of a sudden the dreadful shouts of the mob assailed our ears, and almost at the same instant two women came running as if for their lives, and quite out of breath; they begged us for God's sake to get away, for that the mob were coming, they would be there immediately, and their fury was ungovernable. Such a scene of confusion now followed as cannot be told; all ran about as if not knowing what to do or where to go; there were seven or eight young children [among whom one was T. Eyre Lee, attorney, Birmingham] in the house; some were wrapped up in blankets, others taken from their beds as they were; all ran out of the house, but knew not whither to turn their steps.

"We arrived safe at Mr. G——'s [Greaves], and he not being arrived with the chaise, we took some refreshment offered us by the good lady, and at her earnest request went up stairs to get a little repose. Here a curious scene presented itself: we three ladies were shown into a room with four beds in all, and all but one, whether occupied by men or women we did not know;

but the loud nasal concert, and the different notes of which it was composed, seemed to indicate both. We were amused at our situation, and felt sufficiently at ease to laugh at it. We lay down upon the bed, and our faithful little dog by the side ; but the room was suffocatingly hot, and the number of persons in it made the air very oppressive ; this, together with the music that assailed our ears, and a most numerous swarm of fleas, which attacked us all, kept rest and even quiet at a distance."

From the house of Mr. William Russell the rioters went to those of Mr. Thomas Russell and Mr. Hawkes, at Moseley Wake Green. These they attacked and plundered, but did not burn them. They next repaired to Moseley Hall, the property of Mr. John Taylor, where resided the blind and infirm Lady Carhampton, the mother of the Duchess of Cumberland. One would have supposed that even the hard hearts of the lawless mob would have been softend in the presence of an infirm and aged lady, allied moreover to the throne they professed to honour ; but she lived in a house belonging to a Dissenter, and, therefore, blind and enfeebled with age though she was, she must at once leave the place, to escape molestation. The only favour shown to her by the rioters was to permit her furniture to be removed from the house previous to their attack ; and, when this was done, (Lady Carhampton having been conveyed by Sir Robert Lawley to Canwell,) the hall was set fire to, together with its offices, stables, and hay-stacks. At the same time attacks were made upon the house of Mr. Harwood, not very far distant, and that of the Rev. Mr. Hobson, a Dissenting minister, on the Moseley Road, and the three buildings were all blazing at the same time.

"The terror and distress," says the *Gazette*, "which pervaded the whole town on Saturday, while these dreadful scenes were acting, will be better conceived than described. The magistrates had tried every means of persuasion, to no effect ; large bills were stuck up, requesting all persons to return to their respective homes, to no purpose. Nothing certain was known respecting the approach of the military, and numbers of the rioters, now joined by thieves and drunken prostitutes, from every quarter, were, with blue cockades in their hats, in all parts of the town, and in small bodies, levying contributions on the inhabitants. There was scarcely a housekeeper that dared refuse them meat, drink, money, or whatever they demanded. The shops were mostly shut, business nearly at a stand, and everybody employed in secreting or removing their valuables. Very happily, however, the body of the rioters, overcome with liquor and fatigue, lay all the night in the fields, round their conflagrations in the country, and did not come into the town."

We conclude the narrative of this day's proceedings, as in previous cases, with the old correspondent's summary :—

"*Birmingham, Saturday, July 16.*—In the forenoon, the following hand-bill was distributed : [The hand-bill already quoted on page 238.]

" *Twelve o'clock at Noon.*—The hand-bill has not produced the salutary effects which were wished.

"This moment Mr. Hutton's country house, about two miles from Birmingham, is on fire. Universal despondency has taken place. People of all professions are moving their goods, some to places of private security, others into the country. Plunder is now the motive of the rioters. No *military force* is nearer than Derby, and nothing but *military force* can now suppress them.

" *Eight o'clock in the Evening.*—The rioters are now demolishing the beautiful house of Mr. George Humphreys, and that of William Russell, Esq., a little further on in the Oxford road. The shops are still kept shut up, and no military are yet arrived. Dreadful depredations are expected in the course of this night ! The remains of several poor wretches, who had got drunk, and were burnt to death in Mr. Ryland's cellar, have been dug out ; one so much burnt, that he was recognized only by the buckle in one of his shoes. What could be collected of his remains have been just taken away in a basket. Another has been brought from the ruins of Dr. Priestley's house, who is supposed to have been killed by a fall of some of the buildings.

" The people who demolished Mr. Humphrey's house, laboured in as cool and orderly a manner as if they had been employed by the owner at so much per day."

Writing on Sunday morning, he thus concludes the summary of Saturday's proceedings :

" Last night the people of Birmingham were trembling

spectators of the tremendous conflagration of Mosley Hall, the property of John Taylor, Esq., but in the occupation of Lady Carhampton.

"Fortunately Lady Carhampton, who is blind, was removed to a place of safety, by Sir Robert Lawley, who took her in his own carriage to Canwell.

"About two this morning a most awful scene presented itself! Four dreadful fires within a mile of each other! It is certain that the house of William Russell, Esq., and that of Mr. Hawks of Mosley, have shar'd the fate of Mosley Hall."

Another account of the state of the town at eight o'clock on Friday evening says:

"A gentleman who left Birmingham at the above hour, for the purpose of coming to town, mentioned, that the mob was increasing every hour; and that all the houses above-mentioned were entirely destroyed. Many of the mob had fallen a sacrifice to their own misconduct; near twenty of them, quite drunk, were buried under the ruins of a house by the walls falling in. One poor wretch was found with his legs burnt off, and a bottle of spirits or wine in each pocket.

"A great number of the mob were lying in a state of the most insensible drunkenness on the green, and in other places near where they committed their depredations.

"Several houses were at this time marked out for destruction; no opposition whatever was made to these riots. The town's people seemed to be so panick-struck, as to be capable of no exertion. An officer in Birmingham, offered to lead any number of the inhabitants, and endeavour to repel the mob, but could not prevail upon them to make the attempt.

"No troops had arrived. The mob detained the mail-coach a full hour, but permitted it then to depart unmolested. Such was the state of Birmingham at that time."

CHAPTER XXXVIII.

THE END OF THE RIOTS.

William Hutton's return to Birmingham—Drunken rioters—Lady Carhampton's furniture—Ruins at Bennet's Hill—Second Address from the Magistrates—Kingswood Meeting-House destroyed—Mr. Cox's house at Wharstock—Edgbaston Hall—Arrival of the Military—End of the Riots.

THE narrative of the Hutton family, quoted in our last chapter, left the refugees at Sutton Coldfield, on the third day of the riots, Saturday. It was not long, however, before the panic reached the little town, and once more the Huttons were looked upon with distrust; so that it was thought desirable to continue their flight. Night found them, however, resting quietly at the Castle Inn, Tamworth, where, although they fared frugally, they were unable to discharge their bill.

"On Sunday morning," Miss Hutton writes, "my father was become quite ungovernable. He said it was madness to be at such a distance from the wreck of his property, while we thought it little less that he should expose his person; but, as we could not detain him, we resolved to go with him. We crossed the country to Castle Bromwich, by a road which never chaise went before, and of which we walked nearly a mile, and the first object that met our eyes was our coachman lolling at the door of the inn, and exhibiting, by his livery, a sign that either we or something belonging to us was sheltered there.

"Here we dined in a bed room, and spoke in whispers. When we had dined, no arguments or entreaties could deter my father from going to see the remains of his house at Bennett's Hill, which was little more than three miles distant, and on the road to Birmingham, and my brother, seeing him determined, accompanied him."

What Mr. Hutton saw during this journey into town may be best described in his own words:

"As the storm in Birmingham," he says, "was too violent to last, it seemed prudent to be near the place, that I might embrace the first opportunity of protecting the wreck of a shattered fortune. We moved to Castle Bromwich.

"Ranting, roaring, drinking, burning, is a life

of too much rapidity for the human frame to support. Our black sovereigns had now held it nearly three days and nights, when nature called for rest; and the bright morning displayed the fields, roads, and hedges, lined with *friends and brother Churchmen* dead drunk. There were, however, enough awake to kindle new fires. . . .

" I could not refrain from going to take a view of my house at Bennett's Hill, above three miles distant from Castle Bromwich. Upon Washwood Heath I met four wagons, loaded with Lady Carhampton's furniture, attended by a body of rioters, with their usual arms, as protectors.* I passed through the midst of them, was known, and insulted, but kept a sullen silence. The stupid dunces vociferated, ' No popery ! Down with the pope !" forgetting that Presbyterians were never remarkable for favouring the religion of that potentate. In this instance, however, they were ignorantly right; for I consider myself a true friend to the Roman Catholic, and to every *peaceable* profession, but not to the spiritual power of any; for this, instead of humanizing the mind, and drawing the affections of one man towards another, has bound the world in fetters, and set at variance those who were friends.

" I saw the ruins yet burning of that once-happy spot, which for many years been my calm retreat—the scene of contemplation, of domestic felicity—the source of health and contentment. Here I had consulted the dead, and attempted to amuse the living. Here I had exchanged the world for my little family.

" Perhaps fifty people were enjoying themselves upon those ruins where I had possessed an exclusive right, but I was now viewed as an intruder. The prejudiced vulgar, who never inquire into causes and effects, or the true state of things, fix the idea of criminality upon the man who is borne down by the crowd, and every foot is elevated to

kick him. My premises, laid open by ferocious authority, were free to every trespasser, and I was the only person who did not rejoice in the ruins. It was not possible to retreat from that favourite place without a gloom upon the mind, which was the result of ill-treatment by power without right."

We now enter upon the events of Sunday morning. Another handbill was issued early in the day, signed by all the magistrates of the neighbourhood, as follows :

"IMPORTANT INFORMATION TO THE FRIENDS OF THE CHURCH AND KING.

" *Birmingham, Sunday, 17th July, 1791.*

" *Friends and Fellow Churchmen,*

" Being convinced you are unacquainted that the great losses, which are sustained by your burning and destroying of the houses of so many individuals, will eventually fall upon the country at large, and not upon the persons to whom they belong, we feel it our duty to inform you, that the damages already done, upon the best computation that can be made, will amount to upwards of One Hundred Thousand Pounds ; the whole of which enormous sum will be charged upon the respective parishes, and paid out of the rates.

" We, therefore, as your friends, conjure you immediately to desist from the destruction of any more houses ; otherwise the very proceedings which your zeal for shewing your attachment to the Church and King have excited, will inevitably be the means of most seriously injuring innumerable families, who are hearty supporters of Government ; and must bring on an addition of Taxes, which yourselves, and the rest of the Friends of the Church, will for years feel a very grievous burden.

" This we assure you was the case in London, when there were so many houses and public buildings burnt and destroyed in the year 1780 ; and, you may rely upon it, will be so here on the present occasion.

" And we must observe to you, that any further violent proceedings will more offend your King and Country, than serve the cause of Him and Church.

" *Fellow Churchmen,*

" As you love your King, regard his Laws, and restore Peace.

" God save the King !

Aylesford,	*J. Charles,*
E. Finch,	*R. Spencer,*
Robert Lawley,	*Henry Greswold Lewis,*
Robert Lawley, jun.	*Charles Curtis,*
R. Morland,	*Spencer Madan,*
W. Digby,	*Edward Palmer,*
Edward Carver,	*W. Villers,*
John Brooke,	*W. Wallis Mason.*"

---

* " The rioters assisted in loading four wagons with the goods, and ten of them, armed with bludgeons, formed an escort, and were to march through Castle Bromwich. They were now approaching, and the news of their exploit preceded them."—*Miss Hutton's Narrative.*

This is probably the most extraordinary notice ever issued by a body of magistrates,—*justices of the peace*,—to a mob of lawless persons who had burnt and destroyed property belonging to harmless and peaceable individuals, to the value of nearly a hundred thousand pounds. These worthy magistrates are "convinced" that the rioters, in their holy zeal for Church and King, are "unacquainted that the great loss . . . will eventually fall upon the country at large, and *not upon the persons to whom they* [*i.e., the houses and other properties*] *belong*"! Obviously, the inference to be drawn from this statement is, that if the losses *had* been certain to fall upon the persons attacked, the rioters might have gone on until dissenters were utterly exterminated from the town. But as the burden is likely to fall upon the tax-payers at large, "*the very proceedings which your zeal for shewing your attachment to the Church and King have excited,*" (laudable and praiseworthy as those proceedings doubtless were in themselves,) had better now come to a close, "as you love your King, regard his Laws, and restore Peace"!

But even this loving address failed to restore peace. The lovers of the king, with due regard for his laws, no doubt, proceeded on Sunday morning to pull down and burn the Meeting House at Kingswood,* and in a short time reduced it to ashes. They had previously visited (in their hatred of "false doctrine, heresy, and schism,") the house of Mr. Cox, at Wharstock, which, having been used as a house of prayer by the Dissenters, must come down; and so, after emptying the cellar of its contents—they do not seem even to have entertained the slightest scruple against nonconformists' wine—they left it a heap of smoking ruins.

The next place which required pulling down in the interests of Church and King was Edgbaston Hall, the residence of Dr. Withering,—"who," says Hutton, "perhaps never heard a Presbyterian sermon, and yet is as amiable a character as he who has,"—but, as we have already said in our notice of this most estimable man, he had committed the enormity of receiving and sheltering one of the persecuted families; and had, moreover, a well-stored cellar, and many other valuables, rendering his house a profitable one to attack. The alarm reached him in time to secure and carry off his most valuable books and specimens, also much of the furniture; but, happily, the house was spared, for no sooner had the rioters reached the place, and commenced their attack upon the cellar, than "the words *light horse* sounded in their ears; when this formidable banditti mouldered away, no soul knew how, and not a shadow of it could be found."*

It may be easily imagined with what rejoicings the townspeople received the welcome news of the approach of the military. It was but a small troop,—about sixty-four in all,—but they were sufficient to scare the rioters from their work of destruction. As they marched into the town they were met by a large multitude of the more peaceable citizens, the houses in all the principal streets were illuminated, and every token of joy was manifested at their happy delivery from the rule of King Mob. For now that the rioters had wreaked their vengeance upon the dissenters, and were still insatiable, other inhabitants, whose loyalty was above suspicion, began to fear for their property. The bankers had been compelled to lodge their cash and notes in safe hiding places, lest it should occur to the rioters to run for gold; the carriage traffic in the streets was stopped unless the drivers wore blue cockades; even the mail-coaches had been stopped once or twice; so that the whole populace had cause to rejoice that at last this reign of terror was over.

On Monday morning, however, a fresh contingent of would-be rioters reached the town, viz., a large body of colliers from the Black Country,

---

* "This solitary place had fallen by the hand of violence in the beginning of George the First, for which a person of the name of Dollax was executed, and from him it acquired the name of St. Dollax, which it still bears. He was the first person who suffered after passing the Riot Act."—*Hutton's Narrative of the Riots.*

* Hutton's Narrative.

who had heard of the glorious doings of the Birmingham mob and longed to join in the fray. But the military also received a re-inforcement at the same time, another party of light horse, from Lichfield, so that the grimy contingent found it wisest to retire, with as good grace as might be, to their own regions.

Before the day was over something like order was restored and business was resumed, and although disturbing rumours of a fresh outbreak were current for some time, it was evident that peace was at last fully restored. And thus ended the memorable riots of July, 1791.

CHAPTER XXXIX.

AFTER THE RIOTS.

Conclusion of Miss Russell's Narrative—Dr. Priestley's address—*Aris's Gazette* and the Riots—Advertisements—Conclusion of Miss Hutton's Narrative—The Court of Conscience—Trials of the Rioters—William Cowper on the Riots—Claims of the Sufferers—Narrative of the Trials—The Union Meeting-House—Rebuilding of the Old and New Meeting-Houses.

It is not to be supposed that, when once peace and order had been restored, the subject of the riots was speedily forgotten. On the contrary, there immediately ensued a paper warfare almost as fierce as the actual strife which had just ceased. Letters, Addresses, and Pamphlets were poured upon the inhabitants from all quarters; from churchmen, sufferers, and outsiders, from all who had, or imagined they had, a personal interest in the matter, and many who had not, came augmentations of the deluge of riot literature, until it would have been almost useless to attempt even a complete catalogue of the various publications. But it is not with these that we have to do, so much as with the actual events which followed the memorable disturbances of the four days ending July 17th; and, first, as to the fortunes of the sufferers themselves.

The Russell family at length reached London in safety, and repaired to Bates's Hotel, in the Adelphi. "Mr. Bates," says Miss Russell, "was not up, but soon rose and came to meet us with tears in his eyes, so happy was he to meet us; he had heard reports of the disturbances, and was truly relieved to see us all safe. On sitting down here, for the first time since Thursday had we thought ourselves

safe or at rest. Now we found both, and the greatest refreshment from washing off the dust and filth from our skins, and in changing our clothes. My father soon waited upon Mr. Pitt, and very soon after arriving we learned that Dr. P. was in town, as well as Mr. J. R——'s family, and many other of our Birmingham friends. This evening we went to bed very early, and enjoyed it in such a manner as cannot be imagined. Soon after getting to sleep we were awakened by what we thought most terrible shouting; we jumped up, crying out the mob had followed us; we rose up and in great alarm slipped on our cloaks, and went out to see how matters were; we found the servants, who, in turns, sat up through the night; they informed us that it was as quiet as usual, and we need not be at all alarmed, for the noise we had heard was only *the gardeners coming to Covent Garden Market.* Thus happily relieved, and smiling at our own fears, we returned to comfortable rest.

"After staying a few days in London, we returned to Birmingham, my father, sister, and self; Thomas remained there at school. Nothing material occurred up the journey, but the sentiments I felt on approaching dear Showell Green and first beholding the ruin of our much-loved

32

mansion, I shall not forget. At a distance of two or three miles we discerned the spot, and on a nearer approach descried a part of the shell of the building rearing its head, blackened by smoke, despoiled of its windows, and so defaced and demolished as scarce to leave a trace of its original form. The fine tall elms that grew at the back of the house, which shaded our nursery windows, and which I loved almost as if they were my sisters, still stood; they reared their venerable heads above these melancholy ruins, but had partaken in their fate—their fine foliage was all burnt on the side next the house, and their stems blackened by smoke. What dismal feelings filled my soul on contemplating this sad spectacle! It seemed as if I viewed the distorted and mangled corpse of a dear friend, a parent to whom I was indebted for much of my past happiness, and who could never again be restored to me. Passing on, we beheld Mr. G. Humphreys's house [now J. Bateman's, Sparkbrook], the shell complete, but despoiled of all its windows. Dr. P.'s was as melancholy a piece of ruin as our own. Arriving at New Hall Street [G. Russell's], we met a hearty welcome from our friends there, and took up our residence under the hospitable roof of my good uncle, till my father could procure a house for us. All I saw, felt, and observed seemed like a dream, and it was a long time before I could realize what had passed."*

Dr. Priestley, immediately on his arrival in London, penned the following address, which appeared in *Aris's Birmingham Gazette* of July 25th:

To the INHABITANTS of the
TOWN OF BIRMINGHAM.

My late Townsmen and Neighbours,

AFTER living with you eleven years, in which you had uniform experience of my peaceful behaviour, in my attention to the quiet studies of my profession, and those of philosophy, I was far from expecting the injuries which I and my friends have lately received from you. But you have been misled. By hearing the Dissenters, and particularly the Unitarian Dissenters, continually railed at,

---

* We are indebted to Mr. Councillor R. F. Martineau, for the use of a private reprint of Miss Russell's most interesting narrative.

as enemies to the present Government, in Church and State, you have been led to consider any injury done to us as a meritorious thing; and not having been better informed, the means were not attended to. When the *object* was right, you thought the *means* could not be wrong. By the discourses of your teachers, and the exclamations of your superiors in general, drinking confusion and damnation to us (which is well known to have been their frequent practice) your bigotry has been excited to the highest pitch, and nothing having been said to you to moderate your passions, but everything to inflame them; hence, without any consideration on your part, or on theirs, who ought to have known, and taught you better—you were prepared for every species of outrage; thinking that whatever you could do to spite and injure us, was for the support of Government, and especially the Church. In *destroying us*, you have been led to think, *you did God* and your country the most substantial *service.*

Happily, the minds of Englishmen have a horror of *murder*, and therefore you did not, I hope, think of *that*; though, by your clamorous demanding of *me* at the Hotel, it is probable, that at that time, some of you intended me some personal injury. But what is the value of life, when every thing is done to make it wretched? In many cases, there would be greater mercy in dispatching the inhabitants, than in burning their houses. However, I infinitely prefer what I feel from *the spoiling of my goods*, to the disposition of those who have misled you.

You have destroyed the most truly valuable and useful apparatus of philosophical instruments that perhaps any individual, in this or any other country, was ever possesed of; in my use of which I annually spent large sums, with no pecuniary view whatever, but only in the advancement of science, for the benefit of my country and of mankind. You have destroyed a library corresponding to that apparatus, which no money can re-purchase, except in a long course of time. But what I feel far more, you have destroyed *manuscripts*, which have been the result of the laborious study of many years, and which I shall never be able to recompose; and this has been done to one who never did, or imagined you any harm.

I know nothing more of the *hand-bill*, which is said to have enraged you so much, than any of yourselves, and I disapprove of it as much; though it has been made the ostensible handle of doing infinitely more mischief than any thing of that nature could possibly have done. In the celebration of the French Revolution, at which I did not attend, the company assembled on the occasion, only expressed their joy in the emancipation of a neighbouring nation from tyranny, without intimating a desire of any thing more than such an improvement of our own Constitution, as all sober citizens, of every persuasion, have long wished for. And though, in answer to the gross and unprovoked calumnies of Mr. Madan, and others, I publicly vindicated my principles as a Dissenter, it was only with plain and sober argument, and with perfect good humour. We are better instructed in the mild and forbearing spirit of Christianity, than ever to think of having recourse to *violence;* and can you think such conduct as yours any recommendation of your religious principles in preference to ours?

You are still more mistaken, if you imagine that this conduct of yours has any tendency to serve your cause, or to prejudice ours. It is nothing but *reason* and *argument* that can ever support any system of religion. Answer our arguments, and your business is done; but your having recourse to *violence*, is only a proof that you have nothing better to produce. Should you destroy myself, as well as my house, library, and apparatus, ten more persons, of equal or superior spirit and ability, would instantly rise up. If those ten were destroyed, an hundred would appear; and believe me, that the Church of England, which you now think you are supporting, has received a greater blow by this conduct of yours, than I and all my friends have ever aimed at it.

Besides, to abuse those who have no power of making resistance, is equally cowardly and brutal, peculiarly unworthy of Englishmen, to say nothing of Christianity, which teaches us to do as we would be done by. In this business we are the sheep, and you the wolves. We will preserve our character, and hope you will change yours. At all events, we return you blessings for curses; and pray that you may soon return to that industry, and those sober manners, for which the inhabitants of Birmingham were formerly distinguished.

I am your sincere well-wisher,
J. PRIESTLEY.

London, July 19, 1791.

P.S. The account of the first Toast at the Revolution Dinner in *The Times* of this morning, can be nothing less than a malicious lie. To prove this, a list of the Toasts, with an account of all the proceedings of the day, will soon be published. The first of them was, *The King and the Constitution*, and they were all such as the friends of Liberty, and the true pinciples of the Constitution, would approve.

The same issue of that journal contained a full account of the riots to which we are indebted for some of the particulars. The account opens with the amusing statement that " *In compliance with the wishes of the Magistrates, we forbore to detail in our last the violent proceedings,*" &c.! Let the reader imagine, if he can, the withholding by any newspaper to-day of such startling news as that withheld by *Aris's Gazette* for more than a week, in deference to the wishes of a local authority.

The *Gazette* of July 25th, however, made up for the reticence of the previous week; by far the greater portion of the number was taken up with news and advertisements relating to the riots, besides which the proprietors also issued a supplement, consisting wholly of letters by

Mr. James Keir, in reference to the memorable dinner, giving a list of the toasts, and other information exonerating the dissenters from the charges of disloyalty which had been repeated so frequently in the accounts which appeared in the London newspapers.

Among the advertisements is the following address from the dissenters :—

THE DISSENTERS *of* BIRMINGHAM *desire to return their grateful Acknowledgments to all those Members of the established Church, who in any Manner exerted themselves during the late Riots, in Defence of their Persons and Property ; more particularly to those who in the true Spirit of Christianity received into their Houses, and under their Protection, many families of Dissenters who were obliged to leave their own Habitations ; and also to all those who received and protected their Goods. They trust that good Men of every Denomination, will consider this Protection as highly honourable to the Humanity of those who gave it, and they think it to be the more meritorious, as these generous Protectors did thereby expose themselves to Danger from a lawless Mob, who wanted only Pretence for Depredation.*

Another is inserted by Mr. John Taylor :

JOHN TAYLOR, Esq.

ALL Persons who have in their Possession any Books, Writings, Papers, &c., &c., belonging to John Taylor, Esq., of Bordesley, are particularly intreated to bring them to Charles Taylor's, Esq. in the High-street, or to the Bank, in Dale End, where any Intelligence respecting the same will be thankfully received.

Birmingham, July 23, 1791.

Under this is an address from William Hutton, as follows :—

Birmingham, July 23, 1791.

IT is a material Relief to that Calamity under which I labour, to find, since my Return, every Man my Friend, except the People who composed the Mob of Plunderers, or wished to join them. I shall ever express an Obligation to those who preserved any of my Property from Destruction ; but it gives me great Concern, that much of it has been destroyed through a *Fear* of restoring it, when I have already declared to the World, that I would receive it with Gratitude.—My Friends will add to the Obligation under which they have laid me, by restoring the lost Property as little damaged as possible, particularly the PRINTS and BOOKS, the Value of which is upwards of a Thousand Pounds. Many of the Books are scarce, and in Sets, the Loss of one, diminishes the Value of the Remainder, and is an Injury which Time, Assiduity, or Money, can never repair. There is also lost, Plate, a Gold Watch, beaded Chain, with Gold Trinkets, and Jewels to a considerable Amount, exclusive of Stock in Trade, Furniture, Apparel, Household Linen &c. Should any suspected Articles be offered to Sale

Pawn, I shall be extremely obliged to those to whom they are offered, to stop both Persons and Property, till they give me Information. The Books, the Property of my Son, have generally the Arms on a Copper-plate, two

finding, like Noah's dove, a resting-place for their feet, they returned no more. My mother and I remained at Sutton, where we were not quite so

OLD CARICATURE PRINT OF THE RIOTS.
From the rare original in the possession of W. Bates, Esq., B.A.

Inches Square, pasted on the Inside of the Cover, with **THOMAS HUTTON,** and if torn off the Mark will remain.

W. HUTTON.

"On Monday morning," says Miss Hutton, "my father and brother went to Birmingham, and

happy as during our transports on meeting the soldiers. Birmingham was allowed to be safe now they were in it; but the rioters were supposed to be marching to Sutton every hour, and I had a pair of horses harnessed, to be put to the only post chaise of the inn the moment it came home. Before that arrived we discovered that the alarm was unfounded.

"On Tuesday afternoon my aunt came in our carriage to take us to her house in Birmingham, which had been our first asylum. Our coachman had his stable hat, instead of a laced one, a dirty silk handkerchief round his neck, instead of a white one, a week's beard on his face, worsted stockings on his legs, dirty shoes on his feet, and was excessively drunk. After he had refreshed himself with some more liquor, I went to him and said, 'John, we have changed our minds, we shall not go to Birmingham till to-morrow morning.' 'But you must go now,' he replied, 'for my master ordered me to bring you.' 'No matter for that,' I said, 'we shall not go till to-morrow.' 'I suppose you think I'm not capable of driving you,' said the man, 'and if that's the case, there's my whip, and d——n me if ever I mount the box again.' My blood boiled, but the riots had loosened every tie of subordination, and the greatest blackguard was the master; I therefore only replied, 'I know you are a good driver, but we shall not go to-day,' reserving to myself, however, the right of making him keep his word about mounting the box, at least after he had once set us down in Birmingham. I had soon the satisfaction of seeing him fast asleep in the stable.

"On Wednesday morning our coachman was surly, but silent, and took us in safety to the house of my aunt and cousin, where we now are. He is already paid and discharged. We are now seeking a home. Many of our friends have given us invitations, and, among the rest, your brother; but we have declined them all, for my mother's state of health is such that she must have some little place that she can call her own.

"For some days I had nothing in the world but the clothes I wore; the rest of my apparel, my money, my letters, my papers, my prints, and my music were gone. Odd things are now coming in every hour, such as have been preserved by our friends and the servants at Birmingham, or such as plunderers dare no longer keep. Among the former is my guitar, which some imp of mischief was carrying off in its case, when a neighbour bought it for sixpence. My poor 'Dash' was taken home by a servant who had lived with us, and married, and has also been restored to me, and our cat, with her whiskers burnt off and her feet scorched, was found among the ruins by another, and is now anointed with oil, and fed with a tea-spoon."

A few days afterwards, having settled down temporarily at the inn attached to Vauxhall Gardens, Miss Hutton concluded her narrative in a second letter to the lady to whom the previous portion had been addressed,—Mrs. André, of Enfield, near London. She says :—

"The place from whence I date this tells you our home, and a most delightful one it is; but I need not describe it, for I think you have been here. Upon second thoughts, I think you have not, so I will tell you that it is a kind of tavern, with a bowling green, orchestra, woods, and walks, and that during the summer there is a public night once a week, on which there are musical performances, as at your Vauxhall, except that they, as well as the company which frequent them, are upon a smaller scale, and in a lower style. Here we board and lodge, that is, my mother and myself, for a guinea and a half a week the two. My father sups and sleeps here, paying for his supper. We have a spacious dining room, which we are obliged to quit on public nights, when we sit in my mother's bed-room. We choose to eat alone, but do not require a dinner to be provided for us. Upon the whole, we are as comfortably situated as people can expect to be who have lost two good houses.

"The rioters demolished all the doors, windows, chimney-pieces, wainscots, skirting boards, and banisters, together with the roof of the house. They then began upon the stairs and tore up about six; but they found this work far more laborious, and less amusing, than setting a house in a blaze, and they desisted. To have fired the whole would have produced a glorious scene had not the neighbours prevented it, in consideration of themselves; but the carrying off paper, and tearing to pieces the inside of a house, proved a tedious and fatiguing business, and they gave it up for better sport.

"On Tuesday, the 19th July, my father got boards nailed together for outer doors, old glazed windows put up in front, and again appeared in the shop, though in the most lamentable situation imaginable. In the course of a week he had new doors, windows, and grate put up in the kitchen, new furnished it entirely, and it became the sole eating room for him and my brother and the cook and the housemaid. In about another week they had got two old bedsteads, and my brother and the servants slept in the house, which they continue to do still. If I were to describe the furniture of their apartments, you would for a moment cease to lament the occasion of it to laugh at its oddity. Curtains are a luxury my brother does not know, except to his windows, and one of these is blue and the other yellow. A piece of oil-cloth hung up serves for a door, and, but for this, the room would be open to the court, for there is no outer door below.

"The Court of Requests, which had occasioned the destruction of so much of my father's property, furnished the means of saving a part. The beadle of the Court, who was also a sheriff's officer, shared the plunder of the house at Birmingham, and whatever he and his man could seize was reserved for us in a chamber in his house. I went there, and among broken chairs and sofas, I found some welcome bundles of linen—most welcome to me, for no part of my apparel had been changed during our troubles. Everything was marked with dirt or blood, the tokens of the danger it had escaped."

In another letter to the same lady she writes (October 23, 1791): "Our spirits, except my mother's, have risen superior to our losses; my father has begun to rebuild and repair his houses; my brother to purchase books and prints; and I to collect costumes, and write journals: my mother alone has sunk under terror and anxiety, operating on a frame already diseased." It was shortly afterwards found necessary, on account of Mrs. Hutton's ill-health, to remove to the Hotwells, Bristol; and to this place came many cheery letters from the brave old bookseller to his family, detailing the events in Birmingham during the remainder of the year. In reply to one of these, his daughter writes:

"We intreat you never to go again to the Court of Conscience; it is a duty you owe to yourself and to us. You have devoted every Friday of your life to it during nineteen years, and much of your other time; you have heard a clamour that would have deafened, and breathed an atmosphere that would have poisoned a horse; and your sole reward has been insult and the destruction of your property."

To this he replies: "Do not distress thyself about my resuming the direction of the Court of Conscience; I am as likely to distribute justice while sitting on a bench in the moon." . . . . "Archer, my successor, told me to-day that he was not able to conduct the Court, but would give it up. He wished I would take the reins. Another man observed, that the Commissioners did not know what they were doing; that they could not understand the cases; and that if I did not return the Court would not last a year." Hutton modestly adds, however, "This is not true." Among the other items of news he has to tell his family is, that "Dr. Priestley comes no more. He has taken a house near London for twenty-one years, *provided he lives and the house stands so long.*" A project had been set on foot by the sufferers in the riots to prosecute the magistrates, but Hutton wisely reasons against this. He says: "I supped with William Humphreys a few nights ago. We were a select company of only seven persons, [all sufferers in the riots,] and I estimated our joint property at £400,000. The design was to prosecute the superior powers. John Ryland and I carried it in the negative, which hurt poor William Russell, who is really a good man, so much, that he will resign the direction."

The trials of the rioters themselves, however, came on before those for compensation of the sufferers, at the Warwick Assizes, on August 2nd, in the same year. Only twelve persons were arraigned, and even of these only four were convicted. Against one of the prisoners, named Joseph Careless, it was proved, by two witnesses, that he appeared to be the ring-leader in demolishing Baskerville House; they saw him with an oak rail, about two yards long, knocking down the brick-work of a bow-window; and he was also seen driving away the pigs. Against this, however, it was sworn by his sister-in-law, Elizabeth Grice, that "he came there not as a rioter, but to suppress the riot; inasmuch as he let out two pigs, from an outhouse, which was soon after burnt down." This evidence, together with his good character,—all the rioters seem to have borne, or procured, a good character,—obtained for him his acquittal. Four of the rioters were found guilty and received sentence of death, viz.: Francis Field, John Green, Bartholomew Fisher, and William Hands. All the others were acquitted; and even of the four who were sentenced only two suffered the penalty of death. The leniency of the Court towards these violent supporters of "Church and King" passed into a proverb. On one occasion, not long after the trial, a gentleman who was hunting with Mr. Corbett's fox-hounds, was so sure of killing the fox that he cried, "Nothing but a *Birmingham Jury* can save him !"

On the day of the trial the poet Cowper wrote from Weston, to a clergyman in the neighbourhood, the Rev. W. Bagot : " You live, I think, in the neighbourhood of Birmingham,—what must you have felt on the late alarming occasion ? You, I suppose, could see the fires from your windows.

We, who only heard the news of them, have trembled. Never, sure, was religious zeal more detestably manifested, or more to the prejudice of its own cause."

The claims of the sufferers were heard at the Spring Assizes at Warwick, in 1792. The total bill of costs amounted to £35,095 13s. 6d. Here, as at the trial of the rioters, the whole weight of authority was against the dissenters. No claim was allowed on behalf of the New Meeting House, because the Trustees had lost their License; ultimately, however, a grant of £2,000 was made from the Treasury, upon the application of Mr. Russell.

A very interesting sketch of the proceedings at this trial is given in several letters from a Birmingham tradesman, Mr. Thomas Richards, of 82, High Street, (of whose establishment a full-page engraving is given in Bisset's " Magnificent Directory,") addressed to his daughters at school. As these contain the only accurate account of this event, so far as we know, we make no apology for printing them entire.

"*Birmingham, April 1st, 1792.*—I dare say you will be anxious to hear some news from Warwick assizes, as we are all so much interested in the trials there. They began on Wednesday, the 28th March ; in general they have finished in two or three days, but they are not yet over, nor likely to be for several days. Our friend Dr. Priestley is there, and as I found he did not intend coming to Birmingham, Mr. Saml. Ryland, Sen., Mr. Benton, and myself, went on Thursday last to pay our respects to him. We were so fortunate as to call upon him at a time when he was disengaged, and spent an hour with him by ourselves ; he looks very well, and enjoys his usual and equal flow of spirits. It is evident he is not situated so much to his own wish as he was at Birmingham, but he seems to feel and uniformly expresses himself like a truly Christian Philosopher. We found by our newspaper, that he had received some insults at Warwick, and we asked him about it, but he made very light of it ; and said, he was so used to ill-treatment from the ignorant part of mankind, that he considered it as nothing, but looked upon the kind attention of his friends as clear gain. He was evidently pleased to see us, and pressed us to stay, till we were interrupted by other company. Many of his congregation have followed our example, and have gone over on purpose to see him, and came back the same day. We stayed all night, and Mr. Benton and I were obliged to sleep in one bed, for which we paid the extravagant price of half a guinea, though I was in the court till after two o'clock on

Friday morning, hearing Mr. Ryland's trial, which lasted about fifteen hours. I was there from seven o'clock till two, and got a very good place amongst the Counsel. I much wished to have gone again to-morrow to hear the Dr.'s trial, but Mr. Richards is just set off with Mr. Whately, the attorney, and the Rev. Mr. Lawrence, who is suppoened as a witness on the Dr.'s trial. I expect he will cut a poor figure. The Dr. told me they had got an excellent set of questions to ask him, drawn up by a person well qualified to do it. I think the dissenters have missed

him, if possible, but it is an uncertainty whether they can have him, as the courts are open in London, and I fear he may be engaged. The only two trials that have taken place yet, are Mr. Ryland's and Mr. Taylor's. They have taken off from the former more than £700, and from Mr. Taylor, about £2,600 ; it is expected they will take off more from the Dr. and Mr. Hutton. I am truly sorry for Mr. Hutton's family, they have been used in the most shameful manner ; they have been insulted in the streets ; ludicrous and scandalous prints have been published and

LIVERY STREET (UNION) MEETING HOUSE.

OLD MEETING HOUSE.
Rebuilt 1792-96.

NEW MEETING HOUSE.
Rebuilt 1802.

it very much in not having an eminent counsel to reply to a famous one that the opposite party have brought up on the occasion. He is the most violent, impudent fellow I ever heard in any court ; he spoke two hours upon Mr. Ryland's trial, and began to throw out such invectives and falsehoods against the dissenters, that the judge stopped him, but such was his effrontry that he told the Judge that if he sent him to Newgate he would say what he had to say. I found the Judge told him afterwards that his speech had a very bad tendency, but he is well paid, and seems to be determined to say anything that will please his employers. The dissenters have now sent for Mr. Erskine, the most eminent counsel in the kingdom—I am anxious to know whether they have brought him. Three gentlemen set off on Sunday night, on purpose to procure

sold in the most public manner ; in short, exactly the same spirit seems to have actuated both the great and the little mob of late, as produced and carried on the riots in July. When this wicked spirit will subside I know not, but there is no danger of its shewing itself in the same manner as it has done before.

"The insult that was offered to the Dr. was by an attorney in Warwick. It seems he followed him, either in the hall or the street, and cursed him and used the most audacious language, but the Dr. took no notice of him, but Mr. Edwards saw him in the street last Sunday, and went up to him and fixed his piercing eyes upon him with all the energy he was capable of, said to him 'are you the fellow that dared to damn Dr. Priestley ?' He walked off like a coward, and made no reply."

"*Wednesday Morning, 4th April.*—I have this morning seen one of the gentlemen who went to London for Erskine, and have the mortification to hear that he could not possibly come, but the Chief Baron Eyre is come to relieve the other Judge, and I have no doubt will be a check upon the counsel that has distinguished himself so

dined with Mr. Jno. Ryland and Son, after their *fiery trial.*

THOS. RICHARDS."

"*Birmingham, April 8th, 1792.*—In my last, I gave you some account of Warwick Assizes, which were not finished till Friday night. Dr. Priestley's trial came on

THE OLD "COURT OF REQUESTS."
From a Drawing in the Pershouse Collection, Birmingham Old Library.

much by his contempt of the court. Erskine says if Baron Eyre had been in court when Harding behaved so ill, he certainly would have committed him to prison.

"I suppose the trials will all be over by to-night, but as I think you will be anxious to hear what has been doing, I believe I shall send this by post to-day, and probably write again on Sunday. We called at Rowington when we went to Warwick, spent a short time with your mama, and found her very well, did not call as we came back, as we were induced to come through Knowle, where we

on Thursday, and though they made very large deductions from his claim, I am persuaded they did not make any from his happiness, for I suppose there never was a trial in that court where so respectable a set of evidence were collected together in favour of any man, much less of a man who had by his enemies been treated as the worst of criminals. Three of the most distinguished of the witnesses were the Rev. Augustus Johnson, of Kenilworth, a gentleman of the establishment, a philosophical friend of the Dr.'s, and a man of most amiable character and man-

33

ners, and respected by the whole county round, and of large property; the Rev. Mr. Berrington, a Roman Catholic priest, and an author, who has distinguished himself by several very valuable and ingenious publications, and added to that, a man of most respectable character, and esteemed by all the literati of the present time; Mr. Galton Jun., of this town, a quaker, whom you know, who is universally respected by all parties for his abilities, his generosity, his candour, his public usefulness, and every private virtue which can adorn the gentleman and the scholar. The appearance of such characters as these, would have done honour to royalty itself, and their testimony would have been decisive in any case. Several other persons, of high reputation, were ready to have appeared if it had been necessary, and would have been proud to have had an opportunity of shewing the world that they were the friends of Dr. Priestley, but there were many that were not called upon. The Dr.'s two sons underwent long examinations, and were complimented by both the Judge and Counsel. I have no doubt but the Dr. experienced much more satisfaction from the appearance of these, his friends, and the behaviour of his sons, than he would have done if the jury had given him every shilling he claimed."

The amounts claimed by the various sufferers, together with the amounts allowed by the Court, are given in the following table, prepared by William Hutton:—

NAME.	CLAIM.			ALLOWED.		
John Taylor, Esq.	£12,670	9	2 ...	£9902	2	0
Thomas Russel, Esq.	285	11	7 ...	160	0	0
William Piddock	556	15	7 ...	300	0	0
John Harwood	143	12	6 ...	60	0	0
Thomas Hawkes	304	3	8 ...	90	15	8
B. C. Cox	336	13	7 ...	254	0	0
Parsonage House	267	14	11 ...	200	0	0
St. Dollax	198	8	9 ...	139	17	6
William Russel, Esq.	1971	8	6 ...	1600	0	0
John Ryland, Esq.	3240	8	4 ...	2495	11	6
Old Meeting	1983	19	3 ...	1390	7	5
Geo. Humphreys, Esq.	2152	13	1 ...	1855	11	0
Dr. Priestley	3628	8	9 ...	2502	18	0
Thomas Hutton (my son)	619	2	2 ...	619	2	2
Wm. Hutton (myself)	6736	3	8 ...	5390	17	0
	£35,095	13	6	£26,961	2	3

These amounts, small as they were in proportion to the claims, were paid grudgingly, and, says Hutton, "with as much reluctance as if the sufferers had destroyed their own property." The mere costs of the trial, borne by the dissenters amounted to thirteen thousand pounds.

The congregations of the two Meeting Houses, deprived for a time of their accustomed places of worship, obtained the temporary use of part of a building called the Amphitheatre, in Livery Street, which was opened, under the name of the Union Meeting House, on the 13th November 1791. Mr. Thomas Richards, several of whose letters we have already quoted, wrote on that day to his daughters:

"Our new place of worship, formerly the Amphitheatre, in Livery Street, is made very commodious for our purpose, and was opened this morning by Mr. Coates, who preached an excellent sermon upon the occasion, from the 4th John, 23-24 verses. It was very well filled, both parts of the day, I believe not less than a thousand people in the morning, and I suppose 1,200 this afternoon; and he seemed to be heard by everybody present. It is a much more convenient and comfortable place than the generality of the people expected, and I think will do very well till our own places are rebuilt; we have taken it for three years. Dr. Priestley offered to come to be with us for a few Sundays, but many of the congregation thought it better to deprive ourselves of the pleasure of his company, than expose him to the risk of insult from our Birmingham savages. It was last week determined by the congregation of the late Dr. Price, to invite him as his successor, and I suppose he will accept their invitation."

The congregation of the Old Meeting House commenced to rebuild in June, 1792, on the site of the old building destroyed by the rioters; but did not complete it until 1796. It was built sufficiently strong to stand a siege almost; the basement, which is of stone, forms a piazza; above, the building is of brick, and has but few pretentions to architectural beauty. It is capable of accommodating about 1,100 hearers.

The New Meeting House, in Moor Street, was not opened until July 22, 1802. It was similar in appearance to the Old Meeting; the interior measured 76 feet by 46 feet, and will accommodate about 1,200 persons. Views of both buildings, together with the temporary home of the two Societies in Livery Street, appear on page 254.

CHAPTER XL.

THE THEATRE IN BIRMINGHAM,
From 1775 to the burning of the New Street Theatre in 1792.

Macklin in Birmingham—First attempt to obtain a License for the Theatre—The bill—The debate on the first reading—Mr. Burke's speech—Defeat of the bill on the second reading—Benefits—The Livery Street Amphitheatre—John Collins's Entertainment, " The Brush "—Burning of the New Street Theatre—Suett's Wig—Actors' Benefits at the Amphitheatre.

OUR last notice of matters theatrical brought the history of local theatres down to the year 1775.* At that date, the reader will remember, the town boasted of two newly-built theatres,—those of New Street and King Street. The opening of these two houses marked the beginning of a new era in the history of the stage in Birmingham. Hitherto the dramatic entertainments given in the town hardly equalled those of the strolling players " under canvas," and even these had frequently to give way before the less legitimate performances of rope and wire dancers, conjurors, fire-eaters, and other " entertainers " of a miscellaneous character ; now, a better class of entertainments was promised : " Stars " from the Metropolitan theatres occasionally visited the local houses. On the 12th of July, at the King Street Theatre, Macklin—

———" the Jew
That Shakespeare drew "—

appeared in the character in which he eclipsed all other actors of his time, that of *Shylock* ; and in that of *Sir Archy Macsarcasmn* in the farce of *Love a la Mode* ; other well-known actors also appeared during the same year. But the old liking for miscellaneous performances of a lower order still remained, and we read in the very advertisement announcing Macklin's performances, that the uncommon applause given to Signor Rosignoel's Imitation of Birds, &c., on Friday last, at the above Theatre, has induced Mr. Yates to engage him for a few nights after the expiration of his present agreement at Sadler's

* Public Life and Events (Chapter xxiv., pp. 141-4.)

Wells, which will be some time in the next month, when he will certainly return here, and entertain the publick with several new Performances."

Up to this time all theatrical performances in Birmingham had been, strickly speaking, under the ban of the law, none of the theatres which had arisen from time to time-having been licensed.

As far as Birmingham was concerned, therefore, the old law was still in force regarding all actors as rogues and vagabonds, who were liable, as a local notice pointed out, for " the acting of Plays, Interludes, Comedies, Tragedies, Operas, Farces, and other Entertainments of the Stage, without legal Authority, to condign Punishment." This anomalous position was not one in which the theatre-loving people of Birmingham were inclined to remain contented any longer ; and so we read in the *Gazette*, of February 17, 1777, that " On Monday last Mr. Yates presented a Petition to the House of Commons for leave to bring in a Bill to license the Theatre in New-Street, in this Town ; another Petition was also presented at the same Time, signed by several Gentlemen and respectable Tradesmen, in support of Mr. Yates's Petition : both of which were then read, and referred to a Committee appointed to consider the same, with a Power to send for Persons, Papers, and Records."

In order to strengthen his position, Mr. Yates inserted in the same issue of that journal, an advertisement as follows :—

" To the Gentlemen, Manufacturers, Tradesmen, &c., of the Town of Birmingham, and its Environs. Whereas a Petition is now depending in the Honourable House of Commons, for a ROYAL THEATRE in the Town of Birmingham ; and it having been suggested to several Gentlemen of the said Town, that a bad Use might be made of the Power intended to be vested in the Person to whom it may be granted ; the following Conditions are submitted to their Consideration :

"First, That no public Diversions, such as Rope-Dancing, Tumbling, Puppet-shows, &c., which have been lately exhibited, and are so greatly complained of, shall ever be permitted at the New-Street Theatre.

"Secondly, That the Time for performing Plays shall be limited to four Months ; and if any Attempt shall be made to exceed that Time, the Magistrates for the Time being shall have the same full Power in every Respect to restrain them, as if no such Authority had been granted for a Royal Theatre.

"On the above Conditions (which have already been offered to several respectable Gentlemen) it is presumed that a Royal Theatre would be very acceptable and agreeable, as it is certain nine Parts in ten of the Town are convinced that two Play-houses are greatly injurious. Therefore, whether a Theatre so regulated would not be preferable to those on the present plan is a Question submitted to the candid Public."

A copy of the bill for licensing the theatre, was printed in the *Gazette* of March 10th, 1877. It runs as follows :—

"*A Bill for enabling his Majesty to license a Play-house in the Town of Birmingham, in the County of Warwick, for four months every year.*

"Whereas it may be proper that a Play-house should be licensed in the Town of Birmingham, in the County of Warwick for four months every year :

"MAY IT THEREFORE PLEASE YOUR MAJESTY, That it may be enacted, And be it enacted, by the King's Most Excellent Majesty, by and with the Consent of the Lords Spiritual and Temporal, and Commons, in this present Parliament assembled, and by the Authority of the same, That so much of an Act of Parliament, which passed in the tenth Year of his late Majesty's Reign, intituled, 'An Act to explain and Amend so much of an Act made 'in the twelfth Year of the Reign of Queen Anne, inti-'tuled an Act for reducing the Laws relating to Rogues, 'Vagabonds, Sturdy Beggars, and Vagrants, and sending 'them whither they ought to be sent,' as discharges all Persons from representing any Entertainment on the Stage whatever, in Virtue of Letters Patent from his Majesty, or by Licence from the Lord Chamberlain of his Majesty's Household, for the Time being, except within the Liberties of Westminster, or where his Majesty is residing for the Time being, be, and is hereby*———

——— with respect to the said Town of Birmingham, during the Months of June, July, August, and September in every Year ; and that it shall and may be lawful for his Majesty, his Heirs, and Successors, to grant Letters

* If the Bill passes, this Blank will be filled up with the word REPEALED

Patent for establishing a Theatre or Playhouse, within the said Town of Birmingham, for the Performance of Entertainments of the Stage during the Months of June, July, August and September, in every Year ; which Theatre or Playhouse (during the Time before-mentioned) shall be entitled to all the Privileges and subjected to all the Regulations to which any Theatre or Play-house in Great Britain is entitled and subjected."

The bill was read for the first time in the House of Commons on the 26th of March, and it was during the short debate which ensued that Burke made the now famous reference to Birmingham as "the great Toy-shop of Europe." His speech on this occasion was reported in the *Gazette*, apparently in full, (an unusual circumstance in those days,) as follows :—

"I am sure, Mr. Speaker, that if the Playhouse in Question produces Pieces with half as much Wit in them as the honourable Gentlemen has excited against the Bill, in what I may call the Prologue to the Play, the Town of Birmingham will be most admirably entertained ; —but, Sir, the Honourable Member's Wit stops short even of the *Denouement* of this Piece :—Let us see something more of it : let us hear the Piece before we declare against it. He has brought ancient History to tell you the Circumstances of the City where Iron and Steel were first wrought : but I will likewise tell him that we are indebted to the same Deity for Amusement and theatrical Representation, consequently what he said is an Argument for the Bill.—But, Sir, to be more serious ; I do not know that Theatres are Schools of Virtue :—I would rather call them Nurseries of Idleness ; but then, Sir, of the various Means which Idleness will take for its amusement, in Truth I believe the Theatre is the most innocent :—The Question is not, Whether a Man had better be at Work than go to the Play ?—it is simply this.—Being idle ;—shall he go to the Play or some Blacksmith's Entertainment ?—Why I shall be free to say, I think the Play will be the best Place that it is probable a Blacksmith's idle moments will carry him to. The Hon. Gentleman informs the House, that great Inconveniences have been found from the licensed Houses at Liverpool and Manchester. The Case is not parallel between those Towns and Birmingham.—They have a General Licence —Birmingham asks for a *Four Months' Licence only*— their Theatres are under the direction of the same Strolling Manager, who when he once enters the Town, never quits it, whilst by any Arts he can force Company to his Theatre.—Birmingham Theatre will be under the Direction of a Man very eminent in his Profession as a Comedian ; who in London conducts the most elegant Entertainment in Europe, and who never has been, or wishes to be there, but during the Time the Theatres of Drury-Lane and Covent-Garden are shut up in the Summer. I look upon *Birmingham* to be the *great Toy Shop of Europe*, and submit it to the Members of this

Hon. House, to consider if Birmingham *on that Account*, is not the *most proper Place* in England to have *a licensed Theatre*. The Question before us turns upon this Point —there are already two Playhouses unlicensed ; now the Bill proposes that instead of two in Defiance of Law, the People of Birmingham shall have *one according to Law*— therefore, let us proceed and send the Bill to a Committee, when we shall hear the Evidence of Inhabitants of the first Reputation ; and if they can prove, *that one legal Playhouse* will check Industry, promote Idleness, and do other Mischiefs to Trade, which *two Theatres contrary to Law do not*,—then it will be Time to throw out the Bill."

The unlicensed theatre remained an institution in Birmingham for thirty years after the defeat of 1777 ; several unsuccessful attempts were made by Mr. Yates, of the New Street Theatre, and by the manager of that in King Street, to obtain a licence for the local theatre, and it was not until 1807 that the Act of Parliament was obtained which gave to Birmingham a " Theatre Royal."

Most of the theatrical notices in the old local

JOHN COLLINS, AUTHOR OF "THE BRUSH."

The division on the first reading of the bill showed a majority of twenty in favour of its being read a second time, there being 48 votes in its favour and 28 against it. The second reading was fixed for the 22nd of April, and the local interest in the fortunes of the bill was intense, as is manifested in the lengthy report of the debates on that occasion,—so copious indeed as to drive out many of the advertisements. On the second reading the bill was defeated by a majority of 51, there being only eighteen votes for and sixty-nine against it.

journals refer to benefits, often of actors whose very names are now almost forgotten. The names of Mrs. Robinson, Mrs. Whitfield, Mr. Powell, and others, which occur in the *Gazette* during the period under notice, will, doubtless, be unfamiliar to the reader, even though he may be no stranger to the history of the English Stage. One or two examples of these benefit notices, which sound somewhat curious in modern ears, may be given here. The first-named lady, Mrs. Robinson, was favoured with a second benefit during the season of 1783, in consequence of the want of success on the occasion of her first appeal to the public. The second would appear to have been better received, from the following advertisement, in which the *beneficiere* thanks her patrons :—

"MRS. ROBINSON presents her humble Respects to that *uncommonly* brilliant and crowded Audience, whose Appearance on Monday Night in her Favour must ever be regarded by her as a Mark of the most flattering APPROBATION, and as a Proof of the most exalted BENEVOLENCE.

"To those many—*very* many Friends, whose kind Intentions were frustrated by their being, unfortunately, too late to secure Places in the Theatre, her warmest acknowledgments are also due.

"To the Politeness and Liberality of the MANAGERS she considers herself as *peculiarly* indebted. The only Allay to such heart-felt Satisfaction is—the Consciousness that no Language which *she* can adopt—and, indeed, *no Language in the World*—can do Justice to her *Feelings* on this Occasion ; but she hopes that, when she has the Honour and Felicity of appearing *again* before her indulgent and ever-to-be-revered Patrons, the still happier Exertions of maturer Judgment may afford more *substantial* Evidence of her Gratitude for such unmerited Goodness than it is in the Power of *Professions* to afford, however ardent or however sincere."

Few of our readers would be willing, probably, to credit the fact that Birmingham, a century ago, actually possessed an opera-house. We had no trustworthy evidence of the existence of such an institution, yet such there undoubtedly was, although under the more modest title of the "Concert Booth," a wooden play-house, erected on the Moseley Road early in 1778. An announcement of the performances thereat appears in the *Gazette* of June 8th in that year, as follows :—

"This present MONDAY, June 8th, At the New CONCERT BOOTH, near the Plough-and-Harrow, Moseley Road, will be performed a Concert of Vocal and Instrumental MUSIC.—The Vocal Parts by Mr. Butler, and Mrs. Smith (late Mrs. Woodman,) from the Theatre Royal Covent Garden. Between the several Parts of the Concert will be presented (gratis) a TRAGEDY called The London Merchant ; Or the History of George Barnwell. To which will be added, a Farce, called the King and the Miller of Mansfield. Before the Play will be spoken an occasional PROLOGUE.

"The Proprietors having been at a great expense in fitting up the above Booth in a commodious manner, and being determined to use their utmost Efforts in getting up all the New Pieces performed at the Theatres Royal in London last Winter; hope to meet with the Encourage-

ment of the Ladies and Gentlemen, &c., of Birmingham and its Environs.—Boxes 3s.—Pit 2s.—Gals. 1s.

"The Doors to be opened at Six, and to begin exactly at Seven o'clock. Subscription Tickets to be had of Mr. Graham, at Mr. Heath's in Cross-Street ; of Mr. Cross, at Mrs. Gastrill's, Upper Queen-Street ; and of Mrs. Collins.—No Persons to be admitted behind the Scenes.

"N.B. The Days of performing this Week, are Monday, Tuesday, Wednesday, and Friday ; and for the future, Mondays, Wednesdays, and Friday only."

This building had but a brief existence. It fell a prey to the malice of some incendiary wretch, and was burnt to the ground, with all the scenery, the greater part of the Company's dresses, and other properties, on the 13th of August in the same year. The building being of timber, all efforts to extinguish the flames were fruitless. The melancholy situation of the poor burnt-out players, and the kindly sympathy and assistance accorded to them by the inhabitants are well described by a correspondent of the *Gazette*, who signs himself "No Player," as follows :—

"To the Printers of the Birmingham *Gazette*.—Birmingham, August 24th, 1778.—It is with the sincerest Pleasure that I congratulate the Inhabitants of this Town, on the singular honour they have done their Humanity in contributing to the Relief of the unhappy sufferers by the late Fire. The situation of the Actors was indeed deplorable ; after having taken infinite Pains during the last Months,—after having done all in their power to alleviate the Distresses of some Individuals in this Town, by giving them Benefits, while the miserable Pittance allowed to Themselves afforded them only a bare subsistence—just as they were in Expectation of the Approach of their own Benefits, when they might have shared a few Guineas to discharge their unavoidable Debts ;—at such a critical juncture, to have their fond hopes blasted at once, by a Calamity as shocking as the Authors of it were wicked, must deeply affect every Mind not totally lost to every humane feeling. But the noble Generosity displayed by all Ranks of People upon this occasion, transcends all praise ! Though obvious reasons had prevented their encouragement of the Theatre at Moseley, yet now every other consideration gave way to the generous impulse of Benevolence, and the Proprietors of both Houses evinced the strongest Inclination to render Service to the unfortunate Players. The Justices, too, to their immortal Honour, did not discountenance the undertaking ; and two Plays have been represented at the New-street Theatre* with uncommon applause ;

---

* They performed Sheridan's Opera of "The Duenna," which had been played five times previously, at the Concert Booth ; also, the Farce of "All the World's a Stage."

but whether the violent claps which shook the House proceeded from a sense of the Performer's merit, or compassion for their distress is difficult to determine ; but probably each of these motives had its share in producing the effect. Though the Profits of the nights were not quite equal to the Exigencies of the Company, yet they were considerable, and went a great way towards extricating them from their difficulties ; but if a further application was to be made to the worthy Magistrates, and leave obtained for one or two plays more, at the King-street Theatre (the Proprietors having with great good-nature made an offer of their House), there is no Doubt but every Creditor would be satisfied, and the no longer unfortunate Actors might leave the Town with Comfort and Reputation.

"I am, Your most obedient Servant, No PLAYER."

The "worthy magistrates" granted permission to the proprietors of the King Street Theatre for an additional performance, which was given during the following week, on behalf of Mr. Godso, "the builder and sole proprietor of the Moseley theatre."

Those were the days in which an actor was in reality the *humble servant* of the public, and an old custom still lingered in the profession of calling at the houses of their friends and patrons, in order to sell tickets for benefits. In this manner the great Mrs. Siddons, when a member of a country company of which her father, Roger Kemble, was manager, might have been seen, as described by an eye-witness, " walking up and down both sides of a street in a provincial town, dressed in a red woollen cloak, such as was formerly worn by menial servants, and knocking at each door to deliver the play-bill of her benefit." In the same spirit of almost servility, Mrs. Whitfield announces her benefit in the *Gazette*, of July 26, 1784 :—

" Mrs. Whitfield presents her humble respects to the ladies and gentlemen of Birmingham, having had the honour of appearing before them for four years, and never having before troubled them, she hopes it will not be thought presumptive in her soliciting their patronage on Wednesday next, which is appointed for her benefit ; and as she has upon various occasions experienced their indulgence and urbanity, she now hopes for an opportunity to acknowledge their support. Mrs. Whitfield thinks it incumbent on her to declare she would not have thought of obtruding her name on the public for a night, but that she was in possession of two new pieces which she meant to produce, but Mr. Colman has positively refused to let them be done ; this she was not aware of till it was too late to give up her night. She begs leave to inform them the play of Oroonoko, as it now stands corrected and pruned of every exceptionable passage, by David Garrick, Esq., is one of the most affecting and moral dramatic pieces on the stage.

" Mr. Southern, by every critic of taste and judgment, was declared the most pathetic writer of his time ; his play of Isabella, in which Mrs. Siddons has made so great a figure, is an extant and convincing proof of his genius ; yet, notwithstanding his intimacy with the Tragic Muse, his powers in Comedy were equally commanding, which, according to the fashion of that day, he has most happily blended in the present play ; the story is founded on a well known fact. The Farce of The Devil to Pay, written by the late Henry Fielding, of facetious memory, author of Tom Jones, &c., &c., is too well known to need a comment."

In the same year Dr. Langford quotes an advertisement of an "Annual Night for Ornamenting the Theatre " :—

" Annual Night for Ornamenting the Theatre
(By their Majesties' Servants).
AT THE THEATRE IN NEW STREET,
BIRMINGHAM.
This Present Monday, June 28, 1784,
Will be presented, a Comedy called
"THE MISER."
Lovegold (the Miser) by Mr. YATES
(Being his First Appearance this Season)."

In August, 1787, the New Street Theatre seems to have been the scene of something like a playhouse riot ; " bottles, plates, apples, &c." having been thrown at the actors by the turbulent "gods" of the gallery. A reward was offered by the manager for the detection and apprehension of the offenders, but no further light is thrown upon the circumstance in the local journals.

The Livery Street Amphitheatre, to which we have already made reference in our notice of the riots of 1791, was occasionally used for dramatic performances, principally by amateurs ; and even after the burnt-out congregations of the two meeting-houses had taken a portion of the building, the remainder was still used under the name of "the Gentleman's Private Theatre." A somewhat apocryphal story is told respecting the occasional annoyances suffered by the worshippers, owing to the partition, which divided their portion of the building from that of the sons of Thespis, not reaching to the roof ; the story says that "while one of the buskin was bellowing, 'Thou'rt all a lie, and false as hell,' the pious assembly on the other side of the wall were almost rending the air with 'Hallelujah, Hallelujah!'" This might have been said, perhaps, had the worshippers been Methodists, but a Unitarian congregation is scarcely in the habit of "almost rending the air," either with "Hallelujah" or any other exclamation, in their devotional exercises. Giving this anecdote, however, for what it is worth, the fact remains, that for some time after the riots the building was tenanted by the players as well as the worshippers, as will be seen by the following advertisement, from the *Gazette* of January 14, 1793 :—

FOR TWO OR THREE NIGHTS AT MOST.
" Sport that wrinkled Care derides,
And Laughter, holding both his sides."
At the Gentleman's Private Theatre, in Livery Street, on Wednesday, January 16, 1793, will be presented for the first time in Birmingham,
COLLINS'S NEW EMBELLISHED
EVENING BRUSH,
For rubbing off The Rust of Care,
As exhibited Fifty-two Nights last Winter, at the Lyceum, in London, to overflowing Houses, after One Hundred and Ninety-four Repetitions of the Brush in its original State, at the Royalty Theatre, and the Lyceum before,
BY THE AUTHOR HIMSELF.
The whole interspersed with the following New and Original Songs : The Brush, The King, The Stage Coach, The Glorious Ninety-three, John Bull, Prospect of To-morrow, Gimblet-eyed Kitty, England's Alarm, Rodney's Dirge, Tragic-comic Murder, Von Two Tree Leetel Vords a la Francoise, and the History of England through Two and Thirty Reigns, a copious Subject short in Detail !
Doors open at Half after Six ; Begin exactly at Seven Admittance Two Shillings.
The House will be completely aired, as two large Stoves will be kept constantly burning every Day, and have been so for several Days past.
N.B.—Convenient Lights placed in the Court Yard leading to the Theatre.

The author of "The Brush" was, as our readers will have noticed, from the songs introduced therein, no other than our worthy local poet, John Collins. We do not purpose entering into a biography of the writer here, as that will come in due course in our next chapter of local worthies ; but by the kindness of Mr. Sam : Timmins (who

possesses the author's original MS. of *The Brush*,) we are enabled to give an outline of the entertainment itself.

The author's purpose in this lecture, was to hit off some of "the follies, vices, and absurdities of the age," as "performed off and on the stage." "We beat the bushes," he says, "for no better game than what may be sprung within the walls of a Theatre, but though our object is to point out, and expose, stage imposters, yet not one illiberal idea against the true professors of it, provided they will move in a sphere adapted to their abilities. For, to all be it known, (pronounce it a pun if you please,) I honour the *pillars* of the stage, altho' I think it no crime to expose the *Caterpillars* of it." Then follows a prologue, in verse, the last stanza of which is as follows :—

" You've all heard the story, no doubt, of poor sweep,
Who one morning was found laid out dead on the snow,
Knowing no honest way how from starving to keep,
His brush being lost, and his living also ;
Then put me in his place, and the very same case,
Must be mine, if my labours the Critics should crush ;
Then for charity spare, lest his fate I should share,
For like poor little sweep, I've no bread but my *Brush*."

Talking pleasantly of amateur actors, the lecturer tells an amusing story of a stage-struck tailor who called upon Garrick with the request that he might be permitted to play the part of the hero in " *Romo and Juliet*." The actor, having referred the would-be "Romo" to the description of the huge Colossus bestriding the lazy pacing clouds, said, " Pray tell me, sir, when this huge Colossus was bestriding those clouds, which way would you go, (now supposing his stride to have been much upon a par with a middling-sized rainbow), I say, sir, which way would you go about to measure him for a pair of breeches ?"— "Make a pair of breeches for a rainbow?" exclaimed the astonished snip, " why I don't believe two taylors in London ever did such a thing in their lives, and I'm sure I could as soon make a pair for the Man in the Moon !"—"Then pray, sir, how came you to think of undertaking my business, when you are not master of your own !" Collins then adds a droll parody of Macbeth's

FORWARD

EDWARD CAPERN,

Author of "Wayside Warbles," "Sungleams and Shadows," &c.

PHOTOGRAPHED BY WHITLOCK.

BIRMINGHAM: HOUGHTON & CO, SCOTLAND PASSAGE.

address to the ghost of Banquo, altered to suit the frightened tailor, who " went off in a tangent, perfectly cured of his passion for the stage, and resolved for the future to stick to his shop-board."

Stories of stage-slips, absurd alterations of text, forgetfulness, and other amusing incidents of theatrical life render the lecture more than a mere evening's entertainment. Only a few of these, however, can be quoted here. The first tells how " one of these imperfect gentlemen " had to deliver the lines—

> " Now future fame posterity shall tell
> " No couple lived so happy, died so well,"

from Dryden's *All for Love* (an alteration of Shakespeare's *Antony and Cleopatra*). Instead of these, however, " he came forward, hitching up his small clothes, and wiping his nose on the back of his hand, and in his usual manner said,

> Now fame shall tell posterity that—
> Posterity shall tell Fame—*no*—
> Fame shall tell Posterity—*um*.

Down dropped the curtain and there was an end of the play."

" The very same gentleman," adds Collins, " afterwards in the Norwich Theatre, came forward to give out the play for the next night, it being, by particular desire, for the benefit of the box-keeper, and the last night of performing that season, which he gave out literally in the following manner :—Ladies and Gentlemen— above and below—to-morrow evening will be presented the celebrated Comedy of—of—the Tragedy of—of—no—Opera of—of—the play of—of—the play-bills to-morrow will tell you all about it. To which will be added the farce of the—the pantomine of—the entertainment—of what's to be done after the play, it being by particular desire of the Box-keeper and for the benefit of the last night of the season !"

After several droll stories touching the matter of pronunciation and punctuation,—both on and off the stage,—the author again returns to the curious slips of memory on the part of actors, telling a laughter-moving anecdote of the early

34

days of Foote, when "the English Aristophanes" played *Hamlet* on his own benefit night, at Bath. " He limped tolerably well through the play in his own way till he came to the scene of the quarrel in the last act, with Laertes, and in repeating the lines :

> ' What is the reason that you use me thus ?
> I lov'd thee—but 'tis no matter—
> Let Hercules himself do what he may,
> The cat will mew, the dog will have his day.'

Instead of which, in his usual way, he says :

> ' What is the reason that you use me thus ?
> I lov'd thee—but 'tis no matter—
> Let Hercules himself do what he may,
> The dog will mew—eh ! no, that's wrong—'
> ' The cat will bark— Bark ! no, that's the dog,—the dog will bark—eh ! no, that's the dog again—the cat— the dog—the cat— Pshaw ! d—n the dog, and the cat too— Ladies and gentlemen, it is something about barking and catterwauling, but, as I hope to be saved, I know nothing about the matter.' "

The author quaintly concludes his characteristic entertainment with the following anecdote :— " There was one of the Norwich company, a very eccentric character, who was a tolerable classical scholar, and took no small pains in flashing his learning, but to his shame be it spoken, was never known to be perfect in his part. This gentleman had formerly been a bombardier in the train of Artillery, and his common expression on all occasions, whenever he was gravell'd for lack of matter, was—' Blow me out of the world.' One evening, walking on for the part of Richmond, with all his followers at his heels, when he should have begun :

> ' Thus far into the bowels of the land
> Have we march'd on without impediment '—

and so on to the end of the chapter as he should have done, he says :

> ' Thus far into the bowels of the earth '—

Earth instead of land, but that is much the same you'll say—

> ' Thus far into the bowels of the earth,—
> I say—I have got thus far into the
> Bowels of the earth—and—and '—
> ' Blow me out of the world if I can march a foot further !'

In like manner I find it a difficult matter to carry a recital of these foibles any further, and shall therefore beg leave to dismiss my audience with the sequel to 'Queen Bess's Golden Days— or, the Golden Days we now possess.' "

And with this song our old poet and entertainer closes his most amusing monologue, and doubtless never failed to send his audience home wishing it were longer. Some of the songs he introduces we shall quote in our notice of his life and writings.

And now to return to the theatre. The last event of note of which we purpose making mention in the present chapter is one which for a time cast a gloom over theatrical entertainments in the town for many months, viz., the burning of the New Street Theatre. According to the *Gazette*, there had already been several ineffectual attempts to set fire to the building, but at length the villainous plot met with success, and a little after one o'clock on the morning of Friday, August 17, 1792, the theatre was in flames, which "issued from the front and every part of the building, and illuminated the whole town." All attempts to save it were fruitless ; in about four hours there remained nothing whatever of the principal theatre in the town except the blackened walls.

"That the Theatre was maliciously set on fire," says the *Gazette*, of Aug. 20, "there cannot be a doubt. Those who had the courage to enter it found doors open which were locked when the house was left by the servants the preceding evening, and they observed the fire had been lighted, and was burning with equal fury, in three different parts of the premises, widely distant from, and without any communication with, each other ; but what could be the motive of the perpetrators of this horrid act cannot be conceived. With a view, however, of discovering the villainous authors of so iniquitous a deed, the Proprietors have offered a reward of 200 guineas, which we trust will bring them to light, and to the punishment they so justly merit."

The poor players were, of course, great sufferers in this calamity, by the loss of their wardrobes. The *Gazette* report says, "the dresses of all of them were entirely burnt, except Mr. Marshall's,

who had the intrepidity to enter the dressing-room, and rescue his clothes from the flames." Amongst other sufferers in this respect was the famous comedian Suett, who was a great wig-collector, and had assumed, in one of his performances at the theatre, a large black peruke with flowing curls, that had once been the property of Charles II. "He had purchased this curious relic," says Mr. Dutton Cook, "at the sale of a Mr. Rawle, accoutrement maker to George III. When the wig was submitted for sale, Suett took possession of it, and, putting it on his head, began to bid for it with a gravity that the by-standers found to be irresistibly comical. It was at once declared that the wig should become the actor's property upon his own terms, and it was forthwith knocked down to him by the auctioneer." It need scarcely be said that the loss of a relic so highly-prized was a matter of considerable grief to the actor. With a mournful expression of countenance he would say to every-one he met, "My wig's gone ?" He possessed one of the most valuable stock of wigs in the profession.

In the same issue of the *Gazette* in which appeared the account of the fire, was inserted the following announcement :

August 20, 1792. The late dreadful fire in New Street having deprived several Performers of the accustomed Advantages arising from their respective Benefits,—the Gentlemen of the Private Theatre in Livery Street, have generously stepped forward in this Hour of Distress, and have liberally offered to the Company the Use of their Theatre for the above purpose. The public is, therefore, respectfully informed that the said Theatre, after having been accurately surveyed, is undergoing Alterations which will make it capable of containing near 500 Persons ; but that those Ladies and Gentlemen who wish to patronize this Undertaking may meet with every possible convenience, Tickets for 400 only will be issued.

It will perhaps be appropriate here to allow the curtain to fall for the present on the history of the local stages, so that the next chapter on this subject may open naturally with the rebuilding of the principal theatre.

* *A Book of the Play*, by Dutton Cook, vol ii. p. 55,

CHAPTER XLI.

THE STORY OF SOHO.

PART II.

Extension of Watts's patent to 1800—The first engine—John Wilkinson—Difficulties with the Soho Workmen—The "Waggon and Horses"—William Murdoch and his "timmer" hat—His locomotive engine—Discovery of Gas-lighting—Illuminations at Soho—Bisset's Description of Soho—The New Foundry—Death of Boulton—His Funeral—Death of Watt—Chantrey's Statue in Handsworth Church.

WE now return to Soho,

"—— Where Genius and the Arts preside,
Europa's wonder, and Britannia's pride." *

Our first instalment of the story of this great enterprise† left off at the date of the first attempts on the part of Messrs. Boulton and Watt to manufacture steam-engines for sale.

The Act for extending Watt's patent, vesting in him "the sole use and property of certain steam-engines, commonly called fire-engines, of his invention," for twenty-five years, was obtained in 1775; and now the founder of Soho felt that he could proceed with confidence in the manufacture of "power." Previous to the passing of the Act, he had told Watt "he was afraid to sink many more thousands, in case a better engine appears, and then what becomes of all the fabric we have raised and of the visionary profits?" To have launched into the necessarily heavy expenditure involved in the manufacture of the steam engine, without due protection, would have been ruinous, but now that the Act was obtained, Boulton writes to his partner, "I have made up my mind to make from twelve to fifteen reciprocating engines, and fifty rotative engines, per annum. If we had 100 wheels ready, and 100 small engines like Bow (Liptrap's), we could readily dispose of them; therefore, 'let us make hay while the sun shines,' and before the dark cloud of age lowers upon us, and before any more Tubal Cains, or Doctor Fausts, or Gainsboro's

arise, with serpents like Moses', that destroy all others."

When it became known that the Soho firm were prepared to supply Watt's "fire engine," orders came in from all quarters, and "before long," says Mr. Smiles, "the works at Soho were resounding with the clang of hammers and machinery, employed in manufacturing steam engines for all parts of the civilised world." The first engine made at Soho was one ordered by John Wilkinson, to blow the bellows of his ironworks at Broseley. This engine was, of course, the subject of special interest, both to masters and workmen, as all concerned felt that much of the future success of the Soho foundry would depend upon the manner in which their first engine was turned out. Others, too, were anxiously looking forward to see what Boulton and Watt's engine could do,—the neighbouring iron manufacturers, who were contemplating the erection of Newcomen engines, waited with eager interest until the new engine had been erected at John Wilkinson's works.

"When the materials were all ready at Soho," says Mr. Smiles, "they were packed up and sent on to Broseley. Watt accompanied them, to superintend their erection. He had as yet no assistant to whom he could entrust such work,—on the results of which so much depended. The engine was erected and ready for use about the beginning of 1776. As it approached completion, Watt became increasingly anxious to make a trial of its powers. But Boulton wrote to him not to

---

* Bisset's Poetic Survey round Birmingham.
† Pp. 138-141.

hurry—not to let the engine make a stroke until every possible hindrance to its successful action had been removed; 'and then,' said he, 'in the name of God, fall to and do your best.' The result of the extreme care taken with the construction and erection of the engine was entirely satisfactory. It worked to the admiration of all

In August, 1775, Watt removed with his family to Regent's Place, Harper's Hill, which was then the nearest house to Soho on that side of Birmingham; an engraving of it appears on page 139.

While Watt was at Broseley, Boulton was pushing on with the new buildings at Soho, in

MATTHEW BOULTON.

who saw it, and the fame of Boulton and Watt became great in the Midland Counties."

John Wilkinson's name is worthy of honourable mention in the history of Soho, for the valuable services rendered by him to Boulton and Watt, at a time when they were compelled to sink large sums of money—amounting to nearly £47,000 in all—in perfecting and introducing the steam-engine. During this period of heavy expenditure he supplied them with all the necessary castings for the work to an unlimited extent, waiving all payment until the success of the Boulton and Watt engine was established.

which to carry on the manufacture of " power." Writing to his partner, he says, " The new forging-shop looks very formidable ; the roof is nearly put on, and the hearths are both built. . . . . Pray tell Mr. Wilkinson to get a dozen cylinders cast and bored, from 12 to 50 inches diameter, and as many condensers, of suitable sizes. The latter must be sent here, as we will keep them ready fitted up, and then an engine can be turned out of hand in two or three weeks. I have fixed my mind upon making from twelve to fifteen reciprocating and fifty rotative engines per annum. *I assure you that of all the* *toys and trinkets which we manufacture at Soho, none shall take the place of fire-engines in respect of my attention."* *

In the words italicised Boulton seems to have given his partner a glimpse at the dreams in which he doubtless indulged—dreams which were destined to have a glorious fulfilment—of the

obtained them.   The first difficulty they overcame by confining the men to special classes of work, carrying the division of labour to the farthest possible point ; by continued practice in the same narrow groove, the men acquired considerable proficiency in their special department of work.

The second difficulty, however, was one which

JAMES WATT.

brilliant future in store for the Soho Foundry ; when the two men,—the noble, enthusiastic, and enterprising manufacturer, and the quiet, nervous, modest inventor,—should really be invested with the authority of kingship, dispensing the means of effecting a complete conquest of the world of nature and science.

For a time one of the greatest difficulties experienced by the Soho Firm in their new undertaking was that of obtaining skilled workmen ; another was that of keeping them when they had

required all the tact and spirit of Matthew Boulton to cope with it.   There were tempters from abroad, continually lurking about Soho, offering heavy bribes to obtain access to the works ; and still heavier to lure away skilled workmen.   The " Waggon and Horses " Inn, at Handsworth, was the scene of many a temptation on the part of the " intelligent foreigner," sent out by his Government to worm out the secrets of Soho ; and more than once of a defeat for the Soho firm.   It was here Pickard picked up the idea of the crank steam engine, and thus forestalled Watt in the use of that improvement.   But it is satisfactory to find

* Boulton MSS., quoted in Smiles' *Lives of Boulton and Watt*, (smaller edition, p.p. 161-2.)

that the unscrupulous picker and stealer of other men's brains made but little of his patent, while the fame of Boulton and Watt, and the demand for their engines, increased year by year. "While," says Mr. Timmins, "the nervous, anxious Watt dreaded every new order that came, —hoped some limit would be placed, wanted to sell his interest in the patent for the bare cost of time and labour; the energetic, fearless, brave Boulton grappled with every difficulty, and finally surmounted all. . . . In every relation of their long connection, the cool, clear head and sagacious skill of Boulton were the mainstay of his delicate and nervous friend. The two partners were ever on the very best of terms, although Boulton's patience must sometimes have been severely tried. His bold and vigorous policy always prevailed; and whatever the modest genius of Watt devised, the enterprise and energy of Matthew Boulton brought thoroughly before the world."

In the midst of his difficulties in the matter of his workmen, Boulton was fortunate enough to meet with one who gave promise of becoming a thoroughly trustworthy workman, and a most valuable helper, a young Scotsman, William Murdoch, (or Murdock,) who had, like many of his fellow-countrymen, travelled to England in search of employment. His manner of introduction to the father of Soho is thus related by Mr. Smiles:

"When Murdock called at Soho in the year 1777, to ask for a job, Watt was from home, but he saw Boulton, who was usually accessible to callers of every rank. In answer to Murdock's inquiry whether he could have a job, Boulton replied that work was slack with them, and that every place was filled up. During the brief conversation that ensued, the blate young Scotchman, like most country lads in the presence of strangers, had some difficulty in knowing what to do with his hands, and unconsciously kept twirling his hat with them. Boulton's attention was directed to the twirling hat, which seemed to be of a

peculiar make. It was not a felt hat, nor a cloth hat, nor a glazed hat; but it seemed to be painted, and composed of some unusual material. 'That seems to be a curious sort of hat,' said Boulton, looking at it more closely; 'why, what is it made of?' 'Timmer, sir,' said Murdock, modestly. 'Timmer! Do you mean to say that it is made of wood?' 'Yes, sir.' 'Pray, *how* was it made?' 'I turned it mysel', sir, in a bit lathey of my own making.' Boulton looked at the young man again. He had risen a hundred degrees in his estimation. He was tall, good-looking, and of open and ingenuous countenance; and that he had been able to turn a wooden hat for himself in a lathe of his own making was proof enough that he was a mechanic of no mean skill. 'You may call again, my man,' said Boulton. 'Thank you, sir,' said Murdock, giving a final twirl to his hat."

When next the young Scotsman called he was at once put upon a trial job, which, proving satisfactory, gained for him a permanent situation, at fifteen shillings per week.

Murdoch soon proved himself worthy of confidence, and was despatched to Cornwall, where many Boulton engines were at work in draining the mines, and had hitherto required the almost constant presence of James Watt. While living in Cornwall, as resident engineer, Murdoch turned his attention to the subject of the locomotive engine, and actually brought the idea to a certain degree of perfection, as was evidenced by a model, which, as soon as he had finished, he tried with success, in the long avenue leading to Redruth Church; "and in doing so," says Mr. Smiles, "nearly frightened out of his wits the village pastor, who encountered the hissing, fiery, little machine, while enjoying his evening walk." But Murdoch had not the qualities of Boulton—he was rather of Watt's modest, retiring disposition, —and consequently the locomotive fell into oblivion until George Stephenson took it in hand, and carried the project to a successful issue.

When Murdoch returned to Soho, he was invested with the general supervision and management of the mechanical department, and in this position he was enabled to further justify the confidence and esteem in which he was held by the firm ; he introduced several valuable improvements in the manufacture of the steam-engine, which were embodied in a patent taken out by him in 1799. *

But the invention by which his name will chiefly be perpetuated was that of lighting by gas. The inflammable qualities of coal gas had long been known, but it was left for William Murdoch to apply the knowledge to practical uses. During the long winter evenings at Redruth, he turned his attention to this subject, and dreamed of the brilliant artificial light of the future—which now seems destined to be eclipsed in its turn by one still more brilliant.

Writing in 1808, Murdoch says :—

" It is now nearly sixteen years since (1792), in the course of experiments I was making at Redruth, in Cornwall, upon the quantities and qualities of the gas produced by distillation from different mineral and vegetable substances, that I was induced by some observations I had previously made upon the burning of coal, to try the combustible property of the gases produced from it, as well as from peat, wood, and other inflammable substances ; and, being struck with the great quantities of gas which they afforded, as well as the brilliancy of the light, and the facility of its production, I instituted several experiments with a view of ascertaining the cost at which it might be obtained, compared with that of equal quantities of light yielded by oils and tallow.   My apparatus consisted of an iron retort, with tinned iron and copper tubes, through which the gas was conducted to a considerable distance ; and there, as well as at intermediate points, was burnt through apertures of various forms and dimensions.   The experiments were made upon coal of different qualities, which I procured from different parts of the kingdom for the purpose of ascertaining which would give the most economical

* Patent No. 2340, Aug. 29, 1799.

results.   The gas was also washed with water, and other means were employed to purify it."

He was not long in putting his discovery to a practical use, by lighting with gas his offices and house at Redruth ; and also, in same homely spirit of contrivance which prompted him to make for himself a " timmer hat," constructed a portable gas lantern, which he supplied with gas from a bladder fixed underneath.   With this he lighted himself home at night, across the moors to Redruth.   When he returned to Soho, in 1798, he continued his investigations, and on the occasion of the celebration of the Peace of Amiens, in 1802, the front of the manufactory was brilliantly illuminated with gas, to the astonishment and delight of the inhabitants.   The *Gazette* gives the following description of the

ILLUMINATIONS AT SOHO,

which for elegance and boldness of design, grandeur of effect, and promptness of execution, will remain unequalled amongst the numerous testimonies of joy displayed on the happy occasion of returning peace.   The well known taste and abilities of the liberal proprietors of those premises had given the public every reason to anticipate a very superb and brilliant exhibition ; accordingly, early in the afternoon, the road from this town was crowded with passengers.   The gates of the gardens were thrown open and gave admittance to many thousands of spectators, of whom, it is but justice to observe, that such was their orderly behaviour, that they departed almost without breaking either shrub or tree, or doing any damage.   The house was adorned on the summit of the roof by a magnificent star, composed of variegated lamps, and the centre window was embellished by a beautiful transparency, in glass, of a female figure, in the attitude of offering a thanksgiving for the return of peace.   The manufactory was illuminated throughout its spacious front with upwards of 2,600 coloured lamps, disposed into the forms of G. R., with the word " Peace," above which was placed the crown, with a star of exquisite brilliancy.   In the centre of the front, a transparency represented a dove, the emblem of peace, descending on the globe ; on the left wing, another represented the Caduceus of Mercury between two Cornucopias ; and on the right, a beehive decorated with flowers.   In addition to the above, three very splendid Mongolfier balloons ascended in succession from the courtyard within the manufactory at proper intervals, on a signal from the discharge of cannon. Numbers of sky-rockets also tended to enrich the scene. The whole gave the greatest satisfaction, and produced, in the minds of the spectators, tokens of admiration and sentiments of respect for the munificent projector. Every house in the neighbourhood was also splendidly illuminated; and all the workmen belonging to the manufactory were regaled at public houses.

We have already mentioned Boulton's copper coinage, in the previous chapter of the story of Soho; it will not be necessary, therefore, for us to make further reference to this department of the busy "toyshop" of Soho, except to quote the opinion of Boulton's illustrious partner on this matter. He says, "If Mr. Boulton had done nothing more in the world than he has accomplished in improving the coinage, his name would deserve to be immortalized; and if it be considered that this was done in the midst of various other important avocations, and at an enormous expense—for which at the time he could have no certainty of an adequate return— we shall be at a loss whether more to admire his ingenuity, his perseverance, or his munificence. He has conducted the whole more like a sovereign than a private manufacturer; and the love of fame has always been to him a greater stimulus than the love of gain."

It were almost impossible here, in this brief sketch of the greatest enterprise ever conducted by a private firm, to deal fully with the many and varied products of what has been aptly termed "the world of Soho;" but in order to give the reader a faint idea of the extent and variety of the Soho manufactory, we give from Bisset's "Magnificent Directory" a list of the several distinct "interests" concerned therein :—

"M. Boulton and Button Co.—Buttons in General.
Boulton and Smiths.—Buckles, Latchet's, &c.
M. Boulton and Plate Co.—Silver and Plated Goods.
M. Boulton.—Mint for Governmt. Coin.
M. Boulton.—Medals, Roll'd Metals, &c.
M. Boulton.—Mercantile Trade in Birmingham.
Boulton, Watt, & Sons.—Iron Foundry, & Steam Engines.
J. Watt & Co.—Letter Copying Machines."

In the "Poetic Survey" appended to this Directory, (of which we shall have more to say in

our next chapter,) the author thus describes the residence of Matthew Boulton, at Soho :

" On yonder gentle slope, which shrubs adorn,
Where grew of late, 'rank weeds,' gorse, ling, and thorn
Now pendant woods, and shady groves are seen,
And nature there assumes a nobler mien.
There verdant lawns, cool grots, and peaceful bow'rs,
Luxuriant, now, are strew'd with sweetest flow'rs,
Reflected by the lake, which spreads below,
All Nature smiles around—there stands SOHO ! "

From the contemplation of this seemingly charming abode, he turns to the manufactory :

" SOHO—Where GENIUS and the ARTS preside,
EUROPA's wonder and BRITANNIA's pride ;
Thy matchless works have raised Old England's fame,
And future ages will record thy name ;
Each rival Nation shall to thee resign
The PALM OF TASTE, and own—'tis justly thine ;
Whilst COMMERCE shall to thee an altar raise,
And infant Genius learn to lisp thy praise :
Whilst Art and Science reign, they'll still proclaim
THINE ! ever blended, with a BOULTON's name."

Following the "Poetic Survey," in the same volume, is an allegory in verse, entitled "The Ramble of the Gods through Birmingham," which contains another, and more interesting, notice of Soho. The Gods having visited Henry Clay's establishment,

"——They next resolv'd with speed to go,
To visit BOULTON's, at the great SOHO,
The wonders of that magic place explore,
And with attention, view its beauties o'er.
They went—but here description fails, I ween,
To tell you half the curious works there seen.
Suffice it then, such scenes were there displayed,
The GODS, with rapture fraught, the whole survey'd :
Their NAMES they wrote, and saw, with great surprise,
FAC SIMILES that moment, strikes their eyes ;
Whilst at the MINT, th' invention of the MILL,
Seem'd as if Coin was form'd by magic skill.
But when the ponderous ENGINES were survey'd—
THEY ev'ry tribute due to merit paid :
Then, with reluctance, forc'd themselves away,
Resolv'd to see all that they could by day."

The great demand for the "ponderous engines" rendered it necessary to provide a separate building in which to manufacture them, and on the 28th of January, 1796, the Soho Foundry was "dedicated" with considerable ceremony, as will be seen from the following report, which appeared in the *Gazette* of January 30th in that year :—

SOHO FOUNDRY.

On Saturday last the Rearing Feast of the new Foundry, lately built by Messrs. Boulton, Watt, and Sons, at Smethwick, was given to the engine-smiths, and all the other workmen employed in the erection.

Two fat sheep (the first fruits of the newly-cultivated land at Soho) were sacrificed at the Altar of Vulcan, and eaten by the Cyclops in the Great Hall of the Temple, which is 46 feet wide and 100 feet long. These two great dishes were garnished with rumps and rounds of beef, legs of veal, and gammons of bacon, with innumerable meat pies and plum puddings, accompanied with a good band of martial music. When dinner was over, the Founder of Soho entered and consecrated this new branch of it, by sprinkling the walls with wine, and then, in the name of Vulcan, and all the Gods and Goddesses of Fire and Water, pronounced the name of it Soho Foundry, and all the people cried Amen. A benediction was then pronounced by him upon the undertaking, and a thanksgiving offered for the protection and preservation of the lives and limbs of the workmen during the erection. These ceremonies being ended, six cannon were discharged and the Band of Music struck up God Save the King, which was sung in full chorus by two hundred loyal subjects. After this, many toasts were given suitable to the occasion, by the President of the Feast, Mr. M. Robinson Boulton, which was conducted by him with great spirit and hilarity ; each toast was accompanied with three joyous huzzas and a discharge of cannon. A Ball, with tea, was given in the evening to Venus and the Graces, which ended about ten o'clock, when the concluding guns were fired, and all departed in good humour.

The Address of Mr. Boulton, Sen., upon entering the Foundry, was conceived in the following terms :—After making an excuse to the company for not dining with them, he said, " I could not deny myself the satisfaction of wishing you a happy and joyous day, and expressing my regard for all good, honest, and faithful workmen, whom I have always considered as classed with my best friends.

" I come now as the Father of Soho, to consecrate this place as one of its branches ; I also come to give it a name and my benediction.

" I will therefore proceed to purify the walls of it, by the sprinkling of wine, and in the name of Vulcan and all the Gods and Goddesses of Fire and Water, I pronounce the name of it Soho Foundry. May that name endure for ever and ever, and let all the people say Amen, Amen.

" This Temple now having a name, I will propose that every man shall fill his pitcher, and drink success to Soho Foundry."

Mr. B. then proceeded to give the Establishment his benediction :—" May this Establishment," said he, " be ever prosperous, may no misfortune ever happen to it, may it give birth to many useful arts and inventions, may it prove beneficial to mankind, and yield comfort and happiness to all who may be employed in it.

" As the Smith cannot do without his Striker, so neither can the Master do without his Workman. Let

each perform his part well, and do their duty in that state to which it hath pleased God to call them, and this they will find to be true rational ground of equality.

" One serious word more, and then I have done. I cannot let pass this day of festivity, without observing that these large piles of building have been erected in a short time, in the most inclement season of the year, without the loss of one life, or any material accident. Therefore let us offer up our grateful thanks to the Divine Protector of all things, without whose permission not a sparrow falleth to the ground. Let us Chaunt Hallelujahs in our hearts for these blessings, and with our voices, like loyal subjects, sing God Save Great George our King !"— Which was done in full chorus, and amidst the discharge of the cannon."

Our story of the Soho enterprise may fitly close with the eighteenth century itself, at which date, the patent on the engine expiring, the partnership between the two great master-minds of the firm was dissolved, and the business formally passed into the hands of the younger members of the two families. But the " Iron Chieftain " and the patient, thoughtful inventor still continued to take an interest in the concerns of the manufactory, preferring to " rub " rather than to " rust " out. Matthew Boulton died, at the ripe age of eighty-one, on the 17th of August, 1809 ; he was buried in Handsworth Church, on the 24th of the same month. The funeral was attended by upwards of 700 persons, and included 500 workmen and sixty women employed in the manufactory. A curious old pamphlet describing the ceremony was issued by the undertaker, Mr. George Lander, in order to vindicate himself from certain charges of extortion and of supplying inferior materials, made against him by Matthew Robinson Boulton, the son of the Founder of Soho.

With the quarrel we have nothing to do now ; it is well forgotten, and all who were concerned therein have gone the way of him over whose last obsequies they quarrelled.

From the pamphlet we learn that a special medal was struck in commemoration of the illustrious founder, and was given to every person who was present at the funeral.

James Watt survived his friend and partner

just ten years, dying on the 25th of August, 1819, at the age of eighty-three. He was buried near Boulton, in Handsworth Church, and a noble monument marks his resting place, erected to his memory by the filial piety of his son, James Watt. "This fine work," says Mr. W. Bates, "is the master-piece of the greatest of British sculptors —Chantrey, and consists of an appropriate grey marble pedestal, on which, in a sitting posture, and ordinary costume, is the statue of Watt, in fine white marble. The attitude is unconstrained ; the right hand holds a compass ; the left, a sheet of paper, on which the face—a very personification of abstract thought—is intently fixed : and gazing at it, as we have done, in the mystery of twilight, and the solemn stillness of its shrine, one may well imagine that the cold form, like the wondrous statue of Pygmalion, is gradually becoming instinct with the hues of life and intelligence, and that it is Watt himself in the act of eliminating the sublime conception that immortalizes his name,—

> "The mortal and the marble are at strife,
> And timidly expanding into life."

A statue, almost, if not quite, as noble as Chantrey's, has since been raised to the memory of the great engineer, in the town in whose history the story of Soho is one of the most glorious episodes ; but of this we shall have to speak further at the date of its erection. We may here add, however, that in thus honouring the memory of James Watt, we do ill to forget altogether the brave, fearless, and enterprising Captain of Industry, without whose aid, in all probability, the work of the nervous, modest inventor might never have been accomplished : we do only partial honour to the genius of Soho in perpetuating in enduring marble the memory of one of the partners in that great enterprise,— a partiality which would have grieved none more deeply than James Watt himself.

The story of the Soho manufactory, after the death of its illustrious founders, may best be told in connection with the history of Birmingham manufactures of the nineteenth century in general. Of Gregory Watt and Francis Eginton, and of the famous Lunar Society, we shall have to speak in our next chapter.

CHAPTER XLII.

A SECOND CHAPTER OF LOCAL WORTHIES.

John Collins—His *Scripscrapologia*—His life in Ireland—Poems and Sohgs—Charles Lloyd—The Lunar Society—Gregory Watt—Francis Eginton—James Bisset and his "Magnificent Directory"—Allen's Museum, etc.

ONCE more we pause in the history of the town, to continue our catalogue of local worthies.

First among these comes our old friend of "*The Brush*," John Collins, who, by his exquisite poem, "To-morrow" stands at the head of all local poets.

In one of the best popular collections of songs and lyrics with which we are acquainted,—the *Golden Treasury*, edited by Mr. Francis Turner Palgrave,—the editor re-introduced to modern readers of poetry that delightful poem, as "by

————Collins." In a note at the end of the volume Mr. Palgrave says of its author : "Nothing except his surname appears recoverable with re- gard to the author of this truly noble poem. It should be noted as exhibiting a rare excellence,— the climax of simple sublimity."

The statement that "nothing except the sur- name appears recoverable" respecting Collins called forth several interesting notes from well- known contributors to *Notes and Queries,* and it is to these that we are chiefly indebted for the present notice. The song by which he is best remembered appeared in a rare little volume of songs, published in 1804, with the following quaint title, which we copy entire :—

SCRIPSCRAPOLOGIA ;
or,
COLLINS'S
DOGGEREL
DISH OF ALL SORTS.
CONSISTING OF
SONGS
Adapted to familiar Tunes,
And which may be sung without the Caunterpipe of an Italian Warbler, or the ravishing Accompaniments of Tweedle-dum or Tweedle-dee.
Particularly those which have been most applauded In the Author's once popular Performance, call'd
THE BRUSH.
The Gallimaufry garnished with a variety of
COMIC TALES,
QUAINT EPIGRAMS,
WHIMSICAL EPITAPHS,
&C., &C.
A Kickshaw Treat, which comprehends
Odd Bits and Scraps, and Orts and Ends,—
Mere nicknack namby-pamby Pickings,
Like Fricasees of Frogs or Chickens ;
A Mess with Grub-street Giblets fraught,
And here and there a MERRY THOUGHT ;
In frothy BRAIN SAUCE trimly drest,
But wanting SAGE for perfect zest.
Yet if we countervail that Fault,
With some few Grains of ATTIC SALT,
Sage Critics may withhold their Frown,
And kindly let the Trash go down.
PUBLISHED BY
THE AUTHOR HIMSELF,
AND
PRINTED BY M. SWINNEY, BIRMINGHAM.
1804.

Facing the title-page, is a portrait of the author ; but few copies of this rare little book still contain that embellishment.   As on the title-page, so at the foot of the portrait, the author rigidly suppressed his christian name ; the plate being simply inscribed, "Collins. Scripscrapologiæ Scriptor." It is from this engraving that the portrait on page 259 of this work is copied.

We have already given some account of The Brush, which although popular in the last decade of the eighteenth century, would seem, according to the phrase "once popular" on the title-page of Scripscrapologia to have declined in favour at the beginning of the nineteenth century.   The Brush itself was probably never published ; the original MS, from its appearance—scored here and there with corrections and alterations, directions, (such as—"imitating Smith's tone and monotony in the above lines,") boldly written side-headings to each anecdote or incident, for the direction of the reader, and other marks indicating that it was for personal perusal only—seems to have been the identical copy used by the lecturer in his entertainment ; it is exceedingly dirty in appearance, thumbed, and freely besprinkled with lamp-oil, and would be taken, at first sight, for the prompt-copy of a play.   It is now in the possession of Mr. Sam : Timmins, and has book-plates in it indicating that among its former owners have been two well-known antiquaries, Thomas Bell and William Pinkerton.

Of the life of the author very little indeed is known.   He was born at Bath, (vide "Scripscrapologia," p. 168,) and was the son of a tailor, as the verses entitled "A Frank Confession" indicate.   A report, it seems, had been circulated in that city with a view to injure him in the fashionable world, "which report was nothing more nor less than his being the son of a man who supplied his employers with raiment for the body while he [i.e., the author of The Brush] was furnishing the public with amusement for the mind."   In the verses mentioned, which were inserted in answer to this report in the Bath Chronicle, he says :

"This blot on my 'scutcheon, I never yet tried
    To conceal, to erase, or to alter ;
But suppose me, by birth, to a hangman allied,
    Must I wear the print of the halter ?

        *   *   *   *

And since 'tis a truth I've acknowledg'd through life,
    And never yet labour'd to smother,
That 'a taylor before I was born took a wife,
    And that taylor's wife was my mother.'

        *   *   *   *

Yet, while I've a heart which not envy nor pride,
    With their venom-tipp'd arrows can sting,
Not a day of my life could more gladsomely glide,
    Were it prov'd—I'm the son of a King ! "

According to Pasquin's *Authentic History of the Professors of Painting, Sculpture and Architecture*, Collins was a " miniature painter in profile," and "pursued this diminutive branch of the arts" in Ireland, entertaining the public in the evening with " the amusing lecture called Collins's *Brush*." It would not appear, however, that the

The Elements of Modern Oratory, was evidently the same, substantially, as *The Brush*, as may be gathered from the following thoroughly Collinsian advertisement, which appeared in the *Belfast Newsletter* of January 19, 1776 :

"An Attic Evening's Entertainment.
At Mr M'Kane's Assembly Room° in Belfast,

BINGLEY HOUSE,
The Residence of Charles Lloyd.

lecture was known in Ireland by the name of *The Brush*, but rather as *The Elements of Modern Oratory ;* and its author was known also as an actor as well as a public entertainer. He went to Ireland in 1764, and " proved a very respectable addition to the Irish stage*"—appearing as *Young Mirabel* in " *The Inconstant*," *Justice Woodcock*, *Dick* in " *The Confederacy*," *Peachum*, *Sir Francis Wronghead*, *Bastard* in " *King Lear*," *Major O'Flaherty* in " *The West Indian*," &c., &c. The entertainment which he at that time called

* Hitchcock : *Historical View of the Stage.*

On Saturday Evening, Jan. 20th, 1776, will be presented
for the first Time
A Humourous, Satyrical, Critical, & Mimical
EXHIBITION, call'd The ELEMENTS of
MODERN ORATORY.
In which will be displayed,
The most foreible & striking Examples which this
prolific age affords of the
Great USE & ABUSE of SPEECH,
Particularly in the following Characters, the

Schoolmaster,	Bellower,	Mouther,
Schoolboy,	Growler,	Stammerer,
Public Reader,	Ranter,	Lisper,
Public Speaker,	Whiner,	Snuffler,
Monotonist,	Droner,	Pedant,
Jingler,	Squeaker,	Scotch Orator,

Welch Orator,   And   And Southern
Irish Orator,   The Northern English Provincials.
The whole interspersed with original strictures on
    the Modulation, Variation & Inflection of
    The VOICE in READING and in SPEAKING !
The ludicrous and risible Effects of false Accent,
    Emphasis, and Pronunciation !
The Distortion, Reversion, Maiming, Mangling, and
    Misapplying of WORDS !
The general Abuse of the English Language !
And the present state of Oratory contrasted in the three
Departments of the PULPIT, the BAR, and the STAGE.
    By the Author, J. Collins.
"Whose Stay cannot possibly exceed a Night or two,
as he is on his Journey from London to Dublin, where he
is under Engagements to open by the first of February.
    "To begin exactly at seven, and the Doors to be opened
at six o'Clock.—Admittance two Shillings, English.
    "Tickets to be had at the Donegall Arms, and at the
Printer's hereof.
    "☞ As this Exhibition was repeated forty-two suc-
cessive nights in London, and also several Times with
equal success at the Universities of Oxford and Cambridge, the Author declines the fulsome (tho' too common)
Practice of self Encomium ; chusing much rather to submit the Decision of its Merits to the well-known Candour
and Judgment of an Irish Audience."

Collins probably came to Birmingham as early
as 1793 ; we have already quoted, in our chapter
on the Musical Festivals, his impromptu on hearing Mrs. Second sing at the Festival in that year.
In the Birmingham Directory for 1797 the name
of "John Collins, Great Brook Street," appears ;
and it was in that street, nearly opposite St.
James's Church, that our author is known to have
lived.   At that time he was editor and part proprietor of the *Birmingham Chronicle*, which was
published by the firm of "Swinney and Collins."

And now we return to his poetry, as contained
in his only published volume, the *Scripscrapologia*.
First among these comes the famous song—

TO-MORROW.

In the downhill of life, when I find I'm declining,
    May my fate no less fortunate be
Than a snug elbow-chair can afford for reclining,
    And a cot that o'erlooks the wide sea ;
With an ambling pad-pony to pace o'er the lawn,
    While I carol away idle sorrow,
And blithe as the lark that each day hails the dawn,
    Look forward with hope for to-morrow.

With a porch at my door, both for shelter and shade too,
    As the sunshine or rain may prevail ;
And a small spot of ground for the use of the spade too,
    With a barn for the use of the flail :

A cow for my dairy, a dog for my game,
    And a purse when a friend wants to borrow ;
I'll envy no nabob his riches or fame,
    Nor what honours may wait him to-morrow.

From the bleak northern blast may my cot be completely
    Secured by a neighbouring hill ;
And at night may repose steal upon me more sweetly,
    By the sound of a murmuring rill :
And while peace and plenty I find at my board,
    With a heart free from sickness and sorrow,
With my friends let me share what to-day may afford,
    And let them spread the table to-morrow.

And when I at last must throw off this frail covering,
    Which I've worn for threescore years and ten,
On the brink of the grave I'll not seek to keep hovering,
    Nor my thread wish to spin o'er again :
But my face in the glass I'll serenely survey,
    And with smiles count each wrinkle and furrow ;
As this old worn-out stuff, which is threadbare to-day,
    May become everlasting to-morrow.

This charming production needs no comment ;
we therefore leave it to find its own way to the
heart of the readear—if indeed he be not already
well acquainted with it.   Another poem in the
same volume, which forms an admirable pendant
to "To-morrow," is less known : it is entitled,

HOW TO BE HAPPY.

In a cottage I live, and the cot of content,
    Where a few little rooms, for ambition too low,
Are furnish'd as plain as a patriarch's tent,
    With all for convenience, but nothing for show :
Like Robinson Crusoe's, both peaceful and pleasant,
    By industry stor'd, like the hive of a bee ;
And the peer who looks down with contempt on a peasant,
    Can ne'er be look'd up to with envy by me.

And when from the brow of a neighbouring hill,
    On the mansions of Pride, I with pity look down,
While the murmuring stream and the clack of the mill,
    I prefer to the murmurs and clack of the town,
As blythe as in youth, when I danc'd on the green,
    I disdain to repine at my locks growing grey :
Thus the autumn of life, like the springtide serene,
    Makes approaching December as cheerful as May.

I lie down with the lamb, and I rise with the lark,
    So I keep both disease and the doctor at bay ;
And I feel on my pillow no thorns in the dark,
    Which reflection might raise from the deeds of the day :
For with neither myself nor my neighbour at strife,
    Though the sand in my glass may not long have to run,
I'm determin'd to live all the days of my life,
    With content in a cottage and envy to none !

Yet let me not selfishly boast of my lot,
    Nor to self let the comforts of life be confin'd ;
For how sordid the pleasures must be of that sot,
    Who to share them with others no pleasure can find !

For my friend I've a board, I've a bottle and bed,
   Ay, and ten times more welcome that friend if he's poor ;
And for all that are poor if I could but find bread,
   Not a pauper without it should budge from my door.

Thus while a mad world is involv'd in mad broils,
   For a few leagues of land or an arm of the sea ;
And Ambition climbs high and pale Penury toils,
   For what but appears a mere phantom to me ;
Through life let me steer with an even clean hand,
   And a heart uncorrupted by grandeur or gold ;
And, at last, quit my berth, when this life's at a stand,
   For a berth which can neither be bought nor be sold.

Another short poem, which appears in the MS.
of *The Brush*, is considered by Mr. Pinkerton to
be "much superior to the song of *To-morrow*."
It consists of five verses, and is a paraphrase of
Hamlet's famous Soliloquy on Death.

TO BE OR NOT TO BE.

A Vocal Paraphrase on Hamlet's Soliloquy.

In Shakspere's all-enlight'ning school,
   Where wit and wisdom equal shine,
Where genius spurns at fett'ring rule,
   And, tow'ring, soars to heights divine ;
The Royal Hamlet, wrapt in thought,
   On freedom's pow'r, and fate's decree,
The Question, with importance fraught,
   He states, "To be, or not to be."

Now pond'ring if the noble mind,
   Shou'd tamely suffer fortune's frown,
Or treat her as a mistress kind,
   Whose smiles our tend'rest wishes crown ;
Or, when in dire and troublous siege,
   Strong ills assail, like hostile foes,
Twere best to take up arms in rage,
   Her slings and arrows to oppose.

Revolving then, What 'tis to die,
   He says, 'to sleep,' and nothing more ;
And if from tears it clears each eye,
   And eases hearts that ach'd before ;
Ending at once each cank'ring grief,
   To which devoted flesh is heir,
That sleep which brings such sweet relief,
   Will soon be yours, ye sons of care !

To sleep ;—But then, perchance, to dream ;
   'Ay, there's the rub,' dark doubt replies ;
For whips, and stings, and fire, and flame,
   And widows' moans, and orphans' cries,
Oppression's yoke, pride's rankling gall,
   Love's pangs despis'd, and law's delay,
A bodkin's point might end them all,
   But for that DREAM, which bars the way !

Then, till we quit this mortal coil,
   To reach that undiscover'd bourne,

Where terminates all human toil,
   And whence no trav'ller can return ;
Let smiling hope expand the breast,
   And all from doubt and dread be free ;
Since JOVE has order'd for the best,
   Whate'er's TO BE or NOT TO BE.

How many school-boys—who went to school
before the days of School Boards—are there who
have not learnt "by heart" the quaint mnemonical
verses on the Kings of England? There are
many, we imagine, who are familiar with them,
who do not know that they were written by John
Collins. They were delivered, as the advertisement quoted on page 262 intimates, in the
author's entertainment. We print these verses,
not only as an admirable illustration of Collins's
quaintly humorous style, but as the best set of
verses to enable the student to keep in memory
the order of the English Sovereigns :

"The Romans in England awhile did sway ;
   The Saxons long after them led the way,
Who tugg'd with the Dane till an overthrow
They met with at last from the Norman bow !
   Yet, barring all pother, the one and the other
   Were all of them Kings in their turn.

"Bold Willie the Conqueror long did reign,
But Rufus, his son, by an arrow was slain ;
And Harry the first was a scholar bright,
And Stephy was forced for his crown to fight ;
   Yet, barring all pother, the one and the other, &c.

"Second Henry Plantagenet's name did bear,
And Cœur-de-Lion was his son and heir ;
But Magna Charta was gain'd from John,
Which Harry the third put his seal upon.
   Yea, barring all pother, the one and the other, &c.

"There was Teddy the first like a tyger bold,
Though the second by rebels was bought and sold ;
And Teddy the third was his subjects' pride,
Though his grandson, Dicky, was popp'd aside.
   Yet, barring all pother, the one and the other, &c.

"There was Harry the fourth, a warlike wight,
And Harry the fifth like a cock would fight ;
Though Henry his son like a chick did pout,
When Teddy his cousin had kick'd him out.
   Yet, barring all pother, the one and the other, &c.

"Poor Teddy the fifth he was kill'd in bed,
By butchering Dick who was knock'd on the head ;
Then Henry the seventh in fame grew big,
And Harry the eight was as fat as a pig,
   Yet, barring all pother, the one and the other, &c.

" With Teddy the sixth we had tranquil days,
  Though Mary made fire and faggot blaze ;
  But good Queen Bess was a glorious dame,
  And bonny King Jamy from Scotland came,
      Yet, barring all pother, the one and the other, &c.

" Poor Charley the first was a martyr made,
  But Charley his son was a comical blade ;
  And Jemmy the second, when hotly spurr'd,
  Ran away, do you see me, from Willy the third.
      Yet, barring all pother, the one and the other, &c.

" Queen Ann was victorious by land and sea,
  And Georgy the first did with glory sway,
  And as Georgy the second has long been dead,
  Long life to the Georgy we have in his stead,
      And, may his son's sons to the end of the chapter,
      All come to be Kings in their turn.

The last stanza of this rhymed chronicle has
been altered, and a new one added, in order to
bring the story down to the present reign,—by
whom we do not know ; but as our readers may
be glad to have the story completed, we give the
two additional stanzas as we ourselves received
them in the happy days gone by :

" Queen Ann was victorious by land and sea,
  And Georgy the first did with glory sway ;
  But Georgy the second less favour did gain
  Than kind Farmer George, with his very long reign.
  Yet saving all pother, etc.

" *Next gay George the Fourth, long Regent surnam'd,*
  Was followed by William the Sailor Duke fam'd ;
  And because the Duke of Kent was dead,
  VICTORIA *reign'd on the throne instead."*

And may the time be far distant when any
further alteration of the old rhymes shall be
needed to complete the history !

Space forbids our quoting more than one other
example of Collins's poetry ; and it is one in which
the pathos of our author is finely exemplified. It is
entitled,

DATE OBOLUM BELISARIO.

O ! Fortune, how strangely thy gifts are awarded !
How much to thy shame thy caprice is recorded !
As the Wise, Brave, and Good of thy frowns seldom 'scape
  any,
Witness brave Belisarius, who beg'd for a halfpenny !
      " Date Obolum, Date Obolum,
          " Date Obolum Belisario."

He whose fame from his valour and vict'ries arose,—Sir,
Of his country the shield and the scourge of her foes,—Sir,

By his poor faithful dog, blind and aged was led,—Sir,
With one foot in the grave, thus to beg for his bread,—Sir !
      " Date Obolum,"—&c.

When a young Roman Knight in the street passing by, Sir,
The vet'ran survey'd with a heart-rending sigh, Sir,
And a purse in his helmet he drop'd, with a tear, Sir,
While the soldier's sad tale thus attracted his ear, Sir ;
      " Date Obolum,"—&c.

" I have fought, I have bled, I have conquer'd for Rome, Sir,
" I have crown'd her with laurels, for ages to bloom, Sir,
" I've augmented her wealth, swell'd her pride and her
      power, Sir :
" I espous'd her for life, and disgrace is my dower, Sir !
      " Date Obolum,"—&c.

" Yet blood never wantonly wasted at random,
" Losing thousands their lives with a *Nil desperandum* !
" But each conquest I gain'd, I made both friend and foe
      know,
" That my soul's only aim was *Pro publico bono.*
      " Date Obolum,"—&c.

" Nor yet for my friends, for my kindred or self, Sir,
" Has my glory been stain'd with the base views of pelf, Sir,
" But for all, near or dear, I've so far been from carving,
" Old and blind, I've no choice but of begging or starving !
      " Date Obolum,"—&c.

" Let the brave then when hurl'd from their bright
      elevation,
" Learn and smile, though reduc'd to a slave's degradation,
" And of eye-sight bereft, they, like me, grope their way, Sir,
" *The bright sun-beams of virtue will turn night to day, Sir,*
      " Date Obolum,"—&c.

" For though to distress and to darkness inur'd,—Sir,
" In this vile crust of clay when no longer immur'd,—Sir,
" From the lorn vale of tears they triumphant shall rise, Sir,
" And see all earthly glory eclips'd in the skies,—Sir.
      " Date Obolum, Date Obolum,
          " Date Obolum Belisario."

" We are free to confess," the author adds, in
a note, " that the word ' sir ' has an awkward
appearance at the end of so many lines in this
song ; but the plain truth is, that the TUNE
requires it ; and, as we cannot fill up its measure
without it, we must acknowledge that, like Master
Stephen's Appeal to St. Peter, it is introduced
merely ' TO MAKE UP THE METRE.' "

In an interesting notice of Collins, in *Notes
and Queries*, written by Mr. W. Bates, the author
of *The Brush* is thus described :—

" He was a big, ponderous man, of the

Johnsonian type, and duly impressed with a conviction of his varied talents. Men of this manner are apt to become unwieldy with age; and so it was, I am led to believe, with our friend Collins—whose *Brush* probably ceased to attract the public, with his growing inability to sustain the labours of a sprightly monologue. Even in 1804, the date of his book, he speaks of it as his

These may seem but meagre details of the life of a man gifted as Collins undoubtedly was, yet they are all that can be learned of him. There exist traditions as to the excellence of his singing: it is stated in Dr. Hœfer's *Nouvelle Biographic Générale*, that "he sang with a rare perfection the *Romances* and other *poésies* of his composition." This testimony is corroborated by the

CHARLES LLOYD.

'once popular performance,' and he seems then to have retired into private life. He continued to reside at Great Brook Street, Ashted, with a niece, Miss Brent. This lady, to whose parentage some degree of mystery was attached, was possessed of a fortune, and kept some kind of carriage. The uncle may not have been entirely devoid of means, but, I fancy, was somewhat dependent on his niece for the comforts of age. He died suddenly, a few years later, [in 1808,] and Miss Brent returned to Bath."

Rev. J. Woodfall Ebsworth, M.A.,—editor of several choice volumes of old ballad-literature, —whose father heard Collins sing on many occasions. It is scarcely probable, however, that Dr. Hœfer's statement as to the "*grande fortune*" amassed by the author of *The Brush* as a result of the performance of that "*ouvrage facétieux.*"

Contemporary with John Collins, flourished another local poet, whose writings were of a totally different character from the free and easy verses of the author of *Scripscrapologia*, —bearing traces of ripe classical scholarship, statelier, but none the less true poetry, albeit not so popular as "To-morrow," and other songs of John Collins.

Charles Lloyd,—the friend of Lamb and Coleridge,—was the eldest son of Charles Lloyd, the banker, a member of the honoured firm who established the first Birmingham bank, Messrs. Taylor and Lloyds. The elder Charles Lloyd was a man of refined tastes and no little ability, and was himself occasionally guilty of flirtation with the muses, of which he gave evidence in his translation of the *Epistles of Horace*, (privately printed, 1812), and of the *Odyssey* and part of the *Iliad* of Homer, the 24th book of which was also privately printed. This Charles Lloyd (the elder) was born September 22nd, 1748 ; married, in 1774, to Mary, the only daughter of James Farmer, Esq , of Leicester ; and by her had fifteen children, six of whom survived him. The eldest of these was our author, who wrote, on the 22nd of February, 1822, some "Lines on the Death of Mary Lloyd," his mother, from which we may quote the following fine passage, worthy almost of being placed side by side with Cowper's on a similar occasion :—

My dearest Mother, could a lay of mine
Rescue thy memory from oblivion's gloom,
How gladly would my efforts try to build
Th' imperishable verse ; for thou wert one
Deserving well the love of those that knew thee.
Pious thou wert, sincere, and elevate
Above all vulgar thought : thy heart, the seat
Of every finer sensibility,
Was not for this world's ways. How well do I
Remember, when I yet was but a boy,
And only knew of death by name : ne'er yet
Had felt the nearest interests of my heart
Rent by its cold inexorable hand ;
How well do I still recollect the beam
That brightened in thine eye, and o'er thy face
Spread like a glory, when some lovely scene
Of nature called on thee to gaze ; or when
In book which thou perusedst thou did meet
With sympathetic sentiment, from strain
Lofty, impassioned, generous or devout.
How well do I remember when on eve
Of summer, thou didst sit, and watch the sun's
Last radiance, watch the simple landscape seen

36

From nether windows of thy then abode,
With houses otherwise encompassed, how
Do I remember what serenity,
Bespeaking solemn and unearthly thoughts,
Brooded on all thy person ! How thou lookedst
Still I recall to mind, and too recall
How oft such hour by some appropriate strain
From the Seasons' bard, and him of flight more lofty,
The Poet who did tune his sacred harp
To tell of man's first innocence, his fall,
And restoration,—how such hour was filled
By some appropriate strain from these with taste
Selected ;—thy enunciation graced
Each apt quotation : for thy countenance,
Each gesture, tone of voice, an earnest gave,
Thou lentest more of feeling to the strain
By thee recited, than thou drew'st from thence.
Thou wert meet Priestress for an hour like this !
Thine was a breast tuned to each holier thought !
Thine was a voice which e'en an angel might
Have made its organ, in discourse with man
Rendering thee his interpretress ! so free
From aught of vulgar, sordid, mean, or low,
Were all thy feelings, that not only thou
Didst never to a mood which these inspire
Give utterance, but also in thy breast
Instinct connatural to such impulses
Could not be found !

Charles Lloyd (the elder) died, January 16th, 1828, at Bingley House, in his 80th year. His portrait appears on page 278.

An interesting sketch of the Lloyd family is given by Robert, brother of Charles, in a letter to Charles Lamb. The latter, writing to Coleridge, says :—" Robert Lloyd has written me a masterly letter, containing a character of his father. See how different from Charles he views the old man! *(Literatim):* 'My father smokes, repeats Homer in Greek, and Virgil, and is learning, when from business, with all the vigour of a young man, Italian. He is, really, a wonderful man. He mixes public and private business, the intricacies of disordering life with his religion and devotion. No one more rationally enjoys the romantic scenes of Nature, and the chit-chat and little vagaries of his children ; and, though surrounded with an ocean of affairs, the very neatness of his most obscure cupboard in the house passes not unnoticed. I never knew any one view with such clearness, nor so well satisfied with things as they are, and make such allowance for things which must appear perfect Syriac to him.' By the last he means the Lloydisms of the younger branches. His portrait of Charles (exact as far as he has had opportunities of noting him) is most exquisite :— 'Charles is become steady as a church, and as straightforward as a Roman road. It would distract him to mention anything that was not as plain as sense ; he seems to have run the whole scenery of life, and now rests as the formal precision of non-existence.'"

Bingley House, the home of the Lloyd family, was pleasantly situated on the road to the Five Ways,—now known as Broad Street,— on the site of the modern Bingley Hall ; here the younger Charles Lloyd, our author, was born, in 1775 or thereabout. As he grew up he manifested the greatest disinclination for business pursuits, and preferred the seclusion of the library to the dull routine of the bank. During a short visit of Samuel Taylor Coleridge to Birmingham, an accident brought him into the society of Charles Lloyd, and the latter was so fascinated by the conversation of the great talker that he eventually resolved to remove to Bristol where Coleridge then lived, in order to enjoy the advantage of a closer intimacy with his newly-found " guide, philosopher, and friend."

Arriving at Bristol, he sought out Coleridge, and endeavoured to improve his acquaintance with him. " To enjoy the enviable privilege of Mr. Coleridge's conversation," says Cottle, in his Reminiscences, " Mr. Lloyd proposed even to domesticate with him ; and made him such a pecuniary offer that Mr. C. immediately acceded to the proposal ; and to effect this, as an essential preliminary, removed from Redcliff Hill to a house on Kingsdown." While residing with Coleridge, Lloyd became subject to fits ; writing in 1796, the former says : " I write under great agony of mind, Charles Lloyd being very ill. He has been seized with his fits three times in the space of seven days ; and just as I was in bed last night, I was called up again, and from

twelve at night to five this morning, he remained in one continued state of agonized delirium."

It was in the same year that Lloyd published his first volume of verse, entitled " Poems on Various Subjects," also a thin quarto " Poem on the Death of his Grandmother, Priscilla Farmer," the wife of the James Farmer, of Leicester, before mentioned. Some of these poems were ridiculed by Coleridge, (together with his own and those of Charles Lamb,) in certain " Mock Sonnets," which C. published in the " Monthly Magazine," 1797, under the *nom-de-plume* of " Nehemiah Higginbotham." Not long after this a quarrel seems to have arisen between Lloyd and Coleridge, and early in 1798 they separated ; but about twelve months before the separation Coleridge had introduced his friend to Charles Lamb.

Lloyd's first visit to Lamb is thus referred to by the latter in a letter to Coleridge, in January, 1797 :—" You have learned by this time, with surprise, no doubt, that Lloyd is with me in town. The emotions I felt on his coming so unlooked for, are not ill expressed in what follows, and what (if you do not object to them as too personal, and to the world obscure, or otherwise wanting in worth,) I should wish to make a part of our little volume.

TO

CHARLES LLOYD, AN UNEXPECTED VISITOR.

Alone, obscure, without a friend,
    A cheerless, solitary thing
Why seeks my Lloyd the stranger out ?
    What offering can the stranger bring

Of social scenes, home-bred delights,
    That him in aught compensate may
For Stowey's pleasant Winter nights,
    For loves and friendships far away ?

In brief oblivion to forego
    Friends, such as thine, so justly dear,
And be awhile with me content
    To stay, a kindly loiterer, here ?

For this a gleam of random joy
    Hath flush'd my unaccustom'd cheek ;
And, with an o'ercharged bursting heart,
    I feel the thanks I cannot speak.

Oh ! sweet are all the Muse's lays,
    And sweet the charm of matin bird :

'Twas long since these estranged ears
　　The sweeter voice of friend had heard.
The voice hath spoke : the pleasant sounds
　　In memory's ear in after time
Shall live, to sometimes rouse a tear,
　　And sometimes prompt an honest rhyme.
For when the transient charm is fled,
　　And when the little week is o'er,
To cheerless, friendless solitude
　　When I return as heretofore—
Long, long within my aching heart
　　The grateful sense shall cherish'd be :
I'll think less meanly of myself,
　　That Lloyd will sometimes think on me.

Again, in April of the same year, Lamb writes : " Lloyd tells me he has been very ill, and was on the point of leaving you. I addressed a letter to him at Birmingham : perhaps he got it not, and is still with you. I hope his ill-health has not prevented his attending to a request I made in it, that he would write again very soon to let me know how he was. I hope to God poor Lloyd is not very bad, or in a very bad way. Pray satisfy me about these things."

A week later, (April 15th), after receiving a letter from Lloyd, (who seems to have been staying for a time in Birmingham,) Lamb writes again to Coleridge :—" Poor dear Lloyd ! I had a letter from him yesterday ; his state of mind is truly alarming. He has, by his own confession, kept a letter of mine unopened three weeks ; afraid, he says, to open it, lest I should speak upbraidingly to him ; and yet this very letter of mine was in answer to one, wherein he informed me that an alarming illness had alone prevented him from writing. You will pray with me, I know, for his recovery ; for surely, Coleridge, an exquisiteness of feeling like this must border on derangement. But I love him more and more, and will not give up the hope of his speedy recovery, as he tells me he is under Dr. Darwin's regimen." *

---

* " Poor Charles Lloyd ! These apprehensions were sadly realized. Delusions of a most melancholy kind thickened over his latter days ; yet left his admirable intellect free for the finest processes of severe reasoning. At a time when, like Cowper, he believed himself the especial subject of Divine wrath, he could bear his part in the most subtile disquisition on questions of religion, morals, and poetry, with the nicest accuracy of perception and the most exemplary candour ; and, after an argument of hours, revert, with a faint smile, to his own despair."—*Editor : Lamb's Correspondence. Moxon, 1870.*

The friendship between Lloyd and Lamb, who were to a certain extent similarly afflicted, remained firm and steadfast until severed by death. It is Lloyd who records that tragical scene, often told and always remembered, of Charles and Mary Lamb taking their melancholy way to the asylum, strait-waistcoat under arm !

During the year 1798, the two friends published jointly a thin duodecimo volume, entitled " Blank Verse," in which also appeared one or two stanzas from the pen of Coleridge. This was the " little volume " referred to by Lamb in the letter to Coleridge, dated January, 1797, from which we have already quoted.

The same year Lloyd wrote and published a novel in two volumes, entitled " Edmund Oliver." In 1799 he wrote a " Letter to the Anti-Jacobin reviewers," which brought upon him the abuse of that party, and procured him a place in the poetical pillory side by side with Lamb, (generally spelt by the Anti-Jacobin versifiers *Lambe*), Coleridge, Southey, and others. In one of these verses he is referred to as follows :—

" And ye, five other wandering bards that move
In sweet accord of harmony and love,
C—dge, and S—th—y, L—d*, and L—be, and Co.
Tune all your mystic harps to praise Lepaux !
Pr—tl—y and W—f—ld, humble, holy men,
Give praises to his name with tongue and pen ! "

A note adds :—*" Mr. Lloyd was originally of that fraternity which delights in ' Meetings for Sufferings.' He is descended from an opulent banker, and connected with the first families of *Friends*. Like his relation at Norwich, he has adopted the original principles of George Fox, the Founder, relative to Priests and Kings. . . . Mr. Lloyd continues estranged from the *Thou's and Thee's* . . . for he has not sufficient hypocrisy for the profession.*

Lloyd was also pilloried with his friends in Byron's *English Bards and Scotch Reviewers :*—

" Yet let them not to vulgar Wordsworth stoop,
The meanest object of the lowly group,
Whose verse, of all but childish prattle void,
Seems blessed harmony to Lambe and Lloyd."

---

* See *Beauties of the Anti-Jacobin Examiner*, 1799, p. 306.

In a note the two friends are stigmatised as "the most ignoble followers of Southey and Co.;" and in a letter to the Rev. William Harness, (editor of Shakespeare,) the noble author interpolates the question :—

> " What news, what news ? Queen Oreaca,
>   What news of scribblers five ?
>   S——, W——, C——, L——d, and L——e,
>   All d——d, though yet alive."

and distinguishing,—carried to a pitch almost of painfulness,—Lloyd has scarcely been equalled; and his poems, though rugged in point of versification, will be found by those who will read them with the calm attention they require, replete with critical and moral suggestions of the highest value."

This opinion was severely criticised by a writer

WATT'S HOUSE, HEATHFIELD.

Space will not permit of more than an enumeration of his other writings, the principal and most esteemed of which is a translation of Alfieri; besides this may be mentioned *Nugæ Canoræ*, a little volume of poems, published by Beilby and Knott, 1823, and his *Desultory Thoughts in London.*

"His mind," says Talfourd, "was chiefly remarkable for the fine power of analysis which distinguishes his *London*, and other of his later compositions. In this power of discriminating

in *Blackwood's Magazine*, August, 1849, who pronounced the *London* to be "one stream of mud;" adding that, "there is no trace of verse, and the style is an outlandish garb such as no man has ever seen elsewhere, either in verse or prose." The critic further adds : "Poor Lloyd was a lunatic patient! On him no one would be severe; but why should an intelligent sergeant, unless prompted by a sly malice against all mankind, persuade us to read his execrable stuff."

Charles Lloyd outlived his friend Lamb some

five years.   After the quarrel with Coleridge he
had returned to Birmingham, where Lamb visited
him and stayed a fortnight in the town.   Subsequently Lloyd removed to " a pleasant settlement
on the picturesque Brathay, near Ambleside,"
where he continued his intimacy with Hartley
Coleridge*, whom he had known as a child ; and
finally settled at Versailles, where his mind completely broke up, and he died in 1839.

There may be carping critics, like the writer of
the article in *Blackwood's Magazine*, from which
we have quoted, who may be disposed to disparage
Lloyd's poetry, and to regard the man himself
merely as an amiable lunatic ; but whatever the
quality of his writings may be—and for ourselves
they have a peculiar charm—we cannot but regard
Charles Lloyd as one of the noblest type of hero
worshippers—content to leave the task of heaping
up riches to others, (although, as Cottle observes,
he might have gratified to the utmost the desire
to accumulate wealth,) content to give up position,
and everything which the world counts desirable,
in order that he might enjoy the higher life, in
the world of thought and philosophy, in company
with the noblest minds of his age.

We now come upon a group of worthies,—
most of whose names are " familiar in our
mouths as household words "—whose connection
with the famous Lunar Society sheds a lustre
upon the history of Birmingham, while it
increases considerably the reverence which every
true Birmingham man has for the name of Soho.

" Matthew Boulton," says Mr. Smiles, " was
a man of a thoroughly social disposition, and
made friends wherever he went.   He was a
favourite alike with children and philosophers,
with princely visitors at Soho, and with quiet
Quakers in Cornwall.   When at home, he took
pleasure in gathering about him persons of
kindred tastes and pursuits, in order at the same
time to enjoy their society, and to cultivate his
nature by intercourse with minds of the highest

culture.   Hence the friendships which he early
formed for Benjamin Franklin, Dr. Small, Dr.
Darwin, Josiah Wedgwood, Thomas Day,
Lovell Edgeworth, and others equally eminent ;
out of which eventually grew the famous Lunar
Society."

The necessity for such intercouse with kindred
spirits had called into existence several of these
literary and scientific clubs or coteries, in various
parts of the kingdom, such as that of which
Samuel Johnson and Sir Joshua Reynolds were
the centres, in the metropolis,—Roscoe, at Liverpool,—Sir Humphrey Davy and Dr. Beddoes,
at Bristol, — the Taylors and Martineaus, at
Norwich,—and others elsewhere.   None of these,
however, (if we except the metropolitan coterie,)
seem to have numbered among their members so
many brilliant and distinguished men as were
gathered at *l'hotel de l'amitié sur Handsworth
Heath*, as Boulton, pleasantly called his hospitable
abode, and at the houses of other members of the
society in Birmingham.

The members met once a month, by turns at
each other's houses, always at the full of the
moon, in order that distant members might drive
home by moonlight ; hence the name of the
Society.   At these delightful meetings the
members exchanged views upon all subjects
relating to literature, science, and art.   Here
Murdoch, and Darwin, and Lovell Edgeworth
talked over their pet project of steam locomotion;
here Dr. Priestley told of his marvellous dis-
coveries in chemistry, kindling an enthusiasm
in the minds of Boulton and Watt for the study
of that science which they never suffered to abate,
and which bore fruit in certain of the ingenious
productions of Soho ; and Josiah Wedgwood,
listening with admiration, speedily catches the
enthusiasm for the same fascinating science.   It
was a marvellous gathering of fine intellects, and
one can understand Dr. Darwin,* detained by his
patients at Lichfield, " imprisoned in a postchaise,

---

* *Vide* Hartley Coleridge's Recollections.

* The well-known author of the *Botanic Garden, Zoonomia,
Phytologia*, etc.

joggled, and jostled, and bump'd, and bruised along the King's high-road, to make war upon a stomach-ache or a fever," chafing and repining over his loss, and trying to call to mind " what wit, what rhetoric, metaphysical, mechanical, and pyrotechnical, will be on the wing, bandied like a shuttlecock " from one to another of the " troop of philosophers " gathered at Soho.* Whether the meetings were held at *l'hotel de l'amitié,* — at Watt's house at Harper's Hill,—at Keir's, or Murdoch's or Galton's, or Dr. Withering's,—whether the talk was of Pneumatic Chemistry, the " Priestleyan water-tub " or " mercurial tub,"† Steam Locomotion, or other subject of special interest,— these social gatherings were never unattractive, and absence therefrom was always sorely lamented by the unfortunate " Lunatic " thus detained.

Each member was at liberty to bring a friend with him, and amongst the visitors thus introduced on various occasions were Sir William Herschel, Sir Joseph Banks, De Luc, Dr. Camper, Dr. Solander, Dr. Samuel Parr, Smeaton, the engineer, and many other distinguished men of science. Among these a Frenchman, M. Faujas-Saint-Fond, has preserved to us an interesting description of the house of Dr. Priestley, which, as translated by Mr. Smiles, our readers will thank us for quoting here :

" It is," he says, ' a charming residence, with a fine meadow on one side, and a beautiful garden on the other. There was an air of perfect neatness about the place within and without.' He describes the Doctor's laboratory, in which he conducted his experiments, as ' situated at the extremity of a court, and detached from the house to avoid the danger of fire.'

" ' It consists of several apartments on the ground floor. On entering it, I was struck with the sight of a simple and ingenious apparatus for making experiments on inflammable gas extracted from iron and water reduced to vapour. It con-

sisted of a tube, tolerably long and thick, made out of one piece of copper to avoid soldering. The part exposed to the fire was thicker than the rest. He introduced into the tube cuttings or filings of iron, and instead of letting the water fall into it drop by drop, he preferred introducing it as vapour. The furnace was fired by coke instead of coal, this being the best of combustibles for intensity and equality of heat. . . . Dr. Priestley kindly allowed me to make a drawing of his apparatus for the purpose of communicating it to the French chemists who are engaged in the same investigations as himself. . . . The Doctor has embellished his rural retreat with a philosophical cabinet, containing all the instruments necessary for his scientific labours ; as well as a library, containing a store of the most valuable books. He employs his time in a variety of studies. History, moral philosophy, and religion, occupy his attention by turns. An active, intelligent mind, and a natural avidity for knowledge, draws him towards the physical sciences ; but a soft and impressible heart again leads him to religious and philanthropic inquiries. . . . I had indeed the greatest pleasure in seeing this amiable servant in the midst of his books, his furnaces, and his philosophical instruments ; at his side an educated wife, a lovely daughter, and in a charming residence, where everything bespoke industry, peace, and happiness." '*

Six years before this description appeared in print, the home of Dr. Priestley, and the matchless collection of philosophical apparatus which so delighted the French *savant,* fell a prey to the ruthless mob, and the gentle philosopher himself was driven forth homeless from the town upon which his name has conferred such honour.

We may here appropriately conclude our notice of Dr. Priestley, whom we left at his settlement in London. Soon after his arrival in the metro-

---

* *Vide* letter from Dr. Darwin to Boulton, April 5, 1778, *quoted by Smiles, in " Boulton and Watt," p. 293, smaller edition.*

† Invented by Dr. Priestley for the purpose of collecting and handling gases.

* " Voyage en Angleterre, en Ecosse, et aux Iles Hebrides." Par B. Faujas-Saint-Fond, 2 vols. Paris, 1797. Quoted by Smiles in " *Boulton and Watt,*" pp. 308-9 *smaller edition.*

polis he was chosen successor to Dr. Price, at Hackney, where he remained, however, only a short period ; and in 1794, finding the intense prejudice still cherished against him by many of his countrymen too grievous to be borne, he bade farewell to his native land and settled at North-umberland, in Pennsylvania, for the remainder of his days. From 1801 to 1803 he suffered greatly from indigestion and a difficulty of swallowing, and on the 6th February, 1804, he died, in the seventy-first year of his age. In 1817 his whole works, including his autobiography and correspondence, were published in twenty-five volumes, at Hackney, edited by Mr. John Towill Rutt.

And now to return for a moment to the Society. " The Lunar Society," says Mr. Smiles, "continued to exist for some years longer. But one by one the members dropped off. Dr. Priestley emigrated to America ; Dr. Withering, Josiah Wedgwood, and Dr. Darwin, died before the close of the century ; and, without them, a meeting of the Lunar Society was no longer what it used to be. Instead of an assembly of active, inquiring men, it was more like a meeting of spectres with a Death's head in the chair. The associations connected with the meeting—reminding the few lingering survivors of the losses of friends — became of too painful a character to be kept alive ; and the Lunar Society, like the members of which it was composed, gradually expired."

In the famous group of Soho worthies was one who must have taken great delight in attending, whenever it was possible, the deliberations of the Lunar Society, who, although but a youth, gave promise of becoming as worthy a representative of the genius of Soho in the future as the heads of the firm were then ; we refer to Gregory Watt, generally called the "favourite son" of the great inventor. He was born at Harper's Hill, Birmingham, (a view of which is given on page 139) in the year 1777, a period when Soho was approaching its greatest fame, and his father and

Matthew Boulton were entering upon their long struggles and contests in defence of their patent rights. Of the influence of James Watt upon the training of his son, (whose early death was the great trial of the old man's declining years,) but little is known, yet abundant testimony exists to show that his was a character which would itself have carved a name. He was impetuous, self-asserting, of quick observation, original ideas, bold in language, and with a love for science and literature shewn in few men at his early age. Many of his school letters from Glasgow exist, where, as the fellow and friend of Thomas Campbell, the poet, he discovers to us that he himself was a poet and a translator of considerable merit. His distinguishing characteristic, however, was practical geology, and his letters abound with the result of his observations frequently illustrated with well executed drawings of his specimens ; in fact, he seems to have had a craze for illustrating his epistles wherein the comic element is very prominent. In 1792 he made a tour of observation to Shipston and Stratford, the next year to Malvern, and his descriptions and illustrations in pen and ink or water-colour, as in his journeys to and from Glasgow and the Scotch Coast, as well as allusions to more complete drawings and sketches, show his zeal as a travelling observer. Whilst he would indulge his poetical fancy by composing a number of lines between each stage, and writing them down at each stopping, thus, in turn, the comic—the descriptive—the tragic, and the personal are varied by an ode to the mountains, or lakes, or passes. At one time he is " solitary, melancholy, and cursed by ill-nature," at the absence of Tom Campbell, whose " eccentricities were always a source of amusement," but who was away " at some out-landish place in the High-lands, whose name would defy all England to pronounce," whilst in another he will fill pages, descriptive of his studies, his occupations, and his hopes. In 1794 he is at Heathfield, writing of the illness of his poor sister Jessy, making verses and sketches on her pet lap dog. Poor Jessy Watt's death was felt acutely by her father and mother ; she died in their arms on the 6th June, 1794, when Gregory was but 17. About this time he formed a literary partnership with some friends, and their contributions and interchange of ideas were kept up mainly by correspondence ; but although reference to publishing is often made with the names of Swinney and Pearson, we know of no productions remaining in print.

In 1797 he shows symptoms of consumption, and is sent to winter in Penzance ; he travels there from Heathfield on horseback, and passes his time mainly with " the immense Colony of the Wedgwoods," staying there at the same time. In 1799 he is in London, spending £15 15s. on fossils—so " can't buy a new coat to go to the Theatre." There he becomes acquainted with " all the mineralogists about Town ; " also " the Savants of the Royal Society, with Horne Tooke and Erskine." He can walk to Croydon, ten miles, in two hours five minutes, writes poetry as fast as ever, and constantly refers to his Birmingham printer, Swinney, as "the swine" ; in 1800 he is at Soho, awakening the silent hours of the night, on returning home late with his friends, by reciting aloud the last new poem of Tom Campbell, *con amore ;* or, instead of going to bed, beginning to write at half past eleven and finishing fifty-two lines by the grey dawn. On the 1st October, he starts at five o'clock in the morning, over the Wilds of Sutton Coldfield, for Derbyshire, reaches Lichfield in two hours, and Derby—forty-five miles—at half-past four, in a drenching rain ; thence to Matlock, Stoke, and Ironbridge, where he and Jos. Spode demolished four bottles of "old sport," and "the heroic Josiah roared a song with energy at two in the morning." In May, 1801, he journeys with Murdock on horseback to Scotland, and reports the whole journey in verse, of which the following lines are a sample, after passing through York and Durham, and meeting at Newcastle Dr. Dudgeon,

And yesterday we, by this nice man protected,
Walked full 30 miles, as our business directed.
To-day we rode 40, on Hacks, a fair Trial
Of their powers of persuasion, and ours of denial ;
For they, pious creatures, to praying disposed,
Would have knelt at each stone, if we had not opposed.
But 'tis late—on that Sopha I long to recline,
And combat fatigue with omnipotent wine :
There Murdock, his muscular limbs has disposed,
In transient slumber his eyelids are closed ;
For Sleep, gentle bailiff, arrested his hands,
As he felt for the Bumper that close by him stands.

The winter of 1801 he left for the Continent for his health,—and was ill of fever for a fortnight in Paris—on through Nice to Vienna, Turin, Geneva, Florence, and Rome, sometimes with an escort of soldiers ; mixing his descriptions with fond allusions to smoky Birmingham, his geological pursuits, a dinner with General Soult, or some other great man, and Continental politics. He reached England in October, 1802, desponding at his complaint which then appeared incurable, but wrote always with grim humour. He holds up till the Spring of 1804, when in an alarming state of health he is taken to Bath. He still writes and prints ; his last letter, Aug. 20, acknowledges the printed copies of " that wonderful concoction of wisdom which I engendered last Spring."* His father writes long and hopeful letters, even down to June, but gradually the end comes. He is removed to the sea at Sidmouth, thence to the neighbourhood of Exeter, where he lived only a few days, and died at noon, on Tuesday, the 16th October, 1804.

He was buried in the famous corner of Handsworth Church. In person he was described as tall, with a fine Roman head, his writing was fluent, and his ideas always easily and harmoniously expressed, and, considering the host of friends he made in London, in Birmingham, and in Scotland, it appears strange that his memory receives so little attention from his townsmen.

This chapter of worthies would be incomplete without some mention of Francis Eginton, to whose neglected biography we would recommend

---

Paper on Basalt.

FORWARD

RT. HON. J. CHAMBERLAIN, M.P.

PRESIDENT OF THE BOARD OF TRADE.

PHOTOGRAPHED BY WHITLOCK.

BIRMINGHAM: HOUGHTON & CO, SCOTLAND PASSAGE.

the attention of the historian of industry, Mr. Samuel Smiles.

Very little is known of Eginton's early life; his grandfather was rector of Eckington, in Worcestershire,—and this is the only fact recoverable respecting his relatives. The young artist received his early training at Bilston, where the art of enamelling was at that time

"Eginton was, it appears, the inventor (about the year 1773 it is said) of that curious process by which pictures were mechanically reproduced at the close of last century, and which has of late made so much noise in the scientific world. The process is said to be closely allied to photography, and examples having been discovered among the old papers at Soho, Birmingham, and

THE OLD POST OFFICE.

extensively practised. He was speedily discovered by Matthew Boulton, whose keen insight as to the adaptability of his workmen led him to employ Eginton as a japanner. He was also employed by Boulton in taking copies and casts of vases, statuettes, etc., for reproduction.

We have already (p. 140) referred briefly to Eginton's reproductions of oil-paintings; we may be excused, however, for giving the following further particulars from Mr. Llewellyn Jewitt's interesting *Life of Josiah Wedgwood :*

placed in the Museum of Patents, at South Kensington, have been brought under the notice of the Photographic Society, and produced much discussion at its meeting. What the process adopted by Eginton, who was in the employ of Matthew Boulton, of the Soho Works, was, is at present a mystery; the books which he left, and which contained his recipes, &c., having been abstracted from the family, and lost. The process was called 'Polygraphic,' and the pictures were said to be produced by 'Chymical and

Mechanical process,' and consisted of copies of paintings by different artists—West, Kauffman, Reynolds, Rubens, &c. The following copy of an invoice from Eginton to Boulton, will show the kind of subjects produced by this process, whose peculiarities it is not necessary to inquire into here :

'Handsworth, April 15th, 1791.

'Mr. BOULTON,

'Bt of FR. EGINTON, for Order, S. W. L.

	£	s.	d.
'One Square Mechanical Painting from West—			
Venus and Adonis	1	5	0
One ditto from ditto—Cephalus and Procris .	1	5	0
One ditto, from Angelica Kauffman—Penelope.	1	1	0
One ditto ditto ditto—Calipso . . .	1	1	0
16 *oval pictures in form of Medalions, viz. :—*			
One old man from Sir Joshua Reynolds . .	0	15	0
One Eastern Lady, from Bertalotzi . .	0	15	0
One Vestal, from ditto	0	10	6
One Patience, from Angelica Kauffman . .	0	10	6
One Religion, from ditto. . . .	0	12	0
One Hope, from Rubens	0	12	0
One Shakspear's Tomb, from Angelica . .	0	12	0
One Flora	0	7	6
One Diana	0	7	6
One Dancing Nymph	0	7	6
One Ditto	0	7	6
One Bacante	0	7	6
One ditto	0	7	6
One Apollo	0	7	6
One Una, from Angelica	0	7	6
One Oliver and Orlanda	0	7	6
	£12	6	6
'Finish from the dead Colour and retouching Tragedy and Comedy Heads and Melpomony, 15s. ; and Thalia, 15s. Figures 4 in all, 7s. 6d.	1	1	0
	'£13	7	6'

" SIR,—In the above I have conform'd to the Order as near as the very low prices to which I was limeted would permit. Some alterations I have been obliged to make on that act, particularly in the four historical square ones, which should have been, according to order, from 15s. to 20s.; instead of which you will find one pair from West at 25s. each, and one pair from Angelica at 21s. each, which were the lowest Historical Pictures I could send. The 16 Oval or Medalion formed Pictures are of different sizes; and altho' some of them are something higher priced than what was fixed, others are lower, so that upon the average they will be nearly the price at which they were ordered.

" I hope they will meet yr

" approbation, and

" am, Sir,

" Your obt Sert,

" FR. EGINTON."

" Josiah Wedgwood, the friend of Boulton and of Eginton, the warm patron of art, and the encourager of every useful invention, purchased some of these pictures, as will be seen by the following interesting letter :

'W'hampton, Septr. 22nd, 1781.

'Mr. HODGES.

' SIR,—After considering the great risk you run, in sending the picture by the Coach, with the uncertainty even of its being dry against the time fixed, I conclude it of much less consequence that I should bestow a few days more in rendering the Picture I am now at work on equal to the original, than to have one totally spoiled in the carriage, and the intention of the whole order frustrated thereby. I have therefore sent you the Original, as a companion to the other ; and you may depend upon having the remaining picture returned to you equal to either of the former, and I shall have the satisfaction of compleating my part of the order in due time. If these pictures are not sent away till Monday, there should be some white of egg given to the Time and Cupid, as it is scarcely dry enough to bear the carriage.

' Please, if you can, to return by the bearer the Time and Cupid which is to be painted for Mr. Boulton, with the Circle of the Graces breaking Cupid's bow, for Mr. Wedgwood.

'I am, Sir, Your obt. St.,

'JOSH. BARNEY.'

'Mr. JON HODGES, Soho.'

" Eginton's process was so successful, and was so highly approved by people of taste, that interest was made to get him an annual pension from Government in acknowledgment of his services. Boulton, however, not much to his credit, put a veto on the movement, and thus prevented a fitting and gratifying recognition of his talents from being made. Thus says Mr. Boulton :

'*Copy of a Letter to the Right Honourable the Earl of Dartmouth.*

'MY LORD,—A few days ago I received a letter from Sir John Dalrymple, dated Dublin, May 27, in which he surprises me by saying, 'I have written to Sir Gray Cooper to have a pension of £20 per annum for Mr. Eginton ; so, if there is any stop, write me of it to Scotland, and I will get it set to rights, as I know nothing but inattention can stop it.'

' As I think I cannot with propriety write to Sir Gray Cooper upon this matter, not having the honour of being known to him, and as I have never mentioned the subject to him, or any person besides your Lordship, I hope therefore to be pardoned for thus troubling you with my sentiments and wishes.

'In the first place, I wish to have an entire stop put to the pension ; because Mr. Eginton hath no claim nor expectations. I pay him by the year; and, consequently, he is already paid by me for all the three or four months spent in that business ; and as to an overplus reward for his secrecy, I know how to do that more effectually, and with more prudence, than giving him annually £20, which will only serve to keep up the remembrance of that business, and therefore it is impolitical.

'Besides, it might perhaps be injurious to me, as such a pension would tend to make him more independent of me and my manufacture.

'His attachment to me, his knowing that no use hath been made of the things, the obligation he is under to me, and his own natural caution and prudence, renders me firmly persuaded that the scheme will die away in his memory, or at least will never be mentioned.

'If anybody is entitled to any pecuniary reward in this business, it is myself; because I have not only bestowed some time upon it, but have actually expended between one and two hundred pounds, as I can readily convince your Lordship when I have the honour of seeing you at Soho ; and although I was induced by [　　　] to believe that I was working at the request and under the authority of a noble Lord (whose wisdom and virtue I revere), yet I never intended making any charge to Government of my expenses or for my trouble.

'All that I have now to request of your Lordship is that a negative be put upon the pension.

'My Lord, your Lordship's most dutiful, most obliged, and most faithful humble Servant,

'M. B.'

In our notice of St. Paul's Chapel we mentioned Eginton's fine stained window, of which an engraving appears on page 202. Mr. Jewitt gives a list of his principal works in stained glass, "the first of any consequence being executed in 1784." He enumerates them as follows :

"Arms of the knights of the Garter on the windows on the stalls in St. George's Chapel, Windsor ; some fine windows in Wanstead Church, Essex ; a large representation of the "Good Samaritan" in the private chapel of the Archbishop of Armagh, and another in the chapel of the Bishop of Derry ; *a remarkably fine window in St. Paul's Church, Birmingham;* memorial and other windows in Babworth Church, Nottinghamshire ; *Aston Church, near Birmingham;* Hatton, Warwickshire ; Shuckburgh Church, in the same county ; Pepplewick, Nottinghamshire ; Barr and Bromley Regis, Staffordshire ; Stannor, Berkshire ; Earthing and Llangollen, Denbighshire ; Shrivenham and Frome, Somersetshire ; St. Martin's Gutwich, London ; Tewkesbury Abbey Church, and many other places. Besides these, some of Francis Eginton's principal works were the large window over the altar of Salisbury Cathedral, representing the Resurrection, after a design by Sir Joshua Reynolds, but which has since been removed to make room for memorial windows to Dean Lear ; the west and several other windows in the same cathedral ; the east and other windows of Lichfield Cathedral (1795) ; the windows Merton College Chapel, Oxford (in 1794) ; windows in the Mausoleum at Brocklesby, in the chapel at Wardour Castle, in the Chapel at Pain's Hill, in the banqueting-room and other rooms at Arundel Castle, at Sundorn Castle, and at Fonthill, the charming art-seat of William Beckford."

We cannot speak at length here of his skill as an engraver ; we may, however, refer our readers to the two fine plates of Soho (the manufactory and the mansion), in Shaw's *Staffordshire*, and to the engravings in Bisset's Directory, and Anstey's *New Bath Guide*.

Eginton resided, during the latter part of his life, at Prospect Hill, nearly opposite the Soho factory. He died on the 25th of March, 1805, in the sixty-ninth year of his age, and was buried in Handsworth Churchyard,—in worthy companionship with the founders of Soho.

The last of whom we propose to take note in the present chapter is James Bisset, a worthy of whom we have already spoken in our notice of the Freeth Club, and in the Story of Soho. His name occurs in the *Birmingham Directory* of 1785 as "Miniature Painter, Newmarket," (a place on the site of New Market Street, near Great Charles Street,) and again in 1797, as "Fancy Miniature Painter, New Street"; the latter, which subsequently developed into the establishment known as "Bisset's Museum," was (as appears from a print in his directory,) a little below the Theatre. It was here that he published his several works : *The Orphan Boy*, a pathetic little poem published towards the close of the eighteenth century ; *Flights of Fancy*, (comprising "The Philanthropist," "The "Veteran's Song," and "The Gamester, a parody") ; and, in 1800, the *Poetic Survey round Birmingham, accompanied by a Magnificent Directory*. This work, (by which he is best known,) was designed as a medium for the display of pictorial advertisements of local trades, engraved on copper ; forming a very elegant guide-book to the manufactories and public buildings of the town. The plates were engraved by Francis Eginton and others, in the most approved style of the time. The frontispiece to the volume is a " Plan of Birmingham," drawn by " James Sherriff, of Oldswinford, late of the Crescent, Birmingham," and engraved by Hancock. At first sight it seems to differ but little from the older plans, in the space covered by the town, but a closer examination and comparison reveals to us some of the important changes which were then taking place. Many of the old landmarks still remained, but this was almost the last map on which they would appear ; the Moat, the Parsonage, the Baths, near Lady Well, the open country road between the town and the Five Ways,—these were among the older features which had distinguished most of the previous plans. But there were also new features which had been noted in no survey of the town hitherto published—the " Steam Mills," near Duddeston Row, the open space in front of St. Martin's Church, the Barracks, the several new streets close to the banks of the no longer silvery Rea ; the clusters of new buildings on the road leading to Soho, the new name of that road,—" Great Hampton Street,"—these were for the first time shown in Bisset's Plan of Birmingham.

And now passing from the frontispiece, we proceed to the work itself. After the title-page, (which contains a beautiful vignette engraving of a bust of the Prince Regent), is a list of the plates, and an address to the Public, from which we learn that the charge for engraving single addresses in a general plate in the Directory was 10s. 6d., for half a plate five guineas, and for a whole plate ten guineas ; and various designs were inserted at one and two guineas each. " Thus," says the publisher, " every gentlemen had an opportunity of having his address inserted in the work at whatever price he pleased ; and by paying for the engraving it has enabled the

Author to lay a magnificent work before the Public for only 5s., which otherwise must have cost nearly fifty." The author's prophecy as to the success and result of his publication will at least amuse some of our readers. He says :

"This Book, perhaps, may soon its way explore,
And find a welcome, on each FOREIGN shore ;
Perhaps thro' Europe may, in time be spread,
Or by the tawny AFRICAN be read :
Its novelty may strike, perhaps it may,
In time, reach BORNEO, PEKIN, or BOMBAY ;
At either INDIA, may, perhaps, be found,
Or at KAMSCHATKA seen, or NOOTKA SOUND.
  " Ev'n KINGS and PRINCES, here may deign to look,
Or smiles of BRITSH BEAUTIES grace the book :
My LEARNED COUNTRYMEN* and SAGES rare,
The whole design, perhaps, may scan with care :
And whilst each trophied emblem they peruse,
May feel half tempted to forgive the Muse.
Nay, Foreign MERCHANTS, when they *this* look o'er,
To view this PLACE, may quit their Native Shore :
And when ' The Toy Shop of the World ' they see,
May own (O ! vain surmise) *'twas all thro' me !*
  " In regions yet unknown, or lands remote,
The Natives, thus, may hear of VULCAN's spot :
And whilst, with wonder, they each print survey,
Some information of the Arts convey ;
For whilst, with rapture fraught, they this explore,
And view such sights as ne'er were seen before,
Some CIRCUMNAVIGATORS may, ere long,
Hear BIRMINGHAM extoll'd in SAVAGE SONG ;
And when some progress in the ARTS they've made,
Can tell who formed the HOE, the AXE, the SPADE ;
Or when their great utility they feel,
And learn the use of IRON and of STEEL,
In extacy, may cry, enrapt with wonder,
' Dese English make de GUNS dat roar like tunder ;
' De SWORD, de LANCE, de HATCHET and de SPEAR,
' All dat be grand, and BIR—MING—HAM, be dere.'
  " And when, in mirrors, they themselves behold,
Dress'd out with amber beads, with pearls or gold,
With varnish'd cheeks, of ochre, or red clay,
Like Chimney Sweeps, decked out on first of May,
With bracelets for their THIGHS, their ARMS, their TOES,
Or gaudy pendants for their EARS or NOSE ;
Each martial CHIEF, each sable colour'd Squaw,
Won't cry, in *broken* French ' *Me nong-tong paw,*'†
But cry, in *broken* English, ' O, Manne,
' *Dat Englan be grand place—me go an zee.*' "

Among the engravings were views of the Warstone Brewery, Hockley Abbey, New Street, (showing the Theatre and Bisset's Museum,) the right hand side of High Street, (from the Swan to

---

* " In Scotia."
† "A Corruption of ' Je ne vous entends pas.' *i.e.*, I do not understand you."

the corner of Philip Street, with St. Martin's in the distance,) the Crescent, St. Philip's Church, Deritend, (showing St. John's,) the Soho factory, the Hen and Chickens, and other local places of-

whose names have become part of the history of Birmingham.

We have not space here to quote from Bisset's *Poetic Survey*; we have already given our

THE LOYAL ASSOCIATION.

interest. Here also are engraved advertisements of "Lines's Drawing Academy, Newhall Street," J. Taylor, M. Swinney, Henry Clay, Boulton and Watt, and the Soho firms generally, *Aris's Birmingham Gazette*, and Jabet's *Birmingham Commercial Herald*, the various banking firms, and many other old business establishments

readers a sample of the work in the description of the Soho factory. The *Directory* was reissued in 1808, without the poetry, but with some twenty additional plates by Radclyffe. Bisset also proposed to publish, in a similar form, a "Grand National Directory; or Literary and Commercial Iconography;" but of this he only succeeded in obtaining commissions for thirty plates, of which only one set is believed to exist, viz., that made up for the author himself, now in the possession of Mr. W. Bates. A few of the plates were inserted in some copies of the second edition of the Birmingham *Magnificent Directory.*

Our readers will remember the story of Bisset's visit to Joe Lindon's (the "Minerva") and its result, mentioned in our notice of the Freeth Club; we may here add another anecdote of the mad freaks of the "Twelve Apostles:" One evening,—says the narrator, ("Este")—whilst living in New Street, and suffering most acutely from an attack of the gout, two of the club, agreeable to a preconcerted plan, entered his sitting room disguised as highwaymen, and well-armed, roughly demanded his money, and as was expected, Mr. Bisset resisted, and forgetting his gout, actually chased the supposed robbers to Freeth's house in Bell Street, where the practical joke became at once apparent, and, strange to say, he never again suffered from the same excruciating complaint, to which he had for a long time previously been a martyr."

Later in life Bisset removed to Leamington, where he continued to publish little volumes of verse, and also, a very interesting little work on "the Origin, Rise, and Progress of Leamington Spa." He boasted that upwards of one hundred thousand copies of his different publications had been issued, and that many had reached the fifteenth and sixteenth editions.

He died at the age of seventy-two, Aug. 17, 1832, and was buried at Leamington; his friends erected a monument "in token of their respect to his memory," on which is recorded the previous death of Dorothy, his wife, Dec. 14, 1825. His own epitaph, composed a few years before, does not appear on his monument, and may, therefore, claim a place at the close of this notice:

" What *I was once*,—my Neighbours know full well ;
  What *I am—now*,—there's not a tongue can tell !—
  (My bones lie mould'ring underneath this sod)
  What *I shall be*—is only known to GOD !"

We may appropriately notice here an institution similar to the Museum of James Bisset,—Allin's "Cabinet of Curiosities, and Mart for New and Old Cloaths, Haymarket;" as it is described in Bisset's *Directory.* The building may be remembered by a few in its original form, surmounted by a square turret, from which proudly floated the Union-Jack, as shown in our plate; but nearly all our readers must have known it in its latest form, minus the turret and flag-staff, as "Bryan's." It was removed, in 1873, to make way for the Municipal Buildings. But to return to its original proprietor; he was, like Bisset, of a poetic turn, and published a curious little pamphlet, in verse, describing his heterogeneous collection, which is now very rare. The title-page, which is in itself quite a curiosity, runs as follows:

A L L I N ,

TAYLOR,

Hatter, Haberdasher, Hosier, Linen and Woollen Draper, Grocer, &c.,

AT HIS

CHEAP CLOTHES AND YORK SHOE WAREHOUSE,

T H E   F L A G ,

Opposite the TOP of NEW STREET,

𝔅irmingham :

A   S H O P

For the Accommodation of all Sorts of Customers, who may be provided with every Necessary of Life ; suited from Top to Bottom, from Inside to Outside, from Right Side to Left Side, yea, and on ALL SIDES, *with every Wearable and Tearable, from the Giant of ten Feet high to the Infant just popp'd into the World : Sold*

WHOLESALE AND RETAIL,

AT LITTLE MORE THAN HALF THEIR VALUE,

FOR

READY MONEY ONLY."

We have only space to quote the author's apology for his work, with which we will close the present lengthy chapter.

"Ye wits, ye critics, I love something new,
  Spare then your censure once, I pray you, do ;
  Indulge me now, I only aim at pleasing,
  Not for applause I write, then be not teasing ;
  With lenient eye pass o'er the faults you find,
  And still to mercy ever be inclin'd."

"ALLIN'S CABINET OF CURIOSITIES,"

The Site of the Municipal Hall, (corner of Congreve Street,) as it appeared at the end of the eighteenth century.

CHAPTER XLIII.

PUBLIC LIFE AND EVENTS, 1790-1800.

The Rating of Small Houses—Barracks erected in Birmingham—Local Penny Post established—"The Little Riot"—"Off to the Wars"—
Volunteers for the Navy—"The Scarcity Riots"—The New Library—Birmingham Volunteers—Chapel Wake.

OUR last chronicle of Public Events concluded with the national rejoicings on account of the recovery of his Majesty George III. We now take up again "the story of our lives from year to year," and purpose in this chapter closing up the history of the town to the end of the 18th century.

Towards the close of the year 1790 the people of Birmingham were greatly exercised in mind concerning an important question of rating. At that time nearly three-fourths of the houses in the town were rented at less than £10 per annum, and, in consequence, were not liable to the payment of poor-rates. An attempt was made in the year above-mentioned to remedy this unsatisfactory and unequal mode of rating; and this attempt provoked such a warfare of words as probably had not been experienced before in the town, certainly not since the first attempt to obtain the Lighting and Improvement Act. The first note of the coming strife was sounded in the columns of *Aris's Gazette* on the 27th of September, in the form of an announcement of a general meeting of the inhabitants, to be held "at the great room at the Hotel," on the 20th of October, "to determine the following question, viz.: 'Shall application be made, in the next Session of Parliament, for leave to bring in a Bill to oblige the proprietors of small houses, shops, and other buildings, to pay Parish Rates for those houses, &c.'—And if this question is carried in the affirmative, to appoint a Committee for the management of the Business." In explanation of this notice it is stated that, out of 8,000 houses

built within the previous thirty years, not more than 1,300 paid the parish rates.

Of course all the owners of property of this class stoutly opposed the proposition, and none more so than William Hutton. It is a matter of regret to us thus to expose the "seamy side" of our brave old townsman's character; but we should have produced an unfaithful portrait of the historian if we had omitted this fact, and that of his selfish opposition of the lighting and improvement Acts. It is not necessary to reproduce here all the arguments he adduced against the proposed rating; they resolved themselves, to a great extent, into what has aptly been termed "the argumentum ad *pocket*um." "How well the *landlords' profits* will bear the burden," he says, "has not yet been proved. They can best solve this question who count it. In some instances, I am well informed, it does not exceed 5 per cent. in others the trouble exceeds the profit! As I am possessed of only fourteen pounds a year of this moonshine property, mine is upon too small a scale to decide; nor is the whole worth a contention. Perhaps, from the loss of rent, empty houses, and repairs, I lose about half. But whatever be these monstrous profits, which injustice marks out for plunder, and envy longs to devour, they are the proprietor's *own*, and, as private property, they are sacred. It is a dangerous doctrine to take a man's money because he is rich." In the course of his letter or address on this subject, Hutton referred in his usual quaint, shrewd manner, to several matters respecting the management of parish affairs; and these may be picked out from the dry dust-heap of this discussion, for our readers' amusement. He had been asked some time previously, by one of the overseers of the poor, his opinion concerning the doctrine of the Trinity, the "parochial" dignitary adding that no man would be suffered to transact parochial business who did not believe in that doctrine. "Unable to withhold a smile," says Hutton, "I remarked as religion had long ceased to meddle in the vestry, it would be absurd to refer the question to a perfect stranger; that when I turned Catholic and he turned Priest, I would make my confession." In concluding his address, Hutton referred to the recent attempt to introduce at the workhouse the manufacture of various useful articles; he says: "The fabrication of shanks, toys, shirts, quilts, &c., were solicited of the inhabitants, and established as a manufactory in the Workhouse which was to perform wonders. But, that the foundation of this promising fabric was rotten, and the component parts bundled together with a rope of sand, the increase of the levies sufficiently testified. The profits were like those of the race-horse who won fifty, but cost sixty to keep him. This phantom expiring, the rate upon small houses is now issued forth, which, like a tinkling cymbal, is to din the ear and stifle complaint; or, like charity, is to cover a multitude of sins; or a Betty Canning's tale to amuse the world and hide the errors of government; or a sop to silence the many-headed Cerberus, while the benighted officers are ferried out of danger."

To these points in Hutton's address "Betty Canning" replied in a rather fierce attack upon our historian, published in the *Gazette* of October 18th:

Friend Hutton,

THE Parish of Birmingham is much indebted to thee for thy quaint conceits, droll observations, whimsical similitudes, and the witty old sayings of SOLOMON,* inserted in the newspaper of last week. The present, as well as all former overseers of the poor, cannot but thank

---

* In the Farce called "The Quaker"

thee for thy modest and friendly comments on their parochial management.

The public have much to expect from a person of thy high character, eminence, *liberality*, and experience, in taking up the gauntlet. Already hast thou acted as perpetual high chancellor of the court of tender conscience, one of the honourable commissioners of lamps and scavengers, twice overseer of the poor, and high president of the kirk, F.A.S., all which offices thou didst fill with a dignity peculiar to thyself. If the intended scheme of incorporating this town should take place, we may presage the happy prospect of seeing thee and thy worthy friend fill the magisterial chair, surrounded by the guard with ragged pikes, and the imperial arms of Birmingham on thy carriage of state. Then, no doubt, all the enormities thou and he complains of will be rectified. What a pity that the management and direction of all the public concerns are not vested in the hands of two such SOLOMONS.

But 'Pride, the spring of actions, destroys the most beneficial systems,' totally preventing thee and thy worthy friend from fingering twelve thousand pounds of the town's cash. I thought thee and thy worthy friend were more sagacious philosophers than to suffer the town to see your uneasiness at your disappointment. Have patience, friend William, and all these things may be added unto thee.

I think thou intimates something in thy letter about turning catholic priest: prithee don't: that appearance won't suit thee; a jew rabbi would be more in character for thee. I wish to remind thee of the fable of the Ass in the Lion's skin, who, by his braying and terrible appearance, attempted to alarm the forest, but on close inspection was found to be nothing but an Ass, and derided accordingly.

I have much to say to thee, but as thou art a rigid economist, may be thou wilt blame me for wasting so much time on thy account. I shall, therefore, for the present, content myself with the hope of seeing thee at the Town's Meeting on Wednesday next, when I propose telling thee more of my mind. Till then, farewell, I remain thy old friend,

(I should sign BETTY CANNING, but am) A.B.

On the 20th of the same month, a public meeting was held, at Dadley's Hotel, Temple Row, at which the case of the overseers was presented. The facts laid before the meeting by the overseers, as reported in the *Gazette*, will interest those of our readers who care to compare the old rateable value of the houses in Birmingham with that of the present time :—

The Facts themselves, it is presumed, will not be controverted. Namely,

1st. That the Parish rates have lately increased in an alarming Degree, and are now become extremely burthensome; the Rates for the Relief of the Poor only amounting annually to the sum of £13,000 and upwards.

2nd. That the Rates, under the present System, are very unequally assessed, three Parts in four of the Houses of which the Town consists, and which are calculated to amount to 12,000 in the whole, not being at all rated ; so that the whole Burthen falls upon, and is borne by, the Occupiers of the remaining fourth Part, which Burthen lies very heavy on those who rent Houses between £10 and £20 per Year, who have many of them great Difficulty, with all their Industry and Economy, to support themselves and their families under it.

of unrated Property will have no real cause of Complaint, and that, instead of opposing, it will be their Interest to join with their Fellow-townsmen in the intended Application to Parliament ; for it appears to be a Fact not disputed, that many Proprietors of small Houses set them at higher Rents because they are not rated, so that the Occupiers thereof, virtually and in Effect, contribute towards the Rates, though the same goes (instead of benefitting and increasing the Fund for the Maintenance of the Poor) wholly into the Pocket of the Landlord.   If,

CHRIST CHURCH, NEW STREET.

If these Premises are admitted, it seems expedient that some Method should be adopted to relieve the Inhabitants that are now rated from their present oppressive Payments ; and it is submitted that nothing can so effectually answer this Purpose as the Scheme, now under Consideration, of obliging the Proprietors of small Houses and other Buildings, under the annual Rent of £10, to pay the Rates for the same, by which Means the whole Property will be (as it ought) rated equally, according to its Value, without an Increase to the Number of the Poor, which must be the Consequence of rating and receiving from the Occupiers ; and though it may at first Sight appear a little inequitable that the Landlord should pay a rate, which by the general Law is fixed upon the Tenant, yet, upon an Investigation, it will appear that the Proprietors

therefore, such Proprietors are compelled to pay the Rates, it surely is no more than an Act of Justice and Propriety ; and with Respect to the smaller Houses which are not set at such advanced Rents, a Remedy will be always in the Hands of the respective Proprietors, who may raise the Rents in Proportion to such Rates.

Although the Overseers, willing to make the statement in the Advertisement rather under than over the mark, compute the unassessed Houses at 9,000, it appears from a more strict investigation that there are 10,000, and that they are partly in the following proportions, viz. :—

		£	£ s. d.	
500	from	9 to	9 19 0	per year.
500	,,	8 ,,	8 19 0	,,
2,000	,,	7 ,,	7 19 0	,,

38

```
3,000      ,,      6 ,, 6 19  0    ,,
2,000      ,,      5 ,, 5 19  0    ,,
2,000 under and up to 4 19  0    ,,
—————
10,000
```

If, therefore, a Levy of 6d. in the Pound on such Houses as pay £8 per year and upwards ; of 4d. on such as pay from £6 to £7 19s. per year ; and of 3d. on all under £6 per year, was collected from those 10,000 Houses, which do not now pay, each Levy from them would amount to £970 and upwards, being very near as much as is produced from one of the present Levies ; so, on this calculation, the present payers would be relieved from nearly, if not quite, one half of their present Burthen ; an argument surely of great Weight, and such as should induce the Proprietors of small Houses to consider that they themselves will be thus materially relieved by the Plan proposed. But if the proposed scheme should not take effect, there seems to be no alternative save that of removing all such Persons as are likely to become burthensome ; and then bringing forward a general Rate or Assessment of Houses and Buildings of every Description throughout the Parish ; and the Gentlemen who are Proprietors of small Houses, and who, from apparently interested motives, may be inclined to oppose the present Plan, will do well to consider how in that case the Town in general, and themselves as Individuals, will be affected. In the first Place, it must operate in Reduction of the Rents of unrated Houses and Buildings, most of which are being now set at higher Rents because they are, at present, exempt from the Payment of Rates, must, it is presumed, when rated, sink in their Rents in Proportion, or nearly to the Amount of the Rates which shall be laid upon them. In the next Place, it will necessarily add a great Increase to the Number of Poor, after every endeavour is made by Removal to prevent it, who will become settled in the Parish by Payment of Rates (an evil, which in the proposed Plan, will be avoided) and the additional Expenses of such increased Poor (to which the Proprietors of small unrated Houses who are resident in Birmingham, and who constitute by far the greater part of such Proprietors, will be obliged to bear their part) will be productive of more Disadvantage to such Proprietors, by an increased Assessment upon the Property they now occupy and pay the Rates for, than they can experience by acquiescing in the proposed plan, as they will suffer every Inconvenience and Loss which the plan proposed can bring upon them (without reaping the Advantages which it is calculated to produce to them) as well as the additional Loss occasioned by Removal of their Tenants, and by many of their Houses being unoccupied.

If it should be suggested that the Scheme now in Contemplation savours of Hardship to the Occupiers of the smaller Houses, in depriving them of the Means of obtaining a Settlement by Payment of Rates, though they will in fact contribute thereto by an Increase in their Rents ; it is submitted that this is not an Object of present discussion. This will be properly left to the Wisdom and Justice of the Legislature, which will protect the Rights of Individuals as far as is fitting and expedient. It may,

however, be hoped that the extensive Manufactures and Commerce of the town of Birmingham will lay a particular Claim, under the present circumstances to the Protection and Indulgence of the Legislature more than a Place of less consequence hath a right to expect. As to other Parishes, it is presumed, they can have no Cause of Complaint, because Birmingham employs in its Manufactures a great Number of their Poor, which cannot find employment at Home ; many of whom, as well as their Children, gain Settlements there, whilst very few of the Inhabitants of Birmingham leave their Situations to gain Settlements in other Parishes.

It may upon the whole be concluded, that the Scheme now under consideration will be attended with great advantages to the Town in general, with little, or perhaps no Loss to the proprietors of the present small unrated Houses, and will be no real Hardship to the Occupiers of such small Houses. It is, therefore, hoped that Persons possessed of such Property will meet the wishes of the other Inhabitants, and, instead of opposing, unanimously concur with them in the intended Application to Parliament, or (to avoid that Expense), that they will voluntarily agree to pay the Rates in question (either in the Proportions above stated, or such hall appear most equitable to a Committee which may be appointed for that Purpose), as the Inhabitants of Liverpool, Leeds, and Manchester, under similar circumstances have lately done, and still continue to do.

These interesting and important facts seem to have impressed the meeting with the necessity of adopting the proposals of the overseers, for we read that a resolution was passed " by a great majority " to make application at the next session of Parliament " for leave to bring in a Bill to oblige the Proprietors of small Houses, Shops, and other Buildings, to pay Parish Rates for those Houses."

An opposition meeting was held a week later, at the Shakespeare Tavern, in New Street, at which resolutions were passed declaring that the meeting at the hotel was neither fair nor impartial,—in other words, that it was a "packed" meeting of supporters of the measure,— that the " Paper of facts " contained "a very fallacious Statement of the Business which ought to have been agitated at said meeting,"— and, (after sundry resolutions touching details, &c.,) that a sum of money be raised by voluntary subscription of the owners of the threatened Properties, to defray the expenses of opposing the intended application to Parliament.

The warfare was waged with great vigour on both sides ; William Hutton, Joseph Jukes, and several others returned again and again to the charge on behalf of the opponents of the measure ; and the friends of the overseers replied with equal ability. The latter, early in the new year, 1791, decided also upon endeavouring to obtain leave of Parliament to bring in a Bill to amend the Guardian Act, by including several clauses of the Shrewsbury Act, and ultimately succeeded in obtaining both the rating of small tenements and a New Guardian Act ; and thus one more step was taken toward the better management of the affairs of the town.

The next event of importance in the annals of Birmingham is that which has already thrown its dark shadow over our narrative, and need not further be referred to here : the " Church and King " riots of July, 1791.

Towards the end of the year 1792 the Government, (desirous of relieving the publicans of large towns from the inconvenience caused by the frequent quartering on them of numbers of soldiers passing through those towns), adopted the plan of erecting Barracks, where they might be lodged and provide for themselves. " They have already "—says the *Birmingham Gazette*, of August 17th, in that year—" begun to build them at Manchester, Sheffield, and Nottingham ; and last week Colonel De Lancey agreed with Mr. Brooke for four acres of his land, at Ashted, to erect the Barracks upon, near this town ; the spot is highly approved by all the officers who have surveyed it ; and the adjacent land will, no doubt, soon be covered with other buildings." The first stone of the new Barracks was laid August 28, 1792 ; the cost of erection was, according to Hutton, £13,000, and the annual ground rent one penny per square yard. The building was finished in the summer of 1793, and was intended to accommodate one hundred and sixty-two men. Hutton makes a calculation, in his History, of the cost of maintaining this institution, with a view of showing the superiority and economy of the old system. He says :

As the man who loves his country will rejoice at every saving system to lighten the load of three hundred millions, I shall state the account with precision.

Annual Rent.............................£100   0
Interest upon £13,000..................... 650   0
Loss of principal per annum on the
average during the lease of 80 years 162 10

Perhaps there will not, at a medium, be more than two-thirds of one hundred and sixty-two men, or one hundred and eight accommodated.

We may reasonably suppose £6,000 will be expended, at least during the term, in wear and tear of furniture, alterations, and repairs of buildings. This principal also of £6,000, and half the interest, which is £150 per annum, must be sunk. When all these numbers are added together it will appear that every man's lodging stands the country in about eleven-pence a night, or six shillings and five-pence a week. Half this sum, united to the slender pay of the private soldier, would recruit the army with *men* instead of old age and children, and that without pressing or purchase ; the landlord would then welcome the soldier with a smile, whom he now receives with a frown.

On the 27th of August, 1793, the inhabitants of Birmingham would read with pleasure an announcement in the *Gazette* of the intention of the Postmaster-General to establish a local penny post in the town. The notice ran as follows :

POST OFFICE, BIRMINGHAM.

August 27, 1793.—His Majesty's Post Master General having been pleased to settle and establish a Penny Post, for the Convenience of this Town, the Suburbs thereof, and Places adjacent—Notice is hereby given, that Offices are opened for the Receipt of Letters and Packets, (not exceeding four Ounces in Weight) from Seven in the Morning till Nine o'clock at Night, at the following Places :

Mr. Hewitt's, Grocer, No. 48, Smallbrook Street.

Mr. Steven's, Grocer, No. 72, Digbeth, near Deritend Bridge.

Mr. Murcott's, Grocer, Coleshill-street, opposite Market-street.

Mr. Lutey's, Grocer, Steelhouse Lane, the Corner of Whittall-street.

Mr. Smith's, Grocer, Church-street, Ludgate Hill.

From which Places Letters will be sent to the principal Office, opposite the Theatre, in New Street, four Times a Day, viz.—

At Eight o'clock in the Morning, for the first Delivery, and in Time to be forwarded by the North Mail, via Lichfield ;

At Twelve o'clock at Noon, for the Second Delivery, and in Time for the Mail going to Shrewsbury ;

At a Quarter before Two in the Afternoon, for the London Mail ; and, for the third Delivery, at Half-past Three o'clock ;

And at Four o'clock in the Afternoon, for the Mail going to Bristol ;

On or before which Times Letters should be put into the above Offices, in order to be sent by the earliest Conveyance ; for which One Penny will be charged in the Town, and Twopence for the Suburbs and Places within the Limits of the Penny Post, to be paid on putting in, or on Delivery, at the option of the Writers ; except Letters intended to be forwarded by the London and Cross Road Mails, with which one Penny must be paid on putting into the above mentioned Receiving Offices.

Letter Carriers will be dispatched every day (except Monday) with the Letters to and from Solihull, Knowle, Sutton Coldfield, Hales Owen, Dudley, West Bromwich, Tipton, Wednesbury, Darlaston, Willenhall, Bilstone, and to the intermediate and adjacent Places.

The year 1793 was marked by a scene of disorder which, to the inhabitants of Birmingham at that period, must have caused no little anxiety lest it should lead to a second "reign of terror" such as they had experienced in July, 1791. The disturbance arose out of that of 1791 to a certain extent ; having been caused by the refusal of certain persons to pay their proportion of the levy to pay the riot bill. It has been styled "The Little Riot."

The rate had been levied some time previous to the disturbance, and the amount unpaid had been advanced by the local governing body on behalf of the inhabitants, and on the 9th of September in that year a pressing call was made upon the ratepayers to pay in to the Constables their respective amounts. One Wood, of Lichfield Street, refused to pay his proportion of the riot rate, and it became necessary to distrain his goods for the amount. This was done on Monday afternoon, Oct. 21st, but the defaulting ratepayer resisted, threatening the lives of the officers, and soon succeeded in raising a mob, which, in the evening collected in St. Philip's Churchyard, and attacked the house of Mr. W. Barrs, (one of the Constables) in Temple Row, breaking the windows and doing considerable damage. By ten o'clock at night the riot assumed so serious a character that Mr. Joseph Carles, (one of the local Magistrates), with the police and two troops of horse from the Barracks, found it necessary to attend to restore order.

The mob, however, showed no disposition to desist from further violence, hoping, perhaps, to bring about a state of affairs such as had existed in July, 1791, when the mob for awhile had reigned supreme. Even after the Riot Act had been read they remained deaf to the peaceable overtures of the representatives of law and order, and Mr. Carles found it necessary to order several of the ringleaders into custody, and to instruct the military to disperse the others. Then followed a general street fight between the military and the unruly civilians, and in a brief space of time twenty-six of the latter were safely lodged in the Dungeon, and several others were conveyed to the Hospital. The military paraded the streets during the rest of the night, and quiet was soon restored. But with the dawn of Tuesday the rabble seem to have regretted the easy victory of their opponents ; and once more they rallied on their old battle-ground,—St. Philip's Churchyard,—in front of the obnoxious Constable's house. Again the magistrates and the military appeared, the Riot Act was once more read, and in the course of the day two other troops of horse arrived, from neighbouring towns, and the champions of the defaulting ratepayers were routed.

In the afternoon, a man who had been heard to threaten, in a public house, that the prison should be pulled down that evening, was speedily lodged there himself, (in order, doubtless, to afford him greater facilities for carrying his threat into execution) ; and between nine and ten o'clock at night the mob assembled round the building to further his efforts, and, at the same time, to liberate their companions. As they were attempting to force the door, however, the gaolers fired on them, and two were severely wounded ; the others, seeing the determined resistance made by one man against half a hundred, ignominiously retreated, leaving their wounded companions in arms, (?) as well as those who were lodged in the dungeon, to shift for themselves. One of those who were wounded was a man named Richard

Porter who, according to his own statement, had not joined in the riot, but was shot just as he had reached the mob, and was enquiring what they had assembled for. Wood, who was the cause of the disturbance, absconded, but was arrested a few days afterwards at Walsall. He and another of the rioters, Joseph Darby, (the pothouse desperado who had threatened to pull down the prison,) were committed to Warwick gaol.

money, which they alleged they had not received. Being encouraged by many among the populace to continue in their demands, and several of them being much intoxicated, they forced themselves into their officers' room at the Swan Hotel, and treated them in a very rude and threatening manner. Our Magistrates tried in vain to appease them, and as a large mob began to collect, and add to the tumult, they were obliged to request Colonel Callow to bring the Third Dragoons from the Barracks, to preserve the peace, which they effectually did. A note was then given to all the men by their Lieutenant-Colonel (Montgomery) promising, upon their arrival at head

CHRIST CHURCH :

Medal commemorating the laying of the first stone.   [*Showing the original design for a dome and cupola.*]

The second and third instalments of the obnoxious riot levy appear to have been collected without serious inconvenience or disturbance.

We now come upon the time of war, with all its stirring and enlivening scenes, as well as its horrors and sufferings, experienced alike by those who fought our battles abroad and those who endured at home the privations which a costly war always entails upon a nation. In the *Gazette* of March 16th, 1795, we obtain a glance at one of the scenes witnessed at home during the departure of a regiment for "the wars":

On Monday last great confusion and some alarm was created in this town, in consequence of a party of the 118th, or Fingal Regiment, which had marched in from Ireland on the preceding Saturday, refusing to continue their route until they had been paid all their bounty

quarters, payment of all the money due to them, and signed also by our Magistrates, who engaged to send immediately to the War Office, and see that every man in the regiment had his due. This satisfied most of them; there were some, however, who rejected the notes, and continued in a very mutinous state all the day; but the Magistrates having directed the Constables and their Servants to go at midnight to all the public houses where the men were billeted, and get possession of their arms (which they easily did, assisted by an officer and a party of the dragoons), and every publican being forbidden to give them spirits, or any of the liquor shops to be opened in the morning, Colonel Montgomery was at length enabled on Tuesday to march out with the greatest part of the corps, and the others gradually followed, or were taken by the officers who stayed here to collect them. The Magistrates, we understand, have since received two letters from the Secretary at War; who, in the first, writes that "orders are sent to the Head Quarters, to prevent any difficulty or delay in executing what the Magistrates have engaged for, and a General Officer will be immediately sent, by his Royal Highness the Duke of York, to enforce those orders." And, in a second letter, the Right Hon. Secretary informs the Magistrates, that, "Lieutenant-General Forbes is gone to redress grievances, and, if possible, to prevent such causes of alarm for the future."

An Act having been passed for raising a certain number of men for manning the Navy, from the several counties of England, forty-four men were allotted by the general Session of the Peace held at Warwick, as the number to be raised by Birmingham. Accordingly a meeting of the inhabitants was held March 31st, 1795, at which "it was determined, that a Levy, at the rate of sixpence in the pound, should be immediately made, to defray the expenses of raising the forty-four men for the navy, the quota for this parish." The work of enrolling volunteers, however, does not appear to have proceeded quite so fast as the raising of the money to defray expenses; consequently the few who were induced to enrol themselves were paraded through the principal streets, and their patriotism, gallantry, etc., proclaimed with great flourish in the local papers, as witness the following extracts from the *Gazette*:

April 20, 1795.—The patriotic spirit which has ever been evinced by the Inhabitants of this place to oppose the enemies of their country, will, we are persuaded, at the present moment, when Britannia calls for the best energies of all her Sons, be more ardent than ever ; and we assure ourselves, the Town quota of Men for the Service of the Navy will soon be raised. Eighteen gallant fellows were attested on Saturday, and numbers of respectable gentlemen, we understand, purpose this week to accompany the Church-Wardens and Officers of the Town through the principal Streets (as the chief inhabitants of Liverpool, Leeds, and Sheffield did at their respective places,) and to give every possible encouragement to those who may be desirous of the glorious appellation of Defenders of their country.

April 27, 1795.—On Thursday the High Bailiff, Parish Officers, and many of the principal Inhabitants, paraded the streets of this town with music and flags, to receive and encourage those brave men that might wish to become defenders of their country on board the Royal Navy, and volunteers upon this occasion have come forward in such numbers, that on Saturday only eight men were wanted to compleat the town quota, and which, from the patriotic spirit now abroad, we doubt not will immediately be found.

The town's quota of naval volunteers was completed by the beginning of May.

And now we turn to the sombre side of the picture, and note the effects of war— joined to the calamity of a bad harvest—upon the suffering people at home.

The distress of the country,—caused partly by oppressive war taxation, and partly by the failure of the harvest and the consequent scarcity and dearness of wheat,—drove many among the poorer classes almost to distraction, and their discontent found vent in numerous outbreaks against the millers and farmers, and the moneyed classes of the country. One of these tumults broke out in Birmingham in June, 1795, and led to serious and fatal results. It is thus narrated in the *Gazette* of June 29th, in that year :

"June 29th, 1795.—It is with great concern we state that a misguided populace, too prone to hearken to the suggestions of the designing and evil-minded, has again broken in upon the peace of society, and committed the most culpable acts of violence and outrage. The corn mill and bakehouse of Mr. Pickard, at the bottom of Snow Hill, supplies a considerable number of the inhabitants of this town with flour and bread. The great scarcity of grain which is experienced throughout Europe (but in no country so little as our own), has considerably advanced its price, and of course neither the same quantity of flour, nor the same weight of bread, can be afforded for the like money, as in more abundant times. A few days ago a poor woman, complaining to the maid servant of Mr. Pickard that the loaf she purchased was less than usual, was answered by the maid, that she was sorry for it ; but that wheat was so dear that it could not now be afforded of a larger size at the customary price ; to which she added a just remark, that we surely ought to be contented here, and not complain, as our condition was so much better than in some other countries ; for she understood from the papers the scarcity was so great in France, that the common people were reduced to the necessity of eating grains. The malicious, it seems, soon perverted and fixed the expression on her master, and it was quickly rumoured that Mr. Pickard had said, he would make the poor eat grains in their bread, with the additional calumny, that he had buried under his mill a large quantity of corn. False and improbable as were such reports, they too successfully answered the ends of their vile fabricators, and, irritated by them, a mob (principally composed of women) assembled between one and two o'clock on Monday afternoon, round the mill, and began to break the windows of it. Two of our worthy and active magistrates (W. Villers and W. Hicks, Esqrs.), who happened to be then in town, hastened to the spot; but it was to no purpose that they addressed the deluded multitude on the unlawfulness and impolicy of their proceedings. A rabble, urged on by furious women, made their way into a part of the premises, and the persons of the Magistrates were endangered by the stones and brick-ends which were thrown in every direction. It became, therefore, necessary to adopt the most vigorous measures, and the King's own regiment of Dragoons were sent for from the Barracks. It happened that the men were at this hour watering their horses out of the town; they were, however, with the utmost expedition collected by Colonel Callow, who appeared at the head of a troop in time to save the mill from destruction; but not before the mob had broken into the counting-house, and destroyed many of Mr. Pickard's books of account. In a few minutes after the arrival of the Dragoons, also appeared, headed by Captain Arden, Mr. Legge's Troop of Warwickshire Yeomanry Cavalry, whom (being at exercise a few miles from the town) Captain Arden, upon receiving intimation of the disturbance, immediately brought to our assistance.

"The riot act was now read. The military speedily cleared the premises of the rioters, and parading through the adjoining streets, prevented further tumult during the day. As night came on, the Magistrates considering peace was sufficiently restored, and that the troops on horseback served only to draw crowds of idle people to look

at them, directed that twenty of the Dragoons should be dismounted, and sent into the mill with the Peace Officers; and that the others, with the Yeomanry, should retire to the Barracks, there to wait in readiness for further orders. Not long, however, after the disappearance of the soldiers, another attack was made. The troops within the mill came out, and seized some of the leading rioters; and the Constables then ordered them to load their pieces before the mob, at the same time telling the people, that if the party that was going to convey those they had apprehended to the dungeon were attacked, they had orders to fire. Notwithstanding these precautions, the escort had not proceeded a hundred yards with their prisoners, before a rescue was attempted. The mob beat, pelted, and pressed upon the soldiers on every side; it was in vain that, by slightly wounding some with their bayonets, they endeavoured to keep them off, and that three of them discharged their pieces over the people's heads. This, instead of intimidating, seemed only to increase their violence; and at length, so furious was the attack, that to preserve his own life, and in obedience to the orders he had received from the peace officers, one of the Dragoons fired upon his assailants. A young man of the name of Allen instantly fell dead, and the ball, which passed through his heart and body, lodged deep in the chest of another (Henry Mason), who, after lingering alive until Saturday morning, expired in our Hospital. Upon these sacrifices to the offended laws of our country, the mob instantly dispersed in every direction; nor has the peace of the town been since interrupted; though, we are sorry to say, some wicked incendiary, with a view of renewing the tumult, has been dropping in the streets, at midnight, written papers of the most criminal and inflammatory nature; and for the discovery of the author of which, the magistrates and other gentlemen have offered a reward of one hundred guineas.

"Mr. Brooke, the Coroner, has held an inquest upon the bodies of the dead men, and the Jury have returned their verdict *justifiable homicide*. Two women and a man, Margaret Bowlker, Mary Mullens, and George Hattory, sworn to as being most active in the riot, are fully committed by the magistrates to Warwick gaol, to take their trials for the offence, of which, if they are convicted, the punishment of the law is *death*. Let then those guilty spirits who, by false aspersions, have been exciting public animosity against an individual, reflect upon all the unhappy consequences of their malignant designs, and consider how much they have to answer for. And may the terrible example that has been made, and the punishments that will ensue, be a lesson to all, never to be forgotten, that the disturber of public peace, and the destroyer of private property, cannot escape with impunity.

" Some apprehensions of a riot being entertained last week, by the inhabitants in the neighbourhood of Dudley, and at Bromsgrove, detachments of the Dragoons were sent from our Barracks to each of those places, who effectually prevented any breach of the peace."

Similar riots occurred, as we learn from a MS. note by Mr. Hamper, on Thursday, May 1st, 1800, when a mob assembled in the evening and proceeded to break the windows of several of the principal millers and bakers in the town, and to commit other acts of violence. By the exertions of the Volunteers, (of whom more hereafter,) together with some of the neighbouring Yeomanry, (who remained under arms the greatest part of the night,) the peace of the town was restored. Precautions were also taken on the two following days, to prevent a renewal of turbulent proceedings, as a spirit of lawlessness continued to show itself ; and on Friday, thirty of the ringleaders, who had gone to some of the farms around Edgbaston with the determination to destroy the corn ricks, etc., were taken into custody before they had done much mischief.

Again, in September of the same year, further disturbances occurred, with more serious results. On Monday morning, September 9th. in con-

sequence of the high price of flour and bread in the town, great excitement prevailed among the people, and a well-known corn-dealer was assaulted by a crowd, and compelled to take refuge in an inn in Bull Street, where he remained for several hours, and was at length liberated by an officer of the peace. At night the crowd became more unruly, and a general attack was made upon the shops of the bakers and meal-men in the town ; the mob assumed the right of selling the bread at reduced prices, and large quantities of flour, bread, and other provisions were stolen. The military force at that time quartered at the barracks (the 17th Light Dragoons), and a party of the Birmingham Light Horse Volunteers, were called out, and the disturbance was quelled, for that night at least.

The next morning, however, the mob renewed their attack upon the steam mill of Mr. Pickard, in Snow Hill (the same Mr. Pickard who had dishonestly obtained from a workman at Soho Watt's idea of the rotary crank, and forestalled the inventor in obtaining a patent for the improvment) ; here the proprietor and his workmen, fearful lest the rioters should break into the mill, fired upon them and wounded four persons, one of whom died a few days afterwards. The magistrates were not long in hastening to the spot with the military force from the barracks, under the command of Colonel Grey, and, after the Riot Act had been read, the military speedily dispersed the crowd, a guard was placed over the premises, and the magistrates returned to head quarters at the " Shakespeare " Tavern, New Street, and " immediately," to quote the words of the *Gazette*, " the bugle of the Loyal Birmingham Light Horse Volunteers sounded, and the drums of the Birmingham Loyal Association beat ' to arms,' and these Corps, with Lieutenant Goodall and Captain Lycett at their head, were very soon at head quarters." By and by, the troops of Yeomanry Cavalry, under the command of the Earl of Aylesford and Mr. Legge, reached the town, and the magistrates, having divided the town into eleven districts, and stationed patrols of horse and foot in each, order was restored during the day. Several persons were apprehended and punished for having been concerned in the disturbances, which, after the arrival of the military forces on the Tuesday, seem to have entirely subsided.

On this occasion we meet with an old Birmingham worthy of whom we have not as yet taken account, the pamphleteer who styled himself "Job Nott." Addressing his "dear brother artificers," in a hand bill issued during the riots, he says:

My Advice is now, as it always has been upon such occasions, to keep out of Harm's Way.

Now you see several Persons have been shot at the Mill. Many say they were wantonly fired upon; if so, the Laws of the Country (which protect the Poor and Rich alike) will punish the offenders. At the same Time we all know that a Man's House is his Castle, and that every man has a right to defend himself if attack'd. However, let us suspend our Judgment a little while; for at present, I am told none of the shot Persons are dead. If any of them do die, a Jury and the Coroner will sit upon the Body, and we shall hear what that Jury says. Let us, in the mean Time, pray that none of them may die; and above all, let us keep every one in our own Houses.   Yours ever,

September 9, 1800.   Job Nott.

Addressing "the Farmers who come to Birmingham Market," our old pamphleteer says:

Gentlemen, my Advice to you is, drop the Price of Wheat immediately—that my Betty and her Children, and all my poor Brother Artificers, whose distresses are great indeed, may partake of the Bounty of Providence.

We have great Cause to complain, though it grieves my Heart that Rioting should have taken place. What's more, if you should not fix a moderate Price to Day, it may lie upon your Hands, and you may be glad to take much less for it in a Month; for the Price will come down, that's certain. Don't you see how the weather glass rises? and don't you know that four or five days will get all in?

And my further Advice is that I hope you will sell it to our Millers and Bakers, and such as won't sell it again out of Town, and then we shall have Plenty at a moderate Price. At any rate, don't sell it to Badgers, nor let them whisper in your ears, and persuade you to raise the market for their own Advantage. I say, hear none of their wicked Advice, for the Devil is at the Bottom of all such Advice; and what little you get in that way will never prosper. God Almighty won't bless the Land of that man who does anything to oppress the Poor, but sooner or later it

39

will come home to him, or to his children after him; for what's got over the Devil's Back is sure to be spent under his Belly: so take my Advice, and be good Fellows, and let us have Plenty and Cheap. So no more at present, from your humble Servant,

September 11th, 1800.   Job Nott.

A few words respecting "Job Nott" may not be out of place here.

Towards the end of the last century, when newspapers were merely what their name implies, a collection of the *news* of the day, with little or no comment thereon, when editorial "leaders" were unknown, and when nearly all criticism or expression of opinion upon subjects of the day was conveyed through the medium of pamphlets, there were issued from the Birmingham press a considerable number of pamphlets on local and imperial politics by a writer who signed himself "Job Nott"; so numerous and varied were these pamphlets that no complete set of them is known. The most complete series in existence was probably that in the Staunton collection which has just been destroyed in the disastrous fire at the Reference Library; it included also the numerous replies under the signatures of "John Nott," "Martha Nott," and other members of the supposed Nott family. The original series of Job Nott pamphlets were probably written by Theodore Price, of Harborne; but their authorship is somewhat uncertain. "Job Nott" was supposed to be a Birmingham buckle-maker; in a weekly paper called *The Bristol Job Nott*, (commenced immediately after the Bristol riots, in 1831,) the author, who purports to be the son of the original Job Nott of Birmingham, says:—" Old Job Nott, I have already told you, got his bread by buckle-making; but the best buckles he ever made were his famous *politico-moral* buckles, with which he buckled the people together in one bond of union, in spite of foes without and traitors within. . . My father, old Job Nott, of Birmingham, lived at the time of the former French Revolution; and when the principles of the Revolutionists had got abroad very much in this nation, and there was a great cry about "*liberty and equality*," and "*The Rights of Man ;*" and Tom Paine's infidel principles were being circulated among the people, and a great many other bad notions had got abroad, but when old Nott—(a plain honest fellow who had sense enough to think for himself, and courage enough to speak what he thought), sent forth his little publications amongst the people, presently his wholesome principles spread through the land, altering men's mind just like as a healing medicine changes the whole mass of a man's blood ; Jacobinism was purged out, infidelity skulked into its native darkness, men who had been enemies to all the order of Society, saw the errors of their way, and became loyal subjects and good citizens." By this extract it will be seen that Job Nott was not among the lovers of liberty and progress, but rather of the unreasoning opponents of all reforms, and of those who in Birmingham ceased to exercise any great influence among the people subsequent to the close of the eighteenth century. Among his various publications, (the titles of which, at least may be interesting to our readers) may be mentioned the following, which were in the Birmingham Reference Library : " England in Danger and Britons Asleep," (1798), " A Front View of the Five-Headed Monster, with Ten Sides of his Tongue," (1798), " A Continuation of the " Front View," etc., " Birmingham in Danger, of which Job Nott gives Fair Warning," (1799), " Further Humble Advice," (1800). In 1803, when fears of a French invasion were entertained by all classes, he published two pamphlets which ran through several editions ; partly, perhaps, on account of their sensational titles, which, printed in very large type at the head of the tracts, were certain to attract attention. The first was entitled " The Lion Sleeps ! " and shortly afterwards he issued the sequel," " The British Lion's Rous'd ! and the French Tyrant Trembles ! " He also issued at an earlier date " The Life and Adventures of Job Nott, Buckle Maker, of Birmingham, as

written by Himself, which ran through at least twelve editions, and was thus advertised in the *Gazette :*

JOB NOTT'S THIRD EDITION.

February 11, 1793.—On Wednesday morning next will be published, Price 3d. each, or one Guinea a Hundred,— The Life and Adventures of Job Nott, the Third Edition. In which Miss Spanker is reproved for her ill manners, and made a more proper Companion for the fair Sex.

Brother Englishmen, it is very pleasing to me to hear from my Bookseller that my Life is going at such a Rate ; and is in general so much approved. A great and good Man has said that " Nobody can read it without Laughing, nor leave it off without being more Loyal and more Moral." And, therefore, to all Loyal Masters my Advice is, give your Servants one a piece. To all Loyal Officers my Advice is, give your brave Recruits one a piece for a Knapsack Companion. And to my Brother Artificers, and the small Fry, my Advice is, get a dab of over Work that you may be able to lay out Three-pence in a Book, wrote entirely for your Use, Information, and Amusement, and by one that regards and never will deceive you. Yours to Command, JOB NOTT.

During the riot of September, 1800, " the original *John* Nott " issued a pamphlet, entitled, " A Word to the Wise : or John Nott's (the original *John* Nott's) Opinion of the Riot in Snow Hill, and of and about the Hand-Bill* that was laid in the Streets last Night to Ensnare and Befool us."

Among the minor occurrences of this eventful period may be mentioned an earthquake which, while it does not appear to have caused any damage, must at least have somewhat terrified the inhabitants. Mr. Hamper thus describes it in a MS. note to Hutton's history of the town :—" On Wednesday night, November 18th, 1795, a little before 11 o'clock, an Earthquake was very sensibly felt by the inhabitants of this town and in all the adjoining counties. Those in bed felt themselves raised up in the same manner as if a person had been underneath them, and a shaking of the bedstead, and of the other furniture in the room, immediately ensued. Those who had not retired to their beds were disturbed by an indistinct rumbling noise, apparently proceeding from the cellars, which was followed by a rocking of the house.

* Probably referring to " Job Nott's " Address " to his Brother Artificers."

"At Nottingham the shock was more severe. Several Stacks of Chimnies were thrown down, and the Bells sounded from all the Steeples."

In 1796 some disagreement having arisen among the subscribers to the Birmingham Library, the disaffected members withdrew and formed a new society on a plan similar to that of the parent institution, called the "Birmingham New Library." The room used by the new society was a commodious one in the lower part of Cannon Street, where the library, numbering about three thousand volumes, remained until 1821, when it was removed to a new building, erected specially for its reception, by a tontine subscription, in Temple Row West. The amount of the annual subscription was £1, and the number of members about 250. It was subsequently incorporated with the Old Library, and comprised, at that period upwards of seven thousand volumes.

The name of "Chapel Wake" carries with it an idea of rustic felicity and simple enjoyment such as Wilkie and Collins loved to depict; and one can easily call up ideas of the village festival, with its May-games, and other innocent merriment, and its accompaniments in the shape of a plenteous supply of "the roast-beef of old England" washed down with copious draughts of "nut-brown ale." Alas! that we should rudely disturb such a charming rustic picture by a narrative of the real events of the "Chapel Wake" in Birmingham in 1798. This wake was a festival instituted to commemorate the erection of St. Bartholomew's Chapel, but how the increase of church accommodation could be suitably commemorated by such scenes as that which we have here to describe it is difficult to imagine.

The more brutal among the inhabitants, chiefly those "lewd fellows of the baser sort" who were more frequently to be found at the ale-bench than at the work-bench—had determined to celebrate this wake by a return to those inhuman sports which were by this time discouraged by all well-disposed citizens; and proposed to bait a bull, in a field behind the Salutation Inn, Snow Hill, not far from the General Hospital. On the day appointed, the bull was brought forward and the cruel sport commenced; but the more respectable inhabitants, wishing to see an end of all such pastimes, induced the members of the Birmingham Loyal Association*—a body of Volunteer Militia formed by the trading class—to undertake the perilous task of capturing the bull and putting to flight his tormentors. "The Association assembled"—says a contributor to the Notes and Queries of *Aris's Gazette*, in 1856 —"in the Bull Ring, and marched, with colours flying and drums beating, to the baiting place in Snow Hill. On arriving there they found that the mob, having notice of the attack, had transferred themselves and the bull to Birmingham Heath. Although the day was intolerably hot, the Association gallantly resumed their weary march, and after a due amount of toil reached the scene of action. The bull-baiters scampered off in all directions, taking the dogs with them, but leaving the bull tied to the stake, and the Association leisurely proceeded to secure their formidable prize. A strong cord was made fast to the bull's horns, and tied round his fore-legs, the chain was unloosed from the stake, guards were told off, who, with fixed bayonets, reconducted the poor animal in triumph into the town; a vast crowd, of course, 'assisting' at the novel ceremony. The procession passed through the principal streets, and at last the bull was safely lodged in the yard of the old prison, in Peck Lane. During the night an attempt at rescue was made, but it failed; and for years afterwards the street boys revenged themselves for the disturbance of the sport by singing a song depicting the volunteers in uncomplimentary colours." Our readers will remember, no doubt, a stanza of this song, which we quoted in our notice of the old prison.

* An engraving of the uniforms of members of this Association appears on page 291.

The Volunteers had several other opportunities of distinguishing themselves, as in
the case of the attack on Pickard's mill, and
it was only right that, on the dissolution of

the Association, their colours, which had
seen such valorous service, should be hung
up in St. Martin's Church. Where are they
now?

CHAPTER XLIV.

CHURCHES AND SECTS IN BIRMINGHAM, 1791—1812.

St. James's Chapel, Ashted—Christ Church Founders and Benefactors—Description of the Building—The Original Design for the
Tower—Epigram—Carr's Lane Meeting House—Pastors of the New Meeting Society—Collections for the Distressed Poor.

OUR last chapter of the religious history of
Birmingham closed with the melancholy events
of July, 1791. We now take up the story again,
and enter upon a happier era, in which we shall
find the churches prosperous and undisturbed,
growing in numbers and usefulness, and extending their sphere of labour over a wider area.

Commencing with the churches of the establishment, we have to chronicle—a few months
after the riots—an addition to their number.
Our readers will doubtless remember that after
the removal of Dr. Ash to London, the lease of
his estate at Ashted was purchased by Mr. Brooke,
and the ground laid out for building; and that
very soon "streets covered his fields, and Ashted
became a hamlet to Birmingham."

Dr. Ash's residence was converted into a pro-
prietary chapel of the Establishment, dedicated
to St. James, and was opened by Dr. Crofts, on
Sunday, October 9th, 1791.

The next addition to the churches of Birming-
ham was commenced in 1803. In December,
1802, a communication was made to the High
Bailiff of Birmingham, by Isaac Hawkins
Browne, Esq., to the effect that he and the Rev.
T. Gisborne, as executors of the late ——
Hawkins, Esq., of Burton, had proposed to the
Court of Chancery (and that the Court had
signified their approval), to give to the General

Hospital the sum of £2,000; to the Blue Coat
Charity School, £600; and £500 towards the
erection of a Free Church in Birmingham. The
proposal to build such a church met with universal
approbation; the Bishop of Lichfield offered to
assist the promoters by annexing a Prebend in
the Cathedral Church of that city; Mr. W. P.
Inge offered a plot of land as a site for the
intended church; subscriptions flowed in rapidly
from every quarter,—His Majesty George III.
himself giving £1,000, and offering personally
to lay the first stone. An Act was obtained in
the session of 1803, for building the new church,
to be called Christ Church, the Royal Assent
being given, by commission, on the 11th of June
in the same year. The King was unable, through
indisposition, to fulfil his promise as to the laying
of the first stone, and the Earl of Dartmouth
was deputed to perform the ceremony in his
stead; the stone was, however, actually laid by
Richard Pratchett, Esq., the then high bailiff.
The building was not ready for use until 1813,
and was consecrated on the 6th of July in that
year. With its appearance most of our readers
are too well acquainted; it is a heavy, plain,
stone structure, with a projecting roof, and a
tetrastyle Doric portico at the western end. The
present ugly spire was not erected until 1815,
and was a deviation from the original plan,

as will be seen from the medal of which an engraving is given on page 299 ; according to which it appears to have been the architect's intention to have given the building a dome and cupola, in humble imitation of those of St. Philip's, and far more in keeping with the

the erection of this church amounted to £26,000, which was defrayed with much difficulty. At this church the ancient custom was observed of placing the men on the one side, and the women on the other ; which gave rise to the following epigram :

HEN AND CHICKENS, NEW STREET.

building itself,—heavy and unsightly as it would even then have been,—than the senseless and tasteless combination of a spire intended to be Gothic, (of the most debased order,) with a building supposed to be Classic. The length of the building is about 140 feet, and the width, about 70 feet, and the interior is somewhat more inviting in appearance than the exterior. In the communion recess is an altar piece of carved mahogany, presented by Mr. Stock, of Bristol ; and there is a fine-toned and powerful organ, built by Elliott, of London. The entire cost of

The churches in general we everywhere find,
Are places where men to the women are joined ;
But at *Christ Church*, it seems, they are more cruel-
  hearted,
For men and their wives are brought here to be parted.[*]

The Independent Church meeting in Carr's Lane appears to have grown and prospered considerably during the last decade of the eighteenth century, so that, in 1801, it was found necessary to take down the original meeting-house, which was capable of holding only about 450 persons, and rebuild it ; but

[*] Quoted in Mr. Bates's *Pictorial Guide to Birmingham*, p. 46.

the new edifice was almost as incapable of containing the numerous worshippers as its predecessor, and was several times enlarged. During the period covered by the present notice, the Rev. Edward Williams, D.D., officiated as pastor for several years. His writings have, within the past few years, been republished in four volumes octavo. Our next notice of this place of worship will have reference to the pastorate of the Rev. John Angell James.

We have already referred, in our concluding notice of the riots of 1791, to the rebuilding of the two Meeting-Houses of the Unitarians. We may here add that the Society of the New Meeting, on the completion of the new building, appointed the Rev. John Kentish as pastor, and in the following year, appointed, as his co-pastor, the well-known Joshua Toulmin, D.D., who remained re until his death, which took place on the 23rd July, 1815.

Perhaps the best idea of the number and general condition of the religious societies in Birmingham in the year 1800, is conveyed in the following list of amounts contributed by each place of worship towards the relief of the distressed poor in Birmingham in that year:

	£	s.	d.
St. Martin's	13	12	2¼
St. Philip's	44	16	11¼
St. Mary's Chapel	45	0	0
St. Paul's ditto	13	4	7½
Deritend ditto	6	9	3
Ashted ditto	1	8	2
Friends' Meeting, Bull Street	40	4	2
Union Meeting House*	35	4	3¼
Old ditto	15	2	4½
Catholic Chapel, Broad Street	7	9	9¼
Carr's Lane Meeting	14	4	3
Bond Street ditto [Baptist]	8	14	0
Cannon Street ditto ditto	4	15	7¼
Bartholomew Street ditto	2	1	0
Lady Well Chapel	1	8	7½
Oxford Street Meeting	0	4	3
Bartholomew's Chapel	3	6	5½
King Street Meeting	3	17	6
Paradise Street ditto	2	9	0
Coleshill Street ditto ⎫			
Bradford Street ditto ⎬ [Wesleyan]	6	17	0
Cherry Street ditto ⎭			

£270 9 5½

CHAPTER XLV.

APPEARANCE OF THE TOWN,

At the commencement of the nineteenth century.

Lower end of New Street—The Hen and Chickens—The Old Post Office—Bennett's Hill—"Pratchett's Folly"—Houses round St. Martin's Church—Moat Lane—The Old Parsonage, etc.

WE now pause again in the course of our story to note the appearance of the town, and the fast receding landmarks of *Old* Birmingham at the commencement of the present century. We have already indicated the *extent* of the town at this period, as we turned over the pages of Bisset's *Directory;* we shall, therefore, content ourselves now with a few pictures of Birmingham streets as they appeared when our grandfathers were in their prime; when Birmingham—albeit as yet only a "village" or "lordship"—was quietly taking her place as the metropolis of the midland counties, and began to think of public adornment as well as public utility. But even at this comparatively modern date, how strange does New Street appear to the younger generation of eighteen hundred and seventy-eight! Look at the plate showing the lower end of New Street, where now the handsome shops in the Quadrant

* The New Meeting Society.

THE LOWER END OF NEW STREET. [ABOUT A.D. 1800.]

(From a Drawing in the possession of Mr. J. Hill.)

and at the opposite corner of Worcester Street stand; where the new Aquarium is fast obliterating all the old familiar features of the Hen and Chickens; and the new Joint-Stock Bank, like a pinched-up palace, has taken the place of the old and well-remembered house which few could help still calling "Attwood's Bank." The hotel was at the date of the picture, a new building; the old "Hen and Chickens" in the High Street was vacated by its hostess, Mrs. Sarah Lloyd, early in 1798, for "her new house in New Street," which, her advertisement in the *Gazette* tells us, was "built according to the plan of James Wyett, Esq., of London." The building, as shown in the plate, remained almost unaltered (with the exception of the portico, which was added in 1830), up to the date of the present reconstruction, and forms a prominent feature in nearly every view of the principal street of the town taken during the present century.

From our plate the reader will observe that the old Free School was still standing, the only observable alteration since its erection being the removal of the hideous pillars shown in our first engraving of the building. Between it and the hotel was an old-fashioned little house; beyond, the old "Attwood's Bank" looks just as it did three or four years ago, when it was removed to make way for the present structure.

Coming towards the upper end of New Street, we notice the old Post Office; a quiet unpretending looking private house, with a small one-storey room adjoining, over which we catch a glimpse of St. Philip's Church, picturesquely surrounded with trees. Here came daily the mail-coaches from all parts of the country, and through this office, rustic and un-business-like as it appears, passed all the correspondence relating to the commerce and manufactures of one of the busiest towns in the kingdom.

A good idea of the appearance of the upper part of New Street may be obtained from our engraving of Christ Church. As we proceed in the direction of the site of that unlovely build-ing—which at the time of our survey, existed only on the architect's plans—we pass the place where now Bennett's Hill enters New Street, but which as yet was unknown. The yellow corn waved in the breeze where now the banks and insurance offices stand, and in the glorious autumn, sun-browned children—who as hoary-headed patri-archs have just been laid to rest—romped and tore their clothes as they gathered the ripe black-berries where now nothing grows save interest and lawyers' bills. A few years later, Catherine Hutton, writing to a friend in London, heads her letter—"Bennett's Hill, *near* Birmingham," and adds: "I say *near*, because an upstart of a street has arisen in Birmingham, which has assumed the name of Bennett's Hill."

And now we return into the High Street to note the appearance of the *old* principal street of the town. We have seen in a former survey the removal of the old Market Cross; we have now to witness the passing away of the last of these old crosses, the "Welsh Cross" at the junction of Dale End, High Street, and Bull Street, which was taken down in March, 1803. The clock and other ornaments (?) had probably been disposed of during the previous October, as they had been advertised for sale during that month in the *Gazette*, as follows:

TOWN CLOCK.

Oct. 4, 1802.—To be Sold, the Clock with three Dials, now belonging to the Welsh Cross, Birmingham, also the weather Vane, Iron Works, and Ball thereto belonging. Apply to Mr. Thomas Greaves, Clock-maker, High Street, or Mr. W. Jones, Builder, Snow Hill, Birmingham.

Leaving the site of the Welsh Cross, we proceed towards the Bull Ring, as yet ungraced with Birmingham's first statue, that of the Hero of the Nile; although the project was set on foot as early as 1805,—as soon as the tidings of his death reached the town.

Early in the present century a structure was erected in the Bull Ring, which provoked con-siderable criticism and ridicule,—the Egyptian Conduit, commonly known as "Pratchett's Folly." This, which was supposed to be a considerable improvement upon the more humble pump, was erected at the cost of Mr. R. Pratchett, in 1807, and was thus described by its architect, Mr. W.

tion to remove those prejudices, which, I trust, every candid mind will ultimately allow to have been rather too hastily formed. At a time when the consequences attending the splendid victory attained by our immortal

THE NELSON STATUE, HIGH STREET.

Hollins (father of Mr. Peter Hollins, the sculptor), in one of the local journals :

TO THE PRINTERS.

January 18, 1808.—As a great deal has been said about, and very little, I believe, generally understood of, the architecture of the Egyptian Conduit, lately erected in the market place, and as some, perhaps, think it beneath their notice, others will not take the trouble, and the remainder do not know how, I feel it a duty which I owe the public, my employers, and myself, to endeavour, by a fair explana-

Hero, the late Lord Nelson, at the Nile, have introduced, not only into the palaces of our princes, and the castles of our nobles, but in the houses of our merchants and our manufacturers, a new style of ornamental furniture and decoration, namely, the Egyptian ; at such a time I consider that style of architecture to be the best adapted for a public building, particularly as the Statue, which public gratitude and veneration are about to raise to the memory of that ever to be lamented Hero, is intended to be placed so near the spot. When I contemplated the noble Gothic Basilica, dedicated to Christianity, which

FORWARD

E. O. SMITH, ESQ.,
TOWN CLERK.

PHOTOGRAPHED BY WHITLOCK.

BIRMINGHAM: HOUGHTON & CO. SCOTLAND PASSAGE.

stands at the back of the Conduit, I conceived it might be possible to blend, at least the idea of the Egyptian, the Grecian, and the English architecture. The pyramidical form being, among the Egyptians, emblematical of the Deity, I consider would not appear to be improperly standing near that sacred Fane. The Egyptian Pyramid was likewise an emblem of strength, built to last, to perpetuate, and to hand down to the remotest ages, the wonderful skill of the Egyptian builders of an unknown date, erected for an unknown purpose, and whose massive stones were brought from an unknown place, according to some authors, and according to others, 3,297 years have rolled away since the erection of this mighty pile, for a Mausoleum or Sepulchre, to receive the ashes of their departed kings. But authors of more celebrity contend that it was erected for a more noble purpose ; for as the whole of the Egyptian theology was clothed in mystic emblems and figures, so was the external form of the building a representation of their God Osiris, or the Sun, as being in the form of the Sun's ray ; and that the Deity which was typified in the outward form was to be worshipped within. It contained a trough of granite marble, as a reservoir for the holy water used in their religious ceremonies, which, by means of a well in the Pyramid, was drawn out of the Nile. The propriety of such a building enclosing a well of water for public use, I trust, will not be disputed. I have ornamented it with a representation of the Papyrus, grouped in form of quarter columns at each angle, with Grecian Honeysuckles, and with an Urn at the top, which last may be considered as a symbol of our departed Hero's ashes ; as proper appendages, the Lion's Head is significant of that Hero's strength and prowess in battle, and of his noble disposition when not opposed to an enemy ; as disgorging the water, it is a symbol of the element, for the Egyptians believed water to be the strength and principal of all things. Besides, the Lion's Head is a very ancient ornament for water spouts, and was used in all Grecian Temples. The Pyramid is also in the form of a flame of fire, and within this form the Grecian and Roman statuaries wrought those sublime and beautiful groups of figures which have been the admiration of every age. These, Gentlemen, were the considerations which induced me to adopt such a form for a building which, though so small in bulk that the whole expense of erecting it will not, probably, exceed fifty pounds, is, in my opinion, so great in significance that I do not hesitate publicly to acknowledge myself as the architect.

I am, Gentlemen, yours, &c.,
WILLIAM HOLLINS.

A few days later an exceedingly humorous pasquinade was published in the *Birmingham Commercial Herald*, as follows :

THE HUMBLE PETITION OF THE PUMP IN THE BULL
RING TO THE INHABITANTS OF BIRMINGHAM,

SHEWETH,—That your Petitioner hath been a resident in the town of Birmingham for many years, and hath always been accounted a good neighbour and useful member of society. That your Petitioner hath uniformly borne a good character, both in morals and religion ; and in all the changes which have taken place, he has never forsaken the church, as he can prove by credible witnesses. That your Petitioner, being by nature unostentatious, took up his abode in a narrow passage below the Shambles, where he quietly remained unnoticed, and almost unknown, except by his neighbours. That in this age of innovation, your Petitioner hath found himself suddenly thrust into notice by the destruction of certain buildings behind which he had, for so many years, screened himself, and that, on looking round, your Petitioner could scarcely recognise his old acquaintance, Moor Street, who, like your Petitioner lived in a very retired way, and who was noted for being a disagreeable, close old fellow, began to give himself the airs of a young man, and instead of the dirty garments he formerly wore, shone away in gaudy apparel. That your Petitioner, in his exposed situation, grew ashamed of his old coat and hat, and hearing that a certain ingenious clothier had supplied Moor Street with his splendid habiliments, your Petitioner ordered from him the new garment, which he now wears, and which has so transmogrified him that he is scarcely known by his best friends. That your Petitioner having asked calmly why he supplied a coat of such an outlandish cut, the said clothier broke out into such an incoherent rhapsody about Basilicas, Lotuses, Papyrus, Pyramids, Fire, Ashes and Water, Egypt and Greece, departed Heroes, Urns, Statues, &c., that your Petitioner verily concluded that "much learning had made him mad." That since the said clothier finished your Petitioner's coat, he has dubbed him with the new name of Conduit, whereas the family name of your Petitioner has been from time immemorial plain Pump, which he hopes may be continued, maugre the said clothier. That, although your Petitioner is somewhat stricken in years, he disdains the imputation of having become a Driveller, which it is evident the said clothier has attempted to cast upon him, by having affixed to him a slobbering bib as part of his apparel. That the aforesaid clothier has passed a sentence of denationalization against your Petitioner, who is a trueborn Englishman, although the said clothier asserts that he is a gipsy. That your Petitioner is well disposed to live peaceably, but he fears he shall be involved in a dispute with his opposite neighbour, the statue, in consequence of his having been forced, much against his will, to interfere with the concerns of the said statue. The truth of these premises being made apparent, your Petitioner prays your humane interference to prevent his name from being changed from "the Pump in the Bull Ring," to that of "Egyptian Conduit in the Forum," as proposed in Aris's paper, and you Petitioner shall ever pray.

The old houses around St. Martin's Church are at last removed,—it was by their removal that the old pump was left so prominently conspicuous,— and the patched and unsightly building itself is

40

left bare in all its ugliness. A description of these houses as they last stood was given from the personal recollections of an old lady, in the *Birmingham Daily Gazette*, on New Year's Day, 1866. "At the corner opposite Digbeth," she says, "there were two flights of steps, and at the top of the first flight was a house occupied by the beadle of the church, who was a firework maker, named Neale, and used to make the fireworks for Old Vauxhall, which was then a fashionable place of resort and amusement. Coming to the bottom [of the steps] again towards the Bull Ring, the first shop was a saddler's, named Bassett ; the next, at the corner, Taylor's, a grocer ; while Wright, a combmaker, and Probin, an auctioneer and broker, occupied the two next shops. The well-known printer and bookseller, Belcher, lived at the next house, and his immediate neighbour was Ashmore, who kept a china and earthenware shop. Taverner's shop was the next, and this was followed by what we now call a slop shop. I remember that wagoners' frocks were among the principal articles of trade at that time. Next to this shop was Mr. Hall's, a watchmaker, while Cotton's whip shop completed the row in this direction. Round the corner was a large general tailor's and outfitter's establishment, kept by a man named Deane.

" The church gates were at that time the same as they are now, and situated in the same places. There were houses from the other side of the gate down Spiceal Street to where the gate at the corner is now. The first of these, in the Bull Ring, was a salt shop, kept by Mole, then Craughton's liquor shop, then followed a few shops." From the same article those curious in such matters may learn the names of most of the residents in this locality, (the Bull Ring, Digbeth, Spiceal Street, etc.,) at the same period, from which our space permits only of the following particulars : The Red Lion, an old inn which had stood since the end of the sixteenth century, at least—was still in existence ; the site of the present " Museum Concert Hall" was occupied by

an inn called the George, and two doors below, in the cellar-house, occupied by a quack doctor, named Poole, was the pump from which the famous " Digbeth Water " was taken, and hawked round the town in carts, for sale. Two doors below that was the well-known White Hart Inn, from whence the Plague started ; Allison Street was at that time called "Crooked Lane." On the other side of Digbeth, almost opposite the house which contained the " Digbeth Water," was another equally well known " Cock Pump," (a relic of the days when that thoroughfare was called Cock or Well Street) ; and the writer of the " Recollections " remembered a ballad called " The Cock Pump's Complaint," in which the neglected pump called upon the authorities " to put him in repair and to make him decent." Lower down on the same side of the street was the scale-beam shop of Mr. Balden, the grandfather of Mr. Alderman Avery, who still carries on the same manufactory in the same place. Lower still was the shop of Mr. Zeckariah Parkes, whose family,—in the persons of Mr. Joseph Parkes, one of the leading spirits in the Political Union, and Miss Bessie Rayner Parkes, an able and discreet advocate of woman's rights—have earned the honour and esteem of all lovers of liberty.

The half-timbered house which for so long a time has been known as Assinder's Original Tripe House, was then a fruit shop. What is now called Upper Mill Lane, was a very narrow road, which led to the Moat. The Moat-house, as our readers are already aware, was at that time used as a Manufactory. " Bradford Street," says the author of the Recollections, " now one of the widest streets in the town, was very narrow at that time, and there was a small house at the top nearly round in shape. You went into it down a small flight of steps, and here a very remarkable-looking old woman used to live. The people said she was double-jointed ; and there was a story that she had sold her body to the doctors, so that they might dissect her when she was dead. She sold

OLD VIEW OF THE MOAT, FROM LOWER END OF MOAT LANE.
(From a Drawing by the late Mr. Wm. Robbins.)

sucks and sweets, and children were delighted to spend their money there, in order to see her." There appears to have been "a large sheet of water" in this part of the town, called Mill Pool, which was taken from the Moat. Jamaica Row was then called Black Boy Yard, and the public-house now called the Woolpack was then the Black Boy. Not far from this spot still stood another old land-mark upon which the shadows of decay were fast falling,—the old Parsonage House, with which our readers are doubtless familiar, from the beautiful drawing by David Cox, copied on page 338 of this work. This interesting old house is thus described by one who knew it:* "At the bottom of Worcester Street, where Dean Street, Pershore Street, and the Bath Passages now are, stood St. Martin's old Parsonage House, through the grounds of which ran the Lady Well waters; numbers of large willow-trees grew by its little stream. Its garden was well stocked with fruit trees, and when broken up, I well remember the games we of the Deritend Schools had there." The same writer also pleasantly describes the appearance of the district below St. Martin's. "From the back of Bromsgrove Street," he says, "there was nothing but beautiful and fertile gardens, and many a time have I wandered through them, along the 'pudding brook' walk. This little stream (pudding brook) was a curiosity, inasmuch as on each side of the walk, between the gardens, a stream of water ran, east on one side and west on the other.* In those times the old River Rea was a nice clear stream, always full of water, kept so by the floodgates below Deritend Bridge. A little higher up the stream than the floodgates were some pleasant tea gardens, called Spring Gardens, well wooded down to the river's edge, having pretty walks, grottoes, and arbours. Here, in summer time, I have often seen groups of tea-parties enjoying this rural retreat. The inn, I fancy, is still standing in Floodgate Street. There used to be pleasure boats, for rowing parties up the river, under Deritend Bridge,—then just finished, and put up in place of the old pier bridge. Having passed Bradford Street and Cheapside bridges, they arrive at the lovely sequestered and elegant gardens of the Apollo House, in Moseley Street. The house was originally built for an hotel and gardens, like Vauxhall, but did not answer. It then became the residence of several respectable families, among whom was the talented William Hamper, Esq."

CHAPTER XLVI.

INTELLECTUAL AND LITERARY ACTIVITY OF THE TOWN, AT THE CLOSE OF THE EIGHTEENTH CENTURY.

The Robin Hood Society—A new Debating Society formed—The Society for Free Debate—The Minerva—Local Newspapers—The Birmingham Register—Pamphlets and Miscellaneous Literature.

HAVING endeavoured to obtain some idea of the appearance of our town at the beginning of the present century, we trust our readers will pardon us if we pause still further in our narrative in order to notice briefly the literary and intellectual life of Birmingham at the same period. We have already seen, in our chapters of local worthies, that our town was, at the close of the last century, an important centre of intellectual

---

* Mr. Henry Saytor. See *Birmingham Daily Gazette*, Jan. 22, 1866.

* "Near the place where the small rivulet discharges itself into the moat, another of the same size was carried over it, and proceeded from the town as this advanced towards it, producing a curiosity seldom met with; one river running south, and the other north, for half a mile, yet only a path road of three feet asunder; which surprised Brindley, the famous engineer."—*Hutton's History of Birmingham, sixth edition*, p. 332.

as well as commercial activity; that she boasted among her inhabitants not a few who were eminent in the scientific and literary world: poets and philosophers, artists and inventors, men who had spent a lifetime of research in the

their newspapers, and other current literature, rather than of the greater worthies who have already figured in this history.

On the first of April, 1774, the first meeting of a little society called "The Robin Hood Free

OLD HOUSE IN THE BULL RING.
(Occupied by the late Mr. Thomas Weston.)

domains of nature and philosophy,—Withering and Darwin in botany; Priestley in chemistry, electricity, and pneumatics; Watt in mechanics; and many others in the various departments of scientific research. We have now, however, to speak of our townsmen in general, as we find them in their literary and debating societies,

Debating Society," was held "in Sam Wickins's Long Room, at the Red Lion Inn," (in the Bull Ring, a few doors above Park Street); and the attendance thereat was said to have been "very numerous and respectable." The admission was by ticket, price sixpence, "to be had at the bar;" but ladies (who were allowed to take part in the debates,) were admitted free, on procuring tickets from the hostess, Mrs. Wickins. As a concise description of the aims and objects of the society, we may quote one of its own advertisements :

Birmingham, August 8, 1774.
The Birmingham Robin Hood Free Debating Society will meet in Sam Wickins's Long Room, at the Red Lion Inn, in this town, to-morrow (Tuesday) evening. The President to take the chair exactly at eight o'clock, when the following subjects will be debated, viz. :—
"I. Are vice and virtue innate or acquired ?"
"II. Which merits most admiration—frugality in a low condition, or liberality in a high station of life ?"
"III. Which of the four cardinal virtues is the greatest ?"
"IV. Will open reproof or private admonition tend most to the reformation of vice ?"
Two questions only were debated last Tuesday evening, as the first question took up near two hours. The President returns his sincere thanks to the gentlemen who so ably supported the debates. It is impossible to say, however, that the question was determined, as the speakers resolved the word absurd, as stated in the question, was not applicable either to Pythagoras or Plato. Resolved, the man of knowledge is happier than the ignorant man. An occasional address, "On the Use and Abuse of Debating Societies," by the President, on Tuesday next. The debates to begin at eight o'clock, and end at half-past ten.

J. SHATFORD, President.

A second society was formed,—possibly in consequence of some misunderstanding or dispute among the members of the first,—within a few weeks of the establishment of the Robin Hood Society. A meeting was held on the 20th of April, "to consider the Propriety and Expediency of establishing a Society in this Town, for the Encouragement of free and candid disputation." At this meeting, we read, "it was the unanimous Sense of the Company, that such an Institution might, if conducted with Harmony and Decorum, be generally useful and agreeable." If the "company" comprised members of the older society, it must be inferred from this reservation that the "Long Room at the Red Lion" must have been the scene of one or two rather noisy meetings during the month of April, 1774.

The new society was established, the rules adopted, and the meetings held at Mrs. Ashton's Coffee Room, in the Cherry Orchard, (afterwards Little Cherry Street); at the first meeting, which took place on the 16th of May, 1774, the following subjects were debated :—"I. Is a Drunkard the greater Enemy to himself or to Society ?" "II. Which is most detestable in itself, or most dangerous to Mankind, Treachery in Friendship or Hypocrisy in Religion ?" "III. Which are the greatest, real or imaginary evils ?"

The other questions debated by this and the preceding society during 1774 were advertised in the *Gazette*, and are given by Dr. Langford in his *Century of Birmingham Life ;* but after the first year neither society is heard of again.

The next society of which we find any record is the "Society for Free Debate," which met in a large room in Needless Alley, (afterwards converted into a dancing room); a card of admission to one of the most memorable meetings of this society is preserved in the Birmingham [Old] Library. It contains the following inscription :

"*In veri investigatione versamur.*
SOCIETY FOR FREE DEBATE.
Instituted in Birmingham, 1789.
"On Monday Evening, October 15, 1792, *the following Question will be debated—'Was Brutus justifiable in killing Cæsar ?'*
"The President takes ye chair precisely at Half-past Seven o'clock. No Member to introduce more than two Ladies or one Gentleman."

Coming at the time of the reign of terror in France, this debate so excited the public mind that the Magistrates were compelled to interfere to prevent the further discussion of the subject.

We have already referred to the two political clubs which met at Freeth's Coffee-house and the Minerva Tavern ; the latter, which was kept by Joseph Lindon, (or Lyndon,)—usually known among his companions as "*Joe* Lindon,"—was, perhaps, one of the most respectable and noted, on account of the frequenters of its smoke-room, in the midland counties. Among these—all of whom, as many be judged from former notices, were staunch "Church and King" men—was the late Mr. William Hodgetts, one of the last of the fine old race of Birmingham Tories who flourished in the pre-municipal era of our history. His family, we believe, still preserve his silver pint tankard, of which the smoke-room at the Minerva boasted no less than thirty-seven, each being numbered, and some of them, as in this case, being specially appropriated to the use of the most regular frequenters of the room. Besides, there was a silver tankard which held three pints, called the "*Fine-slapper*," on which was engraved the Lyttelton Arms, in compliment to one of the Lords Lyttelton, and who had on one occasion honoured the company at the Minerva smoke-room with his presence. If anyone committed a breach of good manners, a judge was elected, the case was tried, and the plaintiff or defendant fined a slapper of ale, (*i.e.*, three pints, hence the name of the "*Fine-slapper*,") according to the verdict of the jury which was composed of the company present. It is to be hoped that the person who puffed a whiff of tobacco-smoke in the face of James Bisset, on the occasion of that worthy's visit to this house, was fined the usual slapper, but the violent anti-Jacobin temper of the company almost forbids the supposition. For many years no member of the Radical or Jacobin party as it was then called, was permitted to enter this room, and more than one of these obnoxious interlopers who had the temerity to imitate the author of the *Poetical Survey*, was compelled to take "Bissett's way out," (*i.e.*, through the window,) in order to escape from his tormentors. Gradually, however, the company became more tolerant, and, consequently, more mixed; but not so much so as to permit the Catholic Emancipation Act to pass without offering their most strenuous opposition to the measure. They even turned the portrait of the great duke with its face to the wall, as a mark of their displeasure at the part he took on that occasion. Some of the most influential men of Staffordshire visited this room when they came to Birmingham, and it was no uncommon thing to see two or three magistrates of that county there at one time.

The number of local newspapers and periodicals was as yet limited; *Aris's Birmingham Gazette* still held its own as the representative journal of the town; there was also the *Birmingham Chronicle* published by Swinney and John Collins, and the *Birmingham Commercial Herald*, by R. Jabet. Several little periodicals had been attempted, but all came to a speedy end. The first of these, so far as we can discover, was *The Birmingham Register, or Entertaining Museum*, "Printed by and for J. Sketchley, sworn appraiser, auctioneer, and salesman, in the High Street." It was commenced May 10, 1764, and extended to about twenty-five numbers, expiring in April, 1765. It was conducted on the model of the *Gentleman's Magazine*, its contents being made up of dry moral essays, feebly written; political extracts from the *North Briton;* tales of questionable morality, as befitted the manner of the times; scraps of poetry and lists of bankrupts, the price of corn, and a meagre *resumé* of national intelligence; with short advertisements for "sprightly youths" as apprentices, of "emetic drops," of the "whole art of swimming," the "secret history of Betty Ireland, and her gay life;" and, as in some of the obscure States of Canada and the bush villages of the Far West, lists of letters lying in the Birmingham Post Office, directed to persons unknown. Such were the contents of our first local magazine; yet, poor as they may seem to us who live in the days of high-class monthly reviews and magazines, it is something to be proud of that Birmingham possessed, in 1764, a periodical not very far below those of the metropolis, and that it was, in all probability, the only provincial town in the kingdom that could boast of such a serial.

The Medical Miscellany, which only extended to one volume, was issued about nine years later; a second edition, with an appendix, was published by S. Aris in 1774. No other periodical seems to have been ventured upon until 1817, but from that time to the present our periodical literature, though for the most part short-lived, has been exceedingly prolific,—as will be seen in future notices, and in the bibliographical list which will be printed at the end of the volume.

The pamphlet literature of the period under notice was, as we have already indicated, very considerable. In addition to the numerous tracts of Job Nott and his many imitators, the vast amount of Riot literature, (including pamphlets by Priestley, Madan, Burn, Clayton, Dr. Samuel Parr, Edwards, Foley, and many anonymous writers,) and the poetical pamphlets of Freeth, Collins, and Bissett, mention must be made of Morfitt's *Verses on Birmingham*, the Theological and Controversial Pamphlets of Dr. Priestley, of which the "Catalogue of Birmingham Books in the Reference Library" mentions thirty-three,— (all destroyed in the disastrous fire,) and of the Theological tracts of the Rev. J. Proud, in defence of the doctrine of the New Jerusalem Church.

Nor was the local press less prolific of larger and more important works of permanent value and interest. The Rev. Joseph Berington, a learned and estimable clergyman of the Roman Catholic Church, and an intimate friend of Dr. Priestley, gave to the world, through the medium of the Birmingham press, his *History of the Lives of Abeillard and Heloisa*, (Swinney, 1788, 4to), the *Reign of Henry II., Richard I., and John*, (Swinney, 1790, 4to.), and his *Memoirs of Gregoria Panzani*. (Swinney and Walker, 1793, 8vo. Our worthy historian, William Hutton, who began authorship at the age of 58 with the history of his own town, sent forth therefrom many works of sterling value, and, from his quaint, homely wit, of infinite amusement also. We have already given our readers a few examples of his style in our notice of his *History*

of the Court of Requests ; besides this, mention may be made of his *Dissertation on Juries*, (or the "Hundred Court,")—often bound up with the *Court of Requests*, and now scarce and difficult to meet with ; his *History of the Battle of Bosworth Field*, the *Journey from Birmingham to London*, the Journeys to Coaltham and Blackpool, North Wales, the Roman Wall, and other places of interest ; his *History of Derby*, and his several volumes of verse, which, if they were not poetry, were certainly racy and vigorous. In 1777-8 a bookseller named Earl, in Dale End, published a *History of the Bible in Verse*, by J. Fellows, in four volumes duodecimo, and a *Life of Oliver Cromwell*, in 8vo. Among local reprints of well-known books we may mention those of Robert Dodsley's satirical *Chronicle of the Kings of England, by Nathan Ben Saddi*,— a racy but somewhat irreverent parody of the style of the Chronicles of the Old Testament,— and of his *Œconomy of Human Life*, supposed to be written by an ancient Brahmin* ; Hervey's *Meditations*, (Martin and Hunter, 1808) ; Hugo Grotius *On the Truth of Christianity*, (Piercey, 1797) ; Meyrick's *New Family Herbal*, (Pearson, 1802) ; also a beautiful reprint of Somervile's *Chase*, by R. Martin, with Baskerville's types, in 1767. The Rev. Mark Noble's *Memoirs of the House of Cromwell* was published in Birmingham by Pearson and Rollason, (1784, 2 vols. 8vo.) ; David Simpson's *Sacred Literature*, a work in four volumes, intended to show the superiority of the Holy Scriptures over the most celebrated Writings of Antiquity, was published here by Mr. Swinney in 1784.

---

* A French translation of Dodsley's *Œconomy of Life* was also published in 1799, by Pearson, with the following title : *Manuel du Tous les Ages, ou Economie de la Vie Humaine, par D. P.*

CHAPTER XLVII.

AMUSEMENTS OF THE PEOPLE.

(Including the History of the Birmingham Theatre, 1795-1810.)

Out-door Sports—Guinea Gardens—Old Vauxhall—Re-building of the Theatre—M'Cready appointed Manager—Anecdotes of Mc'Cready—
No Music—Opening of the New Theatre—Description of the Building—Notes from the play bills, 1796-1810.

WE now turn once more to the amusements of the people, and more especially to the history of the local stage during the first decade of the nineteenth century.

The light of advanced civilization was rapidly effacing the rude, boisterous, and cruel sports of earlier days; but there still lingered one or two old-fashioned pastimes of this character throughout the decade, now under notice. Regular cock-fights were announced as entertainments in the public prints,—county was matched against county, and town against town, and even the highest classes of society countenanced and attended these degrading exhibitions They often lasted several days and excited more attention and interest than did the deliberations and acts of the national legislature. Thus, in 1809, we find the following announcement in the local newspapers :—

A main of cocks will be fought in the new pit in Smallbrook Street, between the gentlemen of Warwickshire and Staffordshire, for £5 5s. the battle, and 100 guineas the main.

The "new pit in Smallbrook Street," was the favourite scene of these "sports," and it was not closed until between 1825 and 1830. It is recorded that on one occasion the magistrates, endeavouring to suppress an "institution" so degrading to the public morals and damaging to the reputation of the town, seized about a hundred of the principals and spectators, and, after tying them together, marched them through the principal streets as an example ; but this happened at a somewhat later period than that now under notice. Badger-drawing and bear-baiting also still survived, but in a less degree. These animals were kept for the purpose, and one great black bear in particular, called "Old Nell," kept by a person in Coleshill Street,—was celebrated on account of its great skill in defending itself.

The Old Vauxhall Gardens still remained the chief popular resort of those who sought out-door recreations, and the attractions of music and dancing, fireworks, balloon ascents, variegated lamps, etc., rendered this famous old place of amusement a powerful agent in drawing pleasure seekers from the brutal "sports," previously referred to.

For those of the working classes who cared for the quieter and more healthful pastime of gardening, there were little allotments called "guinea gardens," encircling the town on every side,—little plots of ground, let for a guinea a year, laid out with flowers, or planted with vegetables, currant and gooseberry bushes, strawberries, or other useful "garden stuff," according to the taste of the owner. Besides finding useful and healthy occupation for the amateur gardener, these old-fashioned "guinea gardens" afforded a pleasant retreat, wherein the weary artisan might breathe the pure country air after toiling all day, amid the close surroundings of the factory or the workshop. Alas, their place now knows them no longer. The continually increasing town has spread out its limbs on all sides like a huge octopus, and shabby suburbs have long since covered the pleasant artisans' gardens of seventy years ago.

Among in-door amusements the theatre has ever claimed the first place ; and the first decade of the nineteenth century saw the local theatre in great and increasing prosperity and popularity.

But we must go back a few years into the past century, to the date of the re-erection of the New Street Theatre.

The new building, which was commenced early in 1793, was so far advanced by the end of the following year, that we find the Proprietors in December, 1794, advertising for a manager ; " to engage and manage a Company for the Summer Season ;" announcing at the same time "that their Theatre will be ready for opening the latter

the liberal Manager appears to possess the ability and spirit to form suitable arrangements for opening such a House.

A later advertisement informed the public that " the house would be illuminated with wax," a statement which we frequently meet with in the local playbills of that period.

The new manager was the father of that eminent tragedian, William Charles Macready, and had won "golden opinions" in the

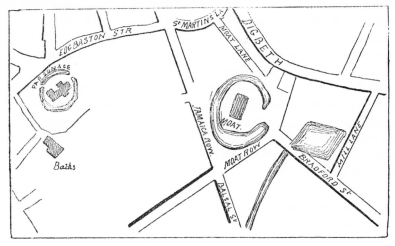

SECTION OF OLD MAP.
(*Shewing the District round St. Martin's, the Old Mill Pool, etc.*)

end of the month of May, 1795." As a result of their advertisement the New Street Theatre passed into the hands of one whose taste and enterprise gave promise of better things than Birmingham playgoers had as yet enjoyed,—a promise which was destined to have a rich fulfilment. The engagement of the new manager was thus announced in the *Gazette* of May, 25th, 1795 :—

The Theatre.—Our new Theatre (which for the present we shall content ourselves with saying will be superior in elegance and grandeur to any provincial one whatever) opens next month. The Gentleman with whom the Proprietors have engaged as Manager of the Company is Mr. M'Cready, the author of the new Comedy called the *Bank Note*, now performing with such applause and success at Covent Garden. The Performers, the names of some of whom we hope to give in our next, are selected from the London Houses ; and from what we can learn,

metropolis, (on the boards of Covent Garden Theatre), both as an actor and dramatic author ; and having also acquired a small fortune, seceded from the Covent Garden company, partly on account of a misunderstanding with regard to salary, and came down to Birmingham to assume the management of the theatre as already stated. This happened about three years after the birth of his son, which took place during his residence in London. The elder Macready (or M'Cready, as he usually wrote himself, and was styled by others), was born at Dublin in 1755. He made his first appearance on the stage of one of the Dublin theatres in a humble capacity, and at the humble salary of fourteen shillings a week. He soon tired, however, of this line of business, and joined a strolling company in a

41

tour throughout the country. He returned to Dublin, and in the beginning of 1786 met with his first success, which ultimately carried him into fame and fortune. It happened that Macklin was "starring it" for the last time in Dublin in some of his own pieces, and among others, "The Man of the World." Of course Macklin was cast for *Sir Pertinax Macsycophant*, and Daly, the manager, as *Egerton*. At the first rehearsal Macklin was peevish, very hard to please, excessively ill-tempered; and Daly, being scarcely so careful or solicitous to please the great star as he ought to have been, irritated him beyond measure. "Sir!" roared Macklin in a fury from the wing, which he nearly battered down with his stick, "Sir! what do you take the character for? By heavens, sir, as Hamlet has it, 'I'd as lief the town-crier spoke my lines!'" The injured Daly replied, with the air of a deeply-injured tragedian, "You may have written the play, sir, but you have no conception of the character." "What does the puppy say?" roared Macklin, more irate than ever, red in the face, and putting his hand to his ear,—for he was very deaf; "I mean to say," said Daly, getting very warm, "that you're a conceited old fool; and more, sir, you may go and find Hamlet or his father's ghost, if you like, to speak your trash." The author of *The Man of the World* found an *Egerton* nearer home than Daly had directed him, in the person of William M'Cready, who played the part so well that Macklin took him to London and brought him before a Covent Garden audience, in the character of *Flutter*, in *The Belle's Stratagem*. This was the beginning of M'Cready's good fortune, and by the time his son, the future tragedian, was born, he had established himself in public favour.

During Macready's engagement at the Covent Garden Theatre a curious incident occurred which illustrates, in an amusing manner, his remarkable superstition. He would not enter a room where there were three candles for any consideration; and it so happened that he had to appear, on one occasion, in a piece called *The Rendezvous*, in which three ladies rush on the stage at once, each carrying a lighted candle in her hand. "Mac" solemnly declared, amid the laughter of the entire company, that he wouldn't go on under such circumstances. The manager became quite furious, and insisted upon his going out, but the superstitious player was obdurate. "He wasn't going to lose his luck for all the Covent Gardens and managers in England." The affair seemed likely to become serious, when someone happily hit upon the suggestion that one of the ladies should carry *two* candles, so as to make four in all; by this means the difficulty was overcome, and M'Cready pacified. When he became manager of the Birmingham Theatre, his superstition remained as strong as ever. He would not bring out a new piece on a Friday, nor any new actor, for worlds. "Both," he said, "would be certain to be hissed."

He had very eccentric notions, too, on the subject of music. On one occasion, during his management of the Birmingham Theatre, he quarrelled with the musicians, and the result was an orchestral strike. When the curtains rose, and the prompter discovered the state of affairs, he rushed in fear and trembling to the manager's room, where M'Cready received the news with the utmost calmness. "Never mind, my boy— never mind," he replied,—"it'll be all right by and by, just ring up, my jewel, ring up," and he at once shuffled on to the stage. Up went the curtain, without overture, and the play proceeded. This absence of musical accompaniment delighted the manager, who wandered about from wing to wing during the representation, rubbing his hands and chuckling audibly, "Och, isn't this beautiful, isn't this heavenly,—how peaceful and quiet we are. It's noisy devils they were, fiddlin' and scrapin' their catgut, the blackguards, and interrupting the performances. Och, and hear how delacious and heaven'y it is,—it's myself that will never have them in the house again—by my soul—for a lifetime. Aye, and isn't it £15 a week that you've saved, too—bedad only think of that. What's that, my boy? The act-drop down—then ring up again, my jewel. Devil the scrape they'll have at all." The drop went up for the second act without a moment's delay, and the whole performance was gone through without the assistance of the musicians. This went on for a month or more, to the great satisfaction of the the music-hating "Mac," if not of the audience, when an event happened which led to the recall of the disaffected band. Miss Kitty Stephens, (afterwards Countess of Essex) had been engaged, and stepping forward at the morning rehearsal to sing her first song, looked to the orchestra,—but not a soul could she discern there. She looked to the wings, but not a mortal fiddler met her gaze; then turning to the manager, she exclaimed, "Dear me, where is the band?" "Heaven knows, my jewel," was the reply, "for bedad its myself discharged them all a month ago." "Well; but Mr. M'Cready, I can't possibly sing without an accompaniment." "Och! an accompaniment, d'ye call it?" roared he, "you mane a parcel of noisy fiddlin' devils to destroy your beautiful singing—to murder that pretty delacious voice of your own. Ah! don't think of it,—not for a moment." Miss Stephens laughed heartily at the old man's compliment to her "pretty delacious voice," but could not sing without the accompaniment nevertheless, and the unhappy manager found himself compelled to re-introduce "the scrapin' blackguards," and, much against his will, to retain them.

The New Theatre was opened on the 22nd of June, 1795, and an elaborate description of its appearance was given in the *Gazette* of the preceding week, which, as the house subsequently met the fate of its predecessor, will be of interest to our readers at the present day.

"Upon entering the House, the eye is struck with its capaciousness, elegance, and richness. Its form, for the audience part of the Theatre, is semi-circular to the box on either side of the stage, which, as far as each extends, takes the line of a circle reversed. Two tiers of Sixteen Boxes surrounded the House; they are decorated with many white enamelled Iron Columns, representing a Bundle of Reeds, the fillet that encircles and binds them, and the vases and capitals, being richly gilt. From above the columns project elegant brackets, which suspend the brilliant glass cut chandeliers. The colour of the inside of the Boxes is a deep pink, the covering of the seats crimson, and the cushions apple green.

"The Pit is most ample and commodious, and here the spectator sees, with perhaps better effect, the whole decoration of the House, which, in executing from the Architect's design, does so much credit to Mr. Dixon. He sees as he directs his view, the elegant ornaments painted on the parapets in Front of the Boxes, the magnificent Ceiling in the form of a Fan, adorned with antique figures and ornaments corresponding with the decoration of the Boxes, and the costly painted Curtain, through which appears, in an opening 38 feet wide, the Stage with the vivid and splendid Scenery of Messrs. Greenwood and Dixon, the masterly execution of which will, we doubt not, confirm and, if possible, increase the celebrity of these eminent Artists.

"The Gallery is, perhaps, the largest, and, we may venture to pronounce, one of the best in Europe; and the public's safety and convenience, in coming to and going from the House, has been particularly consulted. The entrance to Box, Pit, and Gallery, is from different Streets; and there is not, what has been so much complained of in other theatres, any step or descent whatever in the entry from the street to the Pit. A handsome Saloon receives the company before they go into the Boxes, and a communication is made from each lobby to the large ball-room in front of the house, where refreshments will be provided; and whither those Ladies and Gentlemen who may wish to relieve themselves between the acts, and the play and entertainment, may repair. We shall now only add, that as the walls of this large fabric (which enclose a space in length of one hundred and nine feet, and in width of seventy nine) have been erected nearly two years, no apprehension of dampness need be entertained ; and observe, that as the Manager seems to vie with the spirit of the Proprietors, by bringing to the first provincial Theatre a Company of Performers superior to any that

beginning of his career in Birmingham, providing a magnificent production of this description, called *Oscar and Malvini, or the Hall of Fingal,* a descriptive notice of the scenery therein occupied the whole of the back page of the play-bill (which seems in those days to have been generally utilised): this was followed in 1797 by a "Grand Serious Pantomime, entitled *Don*

OLD VIEW OF THE BULL RING.

ever yet left the metropolis, we hope the exertions that have been made, and the great expenses incurred for the public's accommodation and amusement, will not be unremunerated."

A few notes from the unique series of Birmingham playbills in the possession of Mr. Sam: Timmins will give our readers some idea of the spirited manner in which Mr. M'Cready catered for the play-goers of three-quarters of a century ago.

Spectacular display being as popular then as it is to-day, we find the new manager, at the very

Juan." But the manager did not forget, while providing these spectacles, to cater for the tastes of the more intellectual class of playgoers ; and we find Mrs. Siddons in July of the same year, on the boards of the local theatre, playing in *Macbeth, George Barnwell, Henry VIII. King Lear, The Earl of Warwick,* and Home's *Douglas,* The principal male character in each of these pieces was sustained by Mr. Holman.

Pantomime and realism followed in strong force during the same season ; of the former we have *Alonzo and Imogene,* (with the famous ballad on the back of the playbill,) and *Robinson Crusoe*, on the playbill of which there is an elaborate description of the scenery,—and the latter is well provided in one of these same pantomimes, in the shape of a view of the Sea, which changes to a cornfield, "*with plough and horses, as natural as life.*"

The famous "Dicky Suett," already referred to in these pages, was in Birmingham at the close of the same season, "for one night only." The announcement is as follows :—

Last Evening's Entertainment this Season.—Mr. McCready had hoped Mr. Suett's Engagements would have allowed him to have performed more than One Night in this Place ; but he is sorry to find, that the Gentleman being announced to play at Drury Lane Theatre so repeatedly this week, deprives him of the Power of fulfilling his intended engagement. And the Public are therefore respectfully informed, the Theatre will finally close for the Season, with the Entertainments announced for this evening. [September 25, 1797.]

On the occasion of Suett's visit the *Gazette* makes the following remarks :—

September 25, 1797.—Mr. M'Cready, our Theatrical Director, seems bent upon it to make his exit with an universal grace. To say nothing of what he has done, we cannot but look with an admiring eye upon what he this night means to do. Bannister and Suett's attractions combined, in such favourite characters as the Philpots, Lingo, Daggerwood, Fustian, Scout, and Snarl, are too powerful a temptation to resist, even if a man had made up his mind, as the old saying is, to go to the Play no more this season. It is now some years since we had the pleasure of seeing Suett on the Birmingham boards ; but all must well remember that he was the idol of the public then ; and as improvement has kept equal pace with his absence, we may expect to see him now "in all the jocund vein of laugh-provoking humour." Bannister has so recently delighted us, that his merits want no memento, as they are registered, ' where every day we turn the leaf to read them.' Nor do we think it necessary to dwell on what is due to the Manager, whose lavish spirit and inabating ardour to give the public every species of the richest entertainment a Theatre can afford throughout the season, must have entailed upon him an expense enormous, and, indeed, such as, locally considered, is totally unprecedented in the history of the Theatrical World.

During the next season, Birmingham had the pleasure of seeing both Kemble and Siddons : the great John Phillip appeared June 28 and 29, and July 9, in *Hamlet*, *Richard III.*, and *The*

Stranger ; and Mrs. Siddons, in the same characters as before, during the month of August. A great "revival" of Monk Lewis's *Castle Spectre*, with elaborate scenery and startling effects, is the only other event of note during the season of 1798.

In 1799 a piece of some local interest was produced, "a New Poetical Sketch called *Tony Lumpkin's Ramble through Birmingham*, with occasional Remarks on the Theatre, the Squares, the Charity School, Soho, the Stained Glass Manufactory, Clay's Japan Manufactory, Allen's Print-shop, the Museum, the Hen and Chickens, Buckle-making, Gill's and Woolley's Sword Manufactories, &c., &c." On the 22nd of July, Kemble appeared, in "*a new tragedy called Pizarro*, by R. B. Sheridan, Esq.,"—also, in *Othello*, "after which, a new Pantomime Dance, in which Mr. Quantrill will leap through a Hogshead of Fire." Shade of the "Divine William," *Othello* followed by a Pantomime ! In September of the same year, Munden was in Birmingham for a short season, and sustained, on the occasion of his benefit, September 9th, the part of *Autolycus*, in the *Winter's Tale*. At the close of the season of 1799, R. W. Elliston appeared, in *George Barnwell*, and other pieces.

The Birmingham Theatre was, as our readers are aware, open only during the summer months, and usually commenced with a pantomime, in June. To us this may seem very strange, but at that time the reign of pantomime was not confined to the three months between Christmas and Easter, but extended (at intervals) throughout the season. The season of 1800 was opened with one of these, entitled *Harlequin Everywhere, or Jewels new set*, preceded on the first night, (as in the instance previously referred to,) by *Othello*. Other pantomimes followed during the same season, including *Harlequin's Arrival*, (introducing three local scenes ; viz., Birmingham from the Warwick Canal, New Street, and Birmingham Heath,) *The Children in the Wood*, and a **very** curious piece entitled *Obi, or Three Fingered*

Jack, founded on a real incident which occurred in 1780 in the Island of Jamaica, and which is related in Moseley's *Treatise on Sugar, and Medical Observations.* The bill announcing this production contains an elaborate notice of the fact on which it is founded, and gives copious notes from Moseley's work, quoting which the manager says :—

"The learned author of the work we have profited by says,—
'I saw the Obi of the famous Negro Robber, Three Fingered Jack, the Terror of Jamaica in 1780.
'It consisted of a Goat's Horn, filled with a Compound of Grave Dirt, Ashes, the Blood of a Black Cat, and Human Fat all mix'd into a kind of Paste ; a Cat's Foot, a dried Toad, a Pig's Tail, a Slip of Virginal Parchment of Kid Skin, with Characters marked in Blood on it, were found in his Obian Bag. These, with a Keen Sabre, and two Guns, were all his Obi, with which, and his Courage in descending into the Plains, and Plundering to supply his wants, and his Skill in retreating into difficult Fastnesses, among the Mountains, commanding the only access to them, where none dared to follow him, he terrified the Inhabitants, and set the Civil Power and the neighbouring Militia of the Island at defiance for nearly two years.'"

Better things were, however, also provided ; as we find notices of the engagement of Mrs. Siddons' visit, in August, for six nights, when she appeared in *Pizarro, The Stranger,* and other pieces ; of Mr. and Mrs. Johnston, in *Hamlet, Speed the Plough,* etc. ; and of Mr. and Mrs. Pope, in *Pizarro,* etc.

In June, 1801, we find Mrs Siddons again at the Birmingham Theatre, appearing in *Douglas, As You Like It, Isabella, or the Fatal Marriage,* and *Mary Queen of Scots.* On the first of July, Mrs. Second, the lady whose singing called forth the impromptu verses of John Collins—appeared, on the occasion of her benefit, in the *Beggar's Opera.*

In 1802,—August 31st—Shakespeare's finest historical play, *Henry VIII.* was produced "by desire of the Right Honourable Lord Nelson." A new comedy, *Folly as it Flies,* was "acted for the first time, for M'Cready's Benefit, on the 19th of the same month.

The theatrical season of 1804 was perhaps the most successful of any during Mr. M'Cready's management. G. F. Cooke, Dicky Suett, Harley, Blanchard, and other eminent "stars" graced the boards during this season ; but the greatest success was achieved by the Young Roscius, Mr. W. H. Betty. In the engagement of this youthful prodigy Mr. M'Cready's usual perceptive faculties somewhat failed him, and led him into a mistake which amused the Birmingham play-goers amazingly. He had heard of the success which had attended Master Betty's performance in Edinburgh, and wrote, offering an engagement at the rate of £10 a night, which was immediately accepted, and the manager felicitated himself upon his excellent bargain. But when the little actor arrived in Birmingham, and the manager found himself confronted by a boy of thirteen, for each performance of whom he had agreed to pay ten pounds, his apprehensions got the better of his prudence. "No, no," said he, "that won't do, we'll play to empty benches. I have no objection to make him a handsome present for his trouble, but we must cancel the agreement." This the friends of the boy agreed to, and it was finally arranged that, after deducting £60 for expenses, he should divide the profits with Betty.

Never had he made a greater mistake. Instead of the empty benches which he had pictured in his imagination, the house was crammed—literally packed with spectators on every occasion. People who had never entered a theatre in their lives before, came from all parts of the district to see and hear the actor who had barely left off wearing pinafores ; they waited at the doors of the theatre from mid-day until half-past six o'clock in the evening, taking their meals with them in order to prevent the risk of losing their places. Instead of ten pounds, the manager found himself obliged, by his own agreement, to pay the young "star" as much as fifty or sixty pounds for every performance. Commencing with *Young Norval,* in Home's *Douglas*

(August 13, 1804), he astonished old playgoers by appearing during the first week of his engagement in the characters of *Rolla, Hamlet,* and *Richard the Third.* Even after he had left the town his performances continued to excite considerable interest among Birmingham critics and playgoers; James Bisset warmly espoused his cause, and published a pamphlet defending him from the attacks of certain critics who probably had a greater respect for art than for clap-trap sensationalism. The discussion was carried on with great animation until some new sensation arose, in the person of a rival " infant phenomenon," younger, and with even more presumption than Betty,—a Miss Mudie, " a child only seven years of age." As Betty had found a champion in our old friend Bisset, so did the new example of precocious childhood in Mr. Morfitt, who wrote a long letter to the *Gazette* in defence of Miss Mudie, couched in language which would be exaggeration if applied to some of the greatest artists who have graced the stage.

We note also a performance during this season, of the *Merchant of Venice,* on the 9th of July, " by desire of the Three Battalions of Loyal Birmingham Volunteers."

In the earlier part of the year 1806, nothing was talked of except the splendid pageant on the occasion of the public funeral of the Hero of the Nile ; and consequently we find one of the earliest pieces produced on the local stage during that season was " an exact Representation, by moving figures, of the Funeral Honours, Processions by Land and Water, etc., to commemorate Lord Viscount Nelson," of which the play-bill gives a very elaborate description. This season was remarkable, as having witnessed the first appearance on the local stage of Charles Kemble, on the 11th of August, as *Hamlet,* and subsequently as *Shylock, George Barnwell, Richard III.,* and other leading characters. An old favourite also appeared, R. W. Elliston, in Monk Lewis's *Lothair.*

On the 23rd of July, 1807, Mrs. Siddons made her farewell bow to the Birmingham playgoers previous to her retirement from the stage. The following notice of the performance appeared in the *Gazette :*

On Thursday evening, the celebrated Mrs. Siddons, who is now taking leave of her provincial friends preparatory to her retiring from the stage, made her appearance at our Theatre in the character of *Isabella,* and was received with the greatest applause. A correspondent has sent us the following remarks on this eminent actress :—" The surprisingly transcendent talents of Mrs. Siddons have been so long and so universally acknowledged, that to praise her would be to descant on the obvious splendour of the sun ; yet something we must say to gratify the ebullition of admiration her sublime performances excited. Perfection in any art is so rarely arrived at that, when seen, it delights by its novelty as much as it does by its excellence. Mrs. Siddons, in the histrionic art, has reached the utmost boundary of perfection ; so compleat are her powers of assumption that nature, in all her own native loveliness, appears before us. Her attraction can never lose its force ; for however she may cease to be a subject of curiosity, she must still continue to the classic mind ' an ever new delight.' We understand that this is positively her last visit to this county." In justice to the general performances we cannot but observe, that the plays on Thursday and Friday were filled in a manner that did great credit to the Theatre.

The year 1807 is celebrated in the annals of the local stage from the fact that therein our first permanent theatre, worthy of the name, received the designation of " The Theatre Royal," and became a patent house. On the 26th of February a petition was presented and read in the House of Commons, from William Sharpe, James Woolley, Matthew Boulton, and several others, " being proprietors of the Theatre or Play-house in the said town, setting forth that about the year 1792, the only theatre in the town was destroyed by fire ; and that it being " expedient to provide another for the amusement of the inhabitants of the said Town, and that of the Nobility and Gentry of the neighbourhood, some of the Petitioners and other Inhabitants, being the Proprietors of the old Theatre, erected on the site thereof a new and more commodious Theatre or Play-house in the said Town." The petition was referred to a committee, who reported on the 23rd of March, that they had examined the matter and leave was forthwith given to Sir Charles Mordaunt and Mr. Dugdale, to bring in a bill, which, being read for the first time on the 25th of the same month, passed the Commons on the 21st of April, and after receiving a few amendments in the House of Lords, received the Royal Assent on the 1st of August, and the Birmingham Theatre became the Theatre Royal.

In November, 1808, an announcement appeared in the *Gazette* which would doubtless be welcome to all playgoers ; viz., that the Theatre would be open during the ensuing winter season. "The inhabitants of Birmingham," says the manager, "have a claim, and indeed are entitled to every gratification that can be suggested towards rational amusement. Their days are devoted to praise-worthy exertions, which renders the town one of the richest boasts of Britain, and surely it may be expected that a good play (in one of the handsomest Theatres anywhere) will be relished on winter evenings, provided the actors be res-pectable, and the whole well-regulated." The manager further announces his determination "to engage the very best performers that can be had"; and adds that "Stoves are erecting to render the lobbies, etc., warm and comfortable," and that "the most unremitting assiduity shall be exerted on every occasion, to give the amuse-ments of the drama in a correct style, so as to be honoured with approbation, and obtain the sanction of a general public."

During the season of 1809 the lovers of music were liberally catered for by the manager of the Theatre Royal ; Master Dourousset,—"the Young Musical Roscius," as he was called,—Mrs. Emery, Madama Catalani, (whose singing is said by one of the local journals to have "called forth the greatest bursts of applause ever witnessed in the Theatre,") and Mr. Braham, all graced the boards of the local stage during that year ; the latter appeared "for one night only," (Oct. 2,) on the occasion of Mrs. T. Didbin's benefit, and sang "Said a Smile to a Tear," the "Death of Aber-

crombi," and other pieces. During the same season Stephen Kemble appeared, as *Falstaff*, and Mr. Cooke, in his round of characters.

During the summer of 1809 M'Cready entered upon a new speculation, that of the management of the Theatre in Manchester. It was not a success, however, and he retired from it at the end of the year. " Painful as it is to assert," he said, in his closing address to the playgoers of Manchester. "it is the fact that my efforts have not here been attended with success. Indeed, the result is quite the reverse of success—'tis to me *utter ruin*. The money I had in the funds on coming here—which was not inconsiderable— is entirely exhausted : the property I brought, the fruits of my early industry, is at this moment under seizure for rent ; and for the liberty which at this moment gives me the power of addressing you, I am obliged to two friends. Thus situated, I despair of ever having the honour of appearing before you after this night."

During Mr. M'Cready's temporary retirement from the Birmingham Theatre, Mr. J. Watson became the lessee, and may be said to have lavishly consulted the tastes—and especially the musical tastes—of the Birmingham public. He it was who first introduced the welcome innova-tion of a winter theatrical season in Birmingham.

For the services of Madame Catalani, (after the famous "O.P. riots," and the consequent retire-ment of that lady from the boards of Covent Garden) he paid no less a sum than one thousand pounds for six nights' performances.

Mr. M'Cready returned to the Birmingham Theatre in 1810. This year is the most important in the period under notice, on account of the first appearance of William Charles Macready,—the son of the manager,—which took place on Thurs-day, June 7th, in that year. This interesting event is thus recorded in *Aris's Gazette* :—

THEATRE ROYAL.

June 11, 1810.—The Tragedy of Romeo and Juliet was brought forward at our Theatre on Thursday last, for the purpose of introducing a young candidate not 18 years of age (Mr William M'Cready) to the stage, from whose performance we have no hesitation in predicting his future fame and prosperity ; indeed we have never witnessed a better first appearance. He looked the character admirably ; the elegance of his figure, the expression of his countenance, and the very great ease of his deportment, united in forming a perfect representation of what Romeo should exactly appear. He received the most encouraging and flattering applause through the first four acts, and at his dying scene there were several distinct peals, testifying surprise and the highest admiration of talents which have been seldom equalled, if ever surpassed. Mrs. Young seemed much interested, and exerted herself with the happiest effect ; we have never seen her to more advantage. The whole play merited and obtained the warmest plaudits, particularly the Friar, Mercutio, the Prince, and the Nurse. It is to be repeated this evening, with the grand Melodrama of Valentine and Orson, in which Mr. Conway and Mr. Betterton perform.

The miscellaneous entertainments of this period were such as were common in all great towns ; a panorama in New Street, Waxworks in High Street, "the invisible lady" at the Hotel in Temple Row, the "Pandean Band," and "the Patagonian Sampson" at the Shakespeare. There was an amphitheatre, at the back of the Stork, in 1802, where the celebrated Astley used to perform, and other amusements, from time to time, in various parts of the town,—so that our old townsfolk could not have suffered at any time during the first decade of the nineteenth century, for lack of pleasures.

CHAPTER XLVIII.

PUBLIC LIFE AND EVENTS, 1801-1810.

Visits of Celebrated Persons to Birmingham—Nelson—Prince William of Gloucester—Crime in Birmingham—Execution of Philip Matsell—Eight men hanged at Washwood Heath—Riots at Edgbaston—New Street Acts—Street Obstructions—The Peace Rejoicings in 1802—Birmingham Loyal Volunteers and the threatened Invasion—Death of F. Blick—The Public Office—Death of Nelson—The Nelson Statue.

WE now pass to the history proper of the first decade of the nineteenth century. In entering upon the chronicle of the public life and events of this period, we seem to have passed into a new sphere, and to be writing of a new race of men ; hitherto we have found our townsmen, for the most part, interested only in the affairs of the parish, stirred only by parochial feeling, dwelling in what was as yet, despite its size and importance, only an ungainly and overgrown village. But now, as we have seen in the three preceding chapters, more attention was beginning to be paid to the adornment of public offices and private dwellings, as well as in providing for the recreation of the people ; and as we shall see in the present chronicle, considerations of a higher and nobler character began to influence the public of the town. People of note, too, were now attracted to Birmingham in greater numbers than hitherto ; travellers from abroad, desiring to see

the chief objects of interest in England, seldom left without paying a visit to Birmingham. Among the most distinguished visitors during this period was Lord Nelson. On Monday, August 30th, 1802, the hero of the Nile, accompanied by Sir William and Lady Hamilton and others, arrived at Styles's (now the Royal,) Hotel. Thousands of the inhabitants went out to meet him in the afternoon, and crowded round the hotel, shouting their rough welcomes, while the bells clanged peals, and Nelson stood at the windows for hours to gratify their curiosity. In the evening the party visited the Theatre. The hardy Birmingham men took the horses from the hero's carriage, and dragged it in disorderly, but triumphant procession, to the play. The whole house rose at him as he entered, and offered him an ovation which it has fallen to the lot of few men to receive. On his return at midnight, men with torches lined the streets; and in the torchlight, and with hundreds of willing hands at the wheels, he was drawn back along New Street and High Street, up Bull Street, to his hotel. Next day the same demonstrations were renewed. He walked to the manufactory of Mr. Clay, in Newhall Street; the sword manufactory of Messrs. Woolley and Deakin, Edmund Street; the button establishment of Messrs. Smith; the buckle and ring manufactory of Messrs. Simcox and Timmins, Livery Street; and the patent sash manufactory of Messrs. Timmins and Jordan, St. Paul's Square. He was followed by thousands as he went; and when he stepped into his carriage to proceed to the famous stained glass manufactory of Mr. Eginton, at Handsworth, the horses were un harnessed by the multitudes, who drew him thither with their hands, and where he was received by a large party of young ladies, who, in white robes, strewed flowers before him on his path Soho was also seen, where appropriate medals were struck, and where an interview was had with Matthew Boulton in his bed-room. In the evening there was a grand banquet, to which Nelson was invited by the High and Low Bailiffs, as the chief authorities of the town. And there occurred one of those events which look so strange and odd to us by the lapse of only 50 years. We are gravely told that "Lady Hamilton condescendingly gratified the company with several most appropriate charming songs." Again there was a visit to the Theatre, a torch-light procession, crowds, songs in his laudation, and again the populace drew him to the hotel. Next day there was a walking party to Mr. Radenhurst's whip manufactory, the toy warehouse of Messrs. Richards, Mr. Phipson's pin manufactory, and the Blue Coat School. At one o'clock the gallant Admiral, who had won the hearts of the people by his frank sailor-like honesty and bearing, left Birmingham for Warwick Castle, amidst the acclamations of one-half of the population, never to return.

In May, 1805, we had among us a royal visitor,

H.R.H. Prince William of Gloucester. When it was known, on Monday, the 13th of that month, that the Prince intended to stop here on his way to Liverpool, on the following morning, every arrangement was made, considering the shortness of the notice, to manifest the loyalty of Birmingham, to the House of Brunswick. On Tuesday morning, the Loyal Birmingham Volunteers, preceded by a party of the Royal Dragoons from the Barracks. marched to Camp Hill, where they were drawn up in line to receive the Prince, who arrived about one o'clock, and was escorted to Styles's Hotel. (afterwards the "Royal," Temple Row,) where the Magistrates, the High Bailiff, and other gentlemen were assembled to receive him. After the military left the hotel, they paraded in New Street, and on his royal highness being informed of the circumstance, he immediately joined them, walking uncovered along the whole line; "he saluted the officers as he passed, and thanked them and the privates for their polite and marked attention, and observed that he had never seen a finer body of soldiers." The Prince was then conducted to the principal places of interest in the town: the Mint, and other objects of curiosity at Soho, Mr. Eginton's exhibition of stained glass, and Mr. Clay's papier-mâché manufactory, on the Tuesday; and on the Wednesday morning to Wooley's sword factory, Simcox and Timmins's brass-works, and Richards's toy-shop. in the High Street. The *Gazette* records with high eulogium, the patriotism of the Volunteers on this occasion, of whom the greatest part of the three battalions, " when the drums beat to arms . . . assembled at head quarters in little more than half an hour, fully armed and accoutred for the field, unknowing for what service they were so hastily called out, but full of ardent zeal for the cause for which they had associated, and indifferent in their choice whether to pay respect to the family of their sovereign, or to fight the battles of their country." The Prince left the town about three o'clock on Wednesday afternoon, on his way to Liverpool.

Crime increased, and assumed its worst form—that of murder—during this decade, and we have to record in the present chronicle the first and only public execution within the boundaries of the town. A watchman named Robert Twiford, pacing Snow Hill during the night of July 18th, 1806, had occasion to question some suspicious character who was prowling about the silent streets; while the guardian of the peace was questioning him, he was shot by a pistol bullet, and mortally wounded. One Philip Matsell was suspected of the crime, arrested, and, being tried at Warwick, was found guilty, and condemned to be hanged on the spot where the foul deed was committed.

On the morning of August 22nd, a strange grim sight was witnessed in the busy streets of Birmingham, such as had never been seen in the town before. A gibbet was erected near the bottom of Snow Hill,—at the end of Great Charles Street,—with a scaffold below. Large crowds of the idle, the dissolute, and the curious, turned out to see the unwonted sight. Many met the mourning coach containing the wretched criminal at Camp Hill, (on its way from Warwick to the place of execution, and greeted Matsell with yells, groans, and hisses. Here he was brought out in the midst of the dense multitude, pinioned by the executioner with cords, in sight of them all, placed in an open cart covered with black, and with his coffin before him, the hangman on one side, and a clergyman on the other, the doleful procession passed slowly through Deritend on its way to Snow Hill On reaching the fatal spot, a strange spectacle presented itself to the view. Away up the hills on three sides,—up Great Charles Street, up the hill on which Little Hampton Street now stands, and up Snow Hill, was a dense throng of nearly fifty thousand persons; some sobbing hysterically at the unusual sight, some jeering and shouting, and some cursing, and, as it seemed, only one man in the vast crowd calm and collected, and that one the culprit himself. With the reckless spirit of a bravo, spurning all spiritual consolation, casting one glance at the hideous paraphernalia of death, he refused all aid in mounting the ladder, and clenching his hands together, bound as they were, with a "Here goes!" he leaped in the air, and, almost before the shudder which had passed through the vast assembly had become unfelt, the scaffold was instantly removed, and the hapless murderer was left suspended on a gibbet twenty feet high. This was the first and last execution within the boundaries of Birmingham, and the last in the neighbourhood.

Robberies and burglaries were of frequent occurrence; "scarcely a house," says one writer, "was unarmed away from the centre of the town. Every man had to defend his own premises, as the authorities could not do it for him. Sometimes houses were regularly attacked; at short intervals tales of burglars shot, or of inmates wounded, were common. Predatory bands scoured the roads in every direction, and did not hesitate to attack the equipages of travellers, often accomplishing by stratagem what they could not effect by force." The old newspapers of this period afford a curious insight into the condition of affairs in this respect, and the dangers of the road. During 1805 we read that "a trunk was cut from off Lord Derby's carriage upon Hockley Hill," and that "a trunk was stolen from the carriage of Lord Cathcart in Deritend;" and many other instances of daring robberies committed in open daylight might be gleaned from the *Gazette* and *Chronicle* of that time. On the 18th of April, 1804, we read of the discovery of two nests of coiners in the town. "At one place in Thomas Street," says the report, "the constables were obliged to shoot a large mastiff before they could approach the house; but this act so intimidated the fellows that they gave themselves up, throwing some bags of base metal out of the window, to prevent them being found upon the premises." The constables, however, "discovered as many implements as filled a cart; and a quantity of finished coin was found between the beds and the sacking."

Many of these coiners, burglars, and footpads were hanged. A most sickening sight was witnessed at Washwood Heath,—on the spot where Pitmore and Hammond suffered in 1781,—on the 19th of April, 1802, when eight men were

100,000 persons, it was computed, assembled to witness the last sentence of the law carried into execution. The culprits left Warwick at eight in the morning, heavily ironed, and manacled to the transport carriage, attended by peace officers and a squadron of yeomanry cavalry. Thus they slowly advanced until they reached Castle Brom-

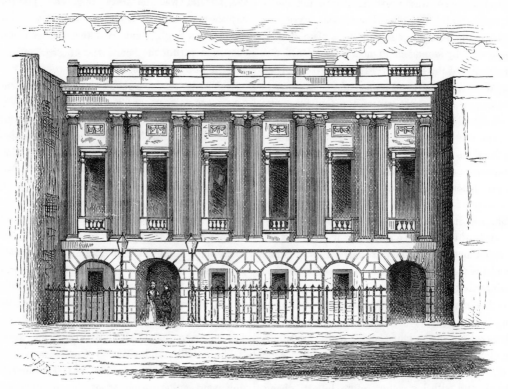

THE PUBLIC OFFICE, MOOR STREET.

executed at one time; four for burglary and four for forgery. The forgers were all Birmingham men, the eldest of them being forty-nine years of age, and the youngest only twenty-seven; the names of these were Joseph Hill, Joseph Carter, Benjamin Baker, and Edward Hill. The four burglars were mere youths,—three of them under twenty-five years of age,—and were named Samuel Bryan, John Parkes, Francis Swiney, and Thomas Moore; these suffered for offences committed in the county. "The day was fine," says an old account of this mournful event, "and nearly

wich. There they ate, and drank a parting cup of ale, and then were drawn at a foot pace and escorted by several troops of dragoons to the drop. Although they had been six hours on the journey, they showed no signs of fatigue when their irons were knocked off, and they were pinioned in sight of the vast concourse of people. They mounted the scaffold one by one, firm and unshaken, and when they had met there, Carter gave out a psalm, and the poor criminals sang that and a hymn. Then one after another they spoke to the people; a few moments after, died;

and yet a little while longer, when they were cut down and delivered to their friends."

In the last year of this decade the town was again the scene of a riot, which began from an insignificant cause, that of a quarrel between two women over the price of some potatoes. It commenced in the market-place, on Monday, May 28, 1810 ; the dispute naturally enough collected a little crowd around the women, and before long the spectators began to manifest a desire to take part in the quarrel. A riot ensued, but very little damage was caused, in consequence of the prompt action of the authorities in quelling the disturbance. The worse-disposed among the crowd, disappointed in their hope of seeing another general riot, started off to the little village of Edgbaston, and there commenced a little riot on their own account, by violently entering the house of a respectable farmer, breaking the windows and the furniture, and leaving the interior of the house almost a wreck. A troop of the seventh dragoon guards soon appeared on the scene, and captured thirteen of the mob, (while in the act of plundering and destroying the farmer's property) bringing them tied together with a rope, into the town, where they were safely lodged in the prison, in Moor Street. On Tuesday morning the mob again assembled, and attacked another farm-house at Edgbaston, (that of Mr. Wheeley, in Wheeley's Lane) where they began to plunder, but were speedily interrupted by the arrival of a troop of the Warwickshire Yeomanry, which had mustered with praiseworthy speed, and, taking five of the rioters into custody, prevented further mischief. There were now, altogether, twenty of these fire-brands, who were brought before the magistrates, and committed to take their trial at Warwick, to which place they were conveyed in three coaches, under strong escort. On Tuesday evening a third attempt at disorder was made at the bottom of Snow Hill ; but the Handsworth Volunteer Cavalry arrived speedily and put to flight the disturbers of the peace, suffering no worse injury than was inflicted by a volley of stones and brick-

bats. The rioters at Edgbaston were tried in July, and sentenced to various terms of imprisonment.

At the same Sessions a case was heard which should interest Birmingham men, inasmuch as it would appear to have been one of the first in which an attempt was made to stifle political opinion, and was the precurser of those persecutions which have rendered the struggle for political freedom one of the most heroic episodes in the annals of our town.

"A decent looking man" named Joseph Fellows," was indicted for having, on the 30th May last, unlawfully endeavoured, by words and gestures, to excite divers of his Majesty's liege subjects to riot against the King's peace. Lieutenant-Colonel Gordon was the prosecutor. He stated that on the 30th May, about ten o'clock at night, he had seen a great number of people collected together at the corner of Temple Street ; that he heard one man haranguing the mob, and speaking very loud, who proved to be the prisoner, Fellows. He heard him say, " I can earn five-and-twenty shillings a week, and that is not sufficient to support me " ; and, further addressing himself to the people, " You must right yourselves, and now is the time." In the gallant Colonel's eyes this was seditious ; he pressed through the mob, and seized Fellows by the collar ; the people rescued him, and in the scuffle the Colonel received a violent blow on the head from a large stone which was thrown, and became insensible. Poor Fellows, however, was re-arrested and thrown into prison ; but was we are happy to say, acquitted by the jury at the Warwick Sessions.

During the Parliamentary session of 1801, an Act was passed to amend and enlarge the previous Birmingham Street Acts of 1769 and 1773. The new Act began by adding to the number of Commissioners, and among those included in the list were Samuel Galton, Richard Tapper Cadbury, George Lander, Thomas Hutton, (son of the historian), John Ryland, and other well-known and respected citizens. The improvements which had been projected so long, and which we have already noticed in our survey of the town during this period as completed, were again included in the third street Act; such as the removal of the Welch Cross and four houses, for the purpose of widening the lower end of Bull Street; the removal of the houses surrounding St. Martin's Church, the Round-about Houses, and the remaining part of the Shambles. Other improvements were also provided for by this Act; viz., the widening of Swan Alley, (upper part of Worcester Street,) also the lower end of the same thoroughfare,—the only portion which then bore the latter name; and the widening of the lower end of Moor Street, (by removing eighteen houses.)

By a further amendment Act in 1812, encroachments and projections are forbidden; the Commissioners may order projecting signs to be fixed flat upon the fronts of the houses, and if this is not done within three months, they may "cause such signs, emblems, sign posts, sign irons, pent houses, shew boards, stalls, window shutters and flaps, porches, sheds, butchers' stalls, bulks and gallowses, shambles, blocks, or pieces of timber, chopping blocks, watering tubs or troughs, posts, rails, and stumps, and all other encroachments, nuisances, or annoyances whatsoever, to be taken down or removed." This list of encroachments affords us a curious picture of the old fashioned appearance of the town, even as late as the beginning of the nineteenth century. The old swinging signs, the sign-posts and watering troughs in front of the old-fashioned inns, the open shop fronts, with projecting show-boards, the quaint projecting "bulk windows," houses with outside window shutters and flaps,—all these are the true signs of a quiet old country town, and may be seen to-day in many such throughout England.

Ninety-nine persons were named in this amendment Act, as Commissioners, and power was given to them to fill up vacancies occurring in their body, it being provided that each Commissioner should be an inhabitant, rated at not less than £15 per annum to the poor rate, and

possessed "really and *bonâ-fide*" of real or personal estate to the value of £1,000.

But by far the most important of the provisions of this Act of 1812 was that empowering the Commissioners to treat with the Lord of the Manor for the lease or purchase of his markets, fairs, and other manorial right, and to buy "a piece of land with the buildings thereon, called the Moat and Moat House," to enclose the same to form the Smithfield Market. But as these changes properly belong to the next decade of our history, we shall defer the more particular notice of them until the next chapter of our chronicle of events.

The signature of the Amiens Treaty of Peace in 1802 was celebrated in Birmingham with great rejoicing, notwithstanding the fact that the prosperity of certain local trades was likely to suffer therefrom. "The joyful information," says the *Gazette*, "was first brought to this town on Tuesday morning, (March 30th,) before three o'clock, by the Balloon Post Coach, which came from London (110 miles) in ten hours and forty minutes. The streets were in a very short time crowded with thousands of people, in anxious expectation of the Mail, which came in between nine and ten, drawn by six horses, and decorated with flags, ribbons, etc. Immediately on its arrival at the Inn the populace took out the horses, and dragged it in exultation round the town for several hours." Bonfires and a general illumination concluded the day's rejoicings, and the next morning the Loyal Association met in New Street, and fired a *feu de joie*, and in the evening another and more splendid illumination (on which occasion the Soho factory was illuminated with gas), concluded the celebrations. At Aston the poor were feasted in honour of the Peace, on the second of April, by the owner of the estates, Mr. Heneage Legge. An ox and two sheep were roasted, and these, with a liberal supply of ale, were distributed to the poorer inhabitants of the village. A day of public thanksgiving was appointed, (June 1st,) and services were held in all the churches and chapels of the

Establishment after which collections were made on behalf of the Sunday Schools of the town ; the following sums were received :—

				£	s.	d.
St. Martin's	...	...	...	13	6	6½
St. Philip's	...	...	...	22	17	8
St. Mary's	...	...	...	24	12	8
St. Paul's	...	...	...	11	1	0
St. Baatholomew's	...	...	...	5	11	7
St. James's, Ashted	...	...	...	4	3	4
				£81	12	9½

The peace which was so joyfully celebrated was of short duration. Early in the following year the country was threatened with invasion by that second "scourge of God," Napoleon Bonaparte, and at once, as in the days of good Queen Bess, the whole nation, fired with patriotic zeal, was roused to arms to oppose the insolent invader. In Birmingham subscriptions flowed in rapidly, and at the first meeting, which was held at Styles's Hotel on the 15th of August, it was announced that already nearly £4,600 had been received for the defence of the country ; the greatest unanimity prevailed in this movement ; "even those persons who have on former occasions so widely differed from their fellow-townsmen on political subjects, now declared their sentiments to be in full unison with the rest of the meeting, and that they were willing to come forward with their last shilling, and to spend the last drop of their blood in support of this now happy country against the threats of the Corsican Usurper."

Nor did our townsmen remain content with the offer of their money ; their persons and their property were also to be at the King's service. Those were the days of slow travelling, compared with our own ; and, odd as it may sound to modern ears, it was an offer by no means to be despised which Mr. Robert S. Skey made, in engaging "to have at the disposal of Government, in case of invasion, ten boats (together of 200 tons tonnage) at his wharf in this town, and fifteen boats (of 300 tons) at Stourport, with men and horses, and also two waggons and horses,

with drivers." Mr. Styles, of the Hotel, also offered "all his chaises and horses to convey his Majesty's troops, free of expense, to the extent of one stage, at any time in case of invasion." One very droll, yet truly noble, instance of patriotism among the working classes is recorded in the *Gazette ;* that of "Wm. Jones, a jobbing smith of this town," who "fearful that his age (73) would preclude him from serving his country, made his return 53, at the same time offering himself as a volunteer." Another, William Cooke, a bolt-maker of this town, on receiving his bounty to serve as a substitute in the Warwick-shire Militia, sent five guineas of the same to the patriotic fund at Lloyd's. Truly these examples of self-devotion and patriotism make us proud of our townsmen, and glad to be able to say, "I, too, am a Birmingham man!"

The old volunteer movement received a new impetus from this threatened invasion ; three battalions were formed, and both cavalry and infantry were put upon permanent pay. The ladies were appealed to for a supply of flannel jackets, to defend the brave defenders from the severity of a cold and wet winter campaign ; and it need scarcely be said that they responded nobly to the appeal. Before the end of the year more than five thousand dresses were promised, and the ladies had also subscribed more than £700 in money. Field-days and reviews followed in rapid succession ; and a curious code of signals for parade was published in the *Gazette,* as follows :—

LOYAL BIRMINGHAM VOLUNTEERS.

Feb. 20, 1804. The following signals for the parade or assembly of the battalions, are in future to be hoisted on St. Philip's Church :—

First Battalion	A Ball.
Second	A Pendant.
Third	Two Pendants.
First, Second, and Third ...	A Ball over two Pendants.
First and Second ...	A Ball and a Pendant.
First and Third ...	A Ball between two Pendants.
Second and Third ...	Two Pendants over a Ball.

The signals to be continued until the battalions are dismissed, and to be withdrawn if any cause prevent their assembling.

This elaborate code of signals was soon found to be confusing, and a new order was issued :

February 27, 1804. The signals arranged for assembling the Loyal Birmingham Volunteers being considered too complicated, the following are to be made use of in future, and displayed at the top of St. Philip's Church : To call out the

First Battalion   ...   .   A Ball.
Second Battalion   ...   .   A Flag.
Third Battalion   ...   .   A Pendant.

On the 29th August, a large and enthusiastic concourse of the inhabitants,—upwards of 30,000 in number, assembled on Moseley Wake Green to witness the presentation of colours to the first and third battalions of the Loyal Volunteers, (the second battalion having already received its colours from the Countess of Dartmouth ;) "the Committee," says the *Gazette*, "had made the necessary preparations to render the spectacle interesting, while at the same time every precaution was taken to avoid every confusion and accident. . . . Not an accident of the least consequence occurred to mar the brilliancy of the scene, although upwards of 30,000 persons were present from the adjacent country." With this scene we take our leave of the Birmingham Volunteers.

We quote from the *Gazette* of June 18th, 1804, notice of the death of its editor (to whom all historians of the town will be deeply indebted), as a memorial of an old local journalist as well as of an old and honoured Warwickshire family, that of the Rev. Francis Blick, for many years vicar of Tamworth :—

"In the performance of a painful duty, we have to add to the catalogue of mortality this week, the name of Mr. Francis Blick, Editor of this Gazette, and son of the Rev. F. Blick, of Bonehill, near Tamworth : he died on Monday morning last, after a few days' illness. It will not be too much to say of his character, that he was at once a pattern to youth and the delight of his friends. Endowed with a penetrating genius, a mind of uncommon strength, and a judgment remarkably acute, this amiable young gentleman had more than equalled all the warmest expectations of a fond and exulting parent. At the age of twenty-three he seems to have gained, and worthily possessed, every honour that moral conduct could merit, every prize that polished manners, and superior abilities, could contend for. But, alas ! the weakness of his frame

owned no kindred to the energies of his mind. He had accumulated upon it a burthen not proportioned to its powers, and, like ill-sorted travellers, they very early parted. He has been torn from the enjoyments of life at a period when the mellow fruit of study, and the rich prospect of independence, beamed full upon him ; and we are persuaded there is not a single individual in the wide-extended circle of his acquaintance who will not long and sincerely lament his loss. The premature dissolution which we are under the sad necessity of recording, affords a striking memorial of the uncertainty of life—an awful admonition to be at all times prepared for death, and for that great event, when we know that the moral conduct, which we commemorate, sprung from faith in Christ, early implanted and deeply rooted, we may humbly hope our young and valued friend was not unprepared."

In 1805, an important and necessary public building was commenced, the need of which, since the removal of the old Market Cross, had been sorely felt. It is thus noticed in the *Gazette* of September 23rd, 1805 :—

"On Wednesday morning, the first stone of the various offices for the convenience of the Magistrates, the accommodation of the town, and the more tranquil and private conveyance of prisoners, was laid by the High Bailiff, and this necessary and important undertaking was honoured by the presence of the Free Masons in their way to St. Martin's Church. The committee for erecting the edifices, by invitation of the High Bailiff, partook of a sociable entertainment at Mr. Freeth's Tavern, in Bell Street."

The most welcome news to the inhabitants respecting this undertaking was conveyed in a paragraph in the same newspaper of October 28th, in which it was announced "that such prudent arrangements have been made by the Guardians and Overseers of this town, that the expenses incurred in erecting the New Public Office and Prison, in Moor Street, *will be defrayed without the burden of any additional levies being laid upon the inhabitants for that purpose.*"

That part of the new building which comprised the Prison House and Prison was completed within twelve months, possession being taken by the keeper, Mr. Payn, on the 29th of September, 1806. The Public Office was not ready until October, 1807, being opened for the first time for the transaction of public business on the 19th of that month. It was erected from designs by Mr. William Hollins, at an expense of nearly £11,000, upon land held under lease from the

RT. HON. JOHN BRIGHT, M.P.

BIRMINGHAM: HOUGHTON & CO., SCOTLAND PASSAGE.

governors of King Edward's School. It is in the Ionic style of architecture, and consists of a massive rusticated basement, with two wide arched entrances, and a lofty story above; there is a balcony in front, surmounted with a deep entablature, which is supported by five pairs of Ionic columns. "The fine forms of the order,"

by congenial spirits, the conquest was achieved. This fell discord marred the general harmony of opinion. Every man smiled at the great news of victory; but when the price was told the *smile* was followed by a *sigh*." The rejoicings were of a subdued character; no illuminations,—no feastings,—and even the joyous clangour of the bells

OLD HOUSES REMOVED TO MAKE WAY FOR THE PUBLIC OFFICES.

says Mr. Bates, "are disfigured by injudiciously placed ornaments and variations, and the general style may be objected to as little consistent with the purposes of its destination."

The "glorious news" of Nelson's final victory gained, like Samson's of old, with the loss of his own life, was received in Birmingham, as elsewhere, with mingled feelings of joy and grief;— "never," says the *Gazette*, "was the victorious banner so darkened and discoloured as this has been by the death of the glorious and intrepid Chief, through whose skilful arrangements, aided

43

was ever and anon softened into a muffled chime for the hero who was no more.

But the people of Birmingham resolved to honour the memory of "the saviour of the silver-coasted isle," and to commemorate the victory of Trafalgar in a worthier and more enduring manner, as they were debarred by grief from the usual boisterous celebration in which they had hoped to indulge. A meeting was held on the 23rd of November, 1805, "to take into consideration some plan for erecting a Monument, Statue, or Pillar, to the memory of the late gallant hero,

Lord Nelson," whereat it was unanimously resolved that some such memorial should be erected by subscription on or near the site of the Old Cross; but the precise form it should take was left open for future consideration. The subscriptions flowed in rapidly, and then ensued the battle of the monuments. One was for a "Naval Pillar," whatever that may be; another supported the suggestion of a pillar, because "our departed hero, who was composed of materials truly British, might be justly compared to a stately English oak, that has long undauntedly stood the ravages of storms and tempests,"—and the pillar "raising its elevated head," seemed to him to typify the giant of the forest. "Our ingenious townsman," Mr. Hollins, was for combining the pillar (which was to be one hundred feet high), with a useful structure, by utilising the basement as "*a dispensary and post-office*, or for other public business." A third suggestion was that a bronze statue should be erected; while another correspondent supported Mr. Hollins's utilitarian pillar, but suggested that it might also combine all the other features; a niche for the bronze statue, sculptured bas-reliefs of "the most splendid Nelsonic victories," and the combined post office and dispensary. The *Commercial Herald* favoured the idea of the bronze statue, giving as a reason that "there at present exists no situation in Birmingham in which a Pillar can be advantageeusly placed;" and this speedily called forth a rejoinder in the *Gazette*, pointing out the suitable position of the Old Square as a site; and that "whatever may be erected in the centre thereof, will not only be seen from the Grand Avenues of the Town, but at the greatest distance from the place, it being *many feet more* elevated than any spot where such a building can with propriety be erected." The discussion was at length set at rest by a resolution of the subscribers, at a meeting held June 13th, 1806, that a statue should be erected from the model presented by Mr. Westmacott, a committee being appointed "to carry the resolution into effect."

The work was at once proceeded with, and was reported, by the end of 1807, to be "in great forwardness." A meeting of the committee was held early in December, at which Mr. Westmacott was present, and it was resolved "that the most eligible place to erect a statue, when finished, will be the centre of the Market Place, nearly opposite the Dog Inn, subject, however, to the approval of the Commissioners of the Street Acts."

The Jubilee Day of George the Third, was appropriately chosen for the inauguration of the Nelson Statue. The scaffold surrounding was taken down at midnight on the 24th of October, 1809, the people enthusiastically assisting the workmen in removing it. On the following day, amid great rejoicing, the statue was uncovered; and the following description of the work, from the pen of the sculptor, was distributed to the spectators :

In this work, intended to perpetuate the greatest example of naval genius, simplicity has been the chief object in the arrangement. The hero is represented in a reposed and dignified attitude, his left arm reclining on an anchor; he appears in the costume of his native country, invested with the insignia of those honours by which his sovereign and distant princes distinguished him. To the right of the statue the grand symbol of the naval profession is introduced. Victory, the constant attendant upon her favourite hero, embellishes the prow. To the left is disposed a sail, which, being placed behind the statue, gives breadth to that view of the composition. Above the ship is a facsimile of the Flag Staff Truck of L'Orient, which was fished up by Sir Samuel Hood the day following the battle of the Nile, and presented by him to Lord Nelson, the same being deposited at Mitford as a trophy of that ever memorable action. This group is mounted upon a pedestal of statuary marble, a circular form having been selected as best adapted to the situation. To personify that affectionate regard which caused the present patriotic tribute to be raised, the town, Birmingham, is represented in a dejected attitude, murally crowned, mourning her loss ; she being accompanied by groups of genii, or children, in allusion to the rising generation, who offer consolation to her, by producing the trident and the rudder.

In front of the pedestal is the following inscription :—

THIS STATUE
IN HONOUR OF
ADMIRAL
LORD NELSON
WAS ERECTED
BY THE
INHABITANTS OF BIRMINGHAM.
A.D. M.DCCCIX.

The whole is enclosed by iron palisadoes, in the form of boarding pikes, connected by a twisted cable, and at each of the four corners is fixed a cannon erect, from which issues a lamp post, representing a cluster of pikes supporting a ship lantern.

A curious little bequest in connection with this statue ought to be mentioned here ; Mr. Joseph Farror, an auctioneer living in High Street, bequeathed the sum of sixpence per week, to be paid for ever out of the rent of a house in Bradford Street, for cleaning the statue and basement.

For nearly fifty years the Nelson statue remained the only monument of the kind in the town. On the 13th of September, 1842, the German traveller, J. G. Kohl, visited the town, and expressed his surprise at the fact that we had only one statue. After some flippant criticism respecting the armless sleeve, and other details, he says : " This statue, small as it is, is the only one, literally the only statue that Birmingham can boast of ! A city of 200,000 living specimens of humanity, and only one marble man among them ! In Rome and Athens there was probably a statue or a monument for every fifty inhabitants ; but even in cities of more modern date, as Berlin or St. Petersburg, there will scarcely be less than a statue for every 4,000 inhabitants. It may be questioned whether in the whole world another town of equal extent and importance could be found, so destitute of public monuments as Birmingham. Not only Liverpool, Manchester and Glasgow, but even Newcastle, Bristol, and Hull, have more of embellishment to boast of, to say nothing of such magnificient cities as Dublin and Edinburgh. Birmingham and Leeds appear to me, among all the large towns of England, to be the two most destitute of taste, ornament, and enjoyment." We have now ' reformed that indifferently,' and if the traveller could visit the town at the present time (1879) he would find eight men of bronze and marble among us, besides busts, portraits, and other memorials,—not counting the statue of George Dawson, now in progress ; he would, moreover, on closer examination of the Nelson, find that at the period of his visit, we had not even one *marble* man, but only one of *bronze.*

CHAPTER XLIX.

LOCAL TRADE AND COMMERCE—1765-1810.

Banks—Wealth in Birmingham—Hutton on Riches –First Steam Engines—Workers in Iron and Steel—The Gun Trade—Sword Making—Brass Work—Jewellery—" Golden Dustmen "—Glassmaking and other trades—Prices of various articles.

WE have now to take our readers back into the eighteenth century for a while, in order to pick up the threads of our commercial history of the town ; and we cannot do better than go back in this second survey of local enterprise, to the date of the establishment of the first Birmingham Bank, as that marks the beginning of a new era in our commercial life. We will, therefore, trace first the history of the local banks during the period under notice.

" Perhaps," says Hutton, " a public bank is as necessary to the health of the commercial body, as exercise to the natural. The circulation of the blood and spirits are promoted by one, as are cash and bills by the other. Few places are without ; yet Birmingham, famous in the annals of traffic, could boast no such claim To remedy this defect, about every tenth trader was a banker or retailer of cash. At the head of these were marshalled the whole train of drapers and grocers, till the year 1765, when a regular bank was constituted by Messrs. Taylor and Lloyd, two opulent tradesmen, whose credit being equal to that of the Bank of England, quickly collected the shining rays of sterling property into its focus."

Our readers have already met with both the founders of this, the oldest Birmingham Bank, in the course of our narrative, on several occasions. The senior partner of the firm was the celebrated bank, and the translator of Homer and Horace, —is preserved in the Hospital. The bank was opened June 3rd, 1765, as appears from a brief notice in *Aris's Gazette*, of June 10th, in that year.

"Success," continues Hutton, "produced a second bank, by Robert Coales, Esq., a third by

OLD ST. MARTIN'S PARSONAGE.

John Taylor, of whom we gave a short notice in our first chapter of Birmingham worthies; the manufacturer whom Hutton styled "the Shakespear or Newton of his day." Mr. Lloyd, the junior partner, was the grandfather of Charles Lloyd, the poet; he it was whom Johnson visited, accompanied by Hector and Boswell, on the occasion of the Doctor's brief sojourn in the town in 1776. The banking firm of Taylor and Lloyd was the first treasurer to the General Hospital; and a fine bust, by W. Hollins, of Charles Lloyd, sen., the son of the founder of the

Francis Goodall, Esq., and Co., and in 1791, a fourth by Isaac Spooner, Esq., and Co."

The year 1804 saw two additions to the local banks; the first was that of Messrs. Wilkinson, Startin, and Smith, opened on New Year's Day, and the second that of "Messrs. Samuel Galton, Joseph Gibbins, and Samuel Tertius Galton, at the house in which the late Samuel Galton, Esq., resided in this town," opened November 19th.

Hutton gives in one of the early editions of his history an approximate estimate of the wealth

of the town in December, 1783. He says :—
" Perhaps we have

3 who possess upwards of	100,000*l.* each.
7	——— of	50,000*l.*
8	——— of	30,000*l.*
17	——— of	20,000*l.*
80	——— of	10,000*l.*
94	——— of	5,000*l.*"

This gives a total, exclusive of smaller sums in
the hands of tradesmen and petty manufacturers,
of two millions and a half, as the estimated
wealth of the town at that date. Our old
historian, in commenting on this subject, makes
a few remarks which, however irrevelant, are
worth quoting for their truth and humour, as well
as for the picture they contain of the old social
life of the town. "*Riches*," he says, "enables
a man with great facility to shake off an old
friend, once an equal; and forbid access to
inferiors, except a toad-eater. Sometimes they
add to his name the pretty appendage of Right
Honourable, Bart., or Esq., an addition much
coveted, which, should he happen to become an
author, is an easy passport through the gates of
fame. His very features seem to take a turn
from his fortune, and a curious eye may easily
read in his face the word *consequence*. They
change the tone of his voice from the submissive
to the commanding, in which he well knows how
to throw in a few graces. His style is convincing.
Money is of singular efficiency; it clears his
head, refines his sense, points his joke. The
weight of his fortune adds weight to his
argument. If, my dear reader, you have been
a silent spectator at the Shakespeare Tavern ; a
general meeting for public business ; the Low
Bailiff's feast ; at Hobson's, or at Jones's, you
may have observed many a smart thing said
unheeded, by the man without money ; and many
a paltry one, echoed with applause, from the man
with it. The room, in silent attention, hears one,
while the other can scarcely hear himself. They
direct a man to various ways of being carried
with great ease, who is too idle to carry himself :
nay, they invert the order of things, for we

often behold two men, who seem hungry, carry
one who is full fed."

Hutton was himself an honourable example of
one who became rich, not by an accident of
fortune, but by long-continued industry and
prudence. In the third edition of his history he
says of himself, " the dejected Bookseller, [of
Southwell, during his early days,] scarcely one
step higher than a *Walking Stationer*, lived to
acquire a fortune of 20,000*l.*" In the historian's
own *MS.* these figures are altered to £40,000 !

Much of what is interesting in the history of
local manufactures during this period has already
been given, incidentally, in our notices of Boulton
and Watt, John Taylor, Henry Clay, Francis
Eginton, and other Birmingham worthies ; but it
will be useful to recapitulate here some of the
salient features in the wonderful story of local
enterprise during the latter half of the eighteenth
century.

There exists a popular error among those who
know our town but imperfectly,— and an error of
very respectable antiquity,—picturing Birmingham as "grimy with the dense smoke of furnaces,
echoing with the clangour of forges, gleaming
with great fires, and busy in the production of
iron." No picture of the town, certainly, could
ever have been wider of the mark. Scarcely a
bar or a pig has ever been smelted within its
boundaries ; but there was, as we have previously
mentioned, a solitary furnace at Aston, until
towards the end of the eighteenth century, which
had existed for many generations. There the
blast was blown by a water wheel, and one of the
first steam engines in this neighbourhood was
erected to supply its place ; one of Newcomen
and Cawley's curious atmospheric engine, which
attracted great crowds at the time of its erection
and for several years afterwards, who used to
stare and wonder at what was then commonly
known as "the fire machine."

The *first* local "fire engine," however, was that
erected in 1760 on the premises of Mr. Twigg,
(afterwards Muntz's), in Water Street, which was

employed to drive four pairs of rolls, and stones for grinding swords and bayonets. This pioneer of Birmingham steam engines was dismantled in 1804. Shortly after its erection several others were brought into use, and at the close of the century there were seven engines at work in the town,—Mr. Twigg's ; Messrs. Pickard's at the Snow Hill Flour Mill, (our readers have already heard more than enough about both the mill and the engine) ; Messrs. Phipson and Son's, Fazeley Street ; Mr. Cotterell's, Deritend Mill ; the New Steam Mill Company ; the lifting engine at Bordesley ; and the Old Union Mill. But none of these were used in the production of iron ; Aston Furnace itself was blown out shortly before 1795, and from that period the iron-smelting was driven away from the town into the district popularly known as "the Black Country."

Workers in iron there were in abundance as well as those who prepared the iron for the manufacturers' use. Among the latter were Gibson's rolling and slitting mill, in Mill Lane, Digbeth, the old Park Mill at Nechells, Bromford Forge and Park Mill, long under the direction of Mr. Finch, (Dr. Priestley's son-in-law,) and afterwards worked by the Spooner family. Of works in iron there had sprung up quite a host of branches ; grates,—rude and barbarous in ornamentation,—sad-irons and furnace-bars, pots and kettles, saucepans, and cart-wheel boxes, (the latter turned out in great quantities at the Eagle Foundry, in Broad Street) ; in the branches mentioned a good business was also done by Mr. William Francis, of Deritend, the Phœnix Foundry, in Henrietta Street, Mr. Francis at the Moat-house, and Mr. Barnes of Bordesley Street. Fenders and fire-irons began to form a separate trade ; steel works, which, for a hundred years had been represented by Kettle's Steel-houses, which gave their name to Steelhouse Lane, were now to be found in Broad Street, (Attwood's,) Holt Street, (Plimley's) and at Bordesley ; and heavy and light steel toys were sent by the Birmingham manufacturer of eighty years ago to all parts of the

world. The implements of the carpenter, the shoe-maker, the butcher, the glazier, and the gardener,—for the plumber, mason, and farrier, and almost every other workman and labourer under the sun ; the thousand-and-one requirements of every-day life,—bodkins, corkscrews, tweezers, sugar-tongs and nippers, tobacco-stoppers, snuff-box, and many similar articles ; chains and manacles for the slaves of America, tomahawks for the red men of the west, axes for the settlers in the backwoods, bells for the vast herds of cattle in Australia,—all these, as well as buckles for the shoes of the English dandy,—dress-swords, stilettos, chatelaines, keys, seals, watch-chains, bracelets, clasps, brooches—all of steel,—these and many other productions in the then fashionable metal were supplied largely from the work-shops of Birmingham.

The American War in 1775 gave a considerable stimulus to the Birmingham gun trade, bringing in a succession of large orders, and these had scarcely been completed when the French War commenced ; the total supply of arms to the Government from Birmingham during this period has been estimated at not less than half a million. It was the practice of the Government to send down Inspectors from the Tower to ascertain whether the arms were fit for use ; and sometimes the barrels were sent up to London to be proved, or were proved at the private proof-houses of the manufacturers, under the superintendence of the Inspector. This was found to be exceedingly inconvenient, and the Board of Ordnance, about the year 1798, purchased a piece of land and erected a proof-house here, where the barrels were not only proved, but the complete fire-arm was inspected before being accepted by the contractors.

Birmingham also supplied fire-arms to the Irish Ordnance department, for use by the military fencibles and yeomanry, called into existence by the rebellion ; to the various companies of Loyal Volunteers throughout England and Scotland, and to the East India Company, besides those for private use. Altogether, if the generally accepted figures be accurate, the Birmingham gun-makers must have turned out at least three-quarters of a million stand of arms between 1775, and the close of the eighteenth century.

The manufacture of swords, which had been carried on so successfully during the seventeenth century, had gradually declined, so that by the year 1780, or thereabonts, it seemed likely to become an extinct local trade, when it was suddenly revived by a somewhat singular occurrence.   On the 1st of October, 1783, the London sword-sellers solicited Government permission to import sword-blades duty-free from Germany. The peculiar character of the application attracted the attention of the Board of Trade, to whom the petition had been referred, and one of its members,—the Earl of Surrey,—opened a communication with Mr. Eyre, a well-known cutler of Sheffield, in order to ascertain the accuracy of the alleged facts against English sword-blades, but, as the Sheffield manufacturers had never engaged in the fabrication of weapons of warfare, his Lordship was referred to Mr. Gill, of Masshouse Lane, Birmingham.   The outcome of the enquiry was that Mr. Gill prayed the Lords of the Treasury, to institute a comparison between his swords and those of the German manufacturers. Three years, however, elapsed, before the request was granted, and then it was only by an accident. The East India Company gave an order for 10,000 cavalry swords, which was distributed indiscriminately among the English and German makers. Every sword sent in was tested by a machine invented by Mr. Boulton, and the result was as follows :

Mr. Gill sent in 2,650, of which 4 were rejected.
Germany sent in 1,400, of which 28 were rejected.
English makers sent in 3,784, of which 1,084 were rejected.

Thus the blades sent in by the German manufacturers were proportionately defective by thirteen to one as compared with those of Mr. Gill ; and out of every five other English blades

two were bad.   Some of Mr. Gill's blades were so exquisitively tempered that they would cut through a gun-barrel, and so elastic that they would twist like a ribbon, and perfectly recover their original straightness again.   This incident gave Birmingham a high reputation for swords, and, together with the troubles in France during the closing years of the eighteenth century, caused the sword trade to flourish in the town.   Nevertheless there were at the close of the period under notice, only four large sword-making firms among us who made the swords complete ; viz., Mr. John Gill, Masshouse Lane ; Messrs. Wooley and Deakin, Edmund Street ; Messrs. Beadel and Bale, Bank Alley, Dale End ; and Messrs. Osborn and Ganby, Bordesley Park.   All these had large manufactories ; but as there were many operations to be performed in the fabrication of a single sword, there were hundreds of persons employed in the town in the various branches of the trade.

The workers in brass still kept the famous old brass-works of Turner fully employed in supplying the metal for their use.   It was estimated that in 1781 not less than 1,000 tons were used in the Birmingham manufactures ; but the rapid and capricious rise in the price of this metal, from £72 to £84 per ton caused the manufacturers who used it to form themselves into a company, in order to resists the demands of the producers. The name of Brasshouse Passage, in Broad Street, commemorates the spot where the company's works stood, and where, through competition, the price of brass was reduced from £84 to £56 per ton.

Jewellery was a comparatively small trade in those days.   The jewellers themselves were not very numerous, there being not quite a dozen establishments in the town ; although there were a number of "small masters," some of whom were earning for Birmingham that unenviable reputation which has rendered the outer world sceptical as to all jewellery which is turned out of the midland hardware metropolis,—unless it happens to be stamped "London" made. Hence has arisen the old saying, "Give a Birmingham maker a guinea and a copper kettle, and he'll make you a hundred pounds worth of jewellery." It was not all undeserved, the odium which was cast upon "Brummagem" trinkets. We read of one ingenious individual who cut and polished some cinders from the calx of Aston furnace, set them in the rings and brooches, and sold them as fragments of Pompey's Pillar.

The profuse use of gold and silver in various manufactures, in ornamentation, gilding, etc., brought into existence a new and lucrative occupation. Previous to 1758 the sweepings of workshops (containing minute fragments of these precious metals), were thrown into the streets, or carted off as an incumbrance. At length, however, one man found out the secret; and, being known at the various manufactories, ingratiating himself with the workmen, was permitted to carry off the sweepings from the floor, and, by way of recompense, he gave the artisans a sort of Christmas treat. By and by a second "golden dustman" arose, and a competition ensued as to which should give the most sumptuous treat; quarrels occurred occasionally among the workmen as to which of the rivals should be favoured, and this attracted the attention of the employers to the subject. They resolved in future to keep the refuse themselves, and found in it a valuable addition to their profit. Mr. John Taylor and several other large manufacturers realised as much as £1,000 a year from this source alone. Thus began the art of refining, which was for many years practised in Birmingham alone, the manufacturers in other towns sending large quantities of sweepings for analysation every year. But the sweepings of the *earlier* period, to the value of many thousand pounds, lie buried beneath the streets of Birmingham, some of which, as an older writer on this subject has remarked, "may be said to be literally paved with gold and silver"; and it is not impossible, as he says, that Macaulay's New Zealander, who in

time to come is to sketch the ruins of St. Paul's from a broken arch of London Bridge, "may find in the deserted streets of Birmingham, another El Dorado or San Francisco "diggings."

Glass-making was another of the trades introduced into Birmingham during this period. The first bit of Birmingham glass was manufactured by Mr. Hawker, who kept a glass-warehouse in Edgbaston Street, and built a small furnace there about the year 1785. His son afterwards erected some large works on Birmingham Heath, afterwards occupied by Messrs. Lloyd and Summerfield. Mr. Johnson, with Mr. Shakespear, followed, and in 1798, commenced working a furnace in Walmer Lane, (Lancaster Street,) from which they soon afterwards removed to the neighbourhood of Soho, and built extensive works there. Previous to Mr. Hawker's first attempt to manufacture glass in Birmingham, in 1785, the midland counties were supplied from Stourbridge, but before the end of the century, Birmingham glass was competing strongly with that of Stourbridge and other neighbouring towns, and its manufacture was rapidly becoming an important local industry.

Our former notice of the manufacture of buckles, buttons, and in the sketch of Henry Clay—papier-mâché, carried the history of those industries to the end of the present period; we have now, therefore, glanced briefly at the commercial and industrial history, of the period, and need only refer for a few moments, to the history of prices during that time.

First then as to the prices of one of the principal materials used in manufactures.

The following table shows the price of English iron in pigs, from 1782 to 1800.

1782	From £6 to £7 10s. per ton.
1783	— 4 to 7 10s. ,,
1784 to 1786 ...	— 3 to 6 10s. ,,
1787	— 3 to 6 ,,
1787 to 1789 ...	— 3 to 7 ,,
1790	— 3 to 7 10s. ,,
1791 to 1793 ...	— 5 to 7 10s. ,,
1794 to 1800 ...	— 5 to 8 ,,

The produce of the coal-mines of South Staffordshire advanced in a corresponding degree. Plot, the historian, writing nearly a century earlier, mentions twelve or fourteen collieries in the district, each of them yielding from 2,000 to 5,000 tons annually,—in all, about 45,000 tons per annum. In 1798, the yield of the South Staffordshire coal-field was about 16,200 tons a week,

	1750.				1800.			
	s. d.		s. d.		s. d.		s. d.	
A cottage and garden, from - - -	20 0	to	30 0	...	30 0	to	50 0	
Wheat, per bushel, Winchester, from	3 0	,,	4 0	...	18 0	,,	23 0	
Barley, per bushel ,,	1 4	,,	2 3	...	3 6	,,	16 0	
Oats ,, ,,	0 9	,,	1 6	...	1 8	,,	6 6	
Salt, per cwt. - ,,	6 9	,,	7 6	...	14 0	,,	26 0	
Malt, per bushel ,,	2 0	,,	3 0	...	5 0	,,	14 0	

OLD VIEW OF TEMPLE ROW WEST, FROM COLMORE ROW.

or a total for the year of 842,400 tons; so that the old annual supply would not have been equal to the demand for three weeks at the end of the eighteenth century.

More interesting, to many of our readers, will be the old prices of articles of every-day use and consumption.

Taking first the common necessaries of life, we quote, from an old volume of the *Gentleman's Magazine*, (1802,) a statement showing the prices of 1800 as compared with those of 1750:

	s. d.		s. d.		s. d.		s. d.	
Common Sugar, per lb., - from	0 3	,,	0 4	...	0 9	,,	1 0	
Soap, per lb. ,,	0 4	,,	0 4½	...	0 8	,,	0 10	
Beef ,, best pieces from	0 2	,,	0 2½	..	0 4½	,,	1 0	
Pork, per lb. ,,	0 2	,,	0 2½	..	0 4½	,,	1 0	
Bacon ,, ,,	0 4	,,	0 4½	...	0 8	,,	1 2	
Mutton ,. ,,	0 2	,,	0 2½	...	0 3½	,,	0 9	
Skimmed Milk, per gallon - from	0 1½	,,	0 2	...	0 3	,,	0	
Pair of Stout Shoes (Men's) - from	3 4	,,	4 0	...	6 10	,,	7 6	
Cheese, per lb. ,,	0 2	,,	0 3½	...	0 4	,,	0 7	
Butter ,, ,,	0 3	,,	0 4½	...	0 8	,,	1 3	

44

	1750.		1800.	
	s. d.	s. d.	s. d.	s. d.
Stuff for gowns, per yard - from	0 8	,, 0 10	... 1 2	,, 1 6
Men's common cloth, per yard - from	2 6	,, 3 6	... 3 6	,, 4 0

It will thus be seen that while war increased the local trade, it increased considerably the prices of the necessary articles of daily life, although some of these seem cheap even at the advanced prices to us of the present day; a few, however, were actually very much higher in price than they now are. The reader will not fail to notice the absence from the above list, compiled by a contemporary writer, of many articles which are nowadays classed among the necessaries of life. Sugar, it is true, we find in the list, but at prices which must have rendered it more of a luxury than a necessary; but tea, coffee, and cocoa find no place among the cottager's necessaries seventy or eighty years ago. How many other comforts, such as are now enjoyed by the humblest, are un-named in this list : hundreds of little luxuries which go to make up ordinary comforts now, were altogether unknown then.

Travelling was, of course, more expensive, as well as less speedy, in those days of stage-coaches, and, in consequence, very few indeed among the artisan and labouring classes took longer journeys than from one neighbouring town to another. Not many Birmingham men of these classes had seen London, or knew what seas and mountains were like, except from the travelling panoramas or other pictorial representations. The fare to London, on the outside of the coach, in 1800, was sixteen shillings, and thirty shillings inside. A guinea was charged for an inside fare to Liverpool, Manchester, or Sheffield, and twelve or thirteen shillings outside. The outside fare to Bath was nine shillings; the outside journey to Wolverhampton even, cost the traveller eighteenpence. These fares do not perhaps seem extravagant as compared with the cost of railway travelling, but think of the inconvenience and discomfort suffered by the economist in a journey on the outside of a coach, in bitter wintry weather! Contrast the journey to London under such circumstances with that now performed by a third-class passenger by rail for little more than half the money.

In our next chapter on this subject we shall have to deal with new industries and more extended commercial transactions, with enterprises of a magnitude undreamed of in the days of which we have been writing. For the present, however, we take our leave of the commercial and financial history of our town.

CHAPTER L.

MORE ABOUT TRAVELLING.

Number of Birmingham Coaches, 1770 and 1820—Speed—The first Royal Mail—Appearance of the English Coaches—Pleasures of the Road—George Eliot's description—The shady side—Thomas De Quincey at the *Hen and Chickens*—Gladstone in Birmingham—Dangers of the Road—Local Conveyances.

THE consideration of the cost of travelling, in connection with the subject of prices generally, at the close of the last chapter, brings us again to the history of the stage coach and other modes of travelling at the period to which we have brought the narrative of local Birmingham events in general.

We have not now to do with the old stage waggon or the loitering packhorse, but with the mail coaches running at the rate of ten miles an hour, making the journey to London in a single day,—the mails, starting almost every hour, with their prancing horses, bright harness, gay guards, armed with pistol and blunderbuss, and furnished with "the twanging horn"—at their rattling speed. A few pictures of the old mode of travelling—so soon to be supplanted by the "iron horse", —will help to complete the picture of Birmingham life during the first quarter of the nineteenth century.

Our former chapter of the history of travelling brought us to the time of the introduction of the " Flying Coaches," which performed the journey from Birmingham to London in two days and a half; we mentioned later, in the chronicle of local events, the introduction of Mr. Palmer's Mail-Coach reform, and the consequent improvement in the speed; but by the end of the eighteenth century many other improvements were effected, in the convenience of the vehicles themselves, the great increase in number, the opening of new routes, and the still further increased speed at which they travelled. In the year 1770 or thereabouts, there were probably not more than half-a-dozen coaches running from Birmingham; in 1820, it was estimated in an article in the *Scots Magazine*, that there were no less than eighty-four coaches belonging to Birmingham, of which forty were daily. At the same time Manchester had but seventy, and Liverpool only sixty. Meanwhile, the improved method of road-making introduced about this time by Mr. Macadam, once more effected an appreciable increase in the speed, so that the older eight-miles-an-hour travelling advanced to upwards of ten miles; between Birmingham, Liverpool, and Manchester, it was found practicable to maintain a rate of ten miles and one furlong, and between this town and Sheffield, Pontefract and Leeds, London and Bath, and on other roads, ten miles an hour was maintained. This was perhaps the highest average speed ever maintained " on the road."

The first Royal Mail from Birmingham to London was established on the 26th of May, 1812. The event was celebrated with some degree of ceremony and rejoicing, as appears from a report in the *Gazette*, of June 1st, in that year. At two o'clock in the day, " the coach, attended by eight mail-guards, in full uniform, adorned with blue ribbons, paraded the streets, under the direction of Mr. Hart, stopped at the residences of the High and Low Bailiffs, the several banks, and many of the principal inhabitants; the procession closed after it had remained some time at the house of Mr. Pratchett, High Street, where, as at other resting places, the attendants were liberally supplied with wine, biscuits, sandwiches, etc. The coach set out from the Swan Hotel, at four o'clock in the afternoon; the bells of St. Martin's Church ringing, and thousands of spectators, assembled on this occasion, greeting it as it passed with cheering shouts."

With respect to the appearance of the English coaches of the later period, we may quote the description given by Baron d'Haussez, in his *Great Britain in 1833*. " The appointments of an English coach," he says, " are no less elegant than its form. A portly good-looking coachman, seated on a very high coach-box, well-dressed, wearing white gloves, a nosegay in his button-hole, and his chin enveloped in an enormous cravat, drives four horses perfectly matched and harnessed, and as carefully groomed as when they excited admiration in the carriages of Grosvenor and Berkeley Squares. Such is the manner in which English horses are managed, such also is their docility, the effect either of temperament or training, that you do not remark the least restiveness in them. Four-horse coaches are to be seen rapidly traversing the most populous streets of London, without occasioning the least accident, without being at all inconvenienced in the midst of the numerous carriages, which hardly leave the necessary space to pass. The swearing of ostlers is never heard at the relays, any more than the neighing of horses; nor are you interrupted on the road by the voice of the coachman, or the sound of his whip, which differs only from a cabriolet whip in the length of the thong, and serves more as a sort of appendage than a means of correction in the hand which carries it."

The pleasures of the road, the delight of rattling along country roads, through old-fashioned villages and towns, through the most charming English scenery; the feeling of importance induced by the excitement created as the "Highflyer," the "Rockingham," or the "Daylight," passed through the country town or village, the various passengers, the coachman and guard, with bar-maids, and the repartees of jocose ostlers; the mail still announced itself by the merry notes of the horn; the hedge-cutter or the rick-thatcher might still know the exact hour by the unfailing yet otherwise meteoric apparition of the pea-green 'Tally-ho' or the yellow 'Independent'; and elderly gentlemen in pony-chaises, quartering nervously to make way for the rolling, swinging swiftness,

ST. PHILIP'S CHURCH.
[From an old view engraved about 1820.

their droll stories and daily repeated jokes—the sunny side, in fact of the journey by coach,—have not these things been described and reported over and over again? We cannot resist the temptation, however, to quote the charming description given by George Eliot in *Felix Holt*: "Five and thirty years ago," she says, writing in 1866, "the glory had not yet departed from the old coach roads: the great roadside inns were still brilliant with well-polished tankards, the smiling glances of pretty had not ceased to remark that times were finely changed since they used to see the pack-horses and hear the tinkling of their bells on this very highway. . . . . The elderly man has his enviable memories, and not the least of them is the memory of a long journey in mid-spring or autumn on the outside of a stage-coach. Posterity may be shot, like a bullet through a tube, by atmospheric pressure, from Winchester to Newcastle: that is a fine result to have among our hopes; but the slow, old-fashioned way of getting from one end of our country to the other is the better thing to have in the memory. The tube-journey can never lend much to picture and narrative; it is as barren as an exclamatory O! Whereas the happy outside passenger seated on the box from the dawn to the gloaming gathered enough stories of English life, enough of English labours in town and country, enough aspects of earth and sky, to make espisodes for a modern Odyssey."

But there was a "shady side" to this picture also. It was not always bright sunshine or clear frosty air; there were deep snows and perilous fogs to be encountered, and driving sleet and drenching rain, to be endured by the outsiders with what patience they could muster. Then there were not unfrequently,—especially in Birmingham, the half-way house of England,—necessary changes at uncomfortable times of the night, and often in the worst of weather. Such was often the experience of Thomas De Quincey, the "English Opium Eater," and one of the most brilliant essayists of the Victorian era, who was several times a guest at the *Hen and Chickens*, in "gloomy, noisy, and at that time dirty Birmingham,"—as he terms it. Speaking of his visits to this town, he says: "There are, I can well believe, thousands to whom Birmingham is another name for domestic peace, and for a reasonable share in sunshine. But in my case, who have passed through Birmingham a hundred times, it always happened to rain, except once; and that once the Shrewsbury mail carried me so rapidly away that I had not time to examine the sunshine, or see whether it might not be some gilt Birmingham counterfeit; for you know, men of Birmingham, that you *can* counterfeit—such is your cleverness—all things in Heaven and earth, from Jove's thunderbolts down to a tailor's bodkin. Therefore the gloom is to be charged to my bad luck. Then as to the noise, never did I sleep at that enormous *Hen and Chickens* to which usually my destiny brought me, but I had reason to complain that the discreet hen did not gather her vagrant flock to roost at less variable hours. Till

two or three I was kept waking by those who were retiring, and about three commenced the morning functions of the Porter or 'Boots,' or of 'Underboots,' who began their rounds by collecting the several freights for the 'High-flyer,' or the 'Tally-ho,' or the 'Bang-up,' to all points of the compass, and too often (as must happen in such immense establishments) thundered into *my* room with that appalling, 'Now, sir, the horses are coming out.' So that rarely indeed have I happened to *sleep* in Birmingham."

The Right Hon. W. E. Gladstone, M.P., describes, in a letter to the publishers of this volume, his experiences of a similar character on several occasions during his journeys by coach through Birmingham. He says: "My recollections of the casual hours in Birmingham, are much less pleasant than those of my visit last year.* The coach inns were bad. The times of stopping chosen with reference to anything rather than the comfort of the passengers. I have repeatedly been turned out of the Liverpool coach, the 'Aurora,' I think, at four o'clock on a winter's morning, sometimes in frost or snow, and offered breakfast, for which this was the only time allowed; while the luggage was charged upon a barrow. Behind this barrow we mournfully trudged along the streets to the other hotel; Castle or Albion, or Hen and Chickens, from which the sister coach was to start for the south. Such was in those days the measure of comfort deemed necessary for travellers. And we must bear in mind that it was a great advance, in point of regularity and dispatch, upon what had been before, though the average rate of coaches during my boyhood did not quite touch seven miles an hour."

These were not, however, the only miseries of the journey by stage-coach. There were, even in the last decade of the coaching days, not unfrequently the most daring robberies committed; and not merely on the open country roads, but even within the boundaries of the town, as the following extract from a Birmingham newspaper of the period will show :—

1877.

December 12, 1822.—Notes to the amount of between £7,000 and £8,000 in two parcels, directed to Taylor and Lloyd's, and Gibbons, Smith, and Company, of Birmingham, were stolen from the box of the Balloon coach just before setting out from the Swan-with-two-necks, Lad Lane.

A similar robbery is recorded two months later :—

February 17, 1823.—A parcel containing 600 sovs., directed to Messrs. Attwood and Spooner, was last week stolen from one of the London coaches, on its way to Birmingham.

There is little to add here respecting the Birmingham inns ; we have recorded, in an earlier chapter, the establishment of the *Hen and Chickens* Hotel in New Street, and have already given two engravings of the building. The only other house of importance not mentioned in our former chapter on the stage-coach is "the Hotel," in Temple Row, to which reference has been made several times in subsequent chapters.

We may, therefore, close this brief chapter with a few notes on the local conveyances *within* the town,—the hackney coaches. These useful vehicles did not find their way into Birmingham until a hundred years after their introduction into the metropolis,—and then only in the singular number, for there was but one in the town in 1775. But by the year 1819 they had increased to thirty ; and at the same period one-horse cars were first introduced, and an attempt was made to popularise the cab, or "two-wheeled car," as it was then called ; "but," we are told, "being very unsafe, they were speedily abandoned." Eleven years later, however, there were about sixty of them, and the old two-horse coaches, having declined in favour, were falling into disuse.

There were as yet many hindrances in the way of traffic of this kind within the boundaries of the town ; there were toll-gates at every outlet towards the country ; the streets were ill-made, and beset with dangers, in the numerous holes and ruts and rubbish heaps, and with numerous obstructions from the old-established out-door markets for pigs, cattle, and agricultural produce ; and there was scarcely any attempt made to observe the rule of the road, so that in 1806 the

Commissioners gave notice to drivers that they should not, by negligence or otherwise, "do any hurt to any person or carriage passing them, or at all prevent the free passage of his Majesty's subjects." They added also "that carts were to give place to coaches ; " and laid down the rule of the road as well to carriages as to pedestrians, (incorrectly, however, as regards the latter,) by quoting the old rhyme :

> " The rule of the road is a paradox quite
> As you drive, ride, or walk it along,
> If you go to the *left* you are sure to go right,
> But if you go *right* you are *wrong*."*

They concluded this notice by proclaiming that " no person was to ride or lead a horse, or wheel a barrow, on the footpaths ; " a drunken driver was to be fined five shillings, and for profane swearing, one, two, or five shillings. The commissioners, however, omitted to make provision as yet for one of the worst dangers of the streets, (arising from the want of an efficient patrol,) that to which we referred in our recent notice of crime in Birmingham, and which is further illustrated in the following paragraphs from the local papers :

February 17, 1800.—On Saturday evening the trunk of the Hon. Captain Macdonald, who was travelling through the town, was cut off by some villains from behind his carriage and carried off. It was lost between Hockley and Birmingham.

December 5, 1805.—On Thursday evening a trunk was cut from off Lord Derby's carriage, at Hockley Hill, near this town ; and on Saturday evening a trunk was stolen from before the front of the carriage of Lord Cathcart, in Deritend.

With these notices we take our leave for the present of "the road," its dangers and its pleasures. When next we take up the story it will be to record the early triumphs of steam locomotion ; we shall view the town under a better aspect, with a better system of local government, improved throughfares, and largely increased facilities for travelling, not only *from* it to other parts of the kingdom, but also through the streets within its boundaries.

---

* The rule of the road as to pedestrians has been epitomized in a like paradoxical couplet :
> " Pass *left* to *left* the passing throng,
> For *right* to *right* is *doubly wrong*."

CHAPTER LI.

THE FIRST CAMPAIGN IN THE STRUGGLE FOR FREEDOM—1811-1820.

East India Company's Charter—The Orders in Council—Success of the Birmingham Opposition—Testimonials to Messrs. Brougham and Attwood—Formation of the Hampden Club—George Edmonds—Disturbance at Mr. Jabet's Shop, Moor Street—Interposition of the Magistrates—The first meeting on Newhall Hill, 1817—The Petitions—The Prince Regent insulted—The Birmingham Loyal Requisition—The Locked-up Meeting—The Newhall Hill Meeting of 1819—The Massacre of Peterloo—Prosecution of the Birmingham Radicals—Loyal Demonstrations, etc.

WE now enter upon the first campaign in that great battle for political liberty which was fought in Birmingham during the second, third, and fourth decades of the nineteenth century, and has caused Birmingham ever since to be the great centre of English Radicalism. We have chosen to separate the story of this struggle from the ordinary chronicle of local events, inasmuch as it forms the central feature in the history of our town.

The united political action of the people of Birmingham may be said to have commenced in 1812, and originated in the perils of their trade, threatened, in the first instance, by the renewal of the East India Company's charter, and second by the promulgation of the Orders in Council, retorting upon Napoleon the Berlin decrees, which crippled the commerce of the country. Twice the people of Birmingham protested, in town's meetings, against this commercial policy of the Government, and forwarded petitions and appointed deputations to represent their case to the Secretary of State; upwards of sixteen thousand persons signing the petition against "John Company's" monopoly. Among those who addressed the town's meetings on these occasions were two young men whose names were destined, in the oncoming time, to be engraven in the history of their town. In these meetings they made their first appearance as public speakers, and immediately commanded a high position amongst their fellow-townsmen. Thomas Attwood and Richard Spooner were at once chosen as the most suitable men to represent to the Government the position in which the manufac-

turing industry of the town and neighbourhood was placed by the Orders in Council; and they amply justified their townsmen's choice. So forcibly did they plead, and so energetically were they supported by Mr. (afterwards Lord) Brougham and others in the House of Commons, that the Orders were speedily revoked. The deputation returned on Wednesday, July 1st, 1812, and made such a triumphant entry into the town as they little expected. The day was wet and stormy, but there were nevertheless many thousands of the inhabitants gathered together on the outskirts of the town to meet Messrs. Attwood and Spooner, and as soon as the carriage came in sight, the men went forward, and having removed the horses, harnessed themselves to the vehicle, and drew their successful fellow-townsmen through the muddy streets to the Shakespeare Tavern in New Street, amid the cheering of the assembled multitude, and the strains "of the joint bands of the two regiments of Warwickshire Militia." On the 7th of the same month a public meeting of the inhabitants was held, at which it was resolved to present a service of plate to Mr. Brougham, as a recognition of the ability and eloquence which he had manifested on their behalf. This handsome present was manufactured at Soho, and consisted of five pieces, of the finest workmanship, bearing the following inscription :

"To Henry Brougham, Esquire, the enlightened Advocate of the manufacturing and commercial interests of his country, this Memorial of Gratitude was unanimously voted at a Public Meeting of the Inhabitants of Birmingham, 7th July, 1812."

Another meeting of the inhabitants was held during the same month, at which it was resolved to present to Mr. Attwood a silver cup weighing 128 ounces, the cost of the same being subscribed in sixpences.

Messrs. Attwood and Spooner, having been successful in obtaining the revocation of the Orders in Council, were not disposed to retire on their laurels, but determined now to take up the other vexed question, that of the Charter of the East India Company. So energetically did they throw themselves into this movement, and so well were they seconded by their townsmen, that they were successful in breaking into the Company's monopoly in three quarters of the globe. Previous to this movement, strange as it may sound in the ears of the present generation, no Englishman was allowed to double the Cape of Good Hope or Cape Horn without the license of the East India Company ; nor was he allowed to navigate any of the seas comprehended between those limits,—including the whole of the Pacific Ocean,—without a similar license. Thus the numerous islands of the Pacific, the western shores of the American continent (from Behring's Straits to Cape Horn), the eastern coast of Africa, Asia, and the new continent of Australia, were practically monopolised by that great Corporation. It is to the opposition originated by our two worthy townsmen that Englishmen to-day enjoy the privilege of navigating the whole world of waters free of any toll or impost whatever.

These proceedings in defence of their industrial liberties by the people of Birmingham, led to the formation of the first political organisation in the town. Certain of the artisan members of the committee appointed to carry out the proposals respecting the testimonial to Mr. Attwood, resolved themselves into a society, called the Hampden Club, with Mr. George Edmonds at their head. They determined to struggle for Parliamentary Reform ; in order to petition for it, effectually and systematically, they formed themselves into an organised body, and formulated

a simple test of membership, in the following series of questions, submitted to each candidate : 1. "Do you highly venerate the constitution of England, as vested in the three estates of King, Lords, and Commons ?"—2. "Do you acknowledge the necessity of Parliamentary Reform ?"— 3. "Are you fully convinced of the obligation to prosecute this great object by legal and constitutional means alone ?" The fact that the society required an answer in the affirmative to each of these questions before accepting any candidate for membership, may be taken as an indication of the constitutional methods they proposed to adopt to carry out their object. Their president, George Edmonds, was the son of the pastor of the Bond Street Baptist Chapel in this town, and kept a school near his father's chapel ; at the time of the formation of this society he would be about twenty-six years of age, being born in 1788.

The Hampden Club was compelled, during its infancy, to meet in public houses, as no other room could be found. They met first at the Saracen's Head, Snow Hill ; then at the Nag's Head, Navigation Street ; and afterwards at the Roebuck in Cox Street. By and by, however, they obtained the use of a private house in Church Street, and subsequently in Peck Lane. They do not appear to have remained in one place for any length of time, being hunted from place to place, watched with suspicion by the magistrates and others in authority, looked upon as seditious and dangerous,—so that no host felt safe in harbouring them long. Perhaps they had good cause, in one sense, to fear this little society of workmen, banded together to agitate against their oppressed condition ;—perhaps conscience whispered to the "respectable classes," that if these toiling, suffering artisans, in a time of dear food and cheap labour, and of oppressive taxation upon the necessaries of life, did not become desperate and violent, ready to break out in open rebellion, they would exhibit more than human patience and submission. But the Hampden Club remained loyal to its own Constitution, and conducted its opposition to the Corn Laws on | than twenty-four hours, 48,600 persons, almost the

STATUE OF THOMAS ATTWOOD,
Stephenson Place, New Street.

strictly Constitutional principles.　A petition was drawn up, and on the 8th of March, 1815, in less whole of the adult population of Birmingham signed their names to the protest against the Corn Bill.

45

The distress, however, continued, and in 1816 the people were growing more and more disaffected towards the persons in authority. Soup was distributed, and large sums were subscribed for the relief of the poor; but with the relief was also administered advice, couched in language which, however well meant, was calculated to arouse and irritate, rather than conciliate, the disaffected classes. On the 28th of October, 1816, Mr. Jabet, the printer of the *Commercial Herald*, and of the first guide to Birmingham, exhibited in his window in Moor Street, a "patriotic address" to the working classes, recommending patience during the depression of trade, etc., which, by a misunderstanding, created an impression among the people that the printer had stated that "nine shillings a week were sufficient for the support of a man, his wife, and six children." A great crowd collected, in consequence, around the window containing the obnoxious address; and Mr. Jabet's premises were in imminent danger of destruction. The crowd smashed the windows, and, as usual, soon became an ungovernable mob. Mr. Hamper, who was at that time one of the magistrates, immediately called out the 15th Light Dragoons to aid him in quelling what threatened to become a serious riot; and soon the crowd was dispersed. The next morning the crowd again assembled, but was prevented from further mischief by the presence of the Dragoons, Yeomanry, and special constables; the Riot Act, however, was read, and immediately afterwards the following bill was posted on the walls throughout the town :

RIOT ACT.
The Riot Act has been read !
Military Aid has been called in !
The public peace must be preserved !
Beware !

Proud of their triumph over "the dangerous classes," as they loved to call the people, the Magistrates issued a proclamation, the like of which had not been seen, perhaps, since those of July, 1791 :

" WE, the Magistrates acting for the Town and Neigh-

bourhood of Birmingham, were much concerned to find that on Monday Evening some of the Inhabitants, misled by seditious and ill-disposed Persons, and especially by some recent Publications, mischievously circulated, showed an Inclination to Riot and Disturbance, and proceeded to Acts of Violence on the Shop and House of Mr. JABET, a very loyal and respectable Printer, who, with the most laudable Views, had published a Letter written by a Gentleman in Lancashire, the sole Tendency of which was to preserve Peace and Order in the Kingdom. We indeed had hoped that we should have to boast of the peaceable and orderly Conduct of all the Inhabitants of this Town ; and having by prompt Exertions quelled the Disturbances, still flatter ourselves that we shall not have again to lament similar Outrages. We are however determined on all occasions to put the law strictly in force against every Disturber of the Public Peace, and intend to have a large body of Special Constables (composed of the principal Inhabitants, who have declared their Readiness to act,) always at Hand to assist us ; neither will we neglect the Aid of the Military, who, under the control of the Civil Power, are strictly legal Preservers of the Peace.

" W. HICKS.   " B. SPENCER.
" W. VILLERS.   " THEO. PRICE.
" WM. BEDFORD.   " W. WITHERING."
" WM. HAMPER.

Major Cartwright replied to this manifesto, showing, in an able and vigorous manner, that according to the constitution, the military are *not* legal preservers of the peace. The reply was, however, disregarded, and a troop of 2,000 soldiers were encamped at Sutton Coldfield, and remained there several months, ready to act in case of sudden emergency.

From this time the members of the political clubs were marked men, throughout the country. Spies were sent by the " persons in authority " to attend meetings of the various Hampden Clubs, and to " report thereon ;" the Press, the magistracy, employers of labour, and the respectable classes generally, set themselves against the new movement on the part of the working classes to assert their independence. Places of public resort were closed against them; they could not meet in public " without the sanction of the High Bailiff;" and, as that functionary was antagonistic to the political clubs, it was impossible, according to all precedent, for them to meet at all. They were, however, determined, for the first time in the annals of the town, to create a precedent for holding public meetings without the sanction of the High Bailiff.

"The importance of this step,"—says an historian of the Political Unions,—"trifling as in the year 1850 it may seem, was vast. It overturned in a day all the traditions, customs, and experience of five hundred years. It was opposed to all pre-conceived notions, and settled ideas of the 'respectable' classes, and completely upset all former experiences. That alone was no slight thing. It set the people thinking about matters that heretofore had not been questioned, and suspicion followed upon many points which before they had not dreamed of doubting. That was a great point gained."

Before setting aside the authority of the High Bailiff, however, they endeavoured to proceed in the customary manner, by a requisition to that functionary, to call an early meeting under his sanction. This was refused, and they then decided to dispense with him. The next question was, where should they meet? Applications were made to owners of the largest rooms in the town, but in vain. In every quarter they met with denials, reproaches, and insults; nobody would harbour the men who seemed determined to turn the world upside down. There was but one resource left to them,—that of meeting in the open air; and so, out of these adverse circumstances, arose *the first open-air political demonstration*. A copy of the requisition to the High Bailiff was prefixed to the announcement of the meeting, which was as follows:

To the High Bailiff of Birmingham.

January 20, 1817.—Sir, — We, the undersigned inhabitants of Birmingham, conceiving it to be the indispensable duty of this town to declare to the Legislature the unexampled distress in which the people are involved, and to petition that every practicable Retrenchment in the National Expenditure may be made, as a mode of present alleviation, and that a Reform in the House of Commons be instituted without further delay, for restoring the Constitution to its pristine purity, as the best security against similar calamities in future, do request you to call an early meeting of the inhabitants, to take this subject into consideration.

[To which were affixed 63 respectable signatures.]

The High Bailiff having refused to comply with the above requisition, we, the undersigned inhabitants of Birmingham, do invite our fellow townsmen to meet on Wednesday next, January 22, 1817, on the open ground to the left of St. Paul's Square, called Newhall Hill, to take into consideration the important objects of the requisition.

The chair will be taken at twelve o'clock.

Joseph Jones,	George East,	S. Lawrence,
Joseph Wareham,	John Bogle, Jun.,	Joseph Luckcock,
E. Thompson,	Edmond Castle,	James Evans,
W. Hawkes Smith,	John Fellows,	Thomas Harrison,
W. N. Whitehouse,	Philip Barrington,	Chas. Maddocks,
J. S. Retchley,	A. Simond,	Thos. Clarke,
John Hincks,	Thomas Wright,	George Barrs,
William Jennings,	George Cox,	W. Moore,
Thomas Amphlett,	Jospeh Benson,	G. Edmonds,
Ralph Heaton, Jun.,	P. Osborne,	George Ragg,
Edwin Hill,	Thomas Cox,	C. Whitworth,
James Bellis,	John Burton,	W. Bullock,
Isaac Smith,	Samuel Eve,	Samuel Burrell,
James Luckcock,	William Probin,	Samuel Bradley,
J. A. Wilkes,	James Harcourt,	S. Wainright,
Joseph Willmore,	W. H. Wignall,	R. Lovatt,

and a great number of other respectable signatures.

As will be seen from the above announcement, the Reformers fixed upon Newhall Hill as their meeting-ground, and therein consecrated it to the great struggle for freedom, as the arena of free debate, a spot which was destined during the fifteen years' war of right against might, to be the scene of some of the most noteworthy events in the history of the nineteenth century.

The meeting was held on the day appointed, and set at naught the sneers of those who described the new movement as the disaffection of a mere handful of pothouse politicians; for there were gathered together on Newhall Hill not less than twenty-five thousand persons. Such a town's meeting had never been heard of before. Accustomed to the old-fashioned meetings of "the respectable inhabitants" in "the chamber over the Cross," they had come to regard the larger gatherings at the new Public Offices in Moor Street in the light of really representative town's meetings; but *this* gathering of from twenty-five to thirty thousand people, as it was variously computed, was far beyond anything they had imagined. Mr. George Edmonds presided, and, quoting the words of Thomas

Attwood, depicted the depressed condition of the people, the poverty of the working classes,—"driven into the workhouse or the grave,"—the stagnation of commerce,—the landlord receiving no rents, and the farmer no profits; the merchant exhausting his capital and industry in vain, and

tivity by night; the excellence of whose works have dazzled and delighted all the nations of the earth. Alas, sir, what is she now? Behold her once valuable artisans hungry and in rags, raking up the filth of her streets, with many of those men who have covered themselves with glory in

GEORGE EDMONDS.

the manufacturer beholding "his hard-earned accumulations gradually passing away."

Following in the same despondent strain, the next speaker (Mr. Moore) described the condition of the Birmingham artisans. "Look around you, sir," he said, "in this once happy Birmingham! this seat of arts and arms; this mine of men and steel, the soldier and the sword; in whose streets the busy hum of prosperous industry was heard by day, and the voice of joy and fes-

the strife of Kings, even with the badge and acknowledgment of their prowess on their breasts; they have fought, they have conquered, and wretchedness and misery is their reward!"

The burden of the same story was taken up by all the speakers in turn; the poverty of the people and the depression of trade. They did not, however, overlook the causes of this distress; they protested against the French War and its object,—that of "restoring the age of political and religious darkness;" they asserted their claim to parliamentary representation, and protested against the corruption of the House of Commons; against the buying and selling of seats, like "stalls in the market," by which "the ruinous schemes of an infatuated Ministry have been submitted to by a generous but misguided people;" against the Corn Bill, "the avowed object of which was to protect the interests of a tenth part of the community, and which by its effects has consigned the remaining nine-tenths to the depths of wretchedness and despair, by prohibiting the importation of food, and consequently preventing the manufacture of those goods which might have been given in exchange;" against sinecures, and public extravagance;—and in favour of reciprocity (the "thin end of the wedge," and perhaps the utmost they then dreamed of, in the direction of free trade,) and of "such a reform in the Commons House of Parliament as will restore frequent elections and general suffrage."

A petition was drawn up embodying the various points above mentioned; and, in conclusion, the following resolution was proposed and carried:

That this meeting shall be adjourned till March 25, 1817; and that it is earnestly recommended to all petitioning bodies throughout the United Kingdom to hold public meetings at the same time and on each succeeding quarter-day, till the grand object of Parliamentary Reform be obtained.

Twenty-one thousand names were appended to the Birmingham petition in a few weeks; and throughout the whole movement there was not the least disposition to riot observable, although the constables and a special detachment of military were in readiness to act in case of disturbance, the 5th Dragoons being quartered in the centre of the town.

The *Gazette* would have taken no notice whatever of the meeting, but that the proceedings had been so generally made public "through the medium of the neighbouring and London prints," that it became "almost necessary to allude to them." As in similar gatherings of later years, that journal treated the whole affair in the most

disparaging manner,—estimating the number present at little more than 10,000, "among whom were a great proportion of women and children;" and denying the statement "that troops were brought from the barracks and quartered in the centre of the town," as "no such measure was considered necessary."

"The speakers," says the *Gazette*, "consisting almost wholly of the members and supporters of the Hampden Club formed in this town, were elevated upon scaffolding at the bottom of the hill near the Parade, from whence they addressed the crowd. *A Mr. Edmonds*, chairman of the Club was the principal speaker, and his address embraced the various topics usually discussed at similar meetings. The Petition was ordered to be presented to the House of Commons by Peter Moore and Joseph Butterworth, Esqs., members for Coventry. At the conclusion of the meeting the populace quietly dispersed to their homes."

The Birmingham meeting was followed, during the week, by various others of a similar character throughout the country, at which the same resolutions were adopted. Six days afterwards, the Prince Regent opened Parliament with a speech from the throne, denouncing these proceedings; and, as he returned from the House, was met with hisses and groans, and not a few missiles; it is said that one of the crowd even fired at him. The High Bailiff of Birmingham (Mr. John Turner) immediately convened a meeting of the inhabitants—"the Magistrates, Gentry, Clergy, Merchants, Manufacturers, and others," not those inhabitants who had convened the Newhall Hill meeting without his sanction,—"to take into consideration the propriety of presenting a dutiful and loyal address to his Royal Highness the Prince Regent, expressive of our unalterable attachment to his illustrious house, and of our utter abhorrence of the late audacious and wicked assault upon his Royal Person, while exercising one of the most important functions of the Regal authority." Yet so far, the reformers of Newhall Hill would have loyally joined with their more respectable neighbours; *they* did not wish to see their cause sullied by an attempt at regicide. But the requisition did not end with this; they were also to "enter into some Resolutions that may declare, that whilst we hold the right of Petitioning to be the undoubted privilege of Englishmen, we strongly deprecate any exercise of that right which in its consequences may lead to scenes of outrage and violence." This was a declaration which they were not prepared to endorse, and they determined to be present at the meeting to oppose it, at the same time, however, "concurring fully in the primary object for which it was called." They succeeded in carrying their point, in a resolution "declaratory of their right and their intention to petition as often and in such a manner as they deemed fitting or necessary." Thus baffled in their endeavours to pass a resolution against the right of petitioning, the requisitionists adjourned to the Public Office, and there, with closed doors, passed the resolution condemning the Reformers' petitions; this circumstance was long remembered by the people as "the locked-up meeting in Moor Street."

The speech of the Prince Regent was not without its effect; reports were presented to the House of Commons on the 18th and 19th of February, by the Secret Committees, (who had employed spies to attend the meetings of the Reformers throughout the kingdom,) alleging that Birmingham and other great centres of industry were filled with revolutionists, members of the various Hampden Club. The Ministry asked for the suspension of the Habeas Corpus Act, and the House readily acceded to the request. This measure brought to a close the career of the Hampden Clubs, including that of Birmingham. Lord Sidmouth, the Home Secretary, issued warrants to apprehend disaffected persons; and many arrests took place in consequence in various parts of the country. Men were dragged from their homes, and were thrown into prison for periods varying from six to eighteen months, and then discharged without trial. The perpetrators

of these acts of despotism, committed under the direction of the Home Secretary, were indemnified by the faithful Commons, by the passing of an Act of Indemnity at the close of the session of 1818.

During this year the reformers of Birmingham, appear to have remained dormant,—paralysed, it may be, by the high-handed procedure of the Government. But in the July of the following year, 1819, they once more took the field, and boldly asserted their right to parliamentary representation. A great meeting was held on Newhall Hill, on Monday, July 12th, at which nearly sixty thousand persons were present. On this occasion they did not stop short at any mere resolution, but boldly appointed Sir Charles Wolseley, as their "Legislatorial Attorney and Representative," and authorised him to claim, on their behalf, admission to the House of Commons, as Member for Birmingham. As one London newspaper of the period expressed it, "in one moment, a public meeting invested the town with the right of sending a Member to Parliament; and without waiting for the Speaker's writ, or any other old-fashioned process, nominated and elected Sir Charles Wolseley to that honour." Among the persons present at this famous gathering, were Major Cartwright, T. J. Wooler, George Edmonds, and many of the members of the old Hampden Club; Sir Charles Wolseley was unable to attend in consequence of the recent death of his mother. The proceedings commenced with a procession from Major Cartwright's lodgings to the place of meeting, and on their arrival, Mr. Edmonds was called to the chair. His opening address, was followed by a speech from Mr. Maddocks, a schoolmaster, who, according to the *Gazette*, had succeeded to the school recently vacated by Mr. Edmonds. A letter of apology for non-attendance, from Sir Charles Wolseley, was next read, and then followed the various resolutions, and the reading of the "Complaint and Remonstrance." This was succeeded by the resolutions of the day, touching the election of Sir Charles Wolseley as

"Legislatorial Attorney and Representative," with the provision that "in the event of his being acknowledged and received as their representative, he is to use his utmost endeavours to secure to them an annual election of Legislatorial Representatives by ballot, and to move for the adoption of Major Cartwright's 'Bill of Rights and Liberties.'" Major Cartwright, Mr. Wooler, and Mr. Edmonds, were then deputed to wait upon the newly appointed representative, and the meeting was brought to a close by votes of thanks to the visitors, Major Cartwright and Mr. Wooler. The Major is described by the *Gazette*, as "spectral" in appearance, and is said by that journal to have "remained almost motionless during the whole of the proceedings," excepting that after the vote of thanks, "he rose and bowed his thanks to the crowd, who in turn testified their respect by taking off their hats while he remained on his legs."

The whole proceedings were mightily disparaged by the *Gazette*, and treated as "farcical"; the numbers were considerably under-estimated, and almost in the same sentence, explained away, by the statement that the majority of the persons present were artisans out of employment. "Not a single individual, resident or holding a respectable situation in society," says the detractor, "took a prominent share in the day's proceedings; and this, we are told, excited chagrin and disappointment to the old Major, who had considered things here to be upon a different footing."

Insignificant as these proceedings appeared to the *Gazette*, however, they were not regarded in the same light by the Government. A cabinet council was held immediately, and a Proclamation against seditious assemblies, with special reference to the Newhall Hill gathering, was issued, commanding Magistrates and persons in authority to make the most diligent inquiry, "in order to bring to punishment those persons who have been, or may be guilty of offences of the kind."

The leaders of the Newhall Hill meeting, Major Cartwright and Messrs. T. J. Wooler,

George Edmonds, Charles Maddocks, and Wm. Greatheed Lewis, (of Coventry), were indicted at the Warwickshire Spring Assizes, "for conspiring to elect and return, without lawful authority, Sir Charles Wolseley, Bart., as a member to represent the inhabitants of Birmingham in the Commons House of Parliament." The indictment was, however, removed into the Court of King's Bench and the trial was postponed, the defendants being liberated on bail.

During the same year occurred the famous "Peterloo Massacre" at Manchester, an event which led the Birmingham Reformers into other grave offences, and rendered some of them liable to further prosecutions. Our readers are doubtless familiar with the story of that shameful act, whereby a peaceable, although it may be somewhat noisy, meeting of Reformers was attacked by the Yeomanry, several persons being killed and others seriously injured; an act which aroused the indignation of all right-minded Englishmen, and led the Reformers of Birmingham to meet once more on the battle-ground of freedom, Newhall Hill.

This gathering took place on Thursday, Sept. 16th, 1819. Shortly before three o'clock in the afternoon, the leaders of the party proceeded to the place of meeting in a mourning coach; the platform was hung with black cloth, and the vast crowd evinced every token of sympathy and compassion for their martyred brethren. As on former occasions, Mr. Edmonds presided; Sir Charles Wolseley had been requested to do so, but declined from prudential motives, having already a prosecution hanging over his head as a result of the previous meeting. He, however, followed Mr. Edmonds in addressing the assembled crowd, concluding by exhibiting a drawing of a memorial column which he proposed to erect in his park at Wolseley, "in commemoration of the brave Reformers who fell on the 16th of August;" a column forty feet high, which should be placed in a situation overlooking the road to Manchester. In an account of the meeting contained in the

Lichfield Mercury, it is stated that "the discharge of ordnance was heard at a distance, and the roll of a drum, which agitated the outskirts of the people—supposed to be a trick of the authorities —a very foolish one—to try the nerves of the meeting. "The great body," says the *Mercury*, "stood firm on the defensive, and we are told that not less than from six to eight thousand had armed themselves with pistols, in case they should be attacked." This report is, however, contradicted by the *Birmingham Gazette*, in a very disparaging notice of the meeting. "It is true," says that journal, "a portion of the crowd became alarmed at some noise which was heard from a distance, and a cry in consequence that soldiers were approaching caused for a few moments considerable confusion, but it soon subsided. The supposition that a discharge of ordnance took place by direction of the Magistrates is too absurd to need contradiction; and the report that a large body of the crowd were armed with pistols we have no hesitation in declaring to be a gross calumny." The same journal states that "the number of persons present was certainly far below any former assemblage on the same spot, notwithstanding the attendance of a numerous concourse from all parts of the surrounding country, who, it being market day, were thus enabled to obtain a sight of Sir Charles Wolseley, an important personage of whom they had heard so much of late."

In reference to this meeting and its objects, one of the conveners of the first Newhall Hill meeting wrote as follows in the *Gazette* of September 27th, the issue containing the account of the proceedings :—

To the Public.

From my known extreme reluctance to public business, and more especially to that description of it so well understood by the term Political, I had hoped to pass unnoticed by the meeting held last Thursday, on Newhall Hill. I had no hand whatever in the two last Town's Meetings, not having seen either Sir C. Wolseley or Mr. Wooler, during the whole of their stay in town ; yet has an appeal been made to my principles by the unanimous voice of my fellow townsmen. Let me not be upbraided with their

being the "riff-raff and scum of society." Wherever I see a human being I recognize the image of God, and however meanly he may be clad, he has a claim on my good-will and fellowship. Let his conduct be correct, and I stop not to ask what cash he has in his pocket, before I shall know if he be entitled to civility or to contempt. I therefore beg leave to state, that I sincerely sympathise with the lower class in their privations and sufferings. A vast portion of the great mass of our population is now working from twelve to fifteen hours a day for the miserable pittance of one shilling—I appeal to our Parliamentary Reports for the truth of the allegation— and even this wretched earning cannot always be obtained, through the want of employment. Is this, or is it not, sufficient cause of complaint ? And if they sometimes err in the mode of seeking redress, with whom lies the reproach ? with those whose wants drive them to use such means as their knowledge affords—or with those who, pretending to know better, at the same time refuse their assistance, protection, and advice ? Whoever tells them that their distresses are temporary, and that it is out of the power of human means to grant present relief, are uttering the foulest libel on the bounty of Providence. The physical resources of nature, and the energies of man, if properly employed, might convert our miserable country into a comparative Eden—but alas ! what has been attempted ?

The late proceedings at Manchester appear to me so perfectly atrocious, anti-christian—so outrageous to every feeling of honour and humanity—so subversive of social order, and of every moral duty,—and so directly opposed to every principle of law and of justice—that I should think it culpable to withhold my humble sanction from the subscription proposed on behalf of the surviving sufferers. If my name will be of service, I willingly lend it, though I am unable to use that exertion in the cause to which I think it so well entitled.

Whatever subscriptions may be deposited in my hands, I hope I need not pledge my name for their faithful appropriation.

St. Paul's, Sept. 23, 1819.   JAMES LUCKCOCK.

It is greatly to the credit of the *Gazette* that a letter expressing sentiments so decidedly antagonistic to the principles advocated by that journal, should have found a place in its columns ; the editor, however, in the same issue, entered a polite but firm and decided protest against the opinions of his correspondent.

It is not to be supposed that during the political events of 1819 the Tory party in Birmingham remained silent, or was by any means a small and unimportant section of the community. Pamphlets, squibs in prose and verse, addresses, sermons, and other wordy missiles were hurled at

FORWARD

G. B. DAVIS, ESQ.,
CLERK TO THE BIRMINGHAM SCHOOL BOARD.

PHOTOGRAPHED BY WHITLOCK.

BIRMINGHAM: HOUGHTON & CO., SCOTLAND PASSAGE.

the heads of the reformers—"*radicals,*" they were now beginning to be called, from their persistent demand for "a *radical* reform," in great profusion. "Joe Shrewd the Die-Sinker"—an a sermon entitled "A Word for my King, my Country, and my God." The inhabitants who "thought themselves *loyal* and despised others," signed a "Loyal Declaration" and forwarded it

ST. GEORGE'S CHURCH, FROM GREAT HAMPTON ROW.

imitator of Job Nott—addressed "A few Words to my Neighbours," and concluded them as other burlesques have since his day been concluded, with a dismally-comic song, called "The Radical Dandy." The Rev. Edward Burn, minister of St. Mary's Chapel, preached and afterwards printed to the Prince Regent, and this Declaration was answered by one of the radicals. The word *loyal* became a shibboleth of the Tory party for a time, and it could not be mentioned even in the theatre without creating an enthusiastic interruption. On one occasion the line "Perhaps some

46

loyal hearts may yet be found" occurred in a play produced at the Theatre Royal; and the lines had scarcely escaped the actor's lips when "the walls of the theatre resounded from every part with one of the most astounding and long-continued bursts of applause ever heard." Another line in the same play, "we would reign undisturbed by civil war," met with a similar reception. On another occasion one of the audience (said to have been in the gallery) demanded *God Save the King*," and the request, says the *Gazette*, "occasioned an instantaneous re-echo from almost every voice." The interrupted performers complied with the request, the audience standing, not content with joining in the chorus, but "actually interposing the most enthusiastic cheers," we are told, "between each distinct sentiment," and when finished, "an universal encore succeeded, and it was again sung, accompanied by the audience with, if possible, increased feeling."

At the same time the 'loyal' party did all in their power to prevent the dissemination of liberal opinion not only in the outdoor gatherings but even through the medium of the press. On the 1st of November, 1819, a Birmingham bookseller, Mr. George Ragg, of Bull Street, was apprehended under a warrant issued by the Magistrates, "for selling a number of 'The Republican,' a blasphemous work still publishing by Carlile." Being unable to find sureties for his appearance at the assizes, he was thrown into Warwick gaol, to await his trial. The author of an 'inflammatory hand-bill' printed by Ragg, Mr. Charles Whitworth, was also taken into custody a few weeks later. Osborne, "a pamphlet vendor, of Union Street," was also apprehended for selling "The Black Book;" Richard Mansfield, for "unlawfully selling in this town, a seditious publication called, An Address to the Reformers;" all these, together with Joseph Russell, Joseph Brandis, and John Osborne, were each sentenced to one year's imprisonment, and required to find sureties for their good behaviour for several years afterwards. After many delays, the leaders of the Birmingham Reform movement were sentenced as follows: George Edmonds, to nine months' imprisonment, T. J. Wooler, to fifteen months, Charles Maddox, to eighteen months, and Major Cartwright, to pay a fine of £100 to the King, after having paid, in travelling, law, and other expenses, nearly a thousand pounds. W. G. Lewis, of Coventry, for a pretended libel in a Coventry newspaper was sentenced to two years' imprisonment in Oakham Gaol. And so ends the first part of the struggle for liberty.

CHAPTER LII.

THE CHURCHES AND SECTS IN BIRMINGHAM—1811-1820.

Necessity for more Churches—St. George's Church—Preparations for building Holy Trinity Chapel—*Ebenezer Chapel*, Steelhouse Lane—Rebuilding of Carr's Lane Chapel—New Roman Catholic Chapel Shadwell Street—Riot in 1813.

THE second decade of the nineteenth century was one of great progress in the churches of the establishment in Birmingham. Not only, as we have already recorded in our last chapter of the history of the churches and sects in the town, was the Free Church completed during this period, but further steps were also taken towards providing additional church accommodation, the need for such provision having long been felt.

At a meeting held in October, 1818, it was

stated that, in the midst of a population of 60,000 souls, (in St. Martin's parish alone,) the churches and chapels of the Establishment could not furnish accommodation for more than 7,630 ; distributed as follows :

At St. Martin's Church	... ...	2,200
— St. Mary's Chapel	... ...	2,000
— St. Paul's Chapel	... ...	1,130
— St. Bartholomew's Chapel	...	800
— Christ Church	... ...	1,500
		———
		7,630

To these, for the accommodation of the rest of the town, may be added,

At St. Philip's Church	... ...	2,000
— St. John's Chapel, Deritend	...	700
— St. James' Chapel, Ashted	...	700
		———
		3,400

Thus making, in all, provision for 11,030 persons, out of a total population of about 80,000.

It was recommended, therefore, that an application should be made to Parliament for the building of three new churches, each to accommodate 2,000 persons, out of the grant of a million provided by the " Act for building and promoting the building of churches in populous parishes."

On the 28th of December, in the same year, the welcome news was announced in the *Gazette* that the Commissioners appointed under the Act just referred to, had " determined, with a liberal consideration of the wants of our numerous population, immediately to build a new Church within the parish of St. Martin, out of the Parliamentary grant, provided a proper site for the building be procured." It was further reported that " the board appointed by the Lord Bishop of the Diocese are now actively engaged in making the necessary preliminary arrangements ; " and that " some gentlemen have kindly engaged to solicit subscriptions from the principal inhabitants, at the commencement of the new year, in aid of the fund already formed for the purpose of providing a site for the intended build-

ing, and defraying any other expenses which may be incidental to the undertaking."

The site was ultimately obtained, partly by the munificence of the Marquis of Hertford and Miss Colmore, and partly by purchase, out of the fund thus raised by private subscription, from the Governors of King Edward's School. The situation was, next to that of St. Philip's, the best in the town, at that period, at the upper end of Hampton Street and Tower Street, and adjoining Great Hampton Row. The church, dedicated to St. George, was the first in Birmingham in which a return was made to Christian architecture. It is built in the early English decorated style, from designs by Thomas Rickman, the author of a popular work on Gothic Architecture, and the first promoter of the Gothic revival. The church consists of a nave, aisles, and chancel, with a lofty square embattled tower at the west end. The nave is divided from the aisles by richly moulded stone piers and arches, upon which rises a lofty clerestory, finished with a battlement and pinnacles. The tower, which is 114 feet high, resembles, in its general features, the Somerset shire towers of the 15th century, and is surmounted by a pierced parapet, with crocketed pinnacles. At the east end is a large stained glass window, of rich flowing tracery, underneath which is a highly decorated altar-piece. The ceiling over the nave and aisles is panelled, partly in wood and partly in plaster ; the open timber roof not having been at that period introduced. Although there are crudities in the design of this structure, as necessarily there must be in all *beginnings*, it will compare favourably with any building of the same early period of the revival of Christian architecture in England. Internally the building is 98 feet in length and 60 feet in width ; the width of the nave is 26 feet, and the height 45 feet. There is accommodation for 1959 persons, the greater portion of the sittings being free.

The first stone was laid by the local commissioners appointed under the Act, in the name of the bishop of the diocese, on the 19th of April, 1820, and the church and churchyard were consecrated by the Bishop of Chester, July 30th, 1822. It was stated in a report of the ceremonies published in the *Gazette* of the following week, that " the entire expense of the church (amount-

On November 4th, 1818, a meeting was held at which it was resolved to build a church or chapel in Bordesley ; and also, that " the upper Part of Mr. John Bradford's Land, adjoining to the Stratford Road Turnpike Road and to Snail's Lane, [now Sandy Lane,] is a desirable situation."

BUST OF THE LATE REV. JOHN ANGELL JAMES.

ing to £12,481) instead of exceeding, as is not uncommonly the case, was contracted for and completed for upwards of *eleven hundred pounds less* than the original estimates ; and that journal is strongly of opinion that, " upon close investigation, it will be found that St. George's Church has been completed for one-third, if not one-half, under the cost of any church of its size and capacity erected of late years."

The sum of £3,000 was raised by voluntary subscription for the purchase of this land as a site for the new chapel, which it was proposed to erect and dedicate to the Holy Trinity. The first stone was laid during the last year of the period under notice, but as the edifice was not completed until 1823 we defer the further notice and description thereof until our next chapter of the religious history of the town.

We turn now to the history of the dissenters in Birmingham.

After the completion of the New Meeting House, in Moor Street, and the consequent removal of the second Unitarian society from their temporary meeting-house in Livery Street, the latter building was used by an offshoot from the Independent congregation in Carr's Lane, under the successful ministy of the Rev. Jehoiada Brewer, previously pastor of Carr's Lane Meeting. The popularity of Mr. Brewer at the Livery Street Meeting-house led to the erection of a larger building for his increasing congregation, in Steelhouse Lane. He died, however, in 1817, just before its completion. The new building, called *Ebenezer Chapel*, was opened on the 9th of December, 1818, the Rev. W. Thorpe, of Bristol, conducting the morning service, and the Rev. S. Bradley, of Manchester, that of the evening. In front of the chapel is a monument to the memory of the minister for whose congregation it was built, and who laid the first stone on the 4th of July, 1816. The chapel contains accommodation for more than 1,200 persons; the cost of its erection was about £7,000.

In the meantime, under the successful ministrations of the Rev. John Angell James at the parent society, the chapel became too small to accommodate the large congregations which assembled there from week to week. For the fame of the preacher was already beginning to spread far and wide, and attracted all classes to Carr's Lane to hear him. After repeated enlargements, it was therefore decided to rebuild the chapel, and the first stone of the new structure was laid by the pastor, on Friday, July 30th, 1819. From a report in the *Gazette* of the period, we learn that the ceremony attracted "a numerous assemblage of spectators," and that the Rev. Timothy East (the pastor of Ebenezer Chapel, Steelhouse Lane,) and the Rev. Isaiah Birt, (pastor of the Baptist Chapel, in Cannon Street,) took part in the proceedings. "Mr. James," says the report, "delivered an animated

and appropriate address to those assembled on the occasion, in his usual impressive and energetic manner." At the time of its removal, the older meeting-house was capable of accommodating about 800 hearers, and it was intended to provide, in the new building, accommodation for 2,100; of which 350 free sittings should be appropriated to the use of the poor, and 300 for the children of the Sunday Schools.

Just three months after the laying of the first stone of the building, the *Gazette*, November 1st, 1819, contained the following paragraph:—

New Meeting House, Carr's Lane.—As an instance of unparalleled dispatch in the erection of public buildings n this town, it is due to the Architect and Committee for conducting the building of the New Meeting House, in Carr's Lane, and especially to the spirited exertions of the Builder, to mention that although the Committee voluntarily extended the time, yet the building was covered in on Saturday, one day within the period originally contracted for.

Upon the last slate was engraved the following inscription :—

"Memoranda.—On the 30th day of July, 1819, the first stone of the building was laid by the Rev. John Angell James, the Minister. On the 30th day of October, in the same year, this, the last slate was laid by Henry Leneve Holland, the builder, in the presence of Stedman Thomas Whitwell, the architect.—*Laus Deo.*"

Some idea of the magnitude of this chapel, may be formed by stating that it contains, within its external boundaries, about 305,000 cubic feet.

The new chapel was opened for divine service in August, 1820. It is a large building of brick, and had until within the last three years, a lofty and imposing cemented front, in the pseudo Grecian style, presenting an arch of large span, within which were placed the entrances. In 1876, however, the old front was removed, and the building somewhat lengthened, the new front being of red brick with stone dressings, in a style of architecture more in harmony with the purpose for which the place was erected; viz., that of Christian worship.

The Roman Catholics, who, up to the commencement of the period under notice, still had but one place of worship in the town,—St. Peter's Chapel, in Broad Street,—began now to build a second, in Shadwell Street, (on the site of the present cathedral); occupying, in the meantime, a temporary place of worship in Water Street. The new chapel was opened in 1813, by the Rev. Dr. Milner, and dedicated to St. Chad.

The other sects in the town appear to have flourished and increased in numbers and influence; small chapels and meeting-houses arose in the various quarters of the town, but none of sufficient importance to call for particular notice.

In the earlier part of this decade, Birmingham was once more the scene of a religious riot. On the night of the 22nd of March, 1813, a crowd broke into the Methodist Chapel, in Belmont Row, broke the windows, destroyed the pulpit Bible, and pulled down the chandelier. From this place the rabble marched to the Jew's Synagogue, in Severn Street, and thence to a meeting-house near Lady Well, and finally to the Baptist Chapel, in Bond Street; in

all these the windows were shattered, pews destroyed, and the places pillaged of everything which could be carried away. An attempt was made to fire the Bond Street Chapel, which happily failed, although the drapery of the pulpit was entirely consumed. The strong arm of the law, however, proved more effective in this case than in 1791, and four young men, named Hanley, Adams, Turner, and Guest, were sentenced respectively to seven years' imprisonment.

"In this town," says Charles Pye, (in his *Description of Modern Birmingham*, published during this period,) "every individual worships his Maker in whatever way his inclination leads him, without the least notice being taken or remarks made; if a person's conduct is exemplary, or if he does not give way to any vicious propensities, no one will interrupt or interfere with him."

CHAPTER LIII.

LOCAL CHARITIES, CHIEFLY MEDICAL.

Establishments of the Birmingham General Dispensary—Description of the Building—Proposal to Establish a Lying-In Hospital—Orthœpædic Hospital—Deaf and Dumb Institution.

In passing from one to another of the scenes which we have endeavoured to reproduce in the last few chapters,—from the public life of our townsmen to their amusements, and from thence to their literary and social life,—our readers have doubtless looked for some particulars as to our local charities, and may perhaps have censured the author for so long delaying any further notice of what has well been described by Pope as "all mankind's concern." But the delay has arisen mainly from the fact that since our notice of the General Hospital, there has been but little to chronicle; from the foundation of that institution, to the commencement of the present century, with the single exception of the General Dispen-

sary, we have had no new charity to record, and but little respecting those already in existence. We now, however, take up the story.

In 1770 the first Dispensary was established in London, by a few private individuals; it was in fact little more than a private institution at first, numbering only 100 subscribers. But in two years the Governors had increased to 300, and by 1778 the institution numbered fourteen thousand subscribers. As the advantages of this useful charity became known, the scheme was adopted by many provincial towns, and especially in Ireland. Towards the end of the year 1792 a proposal to establish a Dispensary in Birmingham was mooted in the columns of the *Gazette*, which resulted in the formation of a private society; and early in the following year, 1793, the infant project attracted the attention of Matthew Boulton, who at once took it under his protection, and elected himself its treasurer, saying, "if the funds of the institution are not sufficient for its support, I will make up the deficiency." A house was thereupon taken, in Temple Row, and the insitution grew and prospered, until, in 1806, it was found necessary to erect a more suitable building. A site was obtained in Union Street, and "our ingenious townsman, Mr. W. Hollins" prepared designs for the intended structure, the first stone of which was laid by Thomas Potts, Low Bailiff, on the 23rd of December, 1806. The new building was opened during the year 1808; it consists of a centre and two wings, the former being surmounted by a triangular pediment, supported by four lofty pilasters, with fluted capitals "Over the doorway," says Mr. Bates, "is an emblematical piece of sculpture by W. Hollins, representing a female crouching beneath an arch; she holds, appropriately, a medicine cup in her hand, but whether on the point of taking a dose herself, or as a nurse of the institution about to adminster a draught to an unseen patient, we have not been able to ascertain, nor is the mystery elucidated by the inscription."* The building is, in fact, one of those monstrosities with which an overweening love for *pseudo* classic art has disfigured our town, and not ours only, but nearly every city and town in the United Kingdom.†

Ugly, however, as the building undoubtedly is, it has yet sheltered an institution which has been the instrument of more usefulness, in proportion to the sums expended, than any other of our local charities. During the year 1794, 280 patients were relieved; in 1802 the number had grown to 1,470; ten years later, (1812) the number of patients admitted exceeded four thousand. During the last year in which both the Vaccination and Midwifery departments existed, 1868,* the number had increased to 9,072, while in 1871 the number of sick patients alone amounted to 10,570, and by 1877 had increased to 19,286. Perhaps the best idea of the usefulness of this institution is conveyed in the total number of patients admitted during the entire period of its existence, which is as follows :—

Sick.	Midwifery.	Vaccine Inoculation.
345,881	35,123.	101,387.

In 1813 we find the first note in the *Gazette* of another useful charity, which did not, however, take a practical form for nearly thirty years after the first attempt to found it :—

Oct. 14, 1813.—It gives us much gratification to hear that a society is about to be established for the express purpose of affording relief to poor lying-in women. A meeting has been held, the result of which gives every reason to believe that the society will be well supported, and we doubt not will be essentially serviceable, as there certainly is not any situation to which the poor are exposed that calls so loudly for relief from those who have it in their power to afford it.

The Lying-In Hospital was not, however, established until 1842.

On the 24th of June, 1817, a meeting attended by all the more influential and benevolently-disposed inhabitants of the town and neighbourhood was held in Birmingham, to consider the propriety of establishing an Institution for the Relief of Persons labouring under Bodily Deformity. It was resolved to establish such an institution, and that it should bear the name above mentioned; that the Earl of Dartmouth be Patron of the Institution; that Mr. Freer be appointed Surgeon to the Establishment, and that Mr. J. W. Whately be appointed secretary. Ultimately the rather clumsily worded title of the institution was changed for that of "the Orthœpædic Hospital," and a building was obtained for the purposes of the charity in New Street. Before the end of September the *Gazette* announced that the society had already been the means of relieving twenty-five patients, and that the applications for ad-

---

* The inscription is "Of the Most High cometh Healing."

† In Birmingham, we are sorry to say, the admiration for this sort of thing has not yet died out.

*The Midwifery department was abandoned in 1869, and Vaccination in 1870.

mission continued to be very numerous. During the first year of its establishment 235 patients were relieved, and the charity has continued up to the present time to prove of incalculable assistance to hundreds of sufferers from various herniary complaints, and has accomplished much valuable work in its limited sphere of usefulness, in a quiet and unobtrusive manner.

In the year 1800 was founded, by a few scientific inhabitants, the Philosophical Institution, of which we shall have more to say in a future chapter; and it is to this society, as we shall presently see, that we owe one of the most useful of the educational charities in our midst. During 1812, Dr. De Lys lectured at the Institution on the advantages which the deaf and dumb might derive from a new system of instruction he (with Mr. A. Blair) had introduced. A young girl, about eight years of age, labouring under these defects, was introduced by the lecturer to illustrate the effects of his system, and this circumstance gave rise to the General Institution for the Instruction of Deaf and Dumb Children.

A private meeting of the principal inhabitants was held on the 30th of November, in the same year, at St. Philip's Parsonage, at which it was determined to take the initiative steps towards establishing such an institution, and this was followed by a public meeting at the Blue Coat School, four days later, when the project was formally set on foot and the first officers of the new institution were elected. We have not space to quote the first annual report of the committee in full, it must therefore suffice to give an outline of the work accomplished during the year. An experienced teacher had been engaged, (Mr. Braidwood) who would reside wholly in or near Birmingham; he was the son of Thomas Braidwood, whose school for the deaf and dumb had received

the approbation of many of the most eminent men of the time. The committee had ascertained that there were, in Birmingham alone "not fewer than twenty poor children, fit objects of this Charity." Further, they reported that at the last Assize at Warwick, "the Gentlemen of a most respectable Grand Jury, and the High Sheriff, unanimously subscribed to this Institution, and kindly honoured it with their powerful Recommendation to the County at large." Thus far, all preliminaries were satisfactorily arranged, and the new institution was ready for work; on the 10th of January, 1814, the school was opened, and the task of instructing the Deaf and Dumb in the useful arts commenced. On the 28th of August Mr. McCready gave a performance at the Theatre Royal for the benefit of the institution, at which an address, written by the Rev. Charles Kennedy, was delivered by Mrs. Edwin immediately after the play of *The Deaf and Dumb*. In February, 1815, the new Asylum, at Edgbaston, handsomely fitted up by Lord Calthorpe, was opened; in it was provided accommodation for sixty-five children, although at first only twenty were admitted, from want of funds for the carrying-out of the further provisions of the institution. In later years the increase of subscriptions, legacies, and donations enabled the managers of the institution to develop still further the intentions of its founders, and there is now accommodation for upwards of 160 children. All honour to those who thus imitate the divine Master, by giving, in a certain degree, ears to the deaf, and voice to the dumb, and thus

—ope new worlds of thought,
With sense and feeling give their eyes to shine
And light up all the human face divine;
Give them, in silent prayer to lift on high
The smile of conscious immortality! *

* Kennedy's Address.

CHAPTER LIV.

PUBLIC LIFE AND EVENTS—1811-1820.

The New Market Places—Destruction of the Moat Buildings—Formation of the New Smithfield—Gas-Lighting—Death of Myles Swinney —-William Hutton—Jonathan Knott—Loyal and Patriotic Celebrations—Miscellaneous Events—Crime--The Mystery of Mary Ashford Murder of Pennington—Booth, the Coiner, etc.

In taking up once again "the story of our lives from year to year," we feel a sense of relief that, during the second decade of the present century, we have to record no riots or public disturbances such as have disfigured previous pages of our history , the turmoil of the first political campaign has already been chronicled, with its attendant disturbances and prosecutions ; we have also referred briefly in a recent chapter to the petty riot in 1813, and there happily remains no further disturbance to record in the present chronicle.

This was a decade of improvement in every respect, of better streets, better accommodation for the various goods in public markets, and of the dawn of a better system of local government.

We noticed briefly, in our last chronicle of events, the fourth Act "for better paving, lighting, watching, cleansing, and otherwise improving the town of Birmingham." The most important of the provisions of this Act was that which empowered the Commissioners to treat with the Lord of the Manor for the lease or purchase of his markets, fairs, and other manorial rights, and to establish agricultural markets in the Bull Ring, and on the site now called Smithfield. In the clauses conferring these powers upon the Commissioners it is set forth that "whereas the town of Birmingham is become a very large and populous trading town, and the markets there have from time out of memory been held in the streets or places called Bull Street, High Street, and Dale End, and whereas the Commissioners have purchased and taken down divers messuages or tenements and buildings situate in the Bull

Ring, for the purpose of enlarging and making more commodious the said market place, and it would greatly tend to the convenience of the inhabitants if the markets were in future held there," it is enacted that "the street or place so widened and enlarged, called the Bull Ring, shall be deemed a public highway, and shall be considered and used as the market place for the town of Birmingham," for "all goods, wares, and merchandises, fruit, vegetables, or garden stuff, butchers' meat, or other matter or thing except neat cattle, horses, sheep, pigs, hay and straw," and that the Lord of the Manor may set up stalls for markets and fairs, and may collect rents and tolls for the same. With regard to the merchandise excluded from the Bull Ring market it is enacted that the Commissioners may purchase "a piece of land with the buildings thereon, called the Moat and Moat House, belonging to Sir Thomas Gooch, Baronet, and Thomas Francis, Esquire," and may lay open the land "so as the same shall form an area of at least one acre and two roods," and "enclose the same for a market place for the sale of neat cattle, horses, sheep, and pigs, hay and straw," and that on the completion of the said market place, the use of other thoroughfares for this purpose shall cease, except at the two public fairs, on which occasions the sale of horses "in a certain street there called the Horse Fair," shall continue as usual.

In accordance with these provisions, the purchase was completed, and the ancestral home of the lords of Birmingham was demolished, and the market tolls and other rights were purchased of the Lord of the Manor, for £12,500, and with

47

these passed away for ever the last vestiges of feudal Birmingham. The house which stood on the very site of the ancient "castle" was destroyed, the almost dry ditch which had erst been "as a moat defensive to a house" was filled up, the old drawbridge, which had long ceased to serve its ancient purpose, was removed, and the lords of the manor of Birmingham passed out of our history for ever.

No compunction as to the destruction of the last link between the past and the present seems to have disturbed the Commissioners; they advertised in the *Gazette* as follows, for plans for converting the Moat grounds into a market-place :—

New Smithfield.

March 27, 1815.—The Commissioners of the Birmingham Street Act do hereby give Notice, that they are in want of a Plan for adapting the Premises, which they have lately purchased, called the Moat and Moat House, for the Accommodation of the intended Smithfield, and they do hereby offer a Premium of Ten Pounds for the Plan which shall be most approved of, and Five Pounds for the next. Ground Sketches of the Premises may be had, and other Particulars known, by applying at our Office in New Street, Birmingham, where the plans are to be delivered in by the respective Candidates on or before the 30th Day of March instant.

By Order of the Commissioners,
Smith and Arnold, Clerks.

On the 5th of April, 1817, it was officially announced that the Land purchased for a Market Place, and commonly called and known by the Name of the "Moat," would be opened as a Market Place, "for the sale of neat Cattle, Horses, Sheep, and Pigs," on Thursday, the 29th of May, (for the Whitsun Fair,) and on the Tuesday following, for the sale of Hay and Straw.

The next improvement we have to record is one which affected the appearance of Birmingham by night. Hitherto, although gas had been in use at Soho since 1802, the town had been content to remain in the most miserable gloom after sunset, the darkness being rendered visible— and nothing else—by the feeble flickering rays of the old-fashioned oil lamps. Even the theatre

was no exception to the rule; and the place where we now look for brilliancy, or at least cheerful brightness, was only rendered a little brighter than the rest of the town by the occasional use of wax instead of oil. It was not until 1817, that a company was formed to "light the town with smoke," as Sir Walter Scott phrased it. On the 6th of January in that year, proposals were published in the *Gazette*, "for lighting up the public Streets of the Town, and the Houses, Shops, and Manufactories of such Persons as may be desirous of the same, by a Company of Proprietors, to be called the "Birmingham Gas Light Company." These proposals were as follows :—

I. That the Capital of this Company be £100,000, in 10,000 Shares of £10 each, and the Shares to be transferable.

II. That each person shall, at the Time of his becoming a Subscriber, pay down a deposit of £10 per Cent. towards the necessary Expenses of Surveys, Plans, Parliamentary and other incidental Charges, to be incurred in procuring the Establishment of the Company's Works ; and in case £20,000 is not subscribed for in three Months, that the Deposit be returned, after deducting the Expences incurred.

III. That no Person be admitted a Subscriber who is not an Inhabitant, or otherwise concerned in Trade in the Town of Birmingham, till after the first Day of March next ; after which Time the Subscription to become open to the Public.

IV. That no Person be allowed to subscribe for more than 40 Shares until the said 1st Day of March next.

V. That when 2,000 Shares shall be subscribed for, a General Meeting shall be held, pursuant to public Notice, to be given in the Birmingham Papers, for the Purpose of Electing a Committee of not less than 15 Persons ; and such Committee to be invested with full Powers to manage the Concerns of the Company till an Act of Parliament is obtained (if necessary), with Power to add to their Number if they shall think fit, so as not to exceed 24 ; and no person to be eligible to serve on the Committee who is not the Holder of 10 Shares, and that six do form a Quorum.

VI. That no Call be made of more than £10 per Cent. on each Share, and that not oftener than every three Months.

VII. That at every General or Special Meeting the Votes shall be taken by Shares, and not by Voices ; and any absent Member to be at Liberty to Vote by Proxy, each Proxy being a Subscriber, and appointed in writing.

The bill for this much-needed improvement was not brought into Parliament until February,

1819; it received the Royal assent on the 14th of May, in the same year. The first shop, so far as we can learn, that was lighted with gas in Birmingham, was Poultney's at the corner of Moor Street, and the first occasion on which the new light was generally used in the town for a public illumination, was at the rejoicing on account of the failure of the proceedings against Queen Charlotte.

During this decade two men well-known to us, one of whom has figured largely in this history of Old Birmingham, passed away to their rest. The first of these was Myles Swinney, the printer, founder of the *Birmingham Chronicle*; the obituary notice in the *Gazette* was as follows:—

Died, on Friday, [October 30th, 1812,] after a long illness, at his house at Ashted, Mr. Myles Swinney, aged 74, nearly 50 years proprietor of "Swinney's Birmingham Chronicle."

The second was our old friend William Hutton. After the turmoil which succeeded the riots of 1791, he had settled down to enjoy that repose he had so well earned by a life of untiring industry. At the end of 1793, he delivered over his business to his son Thomas, and resided for the most part, at Bennett's Hill, coming into Birmingham for a few hours only in each day to assist his son in the shop. In his seventy-ninth year he made the journey entirely on foot into the North of England, and along the line of the old Roman wall. A brief recapitulation of his career, written by himself when at the age of eighty-five, will doubtless interest our readers:—
"At the age of eighty-two," he says, "I considered myself a young man. I could, without much fatigue, walk forty miles a day. But during the last six years I have felt a sensible decay; and, like a stone rolling down a hill its velocity increases with the progress. I have lived to bury two generations and among them many friends whom I loved I do not know, nor am known by any soul living prior to my twenty-seventh year. But although I barely live myself, I may have taught others to live. I was the first who opened a circulating library in Birmingham in 1751, since which time many have started in the race. I was the first who opened a regular paper warehouse in 1756: there are now a great number. I was also the first who introduced the barrow with two wheels; there are now more than one hundred. I may, in another view, have been beneficial to man by a life of temperance and exercise, which are the grand promoters of health and longevity. Some whom I know have been induced to follow my example, and have done it with success. I was never more than twice in London on my own concerns. The first was April 8, 1749, to make a purchase of materials for trade, to the amount of three pounds ! the last April 14, 1806, fifty-seven years after, to ratify the purchase of an estate which cost £11,590 ! One laid a foundation for the other, and both answered expectation."

The first serious symptoms of the approach of death occurred during his ninetieth year ; he had attempted to walk into Birmingham as usual in the morning, but was compelled to accept the eagerly-proffered assistance of several strangers, and at length reached the paper warehouse, in High Street, having been two hours on the way, in walking two miles and a quarter. From this place he returned home in his carriage, being utterly helpless. After this he gradually sank, and died on the 20th of September, 1815, at the age of ninety-two.

Another of our old and honoured townsmen who passed away during this period, was Mr. Jonathan Knott, editor of the *Gazette*. His death is thus recorded in the journal with which he had been connected:—

Died, on Friday Evening, [February 18th, 1814,] in his 48th year, from the sudden rupture of a blood vessel, preceded by an indisposition of a few weeks, which had greatly impeded his bodily frame, Mr. Jonathan Knott, for many years an eminent Bookseller and Printer of this town. His relatives and friends, by whom his private worth was properly appreciated, will long have reason to lament his removal. As editor of this Gazette, his several duties were performed with impartiality, candour, and integrity, carefully excluding from its pages all matter which might injure the character, or even wound the feelings of individuals.

There were, of course, the usual manifestations of rejoicing and of sorrow, during this period, on the occasion of events of national interest. We have previously spoken of the reception of the news of the attack on the Prince Regent, and the subsequent proceedings thereupon ; as well as of the reception of the deputation after the revocation of the Orders in Council The successes of

took place." Then came the defeat of Marshal Soult, in the Pyrenees, a month later ; on the 24th of July, Wellington had besieged Pampeluna, and on the 28th, Marshal Soult was defeated in the battle of the Pyrenees The dispatch announcing these brilliant victories, reached Birmingham, on the 15th of August, and further particulars were obtained soon after

PENN'S LANE, ADJOINING THE SCENE OF MARY ASHFORD'S DEATH.
From a print in the possession of Mr. William Bates.

British arms afforded several opportunities for rejoicing during this period. The Peninsular victories in 1813 were the first to arouse our townsmen ; the news of the brilliant victory at Vittoria, arrived here on the 7th of July, and " so soon," says the local *Gazette*, " as the London Gazette Extraordinary was read on Monday morning, the inhabitants, as it were by common consent, began to make preparations, and in the evening, a most brilliant and general illumination

midnight. " Mr. John Hart, the coach proprietor, of this town," says the *Gazette*, " had, it appears," given directions that so soon as any satisfactory information of these great events could be obtained in London, one of his coaches was immediately to set off with all speed to Birmingham, and the Balloon post coach, through Coventry, was driven at so great a rate that it reached here before one o'clock on Tuesday morning ! bringing a second edition of the *Times* newspaper. The coachman and guard soon gave notice to the inhabitants of the joyful tidings they had brought, and (it being Bell Wake) a large concourse of people very soon assembled, who set the ringers to clang the bells of St. Martin's and St. Philip's, and then drew the coach along the streets with cheers of congratulation and loud huzzas! "About noon the same day many thousand persons assembled to meet the mail coach, which arrived with decorations indicative of victory. The populace took out the horses at the commencement of the town, and dragged the coach to the Post Office, and afterwards through the principal streets. In the evening there was a general illumination."

The news of the glorious and decisive victories at Leipsic, in the same year, reached Birmingham, on the 4th of November, by the same coach which brought the news of Soult's defeat. Placards announcing the gratifying news were issued from the various printing houses, and spread throughout the town, the bells of St. Martin's, St. Philip's, and St. John's, Deritend, rang out a merry peal, tens of thousands of the inhabitants went out to meet the coach, and greeted its arrival with the most enthusiastic shouts, and the illuminations were both brilliant and numerous.

Then came the signing of the Treaty of Peace, in 1814, and more rejoicings, accompanied by the roasting of oxen and sheep, and the plentiful consumption of ale.

The death of the youthful Princess Charlotte of Wales, on the 6th November, 1817, touched the national heart in a more intense degree than had been experienced for many years. The whole nation went into mourning for her loss, addresses of condolence were sent from every town in the kingdom to the Prince Regent, and from Birmingham, the hotbed of disloyalty, as it was then believed to be, the loyal and sympathetic feeling of the masses went with the address of "the respectable inhabitants."

On the 29th of January, 1820, the king, George the Third, passed away at the ripe age of 83, and Birmingham joined in the sorrow of the whole nation for the loss of the patriarch-king. The new king George IV., who had long been monarch in all but the name, was proclaimed in Birmingham on Thursday, February 3rd, and shortly afterwards the usual "suitable address" was adopted by a "highly respectable" assembly of our fellow townsmen.

In 1820 came the shameful trial of Queen Caroline, and who, that has smiled over those wonderful caricature prints of glorious George Cruikshank, does not know how chivalrously the people of England resented the indignities which "the first gentleman in Europe" put upon his unforfortunate Queen. And when the scandalous proceedings were defeated the joy of the whole nation was unbounded. Illuminations, transparencies, (not forgetting the glorious one on Mr. Hone's shop in Ludgate Hill by George Cruikshank), and other tokens of joy were exhibited in the metropolis and elsewhere by the delighted multitudes. In Birmingham a few feeble and foolish somebodies issued a handbill requesting the people to refrain from these exuberant tokens of joy but the manifesto met with the censure it richly deserved ; and was further censured by the more general illumination than might have otherwise have taken place. The streets were brilliantly lighted up, even the humblest contributing to the general display ; and during the evening there was no lack of fireworks, discharging of guns, pistols, &c., on the part of the artisan classes, who thus testified, in a humble manner, their joy at the defeat of the ministerial proceedings. This was the first illumination in which gas was generally used in Birmingham.

Leaving now for a time these loyal and patriotic proceedings on the part of our townsmen, we note a few of the miscellaneous events of this decade.

Among these it becomes our duty first to chronicle the establishment of a Chamber of Commerce in Birmingham. On the 21st

June, 1813, a meeting was held, under the Presidency of Mr. R. Spooner, then High Bailiff, to take steps for the formation of a Commercial Society "for the purpose of collecting and comparing the opinions of its Merchants and Manufacturers; of acting as a Medium of Communications with Ministers and the Legislature on the subject of Trade, and of co-operating, as occasion may require, with other parts of the United Kingdom on questions affecting the general prosperity of the Manufactures and Commerce of the British Empire." The Society was formed; and it was resolved unanimously that it be called "The Chamber of Manufactures and Commerce of Birmingham."

We have already in our chapter on trade and commerce, referred to the establishment of a Proof House in Birmingham. The following account of the ceremony of laying the first stone of the building, from the columns of the *Gazette*, will doubtless interest some of our readers :—

October 4, 1813.—The principal gunmakers of this town, after very considerable pains and expence, having procured an Act of Parliament for the erecting and establishing of a Proof House, proceeded on Wednesday last to lay the first stone of the building, which is situated in Banbury Street, near the Fazeley Canal, and will be of incalculable benefit to the town and the community, as the barrels of all guns manufactured at Birmingham must be full Tower proof, by which persons may use such fire arms with the greatest safety The Guardians, Trustees, and Wardens attended, and deposited within a cavity, previously prepared in the stone, a series of gold and silver coins of his present Majesty, the Bank of England tokens, and the silver and copper tokens of this town, with a narrative of the events which led to the establishment written upon parchment, and enclosed in a glass bottle; over the whole was laid a brass plate, engraved with a suitable inscription, containing the names of the Guardians, Trustees, and Wardens, &c. After the ceremony the parties retired to a dinner prepared for the occasion; mirth and good humour presided, and the festive glass circulated freely to a late hour. At the time of laying the stone the bells of the churches struck up, and continued their merry peals occasionally throughout the day.

On the 24th of March, 1816, another of those slight shocks of earthquake, with which this country seems to have been rather frequently visited during the earlier part of the present **century, was** sensibly experienced in this town and neighbourhood," lasting about twenty seconds.

This year saw the establishment of the first Savings Bank in the town; and on the first day of opening, the sum of £26 was deposited.

Questions of rating houses for the maintenance of the poor appear to have arisen again during this period, out of which arose the following interesting statement, as to the number and rateable value of houses in Birmingham:—

The total number of houses in Birmingham Parish	18,082
Of these contribute towards the maintenance of the Poor	3,893
Houses that pay no Poor's Rates	14,189
The annual value of the whole Parish is	£210,170
The annual value of Premises paying Poor's Rates	£114,665
Ditto ditto that pay no Poor's Rates	£95,505

The outcome of these statistics was the introduction of a bill into Parliament for the rating of the landlords of houses under £12 a year rent, instead of allowing such houses to escape being rated at all, on account of the poverty of the tenant. The bill was however lost, by a majority of 67 in a House of 136 members; the defeat being chiefly owing to the hostility of the landed interest.

The growth of the town westward is illustrated in a striking manner in the notice quoted below. Our readers will doubtless remember the old footpath to the Five Ways of an earlier period; and some idea of the rural appearance of the lower end of Broad Street, at the close of the last century, may be obtained from a glance at the little engraving of Baskerville House, after the riots of 1791. This residence, with its pleasant lawns and avenues of shady trees, remained until within a few years of the date of the notice here quoted; what it was after the completion of Mr. Gibson's undertaking, may be seen by anyone passing along Easy Row at the present day. The old facade of the stately residence of John Baskerville and Rylands, may still be seen amid its grimy surroundings, itself a dingy warehouse;

the beginning of these things may be read in the following paragraph from the *Gazette*, of March 3rd, 1817 :—

It gives us great pleasure to be able to inform the trading World that Thomas Gibson has completed his Canal at Baskerville Place. This is certainly one of the greatest Works any single Individual in this part of the country has undertaken for many years, and we wish him that success he so justly merits. The line of wharfs intended to be erected on this Canal, ought to be called by his own Name, " Gibson's Wharfs." They will be well situated for the Convenience of Trade, being nearly in the Centre of England ; and according to a Level taken by an ingenious Engineer, to determine the Height of this Canal, found to be 3,000 feet above the level of the Thames at London, and 12 feet higher than any other Canal in England.

The first Boats laden will be raised from the lower to the higher Level this Morning at Eleven o'clock.

The troubles into which the too skilful and unscrupulous engravers of our town were prone to fall, owing to their devotion to one branch of their art,—that of imitating the notes of the Bank of England,—led, in 1818, to an enquiry as to the best means of rendering the bank paper as far as possible inimitable. A meeting of the principal inhabitants of Birmingham, was held on the 22nd of April, 1818, Mr. William Cotterill, High Bailiff, presiding ; at which it was resolved—" That this Meeting, observing with feelings of deep concern the increasing number of Prosecutions arising from and out of the Forgery of Bank of England Notes, is of opinion that a due regard to public Morals, as well as public Credit and Security, requires that the utmost endeavours should be made to diminish the evil." It needed, however, more than mere resolutions at towns' meetings to remedy this evil. It was not until George Cruikshank pointed out the moral of the crime and its ghastly punishment in his famous " Bank Note, not to be imitated," that the attention of the authorities was drawn to the terrible facility with which their clumsily engraved notes were copied ; and then the remedy followed speedily.

In May, 1817, a crime was committed within five miles of Birmingham which aroused the most painful interest and excitement, not only in Bir-

mingham, but throughout the country. A pretty country girl, named Mary Ashford, the daughter of a gardener living at Erdington, might have been met on almost any market day on her way to or from the Birmingham market, whither she went with dairy produce, either from her own home, or from her uncle's at Langley Heath, a little village consisting of a few straggling houses not far from Penn's Mills, where she occasionally stayed. On Whit-Monday, May 26th, 1817, she went as usual to Birmingham (from Langley), and stood in High Street, near the Castle Inn ; on her way to the town she had called at the house of Mr. Machell, in Erdington, where a female friend of hers, named Hannah Cox, was in service, and made an appointment to call for her on her way back, to accompany her to a dance at a public house at Tyburn (called " Tyburn House,") about two miles from Erdington. She sold her little stock in the market as soon as possible, in order to keep her appointment with her friend ; and returning to Erdington at about six o'clock, went to the house of her friend's mother, in the village, to change her dress, and at about half-past seven o'clock, set out to the dance. She seems to have won the admiration of most of the rustics assembled at the ball-room, by her beauty and simple modesty ; dressed in a clean and exceedingly neat print dress and white 'spencer,' she looked more than usually pretty that night. Among her rustic admirers at Tyburn House was a young bricklayer named Abraham Thornton, the son of a small farmer, who danced with her the whole of the evening. Her friend Hannah Cox, left the house a little before midnight, and waited at her request on the bridge close by, until Mary Ashford and Abraham Thornton, and a young man named Benjamin Carter joined her. It was then just after midnight and the two couples at once started to walk to Erdington, but Carter appears almost immediately afterwards to have returned to the house. This caused some delay on the part of Hannah Cox, who did not therefore regain her friends until they had gone about a mile of the distance. When they reached the first road leading to Erdington, (a little beyond the *Old Cuckoo*, on the left,) Hannah Cox left them again, and turned along it towards her home. At about two o'clock in the morning a man named John Umpage, who was at the house of Mr. Reynolds in Penn's Mill Lane, (*i.e.*, on the road to Mary Ashford's home,) heard voices in the lane, within a few three, within five minutes' walk of Erdington, walking very fast towards the house of Mrs. Butler, Hannah Cox's mother. Hannah Cox was called up by Mary Ashford, probably a little before four o'clock, and here the latter changed her dress. She appeared very calm and in good spirits, and there were no marks of previous agitation or confusion in her person or her dress. She re-

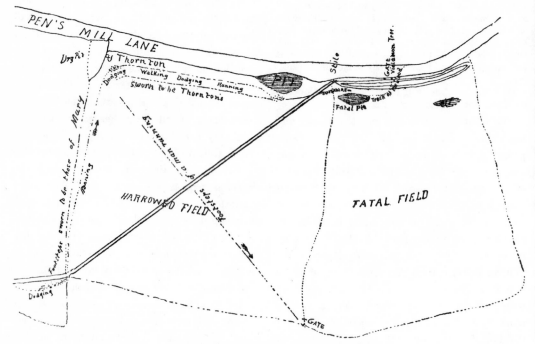

PLAN OF THE SCENE OF MARY ASHFORD'S DEATH.
From a print in the possession of Mr William Bates.

yards of the place where the crime was subsequently committed. The talking continued until he started on his way home to Witton, at about a quarter before three o'clock. After he left Reynolds's house he took the footpath across the field adjoining the fatal pit, which led into a foredrough, and thence in to Bell Lane, Erdington. As he entered the foredrough, he saw two persons on the stile at the further end, and recognised the man as Abraham Thornton The young girl held her head down so that he could not see her face, and appeared desirous of escaping recognition. This would probably be about three o'clock, and **Mary Ashford was again seen**, alone, at half-past dressed and made up into a bundle the clothes worn at the dance, and left the house within about fifteen minutes of the time Hannah Cox was called up, and the latter saw her no more. At a quarter past four o'clock she was met by a labourer named Joseph Dawson, *returning* from Erdington along Bell Lane, towards the place where she had been last seen with Abraham Thornton, and she was then walking very fast, dressed in the clothes she had worn in Birmingham on the previous day, (wearing a *scarlet* spencer in lieu of the white one she had on at the dance,) and carrying a bundle. About the same period, or a few minutes later, she was seen on the same road, a little nearer to the foredrough, by a man named Thomas Broadhurst, and she was still walking very fast.   This was the last person by whom she was seen alive, and it was then perhaps twenty minutes past four,—when the witness reached his home in Erdington, it wanted twenty minutes to five by his clock, which was a quarter too fast; it was therefore at *that* time only twenty-five minutes past four o'clock.

into the pit.   One of the shoes was "all blood", and at the sight he ran and brought a man named Lavell, (who lived close to Reynolds's, aforementioned) to come and look at them.   Blood was visible in various places around; some he saw about a couple of yards round, disposed in zigzag or triangular form; another little pool was observed near a bush, and elsewhere.   Having

ABRAHAM THORNTON.   MARY ASHFORD.

At about half-past four o'clock in the morning a labourer started from Hurst Street, Birmingham, to his work at Penn's; it was just five o'clock when he passed the top of Moor Street, in Dale End, and he reached Erdington about (perhaps a little before) six o'clock.   Taking, as usual, the road leading into Penn's Lane (along Bell Lane, and down the foredrough into the footroad leading to Penn's Lane,) he passed between two pits close to the latter road, and by the side of the one on the left hand side of the path he observed a bonnet, a pair of shoes, and a bundle, lying close by the top of the slope leading down

gathered together several people from Penn's Mills, he did not wait to see the cause, but proceeded at once to his business; it was about half-past six o'clock, when he first reached the scene of what was as yet a mystery.

At about seven o'clock, after several fruitless attempts, the body of the young woman was dragged out of the pit with a rake,—and recognised as that of Mary Ashford.   The dress she wore was that in which she was last seen, and bore marks of blood; and when the scarlet "spencer" was taken off, in the presence of Mr. Joseph Webster, the owner of Penn's Mills, that gentle-

48

man observed, on each arm, what appeared to be marks from the grasp of a man's hand. Footprints, (as shown on the plan engraved on page 374,) were observed along the soft ground of the field adjoining, which was harrowed, of a man and woman, (sworn to be those of Thornton and Mary Ashford), down the field, then back again, alternately running, walking, and dodging ; and terminating within a few yards of the fatal pit ; under a tree opposite, on the other side of Penn's Lane, other marks were observable, indicating a struggle and an ultimate yielding (or compulsion) to the suspected man's guilty purpose. From this place to the pit was the track of blood.

Two of the workmen, Lavell and Bird, carefully traced out at an early hour in the morning, the footprints which traversed the harrowed field from side to side, and, with the assistance of Mr. Webster, measured the woman's footprints with the shoes taken off the deceased ; and they were sworn to correspond exactly therewith.

The first excitement of the discovery of Mary Ashford, being over, they next proceeded towards unravelling the mystery. Daniel Clarke, the landlord of the "Tyburn House," hearing of the affair, started off in search of Thornton, and met him near the Chapel, at Castle Bromwich, on a pony. Clarke says : "I said to him ; ' What is become of the young woman that went away with you from my house, last night ;' he made no answer I said, ' She is murdered and thrown into a pit.' He said, ' Murdered !'—' Yes, murdered !' ' Why,' said Thornton, ' I was with her till four o'clock this morning.' ' Then,' said I, ' you must go along with me and clear yourself.' He said ' I can soon do that ' " * The two then rode back towards "Tyburn House," a distance of more than a mile ; yet, according to Clarke's evidence, neither of them once referred, on their way to the terrible event which had thus brought them together. They talked about farming, and on miscellaneous topics of general

interest ; but of the girl who had been foully treated and so far as they knew, *murdered*, within a mile of the place where they then stood, and with whom Thornton had danced on the preceding evening, and, by his own confession, walked until four o'clock that very morning, not a word was said after the conversation just recorded. No enquiry as to the circumstances under which her melancholy fate had been discovered, no anxiety to unravel the mystery on the part of the man who, so suspiciously implicated in the transaction, yet declared himself innocent ; he simply "talked about farming." On reaching the house of Daniel Clarke, Thornton seems to have taken his ease ; "had something to eat and drink," and remained there until the constable arrived from Birmingham, soon after ten o'clock. He was taken into custody and searched by the latter, assisted by a man named Benson. The search resulted in an admission of the prisoner's criminality, but not as to the murder ; and the confession was qualified by the statement that in his guilt the poor girl had been a consenting party. At one o'clock in the day he was examined by William Bedford, Esq., one of the magistrates for the county ; and deposed as follows :

That he, (ABRAHAM THORNTON,) was by trade a bricklayer—that he lived with his father, at Castle Bromwich —that he had been at a dance at Tyburn House, on the night of the 26th of May last—that he danced with the deceased (MARY ASHFORD,) and came away from the house with her, early the next morning,—that Hannah Cox, and a young man of the name of Carter, went part of the way with them—that after Examinant and Deceased were left by the other two, they walked on by themselves till they came to a stile, and then they went over four or five fields,—that they afterwards came back to the stile again, and sat on it, talking about a quarter of an hour,—while they sat there, a man came by, who wished them a good morning ; Examinant wished him a good morning,—that he soon afterwards went on towards Erdington ; he went to the Green, at Erdington, with Mary Ashford, and then she went on by herself ; she said she was going to Mrs. Butler's, —that he waited on the Green some time for the Deceased,— but as she did not come back, he then went towards home.— In his road home, he saw young Mr. Holden near to his father's house ; he also saw a man and woman in the road there, at the same time,—that after he had passed Mr.

---

* Examination of Daniel Clarke, *vide* Trial of Thornton, p. 42.

Holden's house, he saw John Haydon, Mr. Rotton's game-keeper, taking up some nets at the floodgates, near Mr. Twamley's Mill, and spoke to him; he stopped to talk with him about a quarter of an hour,—that he also saw John Woodcock, Mr. Twamley's Miller, while he stood talking to Haydon, but he did not speak to him,—that he afterwards passed James White, who was at work at Mr. Wheelwright's bank; and then he went straight home. Examinant further said, that when he got home, it wanted twenty minutes to five, by his father's clock,—he took off a black coat which he had on, and put on another,—he also took off his hat and hung it up in the house,—that he did not pull off his shoes, though they were very wet, from walking through the grass,—he said that he had been drinking the whole evening, but that he was not much intoxicated.

The persons referred to all testified to having met the prisoner. The first, William Jennings, a milkman, met him in the lane leading down from Erdington, towards the old Tamworth road, at or about half-past four o'clock; he was then "walking very leisurely along the road, without the least appearance of heat or hurry about him;" Jennings' wife also corroborated his statement. A servant at Mr. Holden's, a house just below the canal bridge, also deposed to having seen from her chamber window a man walking down the road, whom she *thought* she afterwards identified as Thornton; it was then between half-past four and twenty minutes to five o'clock. Her master's son, Mr. John Holden, junr., also saw the prisoner. John Haydon, Mr. Rotton's game-keeper, testified to his having, as Thornton stated, been down to the floodgates to take up some nets, at about five in the morning, and that he saw and spoke to the prisoner. Woodcock, the miller, saw the two men talking together, and "had since calculated that it must have been about ten minutes past five."

The reader will at once see that it is in this portion of the evidence that the principal difficulties present themselves. If the prisoner returned to the fatal field from Mrs. Butler's, (that is, supposing he ever accompanied the girl there, for it must be remembered that all the witnesses deposed to meeting her *alone*, no other person being in sight,) or if he remained at the place until Mary herself returned, it is necessary to suppose that within a quarter of an hour of the time she was last seen, (and she was *then* above five minutes' walk from the field,) he had committed both crimes, crossed the field, (as indicated by the sworn footsteps,) and reached the lane near Holden's house, where he was first seen by the milkman, at *half-past four o'clock*, or at the most thirty-five minutes past. Yet all the witnesses who saw him in that locality declared that he was walking leisurely, and without the least appearance of heat or confusion; and the distance *in a straight line* from the pit to that locality was nearly a mile and a half, and, by the way he himself said he had gone, it was quite two miles. It is therefore impossible to believe all the evidence, for if he had walked with Mary to Erdington, as he stated, then the witnesses who deposed to meeting her alone must have been mistaken, or wilfully perjured themselves. Again, supposing his statement to be true, the footsteps across the field in the direction of Tyburn and Castle Bromwich could not have been his, although they were sworn to have agreed exactly with the boots he wore.

"No trial," says a contemporary report, "since the year 1781, when the unfortunate Captain Donellan was convicted of poisoning his brother-in-law, Sir Theodosius Boughton, Bart.; and Pitmore and Hammond, for shooting Mr. Barrack, butcher, of Birmingham, ever excited so universally the attention of all ranks of people, as the present. By six o'clock in the morning, great numbers of persons had assembled before the gates of the County Hall, using every endeavour, interest, and entreaty to gain admission; and by eight o'clock, the time fixed for the trial to begin, the press at the doors was inconceivably great; and it was with the utmost difficulty that way could be made by the javelin men, for the entrance of the witnesses and other persons who were subpœned, either for the prosecution, or the defence, of the prisoner." The court was crowded in all parts to excess: and the jurors (eight of whom were either farmers or yeomen) having been sworn, the prisoner was charged with having " on the 27th of May last, in the Royal Town, Manor, and Lordship of Sutton Coldfield, in the County of Warwick, not having the fear of God before his

The evidence which we have endeavoured to summarise in the foregoing narrative was elicited, and submitted to a most careful examination, and the jury, without retiring, returned a verdict of " NOT GUILTY."

PORTRAIT OF MARY ASHFORD, IN THE DRESS SHE WORE AT THE DANCE.
From an old print in the possession of Mr. W Bates, B.A.

eyes, but being moved by the instigation of the Devil, wilfully murdered Mary Ashford, by throwing her into a Pit of Water." Thornton, of course, pleaded " Not Guilty," and the trial began; prefaced by the quaint, old-fashioned phrase addressed to the prisoner, " God send you a good deliverance."

To the inhabitants of the locality in which Mary Ashford had lived, as well as to many others who had manifested a deep interest in the case throughout the country, this verdict was most unsatisfactory; and to none more so than to William Ashford, the eldest brother of the deceased. Taking advantage, therefore, of an almost forgotten law, he *appealed* Abraham Thornton ; that is to say, he became, as it were, a private prosecutor, as the direct heir male of Mary Ashford, in a new trial instituted against him for the alleged murder of the appellant's sister. The trial was fixed for November 6th, 1817, but was postponed, at the request of the defendant, until the 17th, on which day the Lord Chief Justice Ellenborough, with other judges, took their seats for the hearing of the case. William Ashford, the appellant, is described in a contemporary account of the proceedings as " a plain country young man, about twenty-two years of age, of short stature, sandy hair, and blue eyes." The Count of Appeal having been read, the prisoner was asked, in the usual manner, whether he was guilty or not guilty of the crime "whereof he stood appealed." His reply,—the last occasion on which such a reply was made—startled the whole court, and brought back to mind a vivid picture of mediæval times : " *Not Guilty ; and I am ready to defend the same with my body.*" At the same time, from the depths of his counsel's bag (in which, for the sake of concealment, they had been brought into Court,) he produced a pair of large gauntlets, or horseman's leathern gloves, and, putting one on his left hand, (which he held up in giving the challenge,) he threw down the other on the floor for the appellant to take up. Both the Court and the audience were literally electrified at this extraordinary proceeding. There had been no " wager of battel " since 1638, and scarcely anyone except the half dozen lawyers who were learned in black letter lore knew exactly what would be the course to take under the circumstances. Ashford was a younger man,—little more than a boy, in fact,—and quite inferior to his opponent in strength and physique, and any trial of battle between him and Thornton would be unfairly matched ; there was, therefore, nothing left but for the former to appeal to the mercy of the Court, that they should not permit the cause to be decided by force. The " wager of battel " could only be resorted to in cases where there existed only circumstantial evidence of the crime, and was refused when the evidence was conclusive of guilt and admitted no denial, when the criminal was taken " red-handed," or in the event of his having " broken prison," or in any other way incriminated himself. The appellant based his plea to set aside the wager, therefore, on the assertion that the guilt of Thornton was sufficiently established to admit of no denial, and that, in consequence, the defendant was not entitled to that mode of trial. The bench, however, had never regarded with favour the appeal of murder, inasmuch as it seemed to imply some doubt of miscarriage of justice in the foregoing trial, and it was not probable, therefore, that the appellant in this case would get more than he was allowed by the strict letter of the law. The Court decided against the view Ashford took of the proven guilt of Thornton, and the former, finding it useless to pursue the matter further, withdrew the appeal, and left the issues of the case to the Judge of all the Earth, before whom both appellant and appellee have since been called ; we do not, therefore, presume to pass judgment, or to offer any suggestion as to the elucidation of the mystery ; but rather to leave it to the Higher Court, where

> ——the action lies
> In his true nature : and we ourselves compell'd,
> Even to the teeth and forehead of *our* faults,
> To give in evidence.*

Other serious crimes were committed in Birmingham during this decade, as we have previously mentioned. In the same year, on the 6th of February, a Mr. Pennington was murdered at Vauxhall ; Booth, the notorious coiner and bank-note forger, was arrested at Perry Barr, on the 28th of March, 1812, and on his premises were found £3,000 in good notes, 200 guineas in gold, £600 in counterfeit silver coin, and a large quantity of forged notes ; for his offences he suffered the extreme penalty of the law, during the same year. These and other instances showed

---

Hamlet, act iii, scene 3.

that while our town was increasing in population, extent, and prosperity, there was at the same time a considerable increase in the number of serious crimes committed in our midst.

CHAPTER LV.

AMUSEMENTS OF THE PEOPLE,
Including the history of the Theatre Royal, from 1811 to 1820.

A curious old playbill—Macready as Orestes—Elliston's address to Birmingham playgoers—His own performances—Miss Booth—Edmund Kean—Mathews—Munden—" Romeo Coates "—Dobb's Reaping Machine—Miss O'Neil—Grimaldi—An Arctic spectacle—Elliston as a humbug—The Bohemian Samson—Alfred Bunn—The third destruction of the Theatre Royal—Other amusements.

WE commence this decade of the theatrical history of Birmingham with a quaint old play-bill, the original of which is in the possession of Mr. Mercer H. Simpson, the present lessee of " the old Theatre." We have heard much of late years respecting the decline of the legitimate drama ; what would the grumblers of the present day think of such a performance as the following, in a ' patent ' theatre ?

Theatre Royal, Birmingham.
Combination of the MOST MIRACULOUS and *Fashionable* ATHLETIC EXERTIONS. Mr. M'Cready respectfully makes known to the Public that he has re-engaged Mr. WILSON for the Remaining Four Nights of the Season. On Monday Evening, December 16, 1811, will be performed Morton's favourite Comedy of *Secrets Worth Knowing.* . . . . End of the Play Mr. Wilson will go through the whole of his Performances on the TIGHT ROPE ! Particularly he will walk from the Stage to the Pit and back again, *wheeling a real Barrow,* and supporting a Boy at the same time. . . . . Likewise a Whimsical Dance, *with Two Boys suspended to his Feet. He will turn a Chair upside down, resting the Top on the Rope, and stand on the inverted Feet.* Also his wonderful Somerset over the Orchestra ; with several other astonishing Feats. After which will be presented Foote's revived Farce of the *Mayor of Garrat.* . . . . In the course of the Farce will be exhibited a Scene from the Metropolis. . . . . *for the purpose of introducing those celebrated and well known Champions,* BELCHER *and* HAMMOND *the Black.* . . . . Affording to the Amateurs and Admirers of the fashionable Art of Boxing, *A Sparring Match,* which must prove a " Gratifying Mill " to the " Brethren of the Fancy." . . . .

The younger Macready, whose *debut* we noticed our last chapter on the theatre, still progressed in favour and popularity. As *Orestes,* (August, 1812) we read that "his appearance altogether brought back departed ages to the imagination ; his acting throughout was dignified and impressive ; his mad scene was finely conceived, and executed with correctness, judgment, and feeling, that merited the repeated plaudits which accompanied his exit." His dress, on this occasion, we are informed on the same authority, was " picturesquely classical ; " an early presage of the reform he was afterwards to initiate in the archæology of the stage.

M'Cready left Birmingham in 1813, and the management of the Theatre Royal fell into the hands of the comedian, Robert William Elliston. Our readers may be curious to read the famous but eccentric manager's address to the Birmingham public :

" Stratford Place, London, May 20, 1813.—Having taken the Theatre Royal in Birmingham, for a term of years, I beg leave most respectfully to intreat your attention to an outline of the plan I mean to pursue in the approaching season. I purpose to open the theatre for a period of twenty weeks, benefit nights included, on Monday, the 31st of May instant. During this period performers in the highest estimation will occasionally appear. The pieces performed will be carefully selected, and diligently superintended ; and it will be my aim to present as often as circumstances permit, the very best example of the British Drama. To so large and populous a town as Birmingham, with a neighbourhood so crowded with opulence and distinction, a theatrical establishment is obviously necessary, in point of policy, as well as of rational recreation. In such a situation, it might be supposed that a theatre would sustain itself without very earnest solicitations for support. The fact, however, is that, even in this situation, unless a marked degree of protection be extended by those who lead and govern the public taste, the best efforts of the Manager must be enfeebled, and, in the end, defeated. By those, therefore, who may be desirous that Birmingham should have the advantage, as well as credit, of a well-regulated Theatre

I shall be excused, I hope, when I suggest that a most effectual aid might be afforded by causing one evening, at least, in the week to be considered fashionable for theatrical amusements. On this evening, without inconvenience, perhaps, to any individual, an expectation might be held out that the best company, or that a considerable portion of the best company, of Birmingham and its neighbourhood, would be collected at the Theatre. An elegant place of periodical assemblage might be thus established; and the Manager enabled to do justice to his own inclinations, and to satisfy the wish the public are always entitled to entertain, that what is done on a stage at all shall be done well. My intention is, that, in the general course of the season, there shall be three performances in the week, namely, on Monday, on Wednesday and on Friday. The Monday night will be commonly devoted to Tragedy; on the Wednesday, the performances will be miscellaneous; and on Friday, some Comedy, or other Drama, of pre-eminent merit, will be represented. If that night were to be distinguished in the manner I have pointed out, all persons coming to the Theatre on Friday would be assured of beholding an interesting performance, and of being surrounded by those they know, and might be pleased to meet. My own personal efforts on the stage will be humbly offered to your notice for a few nights during the season. During the unavoidable discharge of my duties elsewhere, those who act on my behalf will be urged, both by their own sense of respect and my most earnest injunctions, to show every possible attention to the accommodation, and the inclinations of all who may honour the Theatre by their presence or by their encouragement. Anxious as you must no doubt be, for the welfare of Birmingham and its neighbourhood, I trust you will pardon this intrusion on a subject so materially connected with its gratification and public character. The chief object of my ambition is to place the theatrical entertainments of Birmingham on a par with those of other great commercial places. In the pursuit of this object, I shall do my utmost to deserve patronage; and, if I gain it, all I can to show that I am grateful for it. I have the honour to be, your most obedient humble servant, ROBERT WILLIAM ELLISTON."

The new manager had taken care to inaugurate his reign at the Theatre Royal with a strong company. On the 31st of May was presented the favourite comedy of the "Soldier's Daughter," with Mr. Bartley, Mr. F. Middleton, Mr. Mallinson, Mr. Hollingsworth, Miss Wheeldon, Mrs. Grove, Mrs. Payne, Mrs. and Miss Weston, and many other eminent artists, selected from the best metropolitan and provincial companies. It was during Elliston's first season here that the custom was established of regarding Friday as the fashionable night—a custom which has found favour among us from that time to the present day; and

even now, as in 1813, may be observed at the Birmingham theatres during an attractive engagement "an unusual display of beauty and fashion, who by their cheering approbation of the performers, give an additional spur to their exertions."*

The manager reserved the special attraction of his own appearance on the Birmingham boards until July; on the 12th of that month he came for the first time before his new patrons in the part of *Octavian*, in Coleman's play of "The Mountaineers," on which occasion, we are told, "he supported the character with his accustomed excellence." On the following Wednesday "his very successful and spirited representation of the three Shingles (aided by the comic powers of Messrs. Mallinson and Dobbs), convulsed the house with continual bursts of laughter." The following day he sustained the part of *Othello;* and on the Friday, he appeared with Miss Booth, (who made her *debut* here on that occasion) in the comedy of "The Will."

Referring to Miss Booth the *Gazette* says: "Those who witnessed the spirit and vivacity of her performance, and the delicate proportion of her form, will think it almost incredible, that she had played *Angela* in London on the evening preceding, and, after that exertion, had travelled all night and day, to arrive in Birmingham, just in time to dress for *Albina*."

The season of 1814 was one which old Birmingham play-goers may well have looked back upon with loving remembrance. In September Edmund Kean came among us for the first time, and expectation was rife concerning the new star —*meteor*, we might almost have said—who had burst so suddenly upon the theatrical firmament, whose acting Coleridge had compared to the reading of Shakespeare by flashes of lightning. Our readers may perhaps like to hear what a local critic has to say about Edmund Kean :—

Judging . . . from an observation which has been at least attentive, if not accurate, it appears evidently

* *Aris's Birmingham Gazette,* June 14, 1813.

conspicuous that he is a most extraordinary actor ; his representation of passion is not descriptive but imitative ; the silent, yet forcible attacks he makes on the heart and feelings of his auditors are irresistible, and we are involuntary hurried into a sympathy with the character before us. With Mr. Kean the character is never seen to be well exhibited, as in many eminent performers, but is the character itself and we forget the actor in our pity, fear, disgust, or horror of the individual represented. The page of nature has occupied Mr. Kean's attention, and he has read volumes with a facility of attention and exertion which ordinary minds must vainly hope to attain, and which mere study, perhaps, will never accomplish. His eye, his lip, unequalled in expression, his every limb and his every fibre seem to act in unison with the passion, and to unite in promoting one prodigious whole. He must be seen to be truly appreciated ; and if a few sceptics should be slow in belief, the effulgence of such a star must be shortly universally acknowledged.*

But Kean was not the only actor of note who visited the Birmingham Theatre during that season. On the 12th of December we read that "Mr. Mathews, who has been prevented by his late serious accident from appearing on our boards at an earlier period of the season, will this evening introduce an entertainment prepared by himself, called Mail Coach Adventures, in the course of which he will sing most of his popular songs." Mr. Munden—the Hogarth of 'the grand grotesque of farce,' as Lamb styled him— Mr. Elliston himself, Mrs. Jordan, Miss Sally Booth, and other celebrities of the time also appeared on the Birmingham boards during the same season ; but of all who visited us in 1814, none created more excitement than the ridiculous and eccentric "Romeo" Coates. Laughed at for his absurd amateur impersonations of Romeo, and "that gallant, gay Lothario," courted for his immense wealth, his matchless diamonds, he was the talk of society. He rode in a splendid curricle, the body of which was in the form of a cockle-shell, on which, as well as on the harness of his horses, appeared his crest, a cock, with which became associated the motto " Whilst we live, we'll crow." He came to Birmingham in the month of September, 1814, and performed here "in his usual classical style, the part of the

gallant, gay Lothario." In a newspaper report of the period we read that "the house was crowded, and the amateur was received with every attention. . . . An unbounded peal of applause marked his entrance, and the three angular bows with which he returned the compliment were received with 'Bravo! bravo?' The performance proceeded amidst acclamations, occasioned by the singular attitudes and emphasis of the amateur ; the other performers participating in the general mirth, added to the risibility of the audience, who were so much pleased by his dying, that a general *encore* produced an entire new scene not intended by the author—this was a negotiation before the audience, between the *dead man*, the manager, and the characters on the stage, all requesting him to indulge the audience, and to which he consented. The manager accordingly announced that he would repeat the dying scene; but after waiting till the patience of the audience was exhausted, the last act was commenced amid uproar, and this was performed entirely in dumb show. The manager then came forward and said, that as the *dead man* had not spoken quite plainly they had misunderstood him, and that Mr. Coates would speak the address which he had intended to deliver before the Prince Regent and the Emperor of Russia, but which he was prevented from doing, by their not giving him an opportunity.* To this the audience assented— the curtain drew up, the band played 'See, the Conquering Hero Comes," and in marched the amateur in regimentals. The storm was hushed, but scarcely had a couplet proceeded from his lips, than an unlucky wight in the gallery called out 'Sing it.' The blood of the amateur was up ; he took off his hat, and showed as much contempt as the nature of his face would admit of. . . . He ran off the stage to the regret of the whole house, and all the rhetoric of the manager was exerted in vain to induce him to

---

* His invitation to Court on this occasion was one of the cruel and senseless hoaxes of Theodore Hook.

FORWARD

F. SCHNADHORST,

SECRETARY TO THE BIRMINGHAM LIBERAL ASSOCIATION.

PHOTOGRAPHD BY WHITLOCK.

BIRMINGHAM: HOUGHTON & CO., SCOTLAND PASSAGE.

return. The after-piece passed in dumb show, and thus ended this mighty history."

It will scarcely be credited that under the management of Robert William Elliston, an artificial field of standing corn was introduced into a piece for the purpose of showing Mr. Dobb's reaping

During 1816 local playgoers were promised an unusual treat, in the engagement of the celebrated Miss O'Neil; but the fulfilment of that promise seemed for some time a matter of considerable doubt, and they were tantalized from hour to hour, alternating between hope and fear, now

OLD VIEW OF THE TOP OF NEW STREET, SHOWING THE SOCIETY OF ARTISTS' ROOMS.

machine at work. The piece into which this curious incident was introduced, was, according to the play-bill, 'the celebrated Farce of Fortune's Frolic;' the part of *Robin Roughead* was sustained by Mr. Dobbs, who worked the machine and explained its principles during the progress of the farce. We have heard in recent times of a much-advertised sewing machine being introduced into the harlequinade of a Pantomime, but perhaps the episode of the Dobbs Reaping Machine is unequalled in the annals of the British Stage.

49

saying "she will come," and anon, "she will not," and like Gretchen fearing lest the "not," should be the final statement of the case. The actress had, during a short leave of absence from the Covent Garden Theatre, visited several of the principal towns in the provinces, and had concluded an engagement with Mr. Elliston to appear at the Theatre Royal, Birmingham, for six nights, for the sum of six hundred guineas; but on the eve of the engagement the Covent Garden proprietors interfered to prevent Miss O'Neil from performing here, stating that her leave of absence had expired. A delay occurred, during which a letter was received from the lady herself, *confirming* her engagement, but at the same time informing the manager that it would be impossible to reach Birmingham that day. In consequence of the delay, therefore, the theatre was closed from Wednesday, October 2nd, until the following Monday ; and during this period doubts were still entertained as to whether she would fulfil her engagement. Miss O'Neil, imagining from an interview she had had with Mr. Barlow, the Covent Garden manager, that her immediate attendance in town was absolutely necessary, left Manchester with the intention of appearing in Birmingham on the Thursday evening, for the one performance only ; but finding Mr. Elliston absent, she continued her journey to London, and discovered that the Birmingham manager had succeeded in obtaining permission for the fulfilment of her engagement with him, upon which she returned, hoping to perform here on the Saturday. Handbills were speedily printed and circulated, assuring the public that Miss O'Neil had arrived in Birmingham, and would commence her engagement on Monday, October 7th.

The excitement caused by Miss O'Neil's visit is well reflected in the following report from the *Gazette* of October 14th :—

In the memory of the oldest inhabitant of the town, no event in our theatrical history has occasioned a sensation so remarkable as the performances of Miss O'Neil. The *mania* for a view of this interesting and highly gifted young lady has not been confined to any particular class in society, but pervaded all ranks ; even a glance at her in her carriage was considered worthy of contention, and the doors of the Royal Hotel were constantly besieged with spectators, anxious to catch a glimps of her, at her entrance or departure from the house.

Excepting at the periods of our Musical Festivals, we do not recollect to have seen so great an influx of strangers : and certainly on no former occasion do we remember such overflowing houses, or to have witnessed so extraordinary an avidity to obtain admission within the theatre. On almost every night of her appearance, the house filled so quickly that the doors have been closed long before the usual hour of commencement, and hundreds unable to effect an entrance have been obliged to return disappointed. To enter upon a minute criticism of Miss O'Neil's acting is unnecessary, the thousands who

have been present during her performances have only to recall to their minds those touches of deep pathos by which their symyathy was so frequently and irresistibly excited. Her tones and enunciation are peculiarly harmonious and distinct, and her attention to the scene undeviating. Her delineation of the progress of passion appeared to us strikingly correct—her bursts seemed to electrify the whole of her auditors.

Mr. Elliston, who has been unceasing in his efforts to secure her eminent talents, has, we perceive with satisfaction, re-engaged her for a few nights next season.

The exertions of Mr. Conway and Mr. Bartley, during the engagement of Miss O'Neil, have most essentially contributed to give due effect to that lady's performance, by the able manner in which the characters allotted them have been sustained. The former of these gentlemen will take his benefit this evening, being the only remuneration for his valuable services, and Mr. Bartley on Friday. On both occasions, we trust, their friends and the public will convince them that their eminent services on this, and on former occasions, are not forgotten, and will not be allowed to pass unrequited.

The plays represented on the occasion of Miss O'Neil's visit were " Romeo and Juliet," " The Jealous Wife," " Venice Preserved," " The Stranger," and " The Gamester."

During the season of 1817 the famous clown, Joseph Grimaldi appeared, in a new comic pantomime, on the Birmingham boards, delighting large audiences, as he never failed to do, by his broad —yet never indecorous—humour.

Realism and spectacular display seem to have formed the staple attraction during the closing years of Elliston's management. During 1818 a drama was produced entitled " The North Pole, or the Arctic Expedition, with remarkable scenic effects, if the following description of the closing scene was borne out by the representation :—

A Ship of immense size, fully rigged, with a Crew of forty Persons, commanded by a Naval Officer, will effect her passage through floating Islands of Ice, which, on separating, will show an Expanse of Ocean covering the Whole Stage ; she will sa down to the Front Lights with her Bowsprit over the Pit ! producing as novel and powerful effect as can be exhibited on the stage.

Many droll anecdotes are told respecting Elliston's career in Birmingham, especially of the shifts he made to attract, and then to trick his audience. On one occasion, after a long continuance of empty benches, and (consequently) empty coffers, the town awoke one morning to find the walls and hoardings covered with flaming posters announcing that an engagement had been entered into by Mr. Elliston with a *Bohemian Giant* of remarkable strength, who was to perform many extraordinary feats with a huge stone, weighing more than a ton, which he would toss about as easily as an ordinary individual would a tennis-ball. This was an attraction not to be resisted by Birmingham play-goers. *Hamlet* and *Macbeth* might be played to empty houses, the wit of Sheridan might woo pleasure-seekers in vain, but a clap-trap performance exhibiting extraordinary brute force was capable of attracting a crowded house, full almost to overflowing, from floor to ceiling.

When the play which preceded this exhibition was over, the public, who had regarded the legitimate part of the entertainment with the utmost impatience, sat in eager expectation of the intellectual *entr'acte*, and after waiting for some minutes, became clamorous for the appearance of the Bohemian Samson. At length the manager, who was a master of the art of bamboozling, rushed before the curtain in the utmost apparent anxiety. 'The Bohemian has deceived me !' he cried. '*That*, however, I could have pardoned ; but he has deceived you, my friends, *you* ;' and his voice trembled with emotion as he endeavoured to stifle his sobs : 'I repeat, he has deceived me ; he is not here.'

The universal disappointment found vent in a perfect yell, which burst forth from every part of the house. The wily manager, however, was quite equal to the occasion ; drawing a bundle of letters from his pocket, he held them up. 'Here is the correspondence,' he said. 'Does any gentleman here understand German? If so, will he oblige me by stepping forward.'

No, it did not appear that the audience included a single German scholar, or at any rate, if so, he was too modest to step forward.

'Am I, then, left alone?' cried the manager, still sustaining his well-feigned emotion. 'Well, I will translate them for you.'

A few voices in the large assembly were heard above the rest, disclaiming the implied incredulity in requiring vouchers of Mr. Elliston's good faith.

'Your commands, then, shall be obeyed,' he replied, returning the supposed autographs of the perfidious Hercules. 'I will not read them. But, my dear patrons, your kind consideration shall not go unrewarded. You shall not say you have paid your money for nothing. Thank heaven, I can satisfy you of my own integrity, and present you with a portion of the entertainment you have paid to see. The Bohemian, the villain, is not here. But the *stone* is, and YOU SHALL SEE IT.' The orchestra struck up a lively air, and the curtain rose slowly, disclosing a huge piece of sandstone rock, upon which was stuck a label, with the inscription in huge letters, 'THIS IS THE STONE.'

The gullible public was satisfied, the manager's coffers were amply replenished, and the story of the Bohemian Samson who was to have tossed a ton of stone about like a tennis ball was told by many a Birmingham playgoer to his children. Need we say, however, that the only existence the prodigy ever had was in the fertile brain of Robert William Elliston.

In spite of all his resources, however, Elliston was unable to make the theatre pay ; he said that in 1818 he lost £1,500. His trickery (of which the example just recorded was but one out of many similar instances) disgusted the real playgoing public, and at the beginning of the year 1819 he found himself compelled to withdraw from the management of the theatre. He was succeeded by Mr. Alfred Bunn,—"hot, cross Bunn," as *Punch* used to call him,—who announced all kinds of novelty and attraction; caused the theatre to be entirely renovated and re-decorated by Westmacott, and for the first time to be lighted with gas. On the 6th of January, 1820, Sheridan's "Pizarro" was played, and the performance having concluded at an earlier hour than usual, the theatre was in darkness by half-past eleven o'clock, and the actors had left it for the night,—and for ever. The echoes of applause had scarcely died away in the deserted building, when vast columns of smoke and flame were seen breaking out from the windows and issuing from the roof. Thousands of the inhabitants

and 1793. The building was insured for £7,000, and Mr. Bunn had insured his own personal property contained therein for £2,000, but the poor players lost all they had.

There was at that time, it seems, a " Minor Theatre," in Worcester Street, of the perform-

"ROMEO COATES."
From an old print.

came out to see the old playhouse once more perish in the flames. All attempts to save it were in vain ; amid the drizzling rain the roof fell in with a crash which shook the ground for some distance around, and in three hours nothing was left but the bare walls and (curiously enough) the original façade, which thus braved the fury of two destructive fires, and still stands an interesting momento of the old playhouses of 1780

ances at which the *Gazette* contains one or two notices in the year 1818. It was a wooden building, which stood opposite the ' King's Head ; ' and to this humble abode came the burnt-out players, and performed, appropriately enough, " Raising the Wind," " A Cure for the Heartache," and " Blue Devils." Of this pitiable attempt at " raising the wind," Oxberry says, " the humanity of the hardware folks may be surmised when we state as a positive fact that Sherwin shared only 7s. 4d. after performing three nights.

The playgoing public were not altogether without entertainments during the re-building of the theatre. On the 3rd of July, 1820, we read that "the celebrated Mr. Mathews, from the English Opera House, has the Honour to inform the Public of Birmingham and its Neighbourhood, that he will have the Pleasure of being "At Home" in the Royal Hotel Assembly Rooms, on Thursday, the 20th, and Saturday, the 22nd instant, when he will entertain his Friends with his two last popular entertainments—"A Trip to Paris," and his "Country Cousins."

By the end of July, in the same year, the new Theatre was so far advanced towards completion that the manager was able to announce the re-opening for the 14th of the following month, and the performers were by public notice directed to assemble on the 10th; new scenery had been painted by Messrs. Greenwood, Whitmore, and Grieve, and the theatre had been handsomely decorated by Dixon. The new theatre was opened as announced, on the 14th of August, with Sheridan's comedy of "The Rivals," and a new farce entitled "The Promissory Note," written by the architect of the building, Mr. S. Beazley.

Among the other amusements of this decade we notice that Madame Tussaud paid a visit to Birmingham in November, 1813, and exhibited her collection of wax-work, (which had already won for itself a position far above other similar exhibitions) at the Shakespear Tavern, in New Street. Worthy of note, too, both on account of the performer himself and the locality upon which he pitched his tent, is the visit of the famous equestrian, Ryan, who performed at a "New Equestrian Circus" which was erected on the Moat grounds—the last occasion on which they were used for the purpose previous to their conversion into the Smithfield Market—during the Whitsuntide Fair of 1815.

We had also occasional flying visits from Mr. Haddock, with his famous Mechanic Theatre; Ingleby, the Conjuror; Cartwright's Musical Glasses and Philosophical Fireworks; A Spectacular Entertainment, representing the obsequies of the Princess Charlotte, and other miscellaneous shows and sights as in modern times.

CHAPTER LVI.

THE FIRST PHILOSOPHICAL AND ARTISTIC SOCIETIES OF BIRMINGHAM.

The Philosophical Institution—Description of the Building—The Academy of Arts and its First Exhibition—Conditions for the reception of Pictures—The Society of Artists—First Patrons and Subscribers—Erection of the Permanent Building in New Street—Description of the Building—Catherine Hutton on Arts and Artists in Birmingham.

THE second decade of the nineteenth century is memorable in the history of the arts in Birmingham, as having seen the birth of two institutions which have exerted a beneficial influence upon our town, both in respect of mental culture and of artistic training, and ultimately led to the formation of a third institution which remains to this day almost unique, both as to its character and as to the work which it has accomplished. The first of these was the Birmingham Philosophical Society, the germ of which existed, in the form of a small private society, as early as the year 1800. A few scientific inhabitants, having formed themselves into a Society for the study of experimental philosophy, found many others anxious to share in their labours, and in 1813

...rchased commodious premises in Cannon Street, which they fitted up in the same manner as the Royal Institution of London. The first lecture in the Society's new home, was delivered by the Rev. John Corrie (the President), on the 17th of October, 1814. The lecture-room was spacious (for that time), being capable of seating upwards of two hundred persons; it was semi-circular in shape, having raised tiers of benches, and the ceiling was supported by two light pillars of cast-iron. Within the building were various smaller rooms for the pursuit of divers branches of experimental philosophy, amply provided with necessary apparatus; also a museum, a news-room and other apartments: it was, in fact, a complete and admirably furnished scientific institute, and within its walls many of our townsmen, whose names are now familiar in our mouths as household words, received a valuable scientific and philosophical training. As we have already related, we are indebted to this Society for the establishment of the Institution for the Deaf and Dumb, and moreover, in all probability, for the foundation of one of the noblest of our local institutions, of which it was, in a measure the prototype, the Birmingham and Midland Institute.

There was, however, a still more important institution than the Philosophical Society founded during this decade, the forerunner of the Society of Artists—viz., the Birmingham Academy of Arts. In April, 1814, a little society, composed of resident Artists and Amateurs, "convinced by their own experience that Birmingham possesses many local and peculiar advantages for assembling and exhibiting Works of Art, encouraged by the liberal spirit of its inhabitants, and by the particular attention now excited to subjects of Art and Science nearly allied to their own," announced their intention of opening an Annual Exhibition. They pledged themselves for the impartiality of their proceedings; adding that "no considerations shall induce them to swerve from the conduct prescribed to them, by a regard

to the success and reputation of their establishment, and in the general taste of those whose judgment they respect, and whose approbation, therefore, it will always be their principal study to obtain."

The list of honorary members included the names of Benjamin West, Thomas Phillips, J. M. W. Turner, John Flaxman, Richard Westmacott, John Soane, Dr. De Lys, and others of eminence in the world of art and science. The secretary of the new society was the late Mr. J. Vincent Barber, whose works now in the possession of the Birmingham and Midland Institute, and in the engraved "Graphic Illustrations of Warwickshire," are known to all lovers of art in the Midland Counties. The Conditions for the reception of Pictures were as follows :—

1. That those Artists and Amateurs only, who are permanently resident within 30 miles of Birmingham, be eligible as Exhibitors.

2. That the Exhibition shall consist of original Paintings in Oil and Water Colours, Sculptures, Models, Architectural Designs, Engravings, Pictures in Crayons, Miniatures, and Impressions from Medal Dies, and from Engravings on precious Stones.

3. That the Admission or Rejection of all Works sent for Exhibition shall depend on the Decision of a Committee composed of an equal Number of Amateurs and Professors.

4. That Pictures sent for Exhibition shall be properly framed, with or without Glasses, having the Name and Address of the Artist or Amateur, and a Description of the Subject, to appear in the Catalogue, pasted on the Back, and those Works which are intended for Sale must be accompanied by a written Communication, stating the Terms upon which they are to be disposed of.

The Society, however, will not be accountable for Breaking of Glasses, or for any Accidents that may happen to the Works sent for Exhibition, although the utmost Care shall be taken to protect them.

5. That the Exhibition shall open the first Week in September, 1814, and that Pictures and other Works of Art intended for Exhibition must be delivered on the 22nd, 23rd, or 24th of August preceding.

An early Intimation will be given of the Place of Exhibition.

Those Artists and Amateurs who intend to become Exhibitors are requested to communicate their Intention to the Secretary as early as possible, stating the probable Number and Sizes of their Productions, that the Society may calculate accordingly.

Birmingham, April 9, 1814.

J. VINCENT BARBER, Secretary.

SOCIETY OF ARTISTS.

The first exhibition was opened on Monday, September 12, 1814, and was held in a temporary room in Union Street, at the back of the old Birmingham Fire Offices. It was not to be supposed that the members were satisfied with this miserable accommodation, and within a month of the opening of the exhibition we find appended to their advertisement a plan for the establishment of a permanent home for their collections. During the short period which had elapsed since its opening, they had been "induced to hope that a favourable opinion had been formed with regard to the general utility of the establishment, even in its present limited state ;" and "judging by the attention their Plans had already experienced, they indulged a confident expectation that the Taste and Liberality of the Public, would enable them to accomplish the full extent of their designs." Then followed a

Plan of Donations towards the Erection of an Academy of Arts in Birmingham.

A Donor of Five Guineas to have personal admission to the Annual Exhibition.

A Donor of Ten Guineas to have personal admission, and the liberty of bringing *one* friend each Day.

A Donor of Fifteen Guineas to have personal admission, and the Liberty of bringing *two* Friends each Day ; and so on to any Amount of Donations.

The Donations will not be called for until the amount required is subscribed.

A second society of a similar character, but having a more extended scope, was established in 1821. The first note respecting it appeared in the *Gazette* on the first of January in that year, congratulating its readers on " the probability of an Institution being soon established in this town for encouraging the cultivation of the Fine Arts." The projectors of the movement published the following requisition on the 26th of the same month :

We, the undersigned, considering that the due cultivation of the Fine Arts is essential to the prosperity of the manufactures of this town and neighbourhood, and that no society at present exists for this specific purpose, and being of opinion that it is extremely desirable that such a society should be now formed, do hereby invite all persons resident in the town and neighbourhood of Birmingham, who may be disposed to unite in promoting this object,

to a meeting, to be held at the Public Office, in Moor Street, on Wednesday, the 7th of February, at twelve o'clock in the forenoon, in order to take the subject into consideration.

Samuel Galton,	Josiah Corrie,
Edward Outram,	J. A. James,
William Hamper,	John Johnstone,
Edward Johnstone,	Timothy Smith,
J. H. Spry,	S. Tertius Galton,
James Woolley,	John Gordon,
Samuel Ryland,	Thomas Attwood,
William Wallis,	John Towers Lawrence,
H. Galton,	Edward Thomason,
George Yates,	Archibald Kenrick,
W. Wynne Smith,	John Badams,
J. W. Unett,	Theophilus Richards, jun.,
P. M. James,	J. V. Barber.
George Barker,	

The meeting was held as announced, Samuel Galton presiding, and it was resolved that the proposed institution be established, and called " The Birmingham Society of Arts ;" that a Museum be formed for the reception of objects of art ; that suitable accommodation be provided for students in the Fine Arts ; that the Committee be empowered to make arrangements for public exhibitions, and for the delivery of lectures ; and that the Members of the Institution should consist of Patrons (subscribing £100 or more), Proprietors (subscribing £50), and Governors,—the latter being the annual subscribers of two guineas ; certain privileges being accorded to each of the several grades of subscription. A provisional committee was formed, and the following liberal subscriptions and donations were received :

	£
Sir Robert Lawley, Bart., a valuable Collection of Casts.	
Lord Beauchamp	100
Sir Charles Mordaunt	100
H. Legge	100
D. S. Dugdale	100
Timothy Smith	50
F. Lawley	100
T. Lawrence	50
Edward Thomason	50
Samuel Galton	100
S. Tertius Galton	100
Hubert Galton	100
M. R. Boulton	100
James Taylor	100
Samuel Ryland	100
Mark Sanders	100

In May, 1822, we read that the Society's Museum in New Street "is now fitted up, and furnished with the valuable Collection of Casts from the Antique, presented to the Society by Sir Robert Lawley, Bart.," and that it is to be opened on the 4th of June, for the admission of members and students. "The Committee," we read further, "have availed themselves of a favourable opportunity of providing a considerable addition to the present collection, through the assiduity of a gentleman who is visiting Italy, and who has politely offered his services in selecting such specimens of the works of art, as will best promote the objects of the Society." The Society does not appear to have organised an Exhibition of Pictures until the autumn of 1827. Among the artists represented in the first exhibition we meet with the names of J. Vincent Barber, Samuel Lines and his sons (who together exhibited no less than nineteen pictures), Thomas Wyatt, Henshaw, Creswick, Everett, Wallace, Coleman, Walker, Rhodes, Hobday, Room, Jukes, and others of more than local fame. The celebrated sculptor, Chantrey, visited the Exhibition prior to its opening, and "expressed a lively interest in the Institution, and suggested many valuable hints in reference to the Exhibition, 'of which,' we are told, 'the Committee intend to avail themselves.'" *

The Society had not allowed the idea of a suitable block of buildings for the accommodation of the Exhibitions to lie unimproved. By the end of July, 1829, the new building was nearly completed, and the following interesting description appeared in the *Gazette* of July 13 :

The new buildings of the society, which are now so near their completion, consist of a magnificent circular Exhibition-room, 52 feet diameter, with a dome roof, and lighted from the centre by a skylight, 29 feet diameter ; the ceiling is thrown into panels, and the general effect of the room is novel and striking ; indeed, when filled with well painted pictures, we have little doubt of its being considered the finest room of its kind in the kingdom. It is approached from New Street by a spacious flight of steps, and on each side are convenient and well-lighted

rooms, one of which will be used as a library or committee-room, and the other as an exhibition room for sculpture ; between the latter and the circular room is a small octagonal room, forming a communication between the two, and which it is intended to use for miniatures or other small works of art. Beyond the large room is a light and spacious room for the exhibition of water-colour drawings, and adjoining thereto is a long room for exhibiting prints. It will thus be evident that every accommodation has been provided which can be required in an exhibition of works of art ; and care has been taken so to arrange the rooms as to make them available for the other uses to which the Society will appropriate them. In addition to the rooms above enumerated, accommodations have been provided for the keeper, &c., &c. The exterior elevation in New Street is executed in Bath stone, and is of the Corinthian order of architecture. It has a finely proportioned portico, which, by the permission of the Commissioners of the Streets, it was allowed to extend across the footpath ; thus not only affording greater convenience for persons visiting the exhibition in carriages, but also materially adding to the architectural beauty of the edifice. The example which has been chosen by the Architects as their model, and which, although not servilely copied, they have adapted to their purpose, is one of the most chaste and exquisite remains of Roman splendour, the Temple of Jupiter Stator, the purity of which is worthy of the most refined period of Grecian excellence in the arts of design. It is the intention of the Society to erect other buildings beyond the present termination towards the Post Office, so as entirely to exclude any view of the back buildings from New Street, by which the exterior appearance will be greatly increased.

Miss Catherine Hutton, hearing of this movement, writes, in her too frequently cynical manner when she has occasion to speak of Birmingham or its people: "With regard to the arts, I think the genius of the artists of Birmingham is more calculated to paint tea boards than pictures ; and that the fate of their Exhibition will be to die a natural death. I should not wonder if this happens before they have erected a building for the reception of their paintings : but if afterwards, it is no matter ; it will serve for a Methodist meeting house. That society is flourishing enough to take possession of all cast-off public edifices, whatsoever."

As we know, this elegant suite of rooms did *not* fall into the hands of the Wesleyans, or any other religious society ; and the artists, albeit some of them had exhibited their skill in the painting of tea-trays, did not stop at that humble sphere of artistic labour. We purpose in an early chapter to group together a few of those local artists of the earlier period of our art history; meanwhile we take our leave for the present of the artistic and scientific societies of the town.

CHAPTER LVII.

THE CHURCHES AND SECTS IN BIRMINGHAM, 1821-1830.

Holy Trinity Chapel, Bordesley—St. Peter's Church—Burning of St. Peter's—St. Thomas's Church—Rebuilding of Cherry Street Chapel—St. Andrew's, or Mount Zion Chapel, Graham Street—Edward Irving—The Swedenborgians and their Meeting-house—New Synagogue, Severn Street—The first Temperance Society in Birmingham.

In our last chapter of the history of religion in Birmingham, mention was made of the commencement of Holy Trinity Chapel, Bordesley. The site having been purchased, and provision made for the erection of a residence for the clergyman (out of a fund voluntarily raised for the purpose, amounting to £3,000), the cost of erecting the sacred edifice itself was defrayed by the commissioners for building new churches. The first stone was laid by the Earl of Plymouth, on the 29th of September, 1820, in the presence of the Earls of Dartmouth and Aylesford, and a large concourse of the most influential residents in the neighbourhood; and the building was consecrated, January 23rd, 1823. In its general appearance this beautiful structure has been thought by some to resemble the Chapel of King's College, Cambridge, from which, perhaps, the architect (Francis Goodwin) copied the idea of the octagonal turrets, surmounted by dwarf spires, which rise from each of the four corners of the building. The buttresses are finished with decorated pinnacles, and these, combined with the four turrets, give to the roof of the chapel a most pleasing and graceful appearance, unequalled by that of any other building in the town. The architect has imparted to the western front a noble and imposing air, from the bold archway within which he has placed the entrances and the large west window, the whole being surmounted by a gable, in the centre of which is an ornamental clock.

50

At the east end is a shallow projection forming the sacrarium; and above this a large and beautiful Catharine wheel window, which is filled with painted glass, imparting to the interior an exceedingly rich effect, which is heightened by the fine altar piece by Foggo, representing Christ healing the Sick Man at the Pool of Bethesda. The ceiling is lofty and harmonises well with the character of the building, which, although surrounded on three sides by galleries, does not suffer in appearance from the presence of those structures, as Gothic edifices in many instances do.

The cost of the building amounted to £14,235. The living is a perpetual curacy, in the gift of the Vicar of Aston.

On the first of August, 1825, the *Gazette* contained the first note respecting a new church in Dale End :—

August 1, 1825.—The corner stone of a church, dedicated to St. Peter, in course of erection in Dale End, in this town, was laid with due ceremonial, on the part of those officially concerned, on the morning of Tuesday last. Two of the Local Commissioners, the Rev. L. Gardner, D.D., Rector of St. Philip's, the parish in which the structure is to be raised; and James Taylor, Esq., of Moor Green, with their Solicitor, the Architects, and a number of the clergy of the town assembled to breakfast at the Royal Hotel, and soon after ten moved in procession to the spot where the formalities usual on such occasions were observed, and the stone, under which some coins of the present reign were deposited, was lowered into its position. The ceremony being concluded, an appropriate prayer was offered up by Dr. Gardner, after which the procession returned to the hotel. The brass plate embedded in the mortar immediately under the stone, bears the following inscription :—

"The first stone of a new Church, dedicated to St. Peter, was laid on the 26th day of July, 1825, by the Rev. Charles Curtis, the Rev. Lawrence Gardner, D.D., and James Taylor, Esq., the Local Commissioners for building Churches in this district. The expense of the site and

admired"—which is more than can be said at the present day. It was calculated to accommodate about 1,900 persons, and it is gratifying to learn that, like one or two of its predecessors the

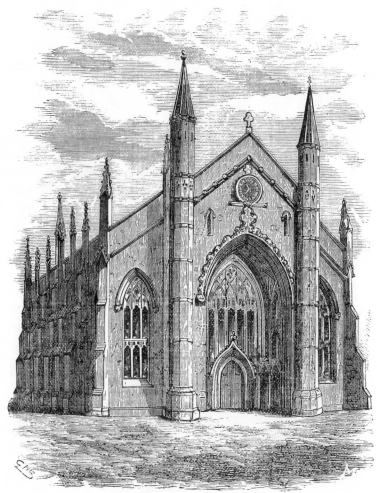

HOLY TRINITY CHAPEL, BORDISLEY.

structure, amounting to £19,676 2s. 11d. was defrayed out of a Parliamentary Grant of £1,000,000. The Hon. and Right Rev. Henry Ryder, D.D., Lord Bishop of the Diocese ; the Rev. Lawrence Gardner, D.D., Rector of the Parish ; John Welchman Whateley, and John Cope, Churchwardens of the Parish ; Rickman and Hutchinson, Architects."

The new church was consecrated on the 10th of August, 1827, when, we read, "the interior, as well as the exterior of the edifice was much

expense of erection was found to be less than the estimate, by nearly £900 ; having been estimated at £13,087, while the total cost of the building amounted only to £12,204 9s. 4d.

The style of the church is Grecian, of the type most favoured by English architects of the Georgian era. It has, at the west end, a massive tetrastyle Doric portico, above which rises an octagonal turret, encircled by a colonnade, resembling that of the Tower of the Winds, at Athens. "It may not be uninteresting," says Mr. Bates, in his excellent Guide, "to learn that in the construction of the portico, the masonry of which is executed in a similar manner to that of its ancient example, [the Temple of Minerva, at Athens,] stones of unusual magnitude were required; the lower blocks of the columns weighing upwards of seven tons, and the centre piece of the architrave measuring more than thirteen feet in length. These large stones were obtained with difficulty from the quarries at Guiting, in Gloucestershire." The east window of the church is filled with stained glass, by Pemberton, representing the Ascension.

On the night of Monday, the 24th of January, 1831, a fire broke out in the roof of this building, and made very considerable progress before any alarm was given; for, in less than an hour after the discovery had been made, the roof fell in, a mass of blazing timbers, and completed the wreck of the interior of the church; involving in one common ruin the whole of the handsome fittings,—pews, pulpit, organ, and altar piece,— leaving nothing save the bare blackened walls to tell of the costly structure which was as yet barely five years old. The fire was supposed by a few at the time to have been the work of incendiaries, but the general belief pointed to a more practical solution of the apparent mystery; viz., that the roof was ignited by the over-heating of a flue at the east end of the church, which communicated with the upper portion of the building. A view of the ruins appears on page 399. The reconstruction of the edifice was not completed until 1837.

Within a month of the laying of the first stone of St. Peter's Church, in 1825, there appeared a brief note in the *Gazette* respecting a further provision for the spiritual needs of our vast and still increasing population :—

October 10, 1825.—The Local Commissioners for the building of Churches in this town met on Saturday morning last, to decide, from among the various designs and estimates submitted to them, upon a plan for the erection of the new Church intended to be built at Holloway Head, when we understand the one made choice of was that furnished by Messrs. Rickman and Hutchinson, under whose superintendence the work will therefore be carried into execution.

The first stone of the new church, to be dedicated to the doubting apostle, was laid by the bishop of the diocese, on the 2nd of October, 1826, and the building was completed and consecrated on the 22nd of October, 1829. The designs for this church were furnished by the architects of St. Peter's, Messrs. Rickman and Hutchinson, and the entire expense was defrayed out of the Commissioners' fund for building churches; again the cost of erection was less than the estimate, amounting, in all, to £14,222 13s. 10d. Accommodation was provided for 2,125 persons, more than six hundred of the sittings being free.

St. Thomas's, like its predecessor, is in the Anglo-Grecian style, the bare and plain exterior of the building itself being relieved by the massive entrance, which is almost semicircular in shape, and consists of two Ionic porticos, from the centre of which rises a tower of the usual Georgian-classic type, not inelegant, albeit slightly out of proportion, o'ertopped by a large gilded ball and cross.

Two of the older Episcopal Chapels of Birmingham underwent important alterations during this decade. In 1823 exertions were made to complete St. Paul's by the long-deferred erection of the spire ; and this time they were successful, and the heavy appearance of the building (to which the square, clumsy, dwarf tower greatly contributed) was relieved by the light and graceful spire. In 1830 the little chapel of St. James, at Ashted, underwent considerable alterations and repairs, at an expense of about £850.

While the churches of the Establishment were thus flourishing and increasing in Birmingham, a corresponding increase and prosperity was at the same time observable among the various Dissenting societies of the town. The Methodists, as indicated by the remarks of Miss Hutton, quoted in our last chapter, were in a most flourishing

erected for the Methodists in St. Martin Street, Islington, in 1825, which has since 1864 been used as a school-room.

In 1824 a large and handsome octagonal

ST. PETER'S CHURCH, DALE END.

condition; the old-fashioned meeting house in Cherry Street—the first building erected by the Methodists in Birmingham—was taken down in 1823, and the present large and commodious chapel—itself in turn now about to be removed to make way for the new thoroughfare—erected at a considerable cost. Another new chapel was

structure was erected on Newhall Hill, (the "Harper's Hill" of Watt's earlier days), at the cost of a private individual (Mr. Robins), who expended upwards of £11,000 upon the undertaking, and thereby ruined himself. When finished it was let to the followers of the able and eloquent Scotch preacher, Edward Irving,

who was at that time in the zenith of his popularity ; and he came down to Birmingham to
conduct the inaugural services, on the 24th of
March, 1824. But the Catholic Apostolic
Church (as it was called) did not get on very
well with the proprietor of the huge chapel, and
the members were all too few to fill the building,
except on the rare occasions on which the founder
of the society himself preached ; and it was not
long before they erected for themselves a smaller
chapel in Newhall Street, and after lying unused
for some length of time the chapel on Newhall
Hill (in what in course of time became Graham
Street) was purchased for the Baptists, and
received the new name, Mount Zion, in lieu of
the older one given to the building by the Irvingites, or " Apostolicans,"—St. Andrews. It has
since become hallowed to Birmingham men by
the memories which cling around it of the earlier
ministrations of George Dawson and the long and
useful pastorate of Charles Vince ; but of these
things we shall have to speak in a future
chapter.

During the last year of this decade the members of the New Church—known to the outer
world as Swedenborgians—erected a new and
more commodious meeting-house in Summer Lane.
It will be remembered that they had, as early as
1791, established a society in Newhall Street,
but the first building passed out of their hands,
owing to an unfortunate omission on the part of the
members, by which, instead of being vested in a
number of trustees, for the benefit of the society,
it became, technically, the private property of an
individual, who subsequently became bankrupt ;
and, in consequence, the building was sold as
part of the effects. The Newhall Street building
being thus lost to them, the members of the New
Church erected for temporary use a small chapel
(in Paradise Street ?) with a view to its ultimate
conversion into a private dwelling ; and with this
restricted accommodation they remained until
1830, the first year of the pastorate of the Rev.
Edward Madeley, when they were emboldened

once more to attempt the erection of a larger
meeting-house. Fearing, possibly, lest the income
of the society should not prove equal to the
expenses of the new building, they made provision to eke out their means by the rents of
several private dwellings which they so constructed in connection with the building as not
to interfere either with the convenience or uni-
formity of the chapel itself. The appearance of
the interior was relieved from the flatness usual
in buildings of the meeting-house-classic order of
architecture, by the arched roof ; and on the
whole it is considerably lighter and more cheerful
than such places usually are.

The year 1827 is memorable in the history of
the Hebrew society of Birmingham as having
seen the completion of a new and (for that
period) commodious synagogue, in Severn Street ;
where, for the first time in Birmingham, their
solemn and impressive service might be conducted
in a more fitting and becoming manner than
in the small building which they had hitherto
occupied.

An important part of the outer manifestation
of the religion of the heart has by all denomina-
tions and sects been admitted to consist in the
sober and temperate life by which, not merely
those who profess and call themselves Christians,
but also the pious disciples of other forms of
religion, should exhibit to the irreligious world
around them the influence of their faith. It is,
therefore, as a note of progress in the outward
religion of morality that we record in this chapter
the establishment of the first Temperance Society
in Birmingham, on the first of September, 1830.
The first anniversary meeting was held on the
30th of August, 1831, at the Public Office ; the
following brief report, from Aris's Gazette, of
September 5th, will serve to show that the
society had already attracted to its cause a
number of highly respectable and influential
inhabitants :

TEMPERANCE SOCIETY.—The first Anniversary of this
Society was held at the Public Office, on Tuesday last.

William Chance, Esq., who was called to the chair, opened the proceedings, and explained the steps that had been previously taken. The Report was read by the Rev. S. Byers, and the adoption of it was moved by the Rev. Thomas Moseley, and seconded by the Rev. B. Slater. The Rev. Dr. Hewitt, from the United States, who had taken a distinguished part in the origin of these Societies in America, then entered into some very interesting statements, by which it would appear that already the beneficial effect of Temperance Societies has extensively appeared in America, where distilled spirits were drank to a very alarming degree, but where a considerable diminution of consumption has taken place since attention has been thus called to the subject. The Rev. Dr. strongly urged the formation of similar societies in England, and produced some very impressive reasons which will no doubt be embodied in the future addresses of the society. The Rev. Mr. James, Mr. Cadbury, and Mr. Chapman, of Ashted, addressed the meeting, which terminated with a vote of thanks to Dr. Hewitt.

CHAPTER LVIII.

THE BIRMINGHAM POLITICAL UNION, AND THE STRUGGLE FOR PARLIAMENTARY REFORM 1828-1832.

Anti-Corn Law Meeting in 1826—A new attempt for the Enfranchisement of Birmingham—Distress of the People—The origin of the Political Union—The Meetings at the Royal Hotel and the Globe—Requisition to the High Bailiff—The first Meeting at Beardsworth's Repository—Objects of the Union—The second Meeting at the Repository—The Union Medal—Death of George IV.—The first Annual Meeting—Dinner at the Royal Hotel—The French Revolution—Petition of Rights—Anniversary of the Union—The first Reform Bill—The Second Reading carried—Defeat of the Measure—Dissolution of Parliament—The second Bill—The Birmingham Petition—Address to the Government—Defeat in the House of Lords—Great Meeting on Newhall Hill—Town's Meeting at the Repository—The third Reform Bill—Great Gathering of the Unions—Their Hymn—The Union Vow—Another Defeat in the Lords—Resignation of the Ministry—Excitement in Birmingham—Threatened Arrest of the Unionists—Proposed March to London—Military Preparations—Return of Lord Grey to Power—Thanksgiving of the People at Newhall Hill—Final Victory.

AFTER the disastrous defeat of the Reform movement in 1821, when the principal leaders were committed to prison, the spirit of the people seems for a time to have been effectually crushed, so that the injustice of those proceedings does not appear to have called forth a single public remonstrance. Now and then, during the half-dozen years which followed, an occasional spasmodic attempt to obtain political justice in one form or other was made; but the active commencement of the second campaign of the united Liberal party in Birmingham, dates from the year 1826. On the 17th of March, in that year, an Anti-Corn Law meeting of the inhabitants was held, at which Mr. Joseph Taylor, presided, and Mr. Spooner was one of the chief speakers; and it was unanimously resolved to petition for the abolition of the obnoxious Corn Laws. In the following July a deputation waited upon the Government and presented a memorial to the same effect, and showing also the distressed state of the town. A further petition was forwarded in the autumn of the same year, from the Birmingham Chamber of Commerce. But they were yet to memorialise and petition for many years, and the burden of the great work was to pass from the shoulders of Birmingham to those of Manchester before the desired object was obtained.

The following year was unmarked by any political excitement; but in 1828, when the petty borough of East Retford was disfranchised on account of the gross corruption practised at the late election, local political excitement was resuscitated by the bill which was brought into the House of Commons, to transfer to Birmingham the forfeited electoral rights of East Retford, and a petition in favour of the measure was signed by upwards of four thousand persons in Birmingham in one day. The measure was strenuously opposed by the Government, with the exception of Mr. Huskisson, who by his vote in its favour, forfeited his seat in the Wellington cabinet. Among those who voted in favour of the bill were Lord John Russell, Lord Palmerston, Sir James Graham, Lord George Bentinck, Sir James Mackintosh, Sir Frederick Burdett, Sir John Cam Hobhouse, Mr. Thomas Duncombe, Joseph Hume, and others. The House, however, rejected the proposal, and when it was reintroduced in the following session, 1829, it met with the same fate; but within a few days of the second failure, Lord John Russell gave notice of his intention, only in the next session, of bringing in a bill to enfranchise, not Birmingham alone, but also Leeds and Manchester.

The people of Birmingham were driven to press their demands for parliamentary representation from the desperate condition of affairs. Owing in a great measure to the restrictions upon trade, and to the unsatisfactory currency system, the trade of the country was paralysed, wages were low, and the people in the direst distress, bordering almost upon desperation. A meeting was held in Birmingham on the 8th of May, 1829, attended by four thousand persons, " to take into consideration the present distressed state of the country." Again they addressed Parliament, praying for free trade and currency reform ; eight thousand signatures were appended to their petition, but their cry was still disregarded. The subject was an uncomfortable one, and members of parliament endeavoured to banish all thoughts of it by the pleasant fiction,—put into words by more than one honourable member—" that every man in the country was happy and comfortable, with plenty of work and abundant remuneration for it." This callous and lying response to the cry of the poor, burned into the heart of Thomas Attwood the fixed determination to organize such a union of the people as should p'ace them in a position to compel the Government to legislate on behalf of the masses, instead of for the benefit of the few. At first the idea existed in his mind only in a vague and shadowy form, but the more he pondered over it the clearer did it become. He was convinced that the public will might be unified, and, under judicious direction, become all-powerful ; and he pursued the project alone, in his own mind, until he had mastered all its details. Then, feeling the solemn responsibility which would attend the guidance of such a movement, and with a pious reverence which is never wholly absent from the truly great man, he went down on his knees, in

his library, at Harborne, in the gray early dawn, —for he had finally resolved upon the undertaking during the night—and prayed to Almighty God that if the great association he contemplated was not calculated to promote the liberty and happiness of the mass of the people it might not prosper. Such was the meek and submissive spirit in which the Birmingham Political Union and its subsequent extension was projected ; is it then, to be wondered at that Attwood's labours were, in the end, abundantly blessed ?

On a bitterly cold night in December, 1829,— the 14th of the month, a meeting was held at the Royal Hotel, Temple Row, at which were present Messrs. Attwood, Scholefield, Muntz, Shorthouse, Lawrence, and other gentlemen, sixteen in all, called together by a private circular ; and on that memorable night " the Political Union for the Protection of Public Rights " was born. On the following Monday an adjourned meeting was held at the Globe (now the Clarendon) Hotel, Temple Street, Mr. Attwood again presiding, and the rules of the Union were submitted and adopted, receiving the signatures of the twenty-eight persons present. It was then resolved to request the High Bailiff to call together the people of Birmingham, and to lay before them the new constitution for their approval, and thereupon to enrol as many as would conform thereto as members of the Union. In less than a week after the meeting at the Globe, the following requisition signed by two hundred respectable inhabitants, was presented to the High Bailiff, Mr. William Chance :—

" We the undersigned, being of opinion that the GENERAL DISTRESS which NOW AFFLICTS THE COUNTRY, and which has been so severely felt at several periods during the last fifteen years, is entirely to be ascribed to the GROSS MISMANAGEMENT OF PUBLIC AFFAIRS, and that such mismanagement can only be effectually and permanently remedied by an EFFECTUAL REFORM IN THE COMMONS HOUSE OF PARLIAMENT ; and being also of opinion that for the legal accomplishment of this GREAT OBJECT, and for the further REDRESS OF PUBLIC WRONGS and GRIEVANCES, it is expedient to form a GENERAL POLITICAL UNION between the LOWER AND MIDDLE CLASSES OF THE PEOPLE, *do request* that you will call a

MEETING of the Merchants, Manufacturers, Tradesmen, Mechanics, Artisans, and other inhabitants of the town of Birmingham, for the purpose of taking these important subjects into consideration."

It need scarcely be added that the High Bailiff refused to call the meeting; he replied that " he could not view it as any part of his duty" to do so. In consequence of this refusal, the leaders of the movement called it themselves; appointing it to be held in Beardsworth's Repository on the 14th of January, 1830, at ten o'clock in the morning. The call was responded to by upwards of 12,000 persons, and the meeting was said to have been the largest, up to that time, ever assembled in this kingdom within the walls of a building. Mr. G. F. Muntz was called to the chair, and, on taking it, he declared himself "not ashamed of presiding at a meeting, the object of which was the promotion of radical reform, meaning by that term, not revolution, but abolition of abuses." Mr. Scholefield and Mr. George Edmonds then addressed the meeting and proposed the first resolution, declaring the necessity for political reform; and then Mr. Attwood read an elaborate document setting forth the plan of the Union, which, although it occupied an hour in reading, was listened to with the utmost attention. From this statement it is worth while to place on record the outline of the objects of the Political Union, which were declared to be as follows:

" 1st.—To obtain by every just and legal means such a REFORM in the COMMONS HOUSE of PARLIAMENT as may ensure a REAL and EFFECTUAL REPRESENTATION of the LOWER AND MIDDLE CLASSES OF THE PEOPLE in the House.

" 2nd.—To enquire, consult, consider, and determine respecting the rights and liberties of the industrious classes, and respecting the legal means of securing those which remain and recovering those which are lost.

" 3rd.—To prepare petitions, addresses, and remonstrances to the Crown and the Legislative Bodies, respecting the *preservation* and *restoration* of PUBLIC RIGHTS, and respecting the repeal of *bad laws* and the enactment of *good laws.*

" 4th.—To prevent and redress as far as practicable all LOCAL PUBLIC WRONGS and OPPRESSIONS, and all LOCAL ENCROACHMENTS upon the rights, interests, and privileges of the community.

" 5th.—To obtain the repeal of the MALT and the BEER TAXES; and in general to obtain an alteration in the system of taxation, so as to cause it to press less severely upon the industrious classes of the community, and more equally upon the wealthy classes.

" 6th.—To obtain the *reduction of each separate Tax and expense* of the Government in the same degree as the *legislative increase* in the *value of money* has increased their *respective values,* and *has reduced and is reducing the general prices of labour* throughout the country.

" 7th.—To promote *peace,* union, and concord among all classes of his Majesty's subjects; and to guide and direct the public mind into uniform, peaceful, and legitimate operations; instead of leaving it to waste its strength in loose, desultory, and unconnected exertions, or to carry out its own objects, unguided, unassisted, and uncontrolled.

" 8th.—To collect and organise the peaceful expression of the PUBLIC OPINION, so as to bring it to act upon the legislative functions in a just, legal and effectual way.

" 9th. — To influence, by every legal means, the elections of members of Parliament, so as to promote the return of upright and capable Representatives of the People.

" 10th.—To adopt such measures as may be legal and necessary for the purpose of obtaining an effectual Parliamentary investigation into the situation of the country, and into the cause of its embarrassment and difficulties; with the view of relieving the NATIONAL DISTRESS, of rendering justice to the injured as far as practicable, and to bring to trial any Members of either House of Parliament who may be found to have acted from criminal or corrupt motives."

The members of the Union were to be "good, faithful, and loyal subjects of the King;" to obey the laws of the land, and, where they ceased to protect the right, liberties, and interests of the community to endeavour to get them changed by just, legal, and peaceable means ONLY; to present themselves at the meetings of the Union, and conduct themselves peaceably and legally thereat; to choose only just, upright, and able men as members of the political council, and to dismiss them and elect others in their stead whenever they ceased to watch over the interests of liberty and right; to obey strictly all the just directions of the political council; and above all never to forget that, while the strength and moral influence of the society lay in the strict observance of "PEACE, *Order, Union,* and LEGALITY, upon any breach of the innumerable and intricate laws which surrounded them, the *lawyer* and the *soldier* would probably break in upon them, and render all their exertions vain." In moving the adoption of the constitution of the Political Union, Mr. Attwood made the following

forward now, that I shall be ready, come weal, come woe, to lead you, through thick and thin, through the dark and dreary scenes which are approaching. As far as the law will justify me,

VIEW OF THE RUINS OF ST. PETER'S AFTER THE FIRE.

declaration, which has frequently since been quoted as illustrating his position in connection with the Union :—

"I feel it my duty to declare to you, that I know the country to be on the verge of dreadful calamities. It may be thought, because I come

I will go with you. When I say I will go with you as far as the law will allow me, I declare to you, most solemnly, that I will not go farther one inch. I know that a great crisis is approaching. I will do all I can to avoid that crisis ; but if the nation is to go through the ordeal of politi-

51

cal convulsions, I will not interfere in those convulsions, but legally and peaceably; and I wish you to bear this in mind. When those dreadful circumstances arise, I know you will come to me, and say, 'Lead us.' My friends, I will not lead you; I will go with you as far as the law will allow; but if the elements of 'Peace, Law, and Order,' are disorganised, I will go with you no farther."

For seven hours the vast concourse of persons stood to listen to the speeches of the reformers, and heartily accepted all their propositions. They were bent upon a thorough reform at last, and would listen to no half-measures. An amendment calling only for the enfranchisement of Birmingham was rejected by 20 to 1, and the thirty-six gentlemen whose names were appended to the declaration of the Union were appointed as the first Council. They also adopted a petition praying the House of Commons to take into consideration "the distresses of the kingdom and the grievances of the people," and their causes, which were stated to be "overwhelming taxation, an enormous and unconstitutional standing army, bands of useless and unmerited placemen and pensioners, profligate expenditure of the public money, an ill-regulated Established Church, and an arbitrary change in the value of money." The petitioners ventured to remind the House that its duty, "upon assembling in Parliament, is to redress the grievances of the people, previous to voting the money out of their pockets;" and they therefore further prayed that the Commons would "vote no estimates, no supplies, nor any mutiny bill," until some steps were taken to better the forlorn condition of the people, and that they would "forthwith repeal all the taxes upon malt and beer, thereby instantly, in some degree, relieving distresses of the labourers and cultivators of that soil which gave them birth, and ought to give them bread."

The meeting had a great effect upon the country; several full reports of the proceedings were published, and the principal speeches, with comments thereon, appeared in nearly every journal in the kingdom. Writing of the new movement, the *Morning Journal* said: "The hurricane has begun to blow, that will sweep the imperious Minister and all his subservient tools from the high places of power, trust, patronage, and official influence. We defy him or them to restrain its fury." The *Times* and the *Morning Chronicle* ridiculed "the whole thing" as nonsense, as might have been expected, but in this case, (which is not a solitary one,) the leaders of public opinion proved to be less prescient than their humbler contemporaries. In four months the Union numbered 2,200 members, and similar unions were already being formed all over the country. The new movement attracted to its forces several Liberal noblemen and members of Parliament, and even Cabinet Ministers began to look forward with apprehension to the effect which the law-abiding unions were likely to produce in Parliament and throughout the country.

The first great display of the strength and power of the Political Union took place on Monday, May 17, 1830. Early in the morning the busiest streets of the town were thronged with the members of the Union from outlying districts, and hundreds pressed into the rooms of the Council to enlist under the banner of political freedom, among whom was the member-elect of 1819, Sir Charles Wolseley. The day was regarded as a general holiday; shops were closed, and their windows filled with spectators; the town was in a general commotion, not a few of the more timorous respectabilities professing to entertain fears of disturbance; but *that* was a thing of bygone days now; the people, under their new leader, had learned the value of peaceable demeanour and the power of moral force.

A monstre procession was organised, and headed by a band, playing "God save the King," marched to the Repository, but long before its arrival the building was more than half filled, and before the Council had taken their places it was estimated that there could not have been less than 18,000 persons present.

"We had the good fortune," says the *Birmingham Journal*, "through the politeness of Mr. Beardsworth, to see the procession as it moved from the end of Moat Street to the Repository, from the site of the famed White Horse. From this elevation we commanded a complete view of the immense concourse from the place of meeting to the end of New Street; and a more animating spectacle was never presented to the human eye. The most remarkable feature in the conduct of the populace was the great attention paid to Messrs. Attwood, Scholefield, and Muntz, who headed the procession. Several sturdy fellows formed a sort of body-guard, and by dint of hard labour and great exertion, succeeded in keeping off the pressure of the multitude from those gentlemen."

Mr. G. F. Muntz was called to the chair, and after a few words from Mr. George Edmonds, who, in his endeavours to preserve order, had unfortunately lost his voice, a most satisfactory report was read, showing the rapid extension of the principle of the Union. "Its effects," said Mr. Attwood, "have not alone been felt in Birmingham or its neighbourhood; its influence has been felt throughout England, and Europe resounds with it. Be assured," he continued, "we have given the enemy a tremendous blow; we have made him reel, as the boxers say, from one side of the stage to the other. By your permission we will repeat the blow again and again, until we are enabled, by God's blessing, to give them what the French call the *coup de grace*, or what we call the finishing blow." This must be done, not only in a morally right manner, but by strictly legal methods, and he again repeated his caution respecting those inexplicable laws which like "devil-traps," hedged about the reformers' footsteps on every hand. "But for our great prudence," said Mr. Attwood, "we should have

been destroyed like the Reformers of old, and I picked out from amongst you, and in all probability lodged in a dungeon."

After declaring in favour of the Marquis of Blandford's Bill of Reform (which was printed and circulated among the members of the Union, together with the declaration), the meeting approved the new Union Medal, the obverse of which contained a representation of the British Lion, rousing himself from slumber, surrounded by the legend: "The safety of the King and of the People; the Constitution, nothing less and nothing more"; and on the reverse, a representation of the Royal Crown, irradiated, and on a scroll underneath, the words "Unity, Liberty, Prosperity," a legend above, "God save the King," and below, "Birm^m. Political Union, 25 January, 1830." It was resolved, "That this medal be adopted as the badge of the Union, attached to a ribbon, on which is enwoven the red cross of St. George, quartered by that of St. Andrew, commonly called the British Union Jack. A standard that has nobly supported the national honour in foreign climes, and which, we trust, will be efficacious in the great moral contest for recovering the national liberty at home." The meeting also voted a gold Union medal to Mr. Attwood for his patriotic exertions.

The Reformers little thought, as they separated at the close of that meeting, that before another public gathering should be held, the King, whose powerful influence had ever been on the side of repression and political injustice, would have passed out of the world; yet such was the case. On the wild and stormy night of the 26th of June, little more than a month after the Union meeting, George IV. died; and the Liberals looked forward to the dawn of a more hopeful state of things. They addressed the country on the eve of the elections, and with powerful effect.

The great sensation excited throughout the country by the two great public meetings of the Union, on the 25th of January and the 17th of

May, caused a wish on the part of the Council that the first Annual Meeting should be attended with similar *éclat* ; and letters of invitation were written to distant members, of rank and standing in the country, to give their countenance and support to the cause by attending on this occa-

Room was engaged to provide accommodation for two hundred gentlemen.

The town was once more thronged, therefore, on the 26th of July, and even a more imposing procession than on former occasions wended its way from the home of the Union, the Globe

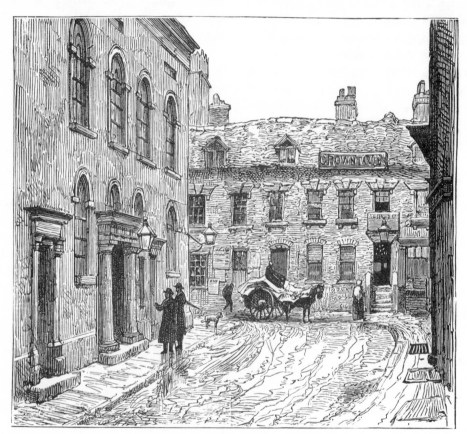

WESLEYAN CHAPEL, CHERRY STREET.

sion. In response to this invitation, Sir Francis Burdett, Bart., who had previously joined the Union, engaged to attend if the meeting could be deferred until after the close of the Parliamentary session. To meet his convenience, therefore, it was postponed from the 5th to the 26th of July, 1830. In order to mark their sense of the public spirit of Sir F. Burdett, the Council determined to invite him to dine on that evening at the Royal Hotel, and the Assembly

Hotel, down Temple Street, along New Street, down High Street and part of Digbeth, up Mill Lane, Smithfield, and Balsall Street ; headed by the band of the Union, in two breaks. Mr. Attwood watched the scene from the " colossal White Horse," and directed the band to move off down Cheapside, to allow the procession to pass to the rear of the Repository, in Moseley Street. When the vast concourse had entered the building, there could not have been less than 20,000 persons present. Sir Francis Burdett was called to the chair, and delivered a vigorous and telling speech concerning the corrupt practices which prevailed at elections; pocket boroughs, the Corn Laws, and kindred topics. Mr. E. D. Davenport, formerly M.P. for the borough of Shaftesbury, Mr. Geo. Edmonds, Mr. Attwood, and other leaders of the Union also addressed the meeting, which was brought to a happy conclusion by a graceful act to one who had rendered them valuable services, the proprietor of the large and most suitable building in which all their public meetings had been held,—Mr. Beardsworth,—to whom they presented a handsome silver tea service.

In the evening, the dinner at the Royal Hotel passed off in an admirable manner. "It was not judged advisable," we are told, in a report of the proceedings, "to invite the neutral milk-and-water-like friends of Reform, or probably a much larger number of the Respectables, as they are called, might have been brought together upon the occasion." The band of the Union (which had just been provided with a "splendid uniform,) played a selection of patriotic airs; the speeches were of the usual after-dinner type, and included many loyal toasts and sentiments; and the various members of the organization were by this pleasant reunion bound more closely together in fellowship one with another, and the Union itself strengthened and benefited thereby.

The same evening, while English Liberals were dining together in peace and amity, their brethren in France were striking a glorious blow for freedom, hurling the last of the Bourbons from the throne, and declaring once more the liberty of the people. Birmingham watched that event with the utmost interest and anxiety, and, on Monday, October 11th, between three and four thousand members of the Union dined together at Beardsworth's Repository, to celebrate the "glorious event," Mr. Attwood presiding. After the Union hymn had been sung by the thousands of voices, Attwood said: "I have made many friends, it seems; perhaps,

some enemies. I have had much to contend with, and have had occasion for some little nerve. I have been told that I should set in motion a tremendous principle, which no human power could control; that I should, like a Frankenstein, create a monster of gigantic strength, endowed with life, but not with reason, that would hunt me to destruction. Is that so? [A "No" thundered through the place.] "What possible mischief can arise," he continued, "from men animated with the same motives which animate you? and, as for me, what possible danger do I incur? Where is the man among you who would injure me? Where is the one amongst you who would not follow me to death in a righteous cause?" [Every one in the vast assembly rose as one man and shouted "All!"]

During the same month they petitioned the King to dismiss the Ministers, and a few weeks later the Wellington and Peel administration resigned, and the Grey administration was formed. Early in December the Political Council called a meeting of the town to support the new cabinet; and once more a large gathering was held at the Repository, on the 13th of that month. At this meeting the famous petition of Rights was adopted, and entrusted to the Earl of Radnor for presentation to the Lords, and to the Marquis of Blandford for presentation to the Commons. It claimed as "the birthright of every Englishman":

1st.—The right of having all *Placemen* dismissed from the House of Commons agreeably to the Great CONSTITUTIONAL ACT OF SETTLEMENT which places the present illustrious Family on the Throne.

"2nd.—The right of having *triennial or more frequent Parliaments*, as recognised and secured by the Great Constitutional Act, the 6th of William and Mary, cap. 2.

"3rd.—The right of sitting and voting in the Commons House of Parliament, *when lawfully chosen* without the *qualification of property*, which was fixed unconstitutionally by the Act of 9th of Queen Anne.

"4th.—The right of having all the Knights, Citizens, and Burgesses of the House of Commons paid the *reasonable wages of attendance* by a rate upon their constituents, in order to enable the common people to have the benefit of the services of persons living under the same circumstances, and having the same knowledge, and the same wants and interests as themselves.

" 5th.—The right of having the large towns and populous districts of the country represented in the House of Commons, in place of those decayed boroughs which return members to Parliament, although now containing but few inhabitants.

" 6th.—The right of every man to have a vote in the election of Members of the House of Commons, who is in any way called upon to contribute to either National or Local taxation, direct or indirect ; by which your petitioners understand that either all the taxes ought to be taken off from those articles necessary for the subsistence and comfort of working men, or that all working men, who are compelled to pay such taxes, should have a vote in the election of Members to your Honourable House.

" 7th.—The right to have elections for Members of the House of Commons *free* and *unbiassed*, and with this view to have arrangements made in the conducting of elections as may effectually prevent all force, fear, or intimidation, and all bribery or undue influence of any kind, from acting upon the minds of the electors."

On the 25th of January, 1831, the members of the Union again dined together to celebrate their anniversary, and many loyal speeches were delivered, in which the King's known sympathy for their cause formed a theme for congratulation, and many " prave 'orts " were uttered concerning the alleged disaffection of certain of the Tories towards his Majesty ; they spoke now of armed assistance : "If the King commanded them," they said, "they would produce a national guard that would be like a wall around his throne." Mr. Attwood said : " It was not too much to say, that if the King required it they could produce him in this district, at his order, within a month, two armies, each of them as numerous and as brave as that which conquered at Waterloo."

A few weeks later the first Reform Bill was introduced into the House of Commons, March 1st, 1831, by Lord John Russell. It was immediately the cause of the utmost alarm and trepidation in both Houses; Lord Sidmouth, addressing Earl Grey, declaring : " I hope God will forgive you on account of this bill : I don't think I can." It was looked upon as almost revolutionary, and many prophesied the speedy overthrow of all our national institutions, and the

total ruin of the nation itself. On the 14th the bill was read for the first time, and the same evening a mass meeting was held in Birmingham, expressing the determination of the people to have " the bill, the whole bill, and nothing but the bill."

The second reading was carried by a majority of *one*—in the fullest house ever known—603 members having voted on that occasion. Great rejoicings following throughout the kingdom, and nowhere more than in Birmingham, where the event was celebrated by popular demonstrations and a general illumination. But on the 19th and again on the 22nd, the Ministers were beaten, and at once placed their resignations in the hands of the King. His Majesty, however, refused to accept them, and dissolved Parliament in order that the feeling of the country might be ascertained. At this act the joy of the Reformers knew no bounds ; in Birmingham they broke open the belfries and set the bells ringing merrily, to the horror and disgust of their clerical custodians. The Political Union issued an address to the electors of the United Kingdom, calling upon them to vote for no candidate who would not pledge himself to support the bill in its entirety ; and the result was that a still greater number of Reformers were returned. A second bill was introduced on the 24th of June, 1831, and the first reading was carried by a large majority, and it was successfully piloted to the committee stage of its existence ; but here it met with obstruction, objection, and every form of hindrance, and the patience of the people was tried to the utmost point of endurance. Then the Union took a bold and decisive step. On the 28th of July, the Political Council addressed the following independent and almost fierce " petition " to the House of Commons :—

" Your petitioners have observed with disgust and indignation the factious and puerile opposition made to the opinions of a majority of your honourable House, and to the demands of an oppressed and insulted people, and with feelings of a nearly similar character they contrast the rapidity with which measures of penalty and spoliation have been enacted by former Parliaments, with the extraordinary tardiness at present displayed in completing a wholesome and healthy measure of wisdom, justice, and conciliation."

Daniel O'Connell presented this " petition of remonstrance," but it was, as might have been expected, rejected as " grossly disrespectful." At length, however, the report of the committee was considered, and after three nights' debate, the third reading of the bill was carried, September 21st, by a majority of 109, the numbers being 345 to 236.

The people were not wanting in gratitude to the Government for their exertions in the cause of reform, and a numerously signed address was presented by the Union to Earl Grey, Lord Althorp, and Lord John Russell. From the latter they received the following reply :

" I beg to acknowledge, with heartfelt gratitude, the undeserved honour done me by 150,000 of my countrymen.

" Our prospects are now obscured for a moment, and I trust only for a moment. It is impossible that the whisper of faction should prevail against the voice of a nation."

There now loomed before the minds of the people the dread—nay the almost certainty of defeat in the House of Lords. The bill was read a second time in the hereditary chamber on the 3rd of October ; and on the same evening Birmingham held a great meeting on Newhall Hill. Shops and factories were closed, the bells were clanged, flags were hung out, and mottoes displayed ; such as : " William the Fourth, the People's Hope ; "—" Earl Grey—the just rights of our order secured, we will then stand by his order ; " " Taxation without representation is tyranny ; " and similar sentiments. They met to petition the Lords to pass the bill.

" We have," said the chairman, " united two millions of men, peaceably and legally in one grand and determined association, to recover the liberty, the happiness, and the prosperity of the country, and I should like to know what power there is in England that can resist a power like this. La Fayette told us forty years ago that ' for a nation to be free it is sufficient that she wills it.' Look around at this vast and magnificent assemblage in the very heart of England, where the English blood is pure and uncontaminated with foreign alloy—see this prodigious mass of brave and upright men assembled together to support their good, and gracious, and patriotic King—and who, with such a spectacle before him, can possibly doubt that the British Nation *wills* that the Bill of Reform shall pass, and therefore that it *must* pass."

Then with reverence he added : " I desire that you will all take off your hats, and that you will look up to the Heavens, where the just God rules both Heaven and Earth, and that you will cry out with one heart and voice, ' God bless the King.' "

In a moment every head was uncovered, every face upturned, and the air was rent with the thunder of voices crying " God Bless the King ! " It is possible that many " unparliamentary " remarks were uttered by the various speakers, respecting our hereditary legislators ; but they felt that they were exercising a solemn duty in thus warning them of the danger of disregarding the people's cry. But the Lords were greatly incensed, and during the succeeding nights of the debate Lord Eldon and others denounced the proceedings of the Birmingham Union as illegal and treasonable ; and on the 7th of October they threw out the bill. The King determined once more to prorogue Parliament, in order that the whole measure might be reconsidered, and on the 20th of October, Parliament was prorogued accordingly.

Notwithstanding the exasperation of the people, (which in Birmingham took various forms, such as the tolling of the bells, the hanging out of black flags, tearing down the names of Wellington and the Queen from the streets, etc.,) there was no riot or mobbing,—nothing but " peace, law, and order," in the streets of Birmingham. On the day following the prorogation of Parliament, a large town's meeting was held at the Repository, the High Bailiff (Mr. Oliver Mason) presiding. They met " for the purpose of expressing to his Majesty, by address, the deep regret and bitter disappointment felt by the inhabitants at the rejection of the Reform Bill." Speeches were delivered by Mr. Joseph

Parkes, Mr. William Redfern, and other leading
Liberals of the town, setting forth in a clear,
calm, and decisive manner, that, while they were
on the side of law and order, yet if the question
should become, reform, accompanied by revolution, or no reform at all, they would not hesitate
to say, " Give us the first, for they *would not
have* the last alternative." But they would not
stoop to a victory by bloodshed ; they would not
imitate the French in this particular. This fact
stood out nobly in their every appeal, as in the
following address to the country, which was
framed at this very meeting :—

" *Friends and Fellow Countrymen !*

" Our road is clear. Our mind is made up. WE WILL
STAND BY LORD GREY. That illustrious Statesman
has declared that the BILL OF REFORM shall *become
Law*, in all its essential principles and provisions. The
whole history of his life forbids us to mistrust his word.
The strength of a United Nation, which he wields, forbids us to mistrust his power. *Therefore we will stand by
Lord Grey.* And if by any possibility he should be driven
from power, we will carry him back upon the shoulders
of the people !

" *Friends and Fellow Countrymen !*

" The King, the Ministers, the House of Commons, and
the People, and are all united. All these have *given proof*
that they are true to the cause of Liberty, and that they
are determined to carry the Bill of Reform into a Law.
This HOLY LEAGUE is invincible. Nothing can shake
its power if no discord or disunion arises within itself.
It is for you, therefore, to shun *discord* as the only *rock*
on which your hopes can be wrecked. *Discord* among
yourselves would give to your enemies the only possible
chance of obtaining a triumph over you. Let no disunion
arise among you ; and nothing can prevent the downfall
of that atrocious Oligarchy which has so long trampled
upon the Liberty and Happiness of the Country.

" *Friends and Fellow Countrymen !*

" At the same time that we show confidence in the
King and in his Ministers, and a fixed determination to
preserve the law, let us show no weakness—no timidity—
no lukewarmness—in the cause of Liberty. Let us all be
united as one man in the enthusiastic and determined
support of this great, this holy cause. Let POLITICAL
UNIONS be formed instantly in every Town, in every
District, and in every Village where they do not already
exist. Let the nation stand forth in its strength ; and in
peaceful and commanding majesty express its WILL ; and
that WILL *is certain to become the Law of the Land.*

" *Friends and Fellow Countrymen !*

" Be patient. Be peaceful. Be firm. Be united. Be
determined. Place your confidence in the King and in
his Ministers. Until *these* shall deceive you, there can be
no fear for the Liberties of England.

" *Friends, Countrymen, and Brothers !*

" Listen to us. The SWORD must not be drawn in
England. The terrible *Knell* of the TOCSIN must not
sound. The tears of the Widow and the Orphan must not
mark our course. *These* are the last dread alternatives of
an oppressed nation. The influence of the Oligarchy,
aided by a corrupt and degenerate BENCH of BISHOPS,
has obtained a momentary triumph in the House of Lords.
By the power of the King and of the Law we will
humble the Oligarchy in the dust. Our gallant neighbours the French effected a glorious Revolution by lifting
the BARRICADES, cemented by the best blood of the
nation. WE will have no BARRICADES. Without *blood*
—without anarchy—without violation of the Law, we
will accomplish the most GLORIOUS REFORMATION
recorded in the History of the World.

" GOD BLESS THE KING.

" By order of the Council.

" THOMAS ATTWOOD, Chairman.

" BENJAMIN HADLEY, Secretary."

The advice contained in this address was
immediately acted upon, and Political Unions
sprang up in every locality. Attempts were
made to stop the formation of such associations,
but all in vain ; the people had at length learned
their own strength, and knew wherein it lay ;—
and once more the reformers were returned to Parliament in an overwhelming majority. The third
Reform Bill was introduced on the 12th of December, 1831, and was read a third time on the 19th of
March, 1832. " What will the Lords do now,"
was the question on every lip ; and the answer
was awaited with breathless interest. The
second reading was fixed for the 9th of April ;
and it was felt that upon this decision rested
the fate of the hereditary Chamber. On the
14th, the debate was protracted until daylight,
and the division resulted in victory for the
Reformers ; the second reading had been carried
by a majority of nine.

Still there was danger. Threats were rife of
serious damage to the bill in committee, and it
must be prevented, or all the labours of the
Union would have been without beneficial result.
A maimed bill the people would not have ; it
must still be " the bill, the whole bill, and
nothing but the bill." In order to convince
their lordships of this determination on the part
of the people, the Council of the Political Union

FORWARD

JOHN JAFFRAY, J.P.

PHOTOGRAPHED BY WHITLOCK.

BIRMINGHAM: HOUGHTON & CO., SCOTLAND PASSAGE.

THE GATHERING OF THE UNIONS ON NEWHALL HILL, MAY 7TH, 1832.

invited the Unions for miles round to meet on
Newhall Hill on the 7th of May, and declare
themselves ; and the people responded nobly to
the call. From the mines and furnaces of the
Black Country came one hundred and twenty
thousand men, with 150 banners and eleven
bands of music ; from the broad acres of Warwickshire, and from the looms of Coventry,
came labourers and silk-weavers, and artificers of
various kinds, five thousand in number ; from
Bromsgrove and Redditch, from the salt-mines of
Droitwich, and from other places in the county
came the Worcestershire contingent, ten thousand
strong ; Birmingham herself contributed to the
vast assemblage no less than fifty thousand souls
—all these—upwards of 200,000 of them in all,
with innumerable banners flying, with bands of
music accompanying the triumphant march of
liberty, assembled on the sacred battle-ground of
freedom, to reiterate their demand for adequate
representation in the Government of their
country. The father of the Unions presided,
and from the whole concourse, like the surging
of a mighty sea, arose the **Hymn** of the
Unions :—

CALL !

Over mountain, over plain,
  Echoing wide from sea to sea,
Peals, and shall not peal in vain,
  The trumpet call of liberty !
Britain's guardian spirit cries—
Britons awake ! awake ! arise !

Sleep no more the sleep of shame :
  Rise and break oppression's chain !
Lulled by freedom's empty name,
  Worse than slaves no more remain,
Freedom's rights, not freedom's name,
Dare to know and dare to claim.

Shall honest labour toil in vain
  While plunder fattens on the land !
Still shall a tyrant faction's reign
  People and King at once command ?
No ! it may not, shall not be,
For we must, we will be free.

Sleep ye still ? while one by one
  Each sacred, dear-bought right is lost,
Rights which your father's broadswords won
  Rights which your father's life-blood cost ;
No ! it may not, shall not be,
For we must, we will be free.

See rises from his bed of fame
  Each chief of glorious Runnymede
With Hampden ! history's noblest name,
  They call us to our country's need ;
They call, and can we heedless be ?
No ! for we must, we will be free.

But not to war and blood they call,
  They bid us lift not sword or gun ;
Peaceful, but firm, join one and all
  To claim your rights, and they are won.
The British Lion's voice alone
Shall gain for Britain all her own.

ANSWER.

Lo ! we answer ; see ! we come
  Quick at freedom's holy call,
We come, we come ! we come, we come !
  To do the glorious work of all.
And hark ! we raise from sea to sea
Our sacred watchword, Liberty !

God is our guide ; from field, from wave,
  The plough, the anvil, and the loom,
We come, our country's rights to save,
  And speak a tyrant faction's doom.
And hark ! we raise from sea to sea
Our sacred watchword, Liberty !

God is our guide ! no sword we draw ;
  We kindle not war's fatal fires.
By union, justice, reason, law,
  We claim the birthright of our sires !
And thus we raise from sea to sea
Our sacred watchword Liberty !

When the echoes of the stirring melody had
died away, and the vast multitude was hushed to
silence by the sound of a trumpet, Mr. Attwood
spoke. He asked them if they intended to be
the slaves of the borough-mongers ; if they would
not rather die ? and with one voice they cried
" All ! All ! " " I say," he declared " that the
people of England stand at this very moment
' like greyhounds on the slip ' ; and that if our
beloved King should give the word, or if the
Council should give the word in his name, and
under his authority, the grandest scene would be
instantly exhibited that was ever witnessed on
this earth before." In like manner did other
leaders of the Union address the multitude, and
before separating they registered a vow,—the
vast sea of faces upturned to heaven, before God,
with heads reverently uncovered, uttering, as
with one voice the pledge :—

"In unbroken faith, through every peril and trial and privation, we devote ourselves and our children to our country's cause."

Before the enthusiasm of the great Newhall Hill meeting had time to cool down—almost before the echoes of the hymn of Liberty had died away—news came that the Ministry had suffered another defeat. The Lords had decided by a majority of thirty-five, to postpone the consideration of the disfranchising clauses until the amount of enfranchisement should be determined. And so, after three days' consideration, Lord Grey once more resigned, on the 10th of May. In Birmingham the people were at the highest pitch of excitement. Business was suspended; most of the factories and workshops were closed; the artisans gathered in angry and excited knots at the street corners; and fears were entertained that the nation was on the eve of a revolution. An actor in these exciting scenes thus speaks of what he saw:

"Early in the morning the muffled peals of the bells of St. Philip's Church fell upon the ear. A black flag floated from the tower. I immediately proceeded to the News Room, in Bennett's Hill; it was filled with gentlemen in a state of great alarm; Earl Grey had gone out of office, and the Duke of Wellington had come in. Up to this time comparatively few of the higher and middle classes had joined the Union, which was composed almost solely of the 'lower orders.' I had belonged to the Political Union from the first, and entered the News Room in a glow of triumph. The people were alarmed; they expected the Political Union would rise and pull down their houses and mob them They were asking what was to be done. As soon as I could obtain a hearing, I said, 'Gentlemen, it is quite clear you will go to the d——l, unless you adopt my recommendation; there is but one way of saving yourselves, and that is to immediately join the Political Union.' 'I'll join,' 'I'll join,' I'll join,' resounded throughout the room. I replied, 'I like to see gentlemen willing to sign what they say they will do;' and many signed at once. I ran like a shot to Barlow's book store, where Roderick's paper shop now is, and got some sheets of parchment, and took them up to the News Room. Mr. Parkes headed one, and the gentlemen signed as fast as they could. While this was going on I ran to Mr. Barlow's, and wrote a placard, 'Great and important political movement. The entire middle classes are joining the Political Union. They are flocking to the News Room by thousands, to sign the declaration. At twelve o'clock there will be a grand procession from the News Room, to the Rooms of the Political Union, Great Charles Street, to hand in their adhesion to Mr. Attwood.'

"In one hour Mr. Barlow had this posted all over the town, in placards about two feet square. At the same time we had a large quantity struck off and sent in bundles by every coach to all the large towns throughout the kingdom, to be there posted up. I then sent to the Union Rooms and got about a 1,000 wands, and brought them to the News Room, and at twelve o'clock a grand procession was formed in double file, Mr. [J. C.] Barlow, [afterwards of Bilston,] and I leading. We proceeded to Great Charles Street, then thronged with thousands of persons, when Mr. Parkes, in an eloquent speech, handed in the adhesion of the middle and lower classes to Mr. Attwood. At the same time these handed in their five and ten pound notes immediately, after which subscriptions poured in from the country, the nobility even, probably partly as an insurance against being molested, contributing largely. The Council was then sitting, and the question then arose, what was first to be done? The people were collecting in masses frightful to those who did not know them. They came pouring in from all parts of the country, and men on horseback to know 'if the people were to move.' It was necessary to do something, and I suggested that Mr. Attwood should give out that there would be a grand procession at four o'clock from the Council Rooms to Newhall Hill, where

a meeting would be held, and a prayer offered up
to the Throne of Grace that the Council and the
people might be directed in the right path in that
hour of their country's agony.   This was adopted.
At the time named the procession was formed,
headed by Mr. Attwood and members of the
Council in one or more carriages.   Newhall Hill
presented one dense mass of men ; and when Mr.
Attwood and others who accompanied him gained
the waggon prepared for the speakers, and the
Rev. Hugh Hutton arose and uncovered to offer
up the prayer, one hundred thousand men, with
their hats off, with frames of iron and hearts of
steel, instantaneously uncovered, and with uplifted eyes joined the fervent supplications of
their reverend leader that the God of kingdoms,
and nations, and people would look down and
save the liberties of their country.   A deputation
was appointed to proceed to London to petition
the King, and the meeting quietly dispersed.
This was, in respect to intensity of feeling, the
grandest meeting held during the whole political
agitation."

The solemn moment when Hugh Hutton
returned thanks to God, and the vast assembly
" cried amen, like the roaring of thunder," was
fittingly selected by the Academician, B. R.
Haydon, as the subject of a great historical
picture, and he made portrait studies of all the
principal persons connected with the movement,
for that purpose ; but unfortunately, owing to
lack of funds, and other hindrances, the work
was never executed.   The sketches, after being
traced by Mr. Sam : Timmins, from one owner to
another, and through the hands of several book-
sellers, were ultimately secured through his exertions and deposited in the Birmingham Reference
Library—only to perish in the lamentable fire of
January last.

The Council of the Union met daily, and soon
became, practically, the ruling power in the
nation.   From all quarters the people looked
towards Birmingham, as the head-quarters of
Liberalism, and, as the *Times* happily phrased it,

" the barometer of the Reform feeling throughout
England."   Since the remarkable change of front
on the part of the middle classes towards the
Reform movement in Birmingham, many others
in various parts of the country had imitated their
action, and now the cause of Reform seemed
stronger than ever.   " People who would have
killed a man," says the writer above quoted, " for
talking of reform of Parliament a short time
before, ' had been Reformers all their lives ; ' all
men became Reformers,"

Then arose disquieting rumours of a great
march of the Birmingham Union, two hundred
thousand strong, for the purpose of encamping on
Hampstead Heath until the bill was passed.   The
Tory papers professed alarm, and counselled the
arrest of the leaders of the Union.   Warrants
were actually made out for that purpose, but
remained unsigned, and were afterwards found at
the Home Office.   These proceedings reached the
ears of Mr. Attwood, and he wrote (confidentially)
to Mr. R. Wallace, Chairman of the Glasgow and
Greenock Unions, and to his brother Charles,
who was president of the Northern Unions, at
Newcastle-on-Tyne ; requesting their presence in
Birmingham to support him during the trying
ordeal which might be expected as soon as the
new Tory Cabinet was formed.   Mr. Wallace
replied, that he felt his proper position, at such
a crisis, to be the head of his own Unions,
and that he could not come to Birmingham, but
added many words of cheering comfort to the
father of the movement.   Mr. Charles Attwood
complied at once, hurrying to Birmingham as
fast as horses could carry him.   Deputies were
appointed in all the Unions, so that, if the
Presidents should be arrested, they might step
into their places, and so preserve the Unions from
disruption.   During these eventful days, an
incident occurred which well illustrates the faithful adherence of the men to their cause, and more
especially to their beloved leader.   One night,
after dark, as Mr. Attwood sat alone in his study,
in the somewhat lonley house at Harborne, he

was alarmed by hearing the hum of voices, and the tramp, as it were, of many feet, quietly moving about in the lane adjoining. He looked out, and was still more astonished, if not startled to find the house sourrounded by armed men. They were his own faithful followers, who had heard the rumour that Mr. Attwood was to be arrested that night ; and they had come out to line the hedges and surround the house, determined to drive back soldiery or police who should attempt to enter.

The excitement of this period paralysed the commerce of the country ; everybody seemed *anxiously waiting* for a revolution. The tories talked of a proclamation of a military despotism ; of police surveillance ; of a system closely akin to that of France in its worst time. In Birmingham, however, the soldiery were well affected towards the people ; many of them were members of the Union, and nearly all had intimated to the leaders that, so long as the people kept within the law, and resorted to no violence, they would not lift a hand against them. They implored the people to abstain from rioting ; window-breaking, or other illegal proceedings, as, in that case, if they (the soldiery) refused to draw the sword, or fire upon them, would be liable to be condemned and shot. " If you do nothing," they continued, " but make speeches, sign petitions, and go peaceably to present them, though you go in hundreds of thousands, the Greys will not prevent you." Among those of the Scots Greys who were at that time in Birmingham, was the celebrated Alexander Somerville and he has described very graphically the doings inside the barracks during these eventful days :—

" Every day for months previously hundreds of people walked into the cavalry barracks yard to see the Greys, who came to Birmingham in the latter part of 1831. On the Sunday before the meeting on Newhall Hill, there were upwards of five thousand people within the gates, most of them well-dressed artisans, all wearing ribbons of light blue on their breasts, indicating that they were members of the Political Union. Next Sunday, [the 13th,] the barrack gates were closed. No civilians were admitted. We were marched to the riding school to prayers in the forenoon, and during the remaining part of the day, or most of it, were employed in rough-sharpening our swords on the grindstone. I was one of the ' fatigue ' men who turned the stone to the armourer and his assistants. It was rumoured that the Birmingham Political Union was to march for London that night, and that we were to stop them on the road. We had been daily and nightly booted and saddled, with ball cartridge in each man's possession, for three days, ready to mount and turn out at a moment's notice. But until this day we had rough-sharpened no swords. The purpose of so roughening their edges was to make them inflict a ragged wound. Not since before the battle of Waterloo had the swords of the Greys undergone the same process. Old soldiers spoke of it, and told the young ones. Few words were spoken. We had made more noise, and probably looked less solemn at prayers in the morning, than we did now grinding our swords. It was the Lord's Day ; and we were *working.* When closed within the barracks, booted and saddled, we had no communication with the townspeople night nor day, and knew nothing of their movements. We did not apprehend an immediate collision until the day of the sword sharpening. The danger now seemed imminent."

The Union did not start on their journey to London, however, nor were the services either of police or soldiery called into requisition. On the same evening, Mr. Scholefield returned from London, with the tidings that "*all was over ;*" Lord Grey now considered his return to power impossible. " Nothing," he said, " is to be done but to keep the people quiet. No doubt the Duke of Wellington will before long bring in a bill of reform nearly as good as that of Lord John Russell. Keep the people quiet," were his parting words to Mr. Scholefield; and with this advice and intelligence that gentleman returned to Birmingham. However this might satisfy lukewarm reformers it was not the result which Mr. Attwood and the Political Council could offer to the people as the outcome of all their toils. They felt that such a conclusion would effectually stifle all popular independence, and render nugatory the influence of that grand display of the power of a united people which had been exhibited in the great meetings on Newhall Hill. The great originator of the movement, therefore, resolved to oppose to the utmost such a crisis as that, and then and there, on that Sunday evening, he drew up the famous Declaration against the Duke, which was adopted by all the Unions throughout the kingdom, and was published in Birmingham on the Monday morning. It ran as follows :

"SOLEMN DECLARATION.

"Birmingham, May 14, 1832.

"We, the undersigned, think it necessary in this awful crisis of our country's fate, to make it known to our fellow-countrymen the alarm and horror with which we are impressed by the report of the Duke of Wellington having been placed at the head of his Majesty's Councils. We entertain this alarm and horror on the following grounds :—

"1st.—The Duke of Wellington's general avowal of Arbitrary Principles.

"2nd.—His speech against ALL REFORM, made only about a year and half ago.

"3rd.—His Protest against the Reform Bill, as entered on the Journals of the House of Lords, on the 17th of April last.

"4th.—His reported Expressions in the late Parliament amounting to those of regret, that the Irish People 'WOULD NOT' break the Law.

"5th.—His being a Pensioner of Foreign Despots ; and as such, exposed to their influence, and unfit to govern a Free People.

"6th.—His conduct to Marshal Ney, who was murdered by the Bourbon Government, in violation of the Convention of Paris, notwithstanding his appeal to the Duke of Wellington, who had signed that Convention.

"7th.—His general support of Arbitrary Power on the Continent of Europe, and the certainty that his policy, if he be true to his principles, will necessarily involve the nation in unjust and ruinous Wars against the Liberties of Europe.

"8th.—His utter incompetency to govern England by any other means than by the Sword, which has never yet been, and never will be, submitted to by the British People.

"For these and various other reasons, we hereby solemnly declare our fixed determination to use all the means which the Constitution and the Law have placed at our disposal, to induce his Majesty to reject from his Councils that faction, at the head of which is the Duke of Wellington, who have, by their arbitrary principles, excited the distrust and abhorrence of the whole population of the United Kingdom, and we declare our firm conviction that the public excitement and agitation can never be allayed until the great Bill of Reform shall be carried into law by that Administration by whose wisdom and virtue it was first introduced.

"These are our fixed and unalterable sentiments, and we hereby appeal to all our fellow countrymen, throughout England, Scotland, and Ireland, and we confidently call on them to unite with us and to sign this our solemn declaration, in support of the liberty and the happiness of our country."

Reminiscences of the old Scottish Covenanters and their league, and of their deeds in the struggle for freedom, suggested to the Birmingham reformers the formation of a solemn league and covenant: and a document was drawn up by Mr. W. Redfern, for signature. It set forth that the inhabitants of Birmingham, " having with hearts stricken with grief and consternation, received the disastrous intelligence that his Majesty has appointed to the highest station in the Government of this country his Grace the Duke of Wellington, the pledged and sworn foe ' of Reform,' and ' truly believing' that ' this ill-boding appointment' threatens a blow to their cause, and that ' unless it be speedily rescinded' it will ' bring down upon our beloved country unutterable woes,' and subject the land ' to the dominion of a stern, jealous, and implacable Oligarchy ;' ' with one common mind, heart and determination, do therefore, by this Solemn League and Covenant, made and entered into in imitation of many worthy and memorable examples of our forefathers, as recorded in history, COVENANT and declare, each one with the others, ... to STAND, ABIDE, and HOLD-FAST, the one by the other, in using and adopting all feasible and lawful ways and means, with which God or Nature, Chance or Circumstances, may furnish us, for the assertion and vindication of all such our just rights and liberties.'"

In the midst of these dark forebodings came hopeful tidings ; on the very day after the people had declared against the Duke, and only two days after the grinding of the swords,—Tuesday, May 15th—Lord Grey received communications respecting the possibility of his resuming office, the Duke having experienced some difficulty in forming a Cabinet. Mr. Joseph Parkes, who was at that time in London, caused slips to be printed to the effect that Lord Grey was again in power ; and immediately set off by post express for Birmingham, scattering the welcome slips by the roadside and amongst the people in every town and village on his way ; and reached Birmingham by six o'clock on the Wednesday morning.

The good news spread like wild-fire ; and in a very few minutes the whole population was roused from its slumbers, and thronged the streets —the bells of all the churches, which had been tolled and muffled, were immediately set ringing joyously—changing " their funeral marches to delightful measures ; " the Royal Standard floated proudly from the dome of St. Philip's, blue ribbons decked all the public vehicles, as well as the persons of nearly all the inhabitants ; printed placards sprang up, as if by magic, calling on the people to rally round the standard of the Premier ; and, as by one consent, a vast concourse of the people moved towards the home of Mr. Attwood, at Harborne, from whence at ten o'clock, a large procession with its attendant music and banners, returned towards Birmingham, and was met, on the outskirts of the town, by upwards of 50,000 of the inhabitants, with a forest of banners, and the various bands of the Union. Old associations, sad, as well as pleasant, led the joyous multitude to march to Newhall Hill, shouting and singing as they went, " Rule Britannia ! " " Britons never shall be slaves ! " " God save the King ! " " Long live Earl Grey ! " and other expressions of loyalty and patriotic feeling. As the morning wore on, large numbers flocked into the town from the

surrounding villages, and when the vast multitude reached the old meeting-ground, such a scene of joy mingled with solemnity was presented as perhaps was unequalled by any previous gathering. With the old feeling of reverence, their first act was one of devotion. The whole multitude uncovered, and then a prayer was offered up, with thanksgiving. A memorial to Earl Grey was then agreed upon, and a deputation appointed to present it.

During these proceedings an interruption occurred which caused considerable alarm to many persons present ; the sound of a drum was heard in the distance, and the cry arose that the soldiers were advancing upon them. Amid the excitement, however, the vast concourse remained unmoved, and all fear very speedily vanished when distance ceased to lend enchantment to the music of a miserable company of mountebanks, who, when they discovered the excitement they had caused, precipitately retreated into a public-house hard by, called the Duke of Marlborough.

The vast assembly broke up peaceably, many of the country people remaining in the town until evening to speed the deputation on its way to London. At half-past six o'clock the same night, Messrs. Attwood, Scholefield, and Parkes, with four others, set out on their journey, to present the memorial to Earl Grey, accompanied, on their way out of the town, by dense crowds of people, loudly cheering.

The victory, however, had not, by the time they arrived in London, been actually won, but was fully assured. On the night of the 17th of May, the Duke of Wellington at last faced the difficulty of his position ; the rank and file of the army could not be depended upon to do his bidding, in putting down the reform movement; the people had already begun to take the dangerous advice of Mr. Edmonds, to " run for gold," and a run upon the banks had been commenced in real earnest, upwards of one million sterling having been already withdrawn in small sums ; these grave facts, together with the threatened commercial ruin and the determined attitude of the masses, led him, on the evening above mentioned, to declare his inability to form a Government, and to retire, with a hundred other peers, from the House of Lords.

The deputation, having thus seen the last of the opposition to the Reform Bill, returned at once to Birmingham, after receiving the most enthusiastic welcome from members of both Houses of Parliament, from the London Unions, the Common Councils of all the metropolitan boroughs, and even from Royalty itself.

Their journey to Birmingham was a march of triumph ; labourers left their toil in the fields to cheer them as they passed ; whole villages turned out to greet them, and raised their simple arches of evergreens ; others presented addresses ; little children scattered flowers in their pathway, and even the stonebreaker by the wayside raised his little flag declaring for " Attwood and liberty."

But when they reached home the joy of the inhabitants knew no bounds. The whole population turned out to meet them as they entered the town, on the 28th of May ; banners hung from almost every window ; every peal of bells in the town clanged out a joyous welcome to the deputation, and the thunders of artillery echoed the same greeting ; but these were both drowned in the deafening cheers of the populace, as from two hundred thousand throats the victors' return was hailed, and the final vanquishing of their opponents was celebrated. Such a scene was never before witnessed in Birmingham ; and at length, when from the pressure of the multitude the pole of Mr. Attwood's carriage was broken, the people joyfully harnessed themselves thereto, and wheeled, or rather carried, the conveyance up the Bull Ring into New Street.

A week later the Reform Bill passed the third reading in the House of Lords, and on the 7th of June received the Royal assent. By this act Birmingham was enfranchised ; and, for the first time in her history, was admitted to a share in the councils of the nation. Preparations were at once made for the election of two Liberal members, and the Council of the Political Union decided to use all its influence for the return of Messrs. Attwood and Scholefield, their president and vice-president. At one period it was feared that they would be defeated, owing to the threatened division of the Liberal party by the candidature of Mr. George Edmonds ; and this condition of affairs aroused the Conservatives to the possibility of their securing one of the seats as a result of the division. But ultimately Mr. Edmonds withdrew from the contest ; and as this action rendered all opposition utterly hopeless, the two candidates nominated by the Political Union found themselves, on the day of the nomination, masters of the situation, there being no other candidate, and they were therefore returned unopposed, as the first representatives of the Borough of Birmingham, in the reformed House of Commons.

CHAPTER LIX.

PUBLIC LIFE AND EVENTS—1821-1830.

Distinguished Visitors—The Prince and Princess of Denmark—Mr. Robinson—Wellington and Peel—The Princess Victoria—Explosion in St. Mary's Square—The *Birmingham Journal*—Town Improvements—Proposal to erect a Town Hall—New Thoroughfares—Town Hall Sites—The Deritend Turnpike Gate removed—Birmingham Botanical Gardens—Obituary Notices—The St. David's Society—The Catholic Question, etc.

WE now return to the beginning of the third decade of the century, to chronicle the various events, and to take note of the public life of that period.

During this decade Birmingham had several distinguished visitors. First among these (in point of time) were the Prince and Princess of Denmark, who came here and remained three or four days, in July, 1822.

In September, 1823, the then Chancellor of the Exchequer, Mr. Robinson, taking the advantage of a temporary residence at Leamington, with his family, paid a visit to Birmingham, in order to inspect some of the leading manufactories in the town; and subsequently accepted an invitation from the High and Low Bailiffs, and other principal inhabitants, to dine with them at the Royal Hotel, on Thursday, September, 11th.

Then came "the great Duke," against whom the people were at that time fighting; he had been staying at the abode of his distinguished colleague, Sir Robert Peel, at Drayton Manor, and his proximity to the home of Radicalism led the High Bailiff, Mr. William Chance, to send an invitation to Sir Robert and his illustrious guest, requesting them to honour him with their presence at his official dinner. The invitation was accepted, and the great leaders of the Tory party and of the Government of the day, accompanied by Lady Peel, Mrs Arbuthnot, and others, arrived at the Royal Hotel at noon, on the 23rd of September, 1830.

As our readers are aware, the popular irritation against the Duke and his party was at that time

53

very considerable, although not at its greatest height, in Birmingham; we are not, therefore, surprised to read in the *Birmingham Journal* of that day that, "on entering their carriages," to proceed to the Society of Arts, "they were assailed by considerable hissing from the populace;" but for the credit of our town we are glad to read further that "if anything, the applause preponderated." The Broad Street bridge of the new canal (where the Church of the Messiah now stands) was then newly opened, and our readers will be at least amused to hear that, in 1830, this was one of the first of the Birmingham "lions" to which our illustrious visitors were conducted; and further, that they entered a barge and "proceeded to examine the works of that stupendous undertaking." They afterwards visited the glass works of Mr. Chance, and the interesting show-rooms of Sir Edward Thomason, in Church Street, returning to the Royal Hotel about half-past five in the evening. "On all occasions," says the *Journal*, "there was a varied demonstration of public feeling, the cheering never being enthusiastic, nor the disapprobation violent."

After dinner the usual toasts were proposed, and speeches made. In responding to the toast proposed in his honour by the High Bailiff, the Duke of Wellington said:

"Gentlemen: I feel much gratified by the honour which your worthy chairman, the High Bailiff, has conferred upon me by affording me the opportunity of meeting you upon this occasion; and it is additionally satisfactory to be thus able to accompany my right hon. friend. The High Bailiff has been pleased to notice in terms of approbation what he has termed the services I have rendered to the country. For this, as well as the manner in which you have expressed your concurrence, I feel highly gratified, but it does not require the flattering expressions of the High Bailiff to enhance the value of your good-will or the gratification I feel in receiving these marks of approbation. Having in the course of this day visited your public institutions, I have witnessed with pleasure your enlightened protection and encouragement of the arts, and that spirit of enterprise and improvement in all the resources of your great community by which you are distinguished—improvements not less important or inferior to any which I have seen in any part of the country. [Cheers.] The approbation of such a society I consider more than a sufficient reward for any service of mine. [Cheers.] Gentlemen, I beg leave to return you my best thanks for the distinguished honour you have conferred upon me in drinking my good health, and in return I drink yours." [Loud cheers.]

In a similar, yet more eloquent strain, Sir Robert Peel followed, making his first speech before a Birmingham audience, saying :

"There could be no time at which a compliment such as the one you have just paid would not be highly gratifying, but the occasion on which it is conferred enhances its value. It is paid on a day on which I have had the honour of introducing my noble friend to many of your public institutions, and those public works which do honour to your town, and which must necessarily raise the impression of every stranger who may visit them. [Cheers.] My chief claim, however, to any mark of your esteem is the deep interest I ever feel in the welfare of the town of Birmingham. [Great cheers.] For this interest I have many motives ; as a Minister of the Crown I should display a gross dereliction of my duty were I indifferent to the welfare of this important seat of manufactures and commerce. Forgetting, however, my relation to the Government of the country, as a private gentleman residing within the district which acknowledges with pride this great town as its metropolis, I cannot but feel interested in all that concerns the welfare of Birmingham. [Cheers.] That district which participates in its prospects, sympathises in its distress, rejoices in its welfare, and languishes in its decay. [Cheers.] Gentlemen, I have indeed another motive for the deep interest I feel in the prosperity of Birmingham. Whatever my present high station may be in the councils of my Sovereign, I assure you I can never forget my own connection and that of my family with the manufacturing industry of this country. [Loud cheers.] On this account I feel personally elevated by all that tends to elevate the manufacturing classes— [cheers]—and when I see around me such an exhibition of public spirit—when I see that there is no community in which there is a greater disposition to promote objects of active benevolence—that here the arts receive encouragement and the hours of relaxation after the toils of business are devoted to the encouragement of science and the cultivation of literature and intellect—I do indeed feel my condition and my character in society raised by such a

connection. [Great cheering.] If then, with these triple motives for an interest in the prosperity of Birmingham, I conclude by proposing as a toast prosperity to the manufactures of Birmingham, I hope I shall not be considered as arrogating to myself a duty which I am not in some measure entitled or qualified to perform." [Cheers.]

Sir Robert then proposed "Prosperity to the Town and Trade of Birmingham"; and the meeting was brought to a close at a rather late hour, the Duke's party retiring by a side door, and entering their carriages, drove away amid the mingled cheers and groans which had greeted their every appearance during the day. And so ended the first and last visit of "The Iron Duke" to Birmingham.

To the same Hotel, during the same year, came our present beloved Queen,—then a mere child,— being on a tour through mid-England with the Duchess of Kent, her illustrious mother. They had visited Guy's Cliff and other objects of interest in Warwickshire, and proceeded to Birmingham, in order to see some of the great manufactories for which it was famous. A guard of honour waited in St. Philip's churchyard, so as to be near the Hotel, commanded by the Hon. Grantham M. Yorke, who afterwards became rector of the noble church hard by, and is now Dean of Worcester. As the time drew near for the arrival of the Royal visitors, the military escort was drawn up in front of the Hotel, chiefly for the purpose of doing the work which should have been done by police, had there been any in that day. Discipline was but indifferently preserved in the large crowd which had assembled, and as the future Queen of England alighted from the carriage, a lady* suddenly rushed forward from the front ranks of the crowd, and snatching the astonished little Royal lady into her arms, fervently kissed her. The crowd cheered loudly at this exhibition of exuberant loyalty and impulsive affection, but the Royal party showed considerable annoyance, and even anger.

---

* A Mrs. Fairfax, late of Great Charles Street.

After visiting some of the principal manufactories in the town, they proceeded to Aston Hall, which then "belonged," says Her Majesty in her private diary, "to a Mr. Watts;" this was *James Watt*, the son of the great inventor, the creative genius of Soho.

If it be true, as Milton sings, that

> " Peace hath her victories,
> No less renown'd than war,"

it is also sadly true that she is not without her scenes of misery and death, which, although happily less frequent and disastrous than those of the battle-field, yet appear to be inseparable from many of the useful arts. In August, 1823, occurred one of the first of those terrible accidents in Birmingham which, to the sons and daughters of toil, have become so many ghastly monuments in the march of time by which its course is marked; "black days" beside which those of the commercial world are insignificant. In *this* accident a near and dear relative was lost, in *that*, a child was maimed and disfigured, and its whole life so blighted that the not-long-delayed visit of the angel of death seemed only a merciful reprieve; in another, the bread-winner of the family lost a limb, entailing long and dreary days of want and poverty, until the disabled man could once more resume his daily work; and so these dreadful accidents have burnt themselves into the history of our town. The record of the catastrophe to which we have referred appeared in the *Gazette* of August 11, as follows :

In the discharge of our public duty through a long series of years, it has not fallen to our lot to record a more appalling and dreadful accident, or from the peculiar domestic affliction under which the family of the principal sufferers previously laboured — one that has excited a more lively and general feeling of sympathy and regret, than that which occurred in St. Mary's Square, in this town, on Monday last. Soon after four o'clock in the afternoon, the inhabitants for a considerable distance around the square were alarmed by the report occasioned by a tremendous explosion, and the fears of those in the immediate vicinity were heightened by effects greatly resembling those of a slight shock of an earthquake, accompanied by the destruction of a number of their windows. It was immediately ascertained that the report proceeded from the premises of Mr. Wilson, formerly in the occupation of Messrs. Wilson, Starkey, and Co., button makers ; and several persons almost immediately proceeded to the spot, when a dreadful scene presented itself. In a back room, or warehouse adjoining the house the body of Mr. Wilson was discovered, almost entirely buried beneath a heap of rubbish, shockingly mutilated and disfigured, and deprived of all signs of life ; and in another part of the same room, but at some distance, one of the females employed in the manufactory was found expiring from the effects of the injury she had sustained. The room in which the bodies were lying, we understand, presented an appearance of the most complete ruin and desolation—the floor was perforated, the ceiling and walls stripped, the roof and part of the laths displaced, and a large counter, at which it afterwards appeared the unfortunate sufferers had been engaged, riven to atoms, and the greater part forced through the aperture into a workshop beneath. In a room adjoining several females were at work, two of whom were also found to be very seriously injured by the effects of the explosion, and two others slightly so. Other more distant parts of the manufactory were much shattered, and the windows, &c., broken. The bodies of the deceased were removed into the house, and the females injured were forthwith conveyed to the hospital, where immediate surgical aid was rendered them. The natural inference as to the cause of the melancholy catastrophe was, that it proceeded from an explosion of gunpowder ; the real cause was, however, soon ascertained, and, dreadful as was the occurrence, the most exaggerated reports were in speedy circulation, and great crowds were in consequence attracted to the spot.

In the course of the evening an inquest was summoned by the coroner, Mr. Whateley, which met on the following morning. The principal evidence was obtained from the under sexton of St. Mary's Chapel, who, it seems was the first to enter the premises after the explosion ; and from several persons employed in the establishment, from whose testimony it appears that Mr. Wilson had been for some time in the habit of manufacturing percussion or fulminating powder—a chemical compound of highly dangerous preparation—now generally used as priming to fowling-pieces. By two of the individuals examined, Mr. Wilson, very shortly prior to the accident, was observed to be occupied at the counter of the warehouse, attended by the female who also unfortunately fell a victim, with a quantity of the powder before him, which he was about to put into a bottle standing near at hand. One of these witnesses passed by him so shortly before the explosion, that it took place before he had time to descend the steps of the warehouse : and that moment he observed that Mr. W. was rubbing some of it between his hands, but by what precise means the explosion was caused, remains, and must still remain, wholly unexplained. It was known that the deceased was sometimes in the habit of collecting the powder with the aid of a knife-blade, when putting it into bottles, but whether he used it on this occasion could not be ascertained ; a blow or friction against some hard substance, no doubt, however, gave effect to the latent qualities of the mixture. It is supposed the quantity that exploded was from four to five pounds weight; and from the testimony of the medical gentleman (Mr. Lloyd) who examined the bodies, it is some slight consolation to know that the deaths of the

In April, 1825 we read the following announcement of a new paper for Birmingham, which ultimately became one of the most thriving of weekly journals, and may be regarded as the

LORD JOHN RUSSELL:
From a pen-and-ink sketch.

sufferers must have been almost instantaneous. After a long and most painful investigation, the verdict returned in both cases was Accidental Death. The females who were conveyed to the hospital, notwithstanding the severity of their injuries, we are happy to say, are in a fair way of recovery. The remains of Mr. Wilson, who was little more than 21 years of age, were interred on Friday, in St. Mary's Chapel-yard.

progenitor of the *Birmingham Daily Post*, a newspaper which has long since taken its place in the front rank of provincial " dailies " :—

NEW BIRMINGHAM PAPER.

On Saturday, the 4th day of June next, will be published a new weekly paper, to be entitled THE BIRMING-

HAM JOURNAL. A prospectus, setting forth the expediency of introducing the same, and the principles of its government, will, in a few days, be circulated throughout the extensive, populous, and important districts of this and the adjoining counties.

The Birmingham Journal, containing the Foreign Intelligence received in London to the last period on the preceding evening, Parliamentary Proceedings, a correct report of the London and Provincial Markets, with a judiciously selected mass of important local information, will be published precisely at *twelve o'clock* every Saturday morning. By this arrangement, and through the medium of its agencies, it will be circulated throughout a district of twenty-five miles round Birmingham THE SAME EVENING, and in the principal towns in the kingdom early on the following morning.

hands of the Tory party; in 1832 it was sold to Messrs. Parkes, Scholefield, and Redfern, and became the organ of the Liberals; but it did not become either a successful or remunerative venture until 1844, when it was purchased by Mr. Feeney, the founder of the *Post*.

There were still certain rights enjoyed by that now almost mythical personage the Lord of the Manor, in Birmingham, in the matter of certain stallages in the market, and these, it appears, stood in the way of a long-needed improvement, the provision of a covered market-place. These

THE REFORMERS' MEDAL.

Printed and published, for the Proprietors, by William Hodgetts, No. 16, Spiceal-street (opposite St. Martin's Church) to whom, or to the Editor, all communications (free of postage) are requested to be addressed.

Agents in London, Messrs. Newton and Co., No. 5, Warwick-square, and Mr. Barker, No. 33, Fleet-street.

The *Journal* was originally started by the little coterie of old-fashioned Tories who used to meet at "Joe Lyndon's"—the *Minerva* tavern; and owed its birth to the annoyance of "the party" at certain remarks on the Birmingham Tories which had appeared in the *Times*. They went through the solemn farce of burning the offending newspaper, it is said, previous to the consideration of the proposed new "organ," and, after subscribing the necessary capital, made arrangements with Mr. William Hodgetts for the starting of the paper which was to reflect their peculiar views. The *Journal* did not long remain in the

were ultimately purchased, in 1825, by the Commissioners; and at the same time measures were taken for the extension of the market-places and for the provision of better accommodation for the increasing number of sellers and buyers therein. Owing to the opposition of certain of the inhabitants, however, these improvements were not effected during that year; but in November, 1827, the Commissioners issued the following notice:—

The Commissioners of the Street Acts, in consequence of applications made to them by the Magistrates and others, have again given the notice required by Parliament of their intention to apply in the ensuing session for an act to enable them to effect sundry contemplated improvements, and particularly to erect a market-house, and to increase the accommodations which are indispensably necessary for the due administration of justice. It therefore remains to be seen whether the Commissioners, acting as trustees for the public benefit, will receive that degree of support from the inhabitants generally which is essential to their success.

These were not, however, the only improvements the Commissioners proposed to effect in the town. Their scheme included the enlargement of Smithfield Market; the widening of Stafford-street; "the opening into Park-street from Digbeth; the widening and improvement of Digbeth, also of the end of Allison-street; the improvement of New-street at the upper end of Worcester-street; Union-passage, from Cherry-street to Bull-street; the widening of Smallbrook-street at the end of Dudley-street; the improvement of Hurst-street; the improvement of Navigation-street and Pinfold-street; the improvement of Masshouse-lane; and the improvement of the bottom of Worcester-street."

But there was still another most important and necessary requirement of public life for which the Commissioners proposed to make provision, along with their other town improvements. It will doubtless be remembered by readers of the earlier chapters that, until late in the eighteenth century, diminutive "town's meetings" were wont to be held "in the chamber over the Cross;" in later years they had been held either in the large room at the Public Offices, or at the Shakespear Tavern, in New Street. Nowadays, however, the only building in which it was possible to hold even a respectable town's meeting was Beardsworth's Repository; and that had the drawback of being in private hands, and was, moreover, not overburdened with elegance of appearance. The next object, was therefore, "the purchase of a proper site for, and the erection of a Town Hall, suitable for the transaction of public business, an object to which the attention of the Commissioners was called, in the first instance, by the Musical Committee of the General Hospital, and which has since been more forcibly urged by a very large proportion of the ratepayers.' On this subject it was thought expedient "to confer with the deputation of the Memorialists, who exhibited to the Committee a plan of a suitable building

capable of containing 3,000 persons, the estimated expense of which, including the purchase of a freehold site, they stated to be about £20,000."

The Town Improvement Bill (comprising the whole of the foregoing provisions) received the Royal assent on the 26th of May in the same year. One of the earliest notes of progress relative to the carrying out of the several projects thus sanctioned, deals with the selection of a site for the Town Hall. In the *Gazette* of July 28, we read that:

At a special meeting of the Commissioners of the New Improvement Act, on Friday, it was resolved, that the intended Town Hall should be erected in Bennett's Hill, near to the Public News Room. Plans, estimates, and specifications will be advertised for as soon as the purchase of the land necessary for the purpose is arranged.

In September, we read further, that "the widening and improving the Stafford Street end of the town has been determined upon, by the Commissioners, as the first public work to be executed under the authority of the new improvement act."

In the August of 1829 we note that "the noble proprietor of the Edgbaston estate, and the owners of the Long Moors and Balsall Heath estate, have agreed immediately to form, at a cost of at least £1,000, a direct line of road, 36 feet wide, from the Worcester Road, opposite the end of the Wellington Road, leading across the Pershore Road and the river Rea, into the Alcester Road, near to Mr. Haden's residence.* This new line of communication has been long wanted by the inhabitants of Edgbaston and Highgate, and will reduce the distance between the two points from two miles to about three-quarters of a mile."

Towards the end of the same year, another most important street improvement was effected. The rapid growth of the eastern end of the the town,—a populous district having arisen

* Or as we should say nowadays: "from the *Bristol Road*, opposite the end of the Wellington Road, leading across Pershore Road and the river Rea, into the *Moseley Road*, near to *St. Paul's Church*." This new thoroughfare took the name of "the Balsall Heath Road."—R.K.D.

between Ashted and the Aston Road, which at first bore the inelegant name of "Duddeston Town,"—the Commissioners wisely took time by the forelock, and, before the whole of the land was built upon, constructed a main thoroughfare from Gosta Green to the Saltley Gate, near Bloomsbury, called Great Lister Street, "thereby opening a direct road from the centre of the town to Castle Bromwich, Coleshill, etc."

The Town Hall Committee experienced considerable difficulty in the selection of a suitable site ; on April 26, 1830, they announce that they "have found themselves compelled to abandon the contemplated site at the further end of New Street, in consequence of the exorbitant prices demanded by the present occupiers of the premises. It would certainly,"—they continue,— "have been a desirable situation on account of its elevation, the open space around it, the excellence of the approaches to it on all sides, and the handsome termination it would have formed to New Street." They trust, however, "that another site will ere long be found," and conclude their report by suggesting " to those persons who may have suitable situations, the expediency of offering them to the Commissioners for the purpose." At last, after much disappointment and delay, the Commissioners were successful in obtaining a site for the building,—the *best* site, as experience has proved, that could possibly have been fixed upon for such a building, had they the whole of the town to choose from. In the *Gazette* of August 16, 1830, we read, that :

At a numerous meeting of the Commissioners of the Street Act on Tuesday last, specially convened, it was unanimously determined that the intended Town Hall should be erected in Paradise Street. This very desirable site, so well calculated to give a good architectural finish to New Street, has, we understand, been contracted for and obtained by the Commissioners at a fair and reasonable price ; and there is now every prospect that the work will proceed without further interruption. In addition to the land required for the building itself, the Commissioners, as a matter of convenience and to prevent the erection of any nuisance in the immediate neighbour-

hood, have purchased, on very advantageous terms, the reversion of the property at the back, extending to Edmund Street and fronting to Congreve Street.

In our next chronicle of events we shall have to record the erection of the Hall.

Another welcome reform in street affairs during this decade was the removal of the turnpike gate in Deritend, in 1828. The *Gazette* of August 25th, in that year, gives a very interesting little "history in brief" of the origin of these tolls, together with a recapitulation of the various incidents in connection with the erection of the last bridge in this ancient thoroughfare, and the formation of the Trust, which although notice has already been taken of these matters, is worth quoting here entire :

The Tolls payable at Deritend Bridge, and at the other Gates in Deritend leading into the town, will cease on the 27th instant, at twelve o'clock at night, and the turnpike gates and houses will be removed. It may not be uninteresting to our readers to give a short account of the origin of these tolls, and the improvements which have been made by the Trustees under the several Acts of Parliament that have been passed for erecting the bridge. At a meeting of the inhabitants, called by public advertisement, on the 17th of January, 1787, it was resolved that an application should be made to Parliament for an act to erect a Turnpike at Deritend Bridge, for the purpose of taking down and rebuilding the bridge, for widening the avenues thereto, and for preventing the lower part of the town from being overflowed. It will be in the recollection of many persons now living, that at this period, in times of flood, the lower part of Digbeth was impassable, and it became absolutely necessary to take down and rebuild the bridge, and to widen, deepen, and vary the bed and course of the river. From an account taken by a Gentleman residing in Deritend, of the number of carriages and horses passing over the bridge, it was calculated that a small toll of two-pence for each four-wheeled carriage, one penny for every two-wheeled carriage, and one half-penny for every horse, would be sufficient in the course of four years to enable the Trustees to take down and rebuild the bridge, and make every other necessary improvement. The amount of the tolls collected during the four years produced, however, but £500 per annum, which was little more than one half the estimated produce ; the consequence was, that the Trustees at the expiration of the act—the tolls having produced so much less, and the work having cost so much more than was expected—found themselves, notwithstanding the receipt of a rate in aid of the tolls, many thousand pounds in debt. In this dilemma, they applied to Parliament to renew the Act for a further term, and for an increase in the tolls ; but in consequence of a powerful opposition, the application was unsuccessful. Thus the matter rested, with a bridge not more than half completed, until 1813, when the trustees renewed their application for and obtained another act to complete the bridge, and make the other improvements required by the first act, and to pay the principal of the amount borrowed, the persons who had lent money on the credit of the tolls having agreed to sacrifice all interest. This act continued in force until 1822, when another act was applied for and obtained, for the purpose of widening the lower part of Digbeth, between Rea-street, and Mill-lane, and widening and repairing the two bridges in Bradford-street and Cheapside. For this purpose power was given to the trustees to continue the tolls until the 1st of January, 1830. The trustee, however, have been enabled to accomplish all the objects of this last act in a shorter period than was given by it, and, as we have before stated, the toll will be discontinued on the 27th instant. The Trustees have diligently, faithfully, and disinterestedly accomplished the object of their trust, and the public should be informed, that whenever expenses were incurred at any of their meetings, such expenses were paid by the trustees out of their own pockets. Out of ninety-five members of the trust who were appointed by the first act of 1788, the following are all that are now living :—Rev. C. Curtis, Rev. Dr. Madan, Samuel Galton, Esq., Mr. Anderton, Mr. Timothy Smith, Mr. Cockle, Mr. John Parker, and Mr. Henry Parker.

In 1829, the first steps were taken towards the formation of a Botanical and Horticultural Society in the town, and the establishment of Botanical Gardens in its vicinity. On the 9th of July, in that year, a meeting was held at the Old Library for this purpose, Thomas Lee, Esq., presiding ; and it was resolved that four hundred shares be raised, at £5 per share, and that each share be subjected to a subscription of one guinea per annum. On the 23rd of September, another meeting was held, at which the Earl of Dartmouth presided, whereat a committee of management was appointed, with full powers to select a site for the gardens, and to carry the objects of the society into effect. The noble earl, we read, was also pleased, at the request of the meeting, to accept the office of president of the institution.

It was not until 1830, however, that the society obtained a suitable piece of land for their gardens. At a meeting held on the 19th of October, in that year, a recommendation from the committee, to establish the proposed gardens " at

Holly Bank, in the parish of Edgbaston,* was unanimously approved ; "the site thus selected being admirably adapted for the purpose," and offering "many peculiar advantages not elsewhere to be met with in this neighbourhood." The effect of this welcome announcement was to stimulate the demand for shares, so that it was anticipated that the whole number required would speedily be subscribed for.

The ground having been secured, (comprising, originally, twelve acres, but subsequently extended, on the recommendation of Mr. Loudon, to sixteen acres,) the committee immediately engaged a competent curator, Mr. Cameron, who, with the advice and practical assistance of the gentleman just named, as well as of the committee, proceeded to lay out the gardens to the best advantage ; and, aided by the natural advantages of the situation, they were successful in forming a most delightful retreat, pleasing alike to the botanist and the admirer of nature's loveliness in whatever shape she reveals herself. A magnificent elliptical conservatory was subsequently erected by Mr. Jones, which was at that time considered one of the finest in the kingdom ; and the entire gardens, with their charming walks, the terrace, the beautiful undulating lawn, and the many interesting features, such as the arboretum, rosarium, pinetum, ferneries, etc., form an irresistible attraction to all classes, (for the grounds are open on certain days at a merely nominal charge for admission,) thus enabling even the humblest artisan to avail himself of these pure and healthful pleasures) ; and the society may fairly take to itself the credit of having cultivated among the masses a taste for that employment which " is the greatest refreshment to the spirits of man," even as it was man's primary occupation ere he lost the innocence of the first Arcadia.

Among the obituary notices of this period we find the name of Richard Pratchet, who at one time filled the office of High Bailiff of the town, and was in every way a useful and energetic public man; a Commissioner of the Street Acts, and one who was ever ready to assist in carrying out improvements. He died "at his home, Sand Pits, near this town," July 4, 1824, aged 67; and a monument was erected in acknowledgment of his public services, in St. Martin's Church, from a design by Mr. Hollins.

which Birmingham, as the Metropolis of the Midlands, had attracted to herself the population of the surrounding counties, even as far off as the Principality. In earlier times, as we know, there was a "Welsh end," and perhaps a little colony of Welshmen, but the latter is somewhat doubtful; in 1824 there was evidently a Welsh

OLD VIEW OF DIGBETH.
From the end of Mill Lane.

On the 16th of January, in the following year, the General Hospital had to mourn the loss of its treasurer,—and one of its most generous patrons,—Mr. Charles Lloyd, sen., of whom a portrait and a brief incidental notice has been given in our sketch of Charles Lloyd the younger. As we have already stated, a beautiful bust was placed in the General Hospital, as a memorial of his services on behalf of that excellent charity.

Among the minor incidents of this period we come across one which indicates the extent to

contingent, which included "a very considerable number of poor persons," and not a few of our more wealthy townsmen. It is pleasing to record that at this comparatively early date the latter were so far mindful of their poorer countrymen to take steps for the formation of a charitable society on their behalf. A meeting was held March 1st, 1824, Mr. Edward Lloyd Williams presiding, at which it was resolved "That a Society be formed, to be called 'The Birmingham St. David's Society,' its object being to assist in educating and clothing Children of Welsh Parentage, not having parochial settlement in Warwickshire or the adjoining counties." The society was accordingly established, and on the 7th of March in the following year the first Anniversary Meeting of the subscribers was held, at the Royal Hotel, at which it was resolved that the committee should place five children, conformably to the rules of the institution, in the Blue Coat School, to be maintained and educated at the expense of the St. David's Society. It was stated at this meeting that there were not less than between five and seven thousand Welsh families residing within fourteen miles of Birmingham, most of whom were of the labouring classes.

In the *Gazette* of December 27, 1824, appeared the following interesting notice of one of the oldest of our local charities, to which reference has already been made on several occasions in these pages :

LENCH'S TRUST.

We have pleasure in giving publicity to the following interesting account of a charity that has long existed in this town, but which, notwithstanding its extent and usefulness, is, perhaps, but little known to the great majority of our readers. Comparing the good it effects with the means employed, it is perhaps unequalled ; and, certainly we are aware of no institution more eagerly sought after by those for whose benefit it is designed. On Tuesday last, being St. Thomas's Day, the Bailiff of Lench's Trust (the present Low Bailiff of this Town) paid the usual gratuity of ten shillings to each of the 112 occupants of the alms-houses, who are principally widows. There are at this time nearly a hundred applicants for admission ; and such is the attention paid by the trust to the comfort of the inhabitants, that but four deaths have occurred during the last two years, though there are forty between 70 and 80 years of age, eighteen between 80 and 90, and five upwards. Several have occupied their rooms from 20 to 30 years, a few more than 40, and one individual not less than 50 years, and who is now nearly one hundred years old, scarcely any of them being under 60. Of late years, to render the charity beneficial to the most needy, it has been the custom not to admit any much under 70 years of age. They receive quarterly five shillings each ; but at this season of the year the trustees have thought it right to double the usual allowance.

The founder of this excellent and well-appropriated charity died in the reign of Henry VIII. and bequeathed a small sum for the benefit of the poor, and in part for the paving and improvement of the town. The present income, however, does not all arise from his bequest, for more than one benevolent individual since his time have bequeathed to the same trust property to be applied by them for the benefit of the poor of this place, at their own discretion. The late Mrs. Scott, of New Street, some few years back, enabled the trustees to build one side row of the almshouses situated in Dudley Street, and at her decease she endowed them.

The original buildings for this purpose are those in Steelhouse Lane, containing 42 rooms ; next, those in Dudley Street, containing 38 ; and lastly, those in Park Street, containing 32 rooms, making a total of 112, which, being erected at an average of perhaps not more than £40 a room, supply as many comforts in proportion to the expenditure as perhaps any institution for the poor can exhibit.

We have been favoured with another account of this most interesting "gild," from documentary sources, which will appear in the Appendix to the present volume.

It was during this decade, as most of our readers are aware, that the great change in the modes of travelling was inaugurated, and the contemporary records are full of allusions to the new "railroad mania" which threatened to become more universal and all-absorbing than even the "canal frenzy" sixty years earlier ; but we must leave the story of this movement for our third chapter of the history of travelling. There is, however, one paragraph which may come here, as showing the attention which the new motor was attracting in all branches of locomotion. In the *Gazette* of October 2nd, 1826, we read the following notice of the arrival of the first Steam Canal Boat in Birmingham :

STEAM CANAL BOAT.

A Steam Canal Boat arrived in this town on Friday last from London, carrying twenty tons, and is the first successful attempt ever made. The steam is generated with the Patent Duplex Generators, upon an entirely new principle, without a boiler, and without danger. The weight of the machinery does not exceed four tons. Her consumption of coal upon the trip was one ton. She has a wheel in the stern, upon an improved construction, that is capable of being raised up on entering a lock. The average of her speed was equal to that of the fly boats. She passed through the long tunnel, one mile and three-fourths, in forty minutes, and towed another boat carrying ten tons, without sensibly diminishing her speed. Great curiosity was excited on the banks of the canal by this novel mode of travelling, and at one time she had no less than fifty passengers upon her deck. The result of this experiment has been perfectly satisfactory, and when the machinery is applied to regular canal boats of a suitable construction, it is calculated that one whole day will be saved in time between London and Birmingham. It is the intention of the proprietors to establish a line of steam boats immediately. This machinery, from its lightness, is peculiarly adapted for shoal rivers and canals; and the Patentee, who is now in town, will dispose of exclusive privileges for any part of the country, upon very reasonable terms.

While Birmingham was thus busy, in the various ways indicated in the present chapter, with her own affairs, and while she was also engrossed with the great question of parliamentary reform, she did not fail to take her part in the various general movements of the time. Birmingham money was liberally subscribed towards alleviating the distress of the Irish peasantry, in 1822; the voice of Birmingham was heard in the cry of righteous indignation which went up from the people of England for the abolition of slavery in the British dominions; and Birmingham men, no longer, as in 1791, afraid of granting religious liberty to all churches and sects, joined in the general memorial in favour of the emancipation of Roman Catholics from that civil disfranchisement which had been their portion ever since the Revolution in 1688. A local Catholic Association was formed in 1824, and in 1829 our townsmen of all sects—the episcopalian Rann Kennedy joining with the nonconformist John Angell James—united in supporting the demand of the Catholics for a greater measure of civil liberty.

CHAPTER LX.

BIRMINGHAM IN 1832.

Gravelly Hill—The Village of Aston—The Old Park Avenue—Lichfield Street and the Old Square—Ruins of St. Peter's Church—The Market Place—New Street—The Old Grammar School—T ·Wheat Sheaf and its Landlord—Mr. Busby and the Duke of Norfolk—The National School in Peck Lane—Dr. Hook and the Schoolboys—Site of the Town Hall—Bingley House—Bennett's Hill—The Pos Office—The News Rooms—1538 and 1832.

FROM the last half-dozen chapters the reader may, by various indications, form some idea of the gradual change which has come over the town since our last survey; it will, however, be of some interest, perhaps, to gather up these scattered threads, and once more to travel with our readers, in imagination, through the streets of Birmingham, to note their appearance at the close of the Georgian era.

It is the year of grace 1832, and the Reform agitation has just culminated in the passing of the great measure for the extension of the franchise. It is about one hundred years since Samuel Johnson paid his first visit to Birmingham, and we are now about to enter the town from the same point. As we stand on the top of the steep ascent called Gravelly Hill, the newly-created Parliamentary Borough of Birmingham stretches out before us, covering the opposite hill and extending almost into the valley which lies at our feet, wherein nestles peacefully the pleasantly rural village of Aston, above which rises the graceful spire of the church, and the minaret-like turrets of the old Hall,—exactly as Washington Irving had seen and described them in his delightful Sketch Book, a few years earlier. The hill on which we stand is considerably higher than the Gravelly Hill of later times. From Erdington to the junction of the Lichfield and Tamworth roads, the former had not, as yet, been levelled by the cutting of the hollow road,* and from the finger-post at the

* As at Holloway Head.

crest of the hill, to the old Salford bridge, was a steep descent, which was afterwards relieved by the erection of the new bridge, and the construction of the embankment over the lower part of the valley.

In the valley we notice on our left the aqueduct which carries the Birmingham canal over the river. As we proceed up the Lichfield Road towards Birmingham, we pass on our right the noble avenue leading up, through Aston Park, to the Hall, and forming an unbroken line of trees, nearly half a mile in length ; so soon to be "curtail'd of this fair proportion," by the Grand Junction Railway. We have yet at least a mile to travel along the highway, before we reach the outskirts of Birmingham ; by the old park wall, through the toll-gate at Aston Cross, and across the brook ; now we are entering the town.

It commences with the row of pleasantly situated houses on the left, near Dartmouth Street, commanding an extensive view of the Lowcells (now corrupted into Lozells), and the upper part of Aston Park. By the time we reach Gosta Green we find ourselves within the grimiest part of the town, the "gunmakers' quarter." Our way is up Lichfield Street, past the old Workhouse, to which age and smoke have given a dingy and miserable appearance, reminding one almost of that grim, prison-like "house that holds the parish poor," which Crabbe describes with such Hogarth-like fidelity, in "The Village."

We reach at length the Old Square, which had only recently been denuded of the pleasant garden shown in the old engraving copied on page 85 ; and turning down the Lower Priory into Dale End, we come in view of the charred walls of St. Peter's Church, which is in course of restoration. A marked improvement has been effected in the principal streets by the erection of iron lamp-posts along the curb-stone, in lieu of the old projecting brackets from the walls which had done duty in the dark days of oil lamps, ever since the Lighting Act of "sixty years since."

We are now in the open market-place in the Bull Ring, which, with its irregular rows of stalls and crowds of market-folk, is so well reproduced in David Cox's familiar picture. On our right hand we take our last look at the old houses between Bell Street and Philip Street, whereon the Commissioners have already decided to erect a convenient market-house. Away in the distance, over the top of St. Martin's Church, we catch a glimpse of the graceful roof of Holy Trinity Chapel, where a populous suburb has arisen since our last survey, covering the whole of the rising ground from which Prince Rupert attacked the town nearly two hundred years ago.

Now let us return into New Street, and take some note of the changes which the last twenty years have wrought there. Take a glance as you pass at the quaint old-fashioned inn-yard of the Swan, for time has marked it to undergo considerable change before we travel this way again. We are once more in New Street, but the improvements and alterations since our last survey have very much changed its appearance. The "Hen and Chickens" has invaded the footpath, across which has been erected a square portico, supported on heavy round pillars. Changes, too, have come over the old Free School : the "sleepy statue," as Hutton used to call it, has been removed ; having verified the sage remark of Doctor Marigold, that "if you don't go off as a whole, when you are about due, you're liable to go off in part, and two to one your *head's* the part." The effigy of Edward the Sixth lost *his* head, that important moiety of his person having rolled off his decayed and mouldy shoulders into the area in front, threatening considerable damage to other heads, less devoid of feeling, below. So, fearing lest the weightier portions of his Majesty's person should follow in the same direction, the governors of the school removed it altogether ; and with it the row of stone vases which had adorned the roof. A little later the vane and cupola were taken down, and the remaining part of the building, bereft of all its adornments and in a

therein almost to the patriarchal age of a hundred. He kept coaches for hire, for funerals;

THE LATE DEAN HOOK, *see p. 429.*

state of total decay, has but a few months longer to stand.

Not far from the school at this time stood an old public-house, called the Wheat Sheaf, kept by a Welshman named Pugh, with whom the air of New Street agreed so well that he lived and for many years regularly drove a coach to Warwick and Leamington which was much used by elderly and cautious persons, for a more careful driver was never known.

On the other side of the street, where Warwick House now stands, lived a wire-drawer named

Busby, about whom a curious story is told. Like most other Birmingham manufacturers of his class, he made the same premises upon which he carried on his business serve also as his private residence; and at the back thereof he kept a pretty considerable litter of pigs, to which he devoted all the time and attention he could spare from his business. He was proud of his porkers, and whenever a customer came to his warehouse who seemed likely to be interested in his hobby he was ever anxious to show them the occupants of his styes. One day, a stout, elderly gentleman came into Mr. Busby's warehouse, and made sundry purchases, which he directed to be sent up to the Royal Hotel for him. The wire-drawer looked rather suspiciously at his customer, who was by no means well-dressed, and inwardly determined to *take* the goods up himself, and to leave them only on condition that he left a receipted bill with them. However, he was determined to be civil to the man at present, especially as he was evidently a countryman, and therefore more or less interested in Mr. Busby's hobby. So, before the stranger departed, the manufacturer said: "You look like a farming gentleman; now, be you any judge in pigs?"

"Well," said his customer, "I am a bit of a judge, and I've got a few of my own."

"Then, you shall see mine," said the wire-drawer, and straightway led his new friend into the yard, to the abode of his porcine pets. "There," he continued, "did *you ever* see such beauties in your life?"

"Well, they are good," said the supposed farmer, "but I think I've got some as good at home."

Of course Busby could not believe that possible, and he felt more determined than ever not to see the last of his goods until he had been paid for them. So, a little while after the stranger had departed, he followed, as directed, to the hotel, his porter walking alongside carrying the goods, while he himself asked to be shown into the presence of his strange customer.

"Walk this way, then," said the waiter, and Mr. Busby followed,—to the room wherein sat the supposed farmer. "This person wishes to see your Grace," said the waiter, deferentially, as he ushered the now bewildered manufacturer into the room.—"What's this?" thought Busby,—"Grace, Grace,—what have I been doing?" and then, in a whisper distinctly audible to the amused customer, he said to the waiter, "Who is the gentleman?"—"The Duke of Norfolk," whispered the latter, and left him in his Grace's presence.

For the next hour the Birmingham manufacturer and the head of all the Howards had the room to themselves, and, before the former left, he had an invitation to go and see the pigs which the Duke had had the hardihood to consider equal to his, but whether he ever journeyed so far we do not know.

Mr. Busby was not singular in estimating the Duke's position in society by the unsuitableness of his costume to his high rank. In Munden's *Reminiscences* it is said that he once went into a hotel in Covent Garden, ordered dinner, and with it a cucumber.

"A cucumber!" exclaimed the waiter, looking hard at his guest's appearance, "why, they are half a guinea apiece!"

"Are they?" replied the Duke, "then, bring *two*."

The waiter appealed to the host, who, taking a peep at his visitor, recognised him, and ordered the dinner to be served as requested.

The general appearance of New Street, although somewhat altered by the various recent structures, was still that of a quiet, semi-private street; more than half the houses on the south side were private residences, and between Cannon Street and Needless Alley, on the other side of the street, were three pleasant, almost rural, residences, with trees and grass-plots in front; the one at the corner of Needless Alley being occupied by the Rev. Dr. Cooke, Head Master of the Free Grammar School. Turning down Peck

Lane, (which entered New Street at the spot now covered by the recently added portions of the Exchange Buildings,) we reach the site of the old Dungeon, which had been pulled down soon after the completion of the prison in Moor Street ; in its stead we find a national school,—a happy indication, let us hope, of the improvement in the social habits and morals of the people. At the period of our survey it is occupied temporarily by the burnt-out congregation of St. Peter's. It was erected in 1813, by public subscription, and was calculated to accommodate nearly a thousand children ; the ascent to the upper, or girls' schoolroom, being by means of a spiral staircase of iron. Among the most frequent visitors to the school was the late Rev. Dr. Hook afterwards Dean of Chichester, who was at this time Lecturer at St. Philip's Church. One who was then a scholar, but is now numbered among "the graybeard boys," says :

"The doctor was a great enthusiast on the question of education, and when he had thoroughly drilled the first class—who always did their best, for they knew their man—used to empty his pockets of all the loose silver he had, telling the master to get change, and then to divide it among the lads. Sometimes it would amount to twopence each ; and then, when the school broke up, there was a scamper to 'Lease Lane,' where a very clean old woman sold 'hot suck,' a sweatmeat much loved by the juveniles of forty years ago. For some reason or other the scholars of Pinfold Street School had acquired the nickname of the 'drowned bulldogs,' and many a fight we had over that unpleasant epithet. I remember a school fight between this and several other schools acquiring such importance that the shopkeepers in the town began to put up their shutters, till the presence of the redoubtable 'Billy Hall,' with his ash plant, put terror into the heels of the combatants, and soon cleared the streets."

It is worthy of remark that at this period the late Mr. Richard Tapper Cadbury, and a number of friends, used to hold meetings every Monday evening in the lower school-room, to advocate the Temperance movement.

Turning up Pinfold Street we soon reach the crest of the hill whereon the Commissioners have commenced the erection of the noble Town Hall. There is not much to be seen at present, however, except scaffold poles and building materials, and these hardly give us an idea of the future appearance of the building ; one thing we note, though, as we walk along in front of the site, namely, that the low roofed houses in Paradise Street come close up to the Hall, so that when finished it will not be seen to the best advantage from this point of view.

We now betake ourselves into Broad Street, which we have not seen since it was a mere field-path to the Five Ways. It is now a thoroughfare, and there are houses and manufactories on either side until we reach Bingley House, the residence of the Lloyd family, with its pretty, park-like grounds in front, across which the tame rabbits scamper, or stop for a moment, to gaze fearlessly at the passers-by. Beyond this point the road has a pleasant half-rural appearance ; most of the houses standing back from the footpath, having pretty little lawns or grass-plots in front.

And now, having reached the outskirts of the town on the western side, and thus passed through it from east to west, we return to take a last glance at the upper portion of New Street, which we have missed in our westward journey by turning into Peck Lane and Pinfold Street. Passing Christ Church, we come to a new thoroughfare called Bennett's Hill, the "upstart street" mentioned by Miss Hutton, which has been constructed since our last survey. It enters New Street at the spot formerly occupied by the Post Office, and there is a new and rather more imposing structure erected for the accommodation of this branch of His Majesty's service at the western corner of Bennett's Hill, which has in later years been occupied by Messrs. Lilly and Addinsell. Here there was a little pent-house under which to stand in order to give or receive letters. If there were four persons standing under this pent-house at once the accommodation was taxed to the utmost, and the unlucky fifth must remain out in the open street, no matter what the weather. But there were not often more callers at one time than the number provided for ; these were not the days of the penny post, and the receipt of a letter was, among the humbler classes, almost as uncommon an occurrence as that of a telegram nowadays.

Turning up Bennett's Hill we come to the new line of street recently opened, called Waterloo Street, where the proprietors of the Birmingham News Room have erected a handsome building for their use* from designs by Messrs. Rickman and Hutchinson. It was opened to the subscribers on the first of July, 1825, and ample provision was made to suit all classes of readers. Here might be found all the leading London, Provincial and Foreign newspapers, Shipping, Commercial, and Law intelligence, together with files of the most important papers, such as the *London Gazette, The Times,* and the local journals ; and our readers will doubtless be astonished to hear that, even in those good old-fashioned days, it was open for a few hours on Sundays.

There are several other new public buildings which have arisen since our last survey ; the elegant little suite of rooms erected on the tontine plan in Temple Row West, for the accommodation of the Birmingham New Library ; from the top of Livery Street we can see in the distance the graceful tower of St. George's Church, and to the left, beyond Great Charles Street, the newly-finished spire of St. Paul's. From an eminence

* Afterwards and still used by the Birmingham Banking Company.

we may now count the spires and towers of thirteen town churches : the older churches, St. Martin's, St. Philip's, and St. John's, Deritend ; the churches of the eighteenth century, St. Bartholomew's, St. Mary's, St. Paul's, and St. James's, Ashted ; and those of recent date, Christ Church, Holy Trinity, St. George's, St. Peter's, and St. Thomas's.

The Roman Catholics have two places of worship in the town ; the Unitarians have two ; the Independents have three (a portion of the old congregation still remaining at the Livery Street meeting-house) ; the various branches of the Baptist community have five, and those of the Methodists the same number ; and there are also places of worship belonging to the Swedenborgians, the Catholic Apostolic Church (Irvingites), Lady Huntingdon's Connexion, the Calvinists (called also *Adullamites*), and the Jews. In all there exist (in 1832, the period of which we are writing) no less than thirty five places of worship within the boundaries of the town, wherein Leland, in 1538, found but two ; and whereas in his day there existed but one public building (the old Guildhall at the end of New Street), the reader will be able to count up at this date more than a score, comprising hospitals, schools, asylums, libraries, reading rooms, Gallery of Arts, philosophical and literary institutions, and, in fact, almost every requirement of public and social life ;—almost, yet not quite ; we have not as yet a Town Hall or a Market House, but these are already promised, and in a short time we shall be able to record their completion. And so at the end of three hundred years of progress, we may be able still to say with the old writer, "Bermingham is a very mete place."

R. W. DALE, M.A.

PHOTOGRAPHED BY WHITLOCK.

BIRMINGHAM: HOUGHTON & CO., SCOTLAND PASSAGE.

INDEX.

OLD AND NEW BIRMINGHAM.

AN ILLUSTRATED HISTORY OF THE TOWN AND ITS PEOPLE.

PRINTED AND PUBLISHED BY

HOUGHTON & HAMMOND, SCOTLAND PASSAGE,

BIRMINGHAM.